PRACTICAL HOUSE BUILDING

Also by Robert Matthews:
TALKING ABOUT SELFBUILD

PRACTICAL HOUSE BUILDING:
A Manual for the Selfbuilder

Robert Matthews

BLACKBERRY BOOKS

Published by Blackberry Books
10 Bartholomew Street, Leicester, LE2 1FA
1991
Reprinted 1992 (with Appendix 4 updated)

British Library Cataloguing-In-Publication Data:

Matthews, Robert
Practical house building
1. Great Britain. Residences. Construction
I. Title
690.941

ISBN 0 9515295 1 X

Illustrations by Sarah Geaves

Typeset from author's disc by Saxon Printing Ltd, Derby
Printed in Great Britain by Biddles Ltd, Guildford

CONTENTS

PREFACE

WRITERS of cookery books sometimes use the preface to justify the publication of yet another book on the subject – aren't there enough of them already? Such a justification is hardly required for this book. When I set out to write it, there was not one book in print on how to build a house – neither for the selfbuilder, nor for the professional. That seemed a glaring omission considering that many thousands of people build their own homes each year. Most of them have done little or no building before, and they are eager to find out all they can.

So there was a need for the book, but was I the person to write it? I had built two homes for myself. The first had been a bungalow, which I built single-handed. Then later, I built a house with the help of subcontractors. These two builds were hardly enough to make me an experienced house-builder. Nonetheless, having done them, I knew vastly more than when I had so blithely started out with a spade to dig the foundation trenches for my bungalow. I have supplemented that hard-won knowledge with much further reading and listening to produce this book.

There are, of course, many books on the different crafts involved in house-building. I have tried to present here, in just one volume, the essence of what is required at each stage of the building process. (In fact, some of it is not to be found in other books.) I have also tried to show how the different stages relate to each other and to the whole. A practical bent is assumed in the reader, but no specialist knowledge. And for people who want a fuller understanding of the processes involved, I have tried to explain the 'why' as well as the 'how'.

The book cannot be exhaustive. It stays in the mainstream of modern building practice and only occasionally wanders along a byeway. Where there are options, these may be mentioned, but only the most popular technique is explained in detail. Few selfbuilders will want to follow exactly the course charted in the book. At various junctures they will prefer other methods, to return to the mainstream later. For a wider and more detailed understanding of house-building, the reader must be prepared to supplement this book with others.

There is no assumption that the selfbuilder is going to do all the work him– or herself. Indeed, the sensible way to selfbuild is to subcontract large amounts of it. But it has been my intention to describe all the stages of house-building in sufficient detail that the reader can obtain a good practical grasp of each subject. Individual selfbuilders can then decide which work to do themselves and which to subcontract. And when they do subcontract, a knowledge of the practicalities will help in choosing between different options and in recognising the difference between good and bad work.

Some words are needed about words:

'Selfbuild' means building your own home. But the word 'build' does not mean that you do all the work yourself. A professional builder often subcontracts out work, and a selfbuilder often does likewise.

On the other hand, 'DIY' does imply that you do the work yourself. The term is widely used, but it can lead to some ugly English. Is it a word, or not? It gives rise to such awkward constructions as 'DIYer' (a person who does DIY). Moreover, the term has a somewhat lightweight feel to it, which is hardly appropriate in the context of the sustained dedication that is required for selfbuild. So in place of 'DIY selfbuild' I've used an invented word, 'ownhands'. This indicates that the selfbuilder is doing the work him– or herself, as opposed to subcontracting it.

And that last sentence, in the paragraph above, brings us onto the thorny question of gender in the language. The ideal nowadays is to write in a neutral gender. (As readers of my other book *Talking About Selfbuild* will know, women are quite involved in selfbuilding.) Unfortunately, the present vocabulary of English makes this difficult. I have occasionally used both genders, as in the sentence earlier, but that is only a token – to use it throughout would be too cumbersome.

There is one word which occurs frequently in the book and which is not be be found in other building books. That word is 'centimetre'. To justify this I must explain my view of metrication in the building industry – that it is both a sham and a shambles. It's a sham because many products that are supposedly metricated are, in fact, just imperial sizes described in metric measurements – the worst of both worlds. And it's a shambles because buildings are designed in metric and built mostly in imperial. Architects produce drawings in millimetres, and tradesmen build them in feet and inches. That's inefficient and leads to mistakes.

This popular rejection of metrication is partly due to inertia, and partly due to the wrong choice of unit. The millimetre is too small for most building work. It should have been the centimetre. In this book it is the centimetre. Some people will find this confusing, but it's my belief that the situation has to get worse before it can get better. (For more about this topic, see the appendix.)

Another point to mention on the subject of words is that in places I've given a number rather than use an adjective. For example, to say that the cost of hiring a JCB is 'moderate' may not be at all helpful to somebody not used to hiring plant. So I give a figure: £14 an hour. Such figures should be used with discretion. On the Isle of Wight, the cost is £11, in London £20. (Prices quoted are appropriate in 1990.)

In a similar vein, I have sometimes written sizes approximately when precision is unimportant. For example, I might write '4 × 4 cm timber' rather than the over-precise '38 × 38 mm timber' – which is the British Standard size that a timber merchant will sell you.

Remember that in building there are virtually always several good ways of doing any particular job. So don't take a prescription in these pages as the only 'right' method. Indeed, you should beware – the prescription may be wrong. The book contains mistakes! What they are I don't know, otherwise I would have removed them. Although I have done my best to check the accuracy of the information, some of it is doubtless wrong. If readers would like to write and tell me about errors, I will be very pleased to incorporate corrections in any subsequent edition.

The book is divided into four parts. The first deals with administrative and managerial matters. The second takes the reader stage by stage through the building of the shell. The third fits it out – and there's quite as much work involved in this as in constructing the shell. The fourth part describes the techniques that are required for the building process.

The purpose of describing the techniques separately is twofold:

Firstly, it avoids needless repetition. For example, the techniques of concreting are explained just once, in Part 4, although they are applied both at the beginning of a build (for the foundations) and at the end (for garden paths).

Secondly, the layout enables the descriptions of house-building, in Parts 2 and 3, to be kept as compact as possible. Readers who are already familiar with basic techniques such as concreting are spared unnecessary reading. They may need to refer to Part 4 only occasionally. Other readers, however, must be prepared to do quite a lot of cross-referencing.

The text is thick with facts, and many of them are expressed in technical terms. For the novice builder, it would be ideal if a technical term were explained when it first appeared in the text. But often the term is only used in passing, and to interrupt the narrative to explain it would be counter-productive. The reader will generally find the term explained later in the text (or in the glossary). Probably the best way to use the book is to skim through it before commencing a build, and then to re-read it more thoroughly as the build progresses.

I must acknowledge the help given by Malcom Thorpe, lecturer at the West Nottinghamshire College of Further Education, Tony Lush, professional advisor on DIY, and Martin Hawes, handyman. From the draft of the book, they each made valuable suggestions for its improvement.

In Edwardian times, British house-building was renowned throughout the world for its excellence; but for the last half-century, it has been pretty banal. It will stay that way unless people take more interest in the design and construction of their homes and become better informed. Selfbuild certainly demonstrates both interest and knowledge. Indeed, it goes further than that and expresses a creative approach to living.

So I hope that many readers will find the book useful. May it help them turn visions into reality. May they build themselves fine homes.

RM – Kinoulton, Nottinghamshire, July 1990.

INTRODUCTION

About 11,000 homes a year are built by individual selfbuilders, and the number is growing. In addition, there are two thousand homes a year built by groups of people in selfbuild housing associations. So altogether, there is in Britain quite a respectable amount of selfbuild. Yet it is still regarded as something of a rarity. Not so in many other countries! In the USA, about 160,000 homes a year are built by their owners. And in many lands nearer to home, from Scandinavia, through Poland to Greece, selfbuild is common. It seems something of an anomaly that Britain, which has such a vigorous DIY tradition, should be somewhat lacking when it comes to the ultimate DIY challenge. But that is changing. And some of the institutions are responding to the growing numbers by catering more adequately for selfbuilders. And so even more people will find that selfbuild is possible for them.

Although selfbuild is a long and arduous task, it brings benefits which more than compensate for the difficulties. The end result is a home which is purpose-designed to meet the needs, wishes and whims of its occupants. No anonymous, spec-built house can be as satisfactory. And the owner-built house is usually better built because more care has gone into it – not for the selfbuilder the 'out of sight out of mind' mentality of many commercial builders.

Another benefit of selfbuild is the substantial financial gain. Indeed, the question that comes first to many people's minds is "How much do you save?". The short answer is "Twenty to thirty-five percent of the value of the finished house". The saving is considerable. But if you are interested in selfbuild just for profit, think twice. Selfbuild is hard work that will seem even harder unless you find the work itself interesting and satisfying.

And there is another, less tangible, benefit in selfbuild – a benefit in another sense of the word 'selfbuild'. This is the development of the selfbuilder himself (or, perhaps even more so, of 'herself'). Most obviously, the selfbuilder will have acquired several skills and much know-how in the course of the project. Less obviously, he will have gained confidence in himself and his ability to control his own life. He will have been a creator, rather than another of society's manipulated consumers.

The easiest way to get your own house built is to engage somebody else to do it for you. You can engage a builder; or your architect may undertake to control the work. Either way, this can hardly be called 'selfbuild'.

Rather, the term 'selfbuild' implies the active participation of the owner in the construction of his home. Even so, there is a wide spectrum of possible involvement. The least strenuous way is to take on the managerial work only, subcontracting out the physical work. This way, the selfbuilder wears two hats: one the boss's, telling the workers what to do, and the other the teaboy's, keeping them happy and clearing up after them. If this is the course you wish to pursue (and it's a very sensible course), then a lot of the detail in this book won't be needed. Yet the book should help you to make informed judgements about the many technical choices involved along the way, and to recognise the difference between good work and bad by your subcontractors.

At the other end of the spectrum is the selfbuilder who does all the work himself, 'ownhands' – to use the word introduced in the preface. This is a very arduous course, and probably not rational! Yet like the mountaineer, you may feel impelled to accept the challenge, 'because it's there' – or more prosaically, because of a lack of money.

It may be encouraging to know that ownhands building becomes easier by the year as technology simplifies the building processes. The forerunner of this present book was Stuart Martin's *Build Your Own House*, the seventh and final edition of which came out in 1978. Here is a list of some of the differences between the two books. The first item of a pair refers to the earlier book:

Foundation trenches:	then – dug by spade now – dug by JCB
Concrete:	then – mixed on site now – ready-mixed
Off-loading of bricks:	then – by hand now – mechanical
Inner leaf of cavity walls, and internal walls:	then – brickwork now – blockwork
Roof timbers:	then – constructed on site now – prefabricated trusses
Lintels:	then – concrete, cast *in situ* now – lightweight steel, factory made
Jointing of floor joists:	then – tusk tenon joints cut on site now – steel joist hangers nailed in place
Drain laying:	then – mortar and hemp joints now – push-fit plastic joints
Inspection chambers:	then – brickwork, built *in situ* now – plastic
Bath:	then – heavy cast iron now – plastic.

That is by no means an exhaustive list, but it does show how much easier house-building has become.

Anyway, most selfbuilders will be somewhere between the two extremes of doing all or none of the physical work. They will subcontract out some work and do the rest themselves – nearly all DIYers are capable decorators at least!

A rather different situation is met with in selfbuild groups. The composition of these is usually chosen so that most of the required trades are represented in the group, ie, there is at least one bricklayer, one carpenter, etc. Other members of the group can learn the easy way, directly from the skilled tradesperson.

Selfbuild housing associations receive quite a lot of institutional backing. Selfbuild individuals have been largely on their own, but support for them is growing. Most building societies, having their origins in self-help movements, have catered for selfbuilders for many years by granting an increasing loan or mortgage as building progresses. However, in the past, the selfbuilder has had to have enough capital to purchase the plot outright. This, of course, was beyond the means of many people. Fortunately, some building societies (and banks) are now willing to make an initial advance for the plot itself, so making selfbuild financially possible for many more people.

Selfbuilders also receive support from an unlikely source. The Customs and Excise, in a rare example of bureaucratic enlightenment, allow selfbuilders to reclaim VAT on the materials used in their new dwelling. This comes as a sizable 'bonus' when the house is complete – enough perhaps to fit the place out in carpets and curtains.

More support for selfbuilding is coming from an insurance company which has set up the 'Foundation 15' certification scheme to guarantee new houses for 15 years. Unlike the National House-Building Council certificates, these certificates are available to selfbuilders, and they will reassure any future purchaser of the house.

One last point to note about building is that there are still, fortunately, some regional variations. Scotland and Northern Ireland have their own laws, customs and Building Regulations. For these areas, information in this book must be treated with caution. Other regions may have more informal differences. For example, 'setting out', which is the process of marking out the plans of a building onto the ground, may be done by groundworkers, bricklayers, or surveyors, depending on the region. And there are still some regional variations of styles and materials, although they are fading fast.

Part One

PREPARATIONS

☆ ☆ ☆ ☆ ☆ ☆ ☆ ☆ ☆ ☆ ☆ ☆ ☆ ☆ ☆ ☆ ☆ ☆ ☆ ☆

1

OPTIONS

☆ ☆ ☆ ☆ ☆ ☆ ☆

Individual selfbuild or group build?
Conventional construction or not?
All your own work?

If you intend to build yourself a house, you have some major choices to make:

> Whether to build as an individual or as part of a group.
>
> Whether to build with bricks and blocks, or with prefabricated timber panels ('timber-frame'), or to use some unconventional technique.
>
> Whether to do all the work yourself or to subcontract some of it.

Let us look more closely at these various options:

Individual selfbuild or group build?

As an individual selfbuilder you have a good deal of freedom of choice. Within your financial constraints, you can choose the plot, the design of the house, and how much work to subcontract. You can work the hours that suit yourself. But without support from other people, there will be a heavy responsibility on your shoulders. You need a lot of justified confidence in yourself to embark on such a major project alone (or with your family).

Selfbuilding as part of a group is rather different. There is little choice about the site, and at best, the house design is limited to the selection of one from a handful on offer. The working hours are generally prescribed: all day Saturday and Sunday, and three evenings during the week. But responsibility is shared, and there is usually more skill and experience to hand. Very little capital is required.

Most selfbuild groups are set up and managed by selfbuild consultants. Briefly, the consultants arrange the purchase of the land for the scheme and advertise locally for people to join it. Ideally, they select the people so that a good number already have building skills. The group initially consist of a bunch of strangers without any common bond except the wish to build homes for themselves. Throughout that hard experience, discipline is needed to keep them all working together. Members record their hours worked, and they must put in a minimum number each month or else be fined by the group.

Contrast this with the individual selfbuilder who can often become so absorbed in his work that he doesn't know when to stop. There's a temptation to squeeze one more mix in before it gets dark. The likelihood is that he rushes the work, he still doesn't finish before dark, and he doesn't clean up properly until the morning after when it takes twice as long. Be on guard against such excessive enthusiasm!

Another contrast is that in individual selfbuild the whole family is usually involved. With group build, children are banned from the site, and wives generally do little of the work.

Besides acquiring the site, the consultants select the house designs and obtain Planning permission and Building Regulations approval for them. Most importantly, they arrange corporate finance for the whole scheme. As a result of this, members joining the scheme need very little capital – only a matter of a few hundred pounds, mainly to buy equipment for the housing association to build with. (A member must, of course, be eligible for a mortgage so that he can purchase his house from the housing association when the scheme is complete. It is presumed that members will be in full-time employment.)

Although the consultants set up the housing association, once it has been formed, the association is responsible for the scheme, and, in fact, employs the consultants as managers. The consultants charge a fee for their services, but this is more than recouped by the the savings that are possible in bulk buying. Like anything else, land is cheaper in bulk, and a number of plots together are cheaper, per plot, than an individual one. Materials can be obtained at a bigger discount, and there can be savings on fees to architects, solicitors, and the like.

The association will have regular meetings to make democratic decisions about the project and to monitor progress. (Some words of warning to those not experienced in the working of groups: A great amount of time can be taken up with meetings and they can be very boring. On the other hand, sometimes passions become inflamed and then the meetings are not boring enough!) Some groups are fun; a few are beset by acrimony.

The schemes usually take one to two years to complete. Members move into the houses as they are completed and pay a rent to the housing association until all the houses are built. Only then does the association sell the houses to its members. People don't particularly work on their own house, but rather they help in the building of all the houses. They usually specialise in their work, keeping to just one or two trades. With skilled craftsmen in the group, there is a good deal of knowledge and experience available, and the consultants also contribute a lot of practical expertise.

However, not all selfbuild groups are set up by consultants. Some arise spontaneously, as a result of local initiatives – it needs only seven people to start a selfbuild housing association. Local Authorities are encouraged by the Government to help such groups find building land. In fact, some Local Authorities are keen to promote these groups. You could be surprised how warmly an initiative on your part would be received.

There are possibilities of finance even for people who think that selfbuild is way beyond their pocket. Since 1988, the Housing Corporation can make Housing Association Grants to selfbuild groups (up to 87% of the costs). The housing has to be primarily for people in housing need; and it cannot be privately owned. This last restriction does not apply to funding from the Community Self-Build Agency – sponsored by the Housing Corporation and some building societies. The Agency can make 100% mortgages available to members of the housing association.

So these developments help those in housing need. What about the unemployed, people who have plenty of time to put into selfbuild? The Department of the Environment now deems unemployed selfbuilders to be 'technically' available for work and so eligible for benefit. So far, so good. A difficulty is that housing benefit is only due on the interest repayment of a mortgage, not the capital repayment. Some building societies have helped to overcome this by asking, in the initial years, only for interest repayments. With all these benign developments, this sort of selfbuild looks likely to expand rapidly in the coming years.

Not all selfbuild groups follow the very disciplined corporate approach outlined previously. There are groups where people work more as individuals on their own homes. Housing associations using Segal's easy-to-build method (see later) usually follow this more relaxed approach. Co-operation is rather informal: People work on their own houses, but lend a hand to a neighbour when called upon. Common works, like drains and paths, are worked upon together.

So there are pros and cons for both individual selfbuild and for group build. In the end, it may depend upon your temperament whether you prefer the comradeship of a group, or the freedom of going your own way. But if you have very limited capital (a few hundred pounds), group build is your only possibility.

Conventional construction or not?

Unlike the house buyer, who is only interested in a house as a finished product to live in, the selfbuilder has another interest: the process of construction itself. How easy is it to build, and how long does it take? Let us look briefly at the pros and cons of different methods:

Conventional construction

This usually gets called 'traditional', though cavity walls have been widespread only for 40 years, and prefabricated roof trusses for just 20. How old is 'tradition'? The British seem to go dewy-eyed at the word, which must be why it is so widely used about buildings and the British way of life in general.

More specifically, in this context it means brick-and-block cavity walls and a tiled roof. A prime advantage of this method comes if and when you wish to sell up – a house of conventional construction is readily marketable.

There are advantages during construction too. The building industry is geared up to producing for this style of building, so the requisite materials and skills are widely available – unless a building boom produces shortages! For the selfbuilder wishing to learn the necessary skills and techniques, there is a lot of information available – such as this book. The techniques allow a fair degree of flexibility in design, and have been widely tried and tested.

However, this can't be called an easy method of construction, nor is it fast.

Prefabricated timber-panel construction ('timber-frame')

With this form of construction, external wall panels are made up in a factory from timber studwork, sheathed on the outside with plywood to give it stiffness. Thick insulation is added to the panels, and in the past they have had better U-values than the conventional cavity walls. The inner surface of the panels is sealed with a vapour barrier of polythene or aluminium foil to prevent the humid air from the rooms condensing inside the panels – which could lead to rot. Usually, an outer leaf in brickwork is added, and the roof is pitched; the house takes on a traditional appearance. There are plenty of other possibilities for the cladding, although in the past they have been little used in Britain. Some options are: vertical or horizontal boarding, tiling, cement-based sheet materials (eg, Masterboard), or rendering. (This last needs metal lath to hold it in place. Pebble dash gives an attractive finish to rendering.) Because of its 'engineered' structure, a prefabricated timber-frame house is not so amenable to future alterations as a brick-and-block one.

The method is said to have been first used for the building of a warehouse in Chicago in the 1830's. The use of sturdy posts and beams for building is much older. These may also form a framework, of course, but the term 'timber-frame' is usually taken to mean the panelled construction.

The big advantage of the timber-frame method is the speed with which the shell can be erected. Once the base has been prepared, the panels can be put up and roofed in within a week. Then, while the plumber works inside, the brickies can be taking up the brickwork outside.

The cost of materials is higher (maybe 20% on the cost of the shell), and this out-weighs the savings in subcontracted labour. Nevertheless, for the selfbuilder in a hurry, this option may be advantageous. There are several firms which will supply the selfbuilder with 'kits' for putting up a timber-frame house. Such a kit is obviously beneficial to a self-builder. Having the right parts to hand is a big step forward.

(Kits are also available for brick-and-block houses. See 'House kits', Appendix 4.)

The shell does go up fast, but it needs several helpers to assemble it – no problem on a group build, but a difficulty for an individual selfbuilder. The number of people required depends on the size of the panels: Four is often sufficient, but six more comfortable. In a wind the panels can be difficult to control. Sometimes a crane is used, and then the panels can be made larger and pre-glazed. (The hire charge for a crane is about £120 a day.) Nowadays, only the 'platform' method of timber-frame is used – the panels are one-storey high. (In the former 'balloon' method, two-storey panels were used.) Nonetheless, different manufacturers produce panels in different sizes, and this is a matter to be clear about before placing an order.

On a practical note, the foundations for a timber-frame house need to be set out more accurately – foundations and frames must match exactly together. One selfbuilding couple found that their floor slab was a couple of centimetres too small for the sole plate – even though they had employed experienced subcontractors to build the slab. The foundations had to be dug up on two sides and rebuilt.

Plastering, however, is easier – the walls are dry lined, a process which does not require great skill. Because timber-frame is a lighter construction, sound insulation and thermal stability may not be as good as in a brick-and-block house.

There are a lot more timber-frame houses about than you might imagine – they are disguised to look like traditional houses. There have been scare stories in the media about the vulnerability of the panels to rot if put up carelessly. This obviously is not something that applies in selfbuilding.

Unconventional

The possibilities, in theory, are boundless. In practice, sadly, the variations from the orthodox are minimal.

A lone pioneer has been an architect, the late Walter Segal, who promoted a system designed for selfbuilders. The system is simple yet flexible. The foundations consist only of concrete piers. The structure is basically a modular, post-and-beam frame which is topped with a flat roof and which is constructed on site. The simple method of construction requires fewer skills (eg, no bricklaying or plastering) and gives quick results. Walter Segal claimed that a bungalow could be built by a couple alone in six months. Disadvantages are less sound insulation, and some constraints in the design due to its modular nature. Flat roofs are generally disliked, although Segal used an unusual design which has so far been trouble-free.

Several individual houses and bungalows have been built in the Segal style, and in Lewisham, London, a selfbuild housing association built their houses to his design. Ten years after completion, nobody had moved away – an indication of a high degree of satisfaction. Contrast that with the comings and goings on a speculative housing estate!

The role of pioneers in innovatory selfbuild has now been taken over by Constructive Individuals. Their designs have several similarities with the Segal method. They use a post-and-beam technique to give easy and rapid construction; but the roofs are pitched. Their houses are very energy efficient.

Other examples of unconventional house-building are very few and far between. But if you want inspiration, read Ken Kern's book, *The Owner-Built Home*. As you proceed from chapter to chapter, you'll be wanting to build in earth (there's still a lot of Devon cob standing), stone (but pricey for most of us), concrete, timber, bamboo, or even, perhaps, with salvaged materials (the ultimate in recycling?). Then come down to earth. With our conformist Planning authorities, the chances of obtaining consent are virtually nil. You'll have to emigrate!

All your own work?

The degree to which you do the physical work yourself and the degree to which you subcontract it is influenced by many factors. Time and money are major ones. Let us look at these.

For some particular job, a rule of thumb is that an amateur who is competent in the techniques takes three times as long as a professional. A real beginner may take ten times as long – a truly daunting figure. However, by the time the beginner has done a houseful of whatever it is, he will have become a competent amateur. So over the whole job, he may take about five times as long as the professional. If, for some particular job, a tradesperson would charge you £5 an hour, are you prepared to do it to save money at the rate of £1 an hour? Superficially, the answer for most of us would be 'No'. But there are other considerations.

One ameliorating bonus is that there is no tax on your efforts. The professional may be working one hour in five to pay income tax. And another bonus, if you are living on site, is the saving on transport costs. While the professional is motoring to and from work, you can be productively working. You may well be getting from these bonuses, the equivalent of three 'free' hours a day. That must be encouraging!

If your budget is very tight you may have no choice. You may not be able to afford to pay wages to others. Do not be down-hearted. See, for example, what some of the self-builders in *Talking About Selfbuild* accomplished by their own labours. Nor is money saved the only item worth consideration. You acquire skills and that must have its own worth. Building a house can be a useful rounding-off of your education that could stand you in good stead in the future. But above all, there is the enduring satisfaction of living in a home built by yourself, a satisfaction that no amount of money can buy. We all have some creativity. To have expressed it in such a useful and lasting form must always be gratifying.

How all these factors are assessed varies from individual to individual. You choose your own degree of involvement according to your inclinations and circumstances. Let's look at the options in more detail:

Managerial selfbuild

If intangible factors are left out of account and only utilitarian ones considered, managerial selfbuild is usually the prudent course. A modicum of organising skill is required to manage the flow of materials, labour, money and tea. The time required is not excessive, and it's quite feasible to be in some other full-time employment. Tradespeople can often be found who are willing to work at weekends or in the evenings, when you can be on site if required. As a rough guide, the cost of buying in all the labour may be about half the cost of the materials.

This is the fastest way to build. After Planning permission had been obtained, a typical house could be built in about six months.

It is also lucrative. The cost saving due to your managerial and entrepreneurial effort is likely to be about 20% of the value of the finished property. Organising the build saves more than actually doing all the physical labour.

Ownhands selfbuild

This is the other extreme. You do all the work yourself. The cost saving in doing the manual work is quite considerable (say 15% of the final value), but the time taken is very considerable. A bungalow could take a couple of years to build. Anybody following this course must surely devote themselves full-time to the project. There could be no energy or time to spare for paid employment.

Unless you have a real urge for total ownhands building – don't! However, if that is what you want to do, why not climb your own Everest? It will probably be the most arduous task that you undertake in your life. Most ownhanders say "Never again" when they've finished, their urge satisfied.

For ownhands building, you need a determination to meet a great challenge, and confidence in your abilities – not that you already have the skills, but that you can learn them on the job. You need to be sound in body and mind. If you already have a history of back trouble, or whatever, then don't risk it. If you're a worrier, you'll have so much to worry about that it might be a case of kill or cure!

Of course, if you do set out on the ownhands course and find that you've over-committed yourself, you can change tack and call in subcontractors. You could even get a builder to finish the project off – though he might also finish off your profit!

Sensible selfbuild

Neither of the two extremes above is common. The usual and sensible course is that you do the work in which you are reasonably competent, or which you can quickly learn. Most people, for example, can decorate themselves, but many leave bricklaying and plastering to the professionals.

Of course, the amount of time taken to build by this option will depend on the proportion of subcontracting, but a year is typical. You could stay in full-time employment, as long as generous holidays were available when required!

Training

If you foresee becoming involved in selfbuild, then it helps to learn some skills beforehand. There may be relevant courses at evening classes or technical colleges. Some private centres hold short courses for selfbuilders.

There are plenty of DIY books to read. These are strong on the fitting out of the shell (eg, the plumbing and electrics), but weak on how to build it. For a more theoretical approach, try building textbooks.

Visit building sites and become familiar with the different stages of construction. Watch tradesmen at work and think about what they're doing and why. Look at housing around you more closely and analytically. Renovating an old house, or building an extension, is obviously a good and profitable way to gain practical experience.

2
PRELIMINARIES

☆

☆

☆

☆

☆

☆

☆

Finding a plot
Requirements of a plot
Producing a design
Specification
Bill of quantities
Costings
Obtaining finance
Applying for Planning permission

LET US ASSUME that you have decided to 'go for it' as an individual selfbuilder. You must now set about obtaining the fundamental necessities: a plot, a design for your house, finance, and Planning permission. These are big issues and are likely to take many months.

By the way, don't be put off if the building industry is in one of its periodic slumps. On the contrary, this is the best time to build – plots are plentiful, there are no shortages of materials, and subcontractors are readily available.

Finding a plot

This used to be among my prayers – a piece of land, not so very large, which would contain a garden, and near the house a spring of ever-flowing water, and beyond these some trees – Horace (65 – 8 BC).

Despite 'Progress', such simple bounty is no more plentiful nowadays than it was two-thousand years ago. Even if you find your idyllic patch of land, can you build on it? It is the crucial Planning permission that turns a piece of land into a building plot. The high price of a plot is due to this essential consent from the Local Authority rather than for the land itself.

Plots usually come with 'Outline' Planning permission. This gives the general type of development allowed. Invariably there are some conditions attached, and these 'Reserved Matters' must be approved for your particular house. (See the end of the chapter for more about Planning permission.)

The availability of building plots varies greatly with the area of the country and the buoyancy of the house-building industry. In the crowded South-East, when house-building is booming, plots are rare and expensive. In the more neglected parts of Britain, when the building industry is stagnant, they are plentiful and cheap. (Advertisements in the *Exchange and Mart* give an idea of where plots are easily found.) The straightforward way to find a plot, once you have decided upon a particular locality, is through estate agents. This involves a lot of phone work. You need to track down which ones commonly deal with plots and ask to be put on their mailing list. Local newspapers are another source. Local Authorities sometimes have plots to sell. (Contact their Estates department). And occasionally, so also do large estate developers. (If house sales on an estate are slow, the developer may sell off the remaining plots; and they may well prefer to sell to selfbuilders rather than to rival builders.)

The magazine devoted to selfbuild, *Build It!*, has a section with details of plots available nationwide. Other nationwide lists are put out by some commercial organisations, such as house-kit suppliers. One company, Package Deal, offers lists of plots to its subscribers. The 'package deal', in this case, is that finance for selfbuild can be included with the plot, if required.

Once you have details of plots, some will need to be inspected. All this takes time. And unfortunately, it is not uncommon for plots to be sold at auction (especially when house-building is booming). This does not help the self-builder, who needs more time to get his act together than a professional builder.

If plots are not forthcoming through the above channels, then you will have to go out and more actively search for them. You can look for some land and apply yourself for Planning permission. But before doing this, it's advisable to see the 'Structure Plan' for the area, which you can inspect in the Planning office of the Local Authority or in the Public Library. The Structure Plan gives the broad outlines for development in the area, and criteria for judging applications. Finer detail is given in Local Plans. These will give you a good idea of the likelihood of Planning permission being granted for some particular piece of land.

You don't need to be the owner of the land to apply for permission. But you must inform the owner of your application. In other words, if Planning permission is granted, it will be the owner that profits from it, not yourself. (As from 1991, many years overdue, the ownership of registered land can be traced through the Land Registry for a fee of £12. Contact the appropriate District Land Registry.)

Another possibility is to go in for demolition! Commercial developers have got redevelopment a bad name, often putting up buildings inferior in quality to what they knock down. It doesn't have to be so. In the South-East, a few selfbuilders are using this method. Demolition is sometimes 'free', the materials salvaged paying for the cost of the work.

Some businesses with land, eg, smallholdings, are specially favoured in Planning applications, though the Planners may want proof that the business has a record of commercial viability. To stop the get-rich-quick developer, the Planning consent will probably stipulate that the house cannot be sold off separately from the land.

Altogether, finding a plot is likely to involve a lot of perseverance – a suitable initiation into selfbuild!

Requirements of a plot

With such a limited choice, it is unlikely that anyone is going to find their ideal plot. Nonetheless, it does help you to reach the right decision if you do know what you really want. In fact, the main requirements of a plot are the same whether it has a house already on it or not. Experienced house owners will know what they are looking for, and this is not discussed here.

However, a few words of warning: Some selfbuilders will be tempted to move to an area of the country where plots are plentiful and cheap. But consider first whether such an area would be the right place for you to live, not just to build. If it means leaving friends, relations, and your own cultural environment, you may end up living a lonely life in a fine house.

Another factor to bear in mind is that economically it is not worth building better than the neighbourhood warrants. Or, as somebody else has expressed it, "You don't build a palace next to a chip shop". As a very rough rule of thumb, the ratio of construction cost to plot price is generally about 2 in the Midlands, 3 in Wales, and 1 in the South-East where plot prices are so high.

The size of a plot is an important factor in its price. In fact, neighbouring plots are often priced directly according to their areas. The frontage is also a factor, a wide frontage looking more impressive. Typically, a plot for a detached house might be 500 square metres with a frontage of 16 metres. A bungalow generally needs a wider frontage, say 22 metres for a typical figure. By detaching the garage, or by turning a gable end to face the road, narrower frontages can be utilised.

There are some features of a plot in which you, as a selfbuilder, will be particularly interested:

Levelness is one. It is easier and cheaper to build on a level plot. A marked slope will mean extra excavating or infilling and more complicated foundations.

The nature of the subsoil is another. Don't just poke the ground with your foot. Take a spade and dig down half a metre or so. The nature of the subsoil will affect the foundations. If there are neighbouring buildings, that is reassuring. If not, the ground may be difficult to build on. If in doubt, contact the local building inspector for advice.

Are services close by? Water and electricity are usually considered essentials. Gas and a telecom cable are desirable. Foul sewers are convenient, though it is possible to install a septic tank if the effluent can be drained away. Surface-water sewers may be available, though your own soakaways are often an easy alternative that you may prefer.

A spacious plot is easier to build on than a cramped one. You need room for bricks and blocks, sand and cement, roof trusses, spoil, a store, and possibly a caravan to live in. You need space around the building for scaffolding.

Additionally, there may be legal considerations. Are there restrictive covenants on the land, or are there easements giving you rights over adjacent land? Rights of drainage and other services are often involved in these matters.

Producing a design

A good design results from combining your needs of a house with the qualities of a particular plot. The plot usually comes first, and the detailed design follows. (See Chapter 19: *Design*.) There is a wide choice of options for producing a design:

Your own design

If you already have some familiarity with house-building, you may feel confident enough to draw up your own design. Many people are aware of the glamorous aspect of design – the layout and overall appearance of the house, and they can produce a satisfactory design in this respect. Few people have enough technical familiarity with the details – for example, the design of foundations or eaves. (But there are books of 'details' which help in this respect.)

If you do draw up your own design, it may still be a good idea to have it checked over by a professional. Some of the details will be checked by the building inspector, but your professional adviser may well make other useful suggestions.

Architect

To claim to be an 'architect', a person must be registered with ARCUK (Architects' Registration Council of the United Kingdom), and to do this he (or she) must have specified architectural qualifications.

Many architects are also members of the Royal Institute of British Architects, and like to put RIBA after their names. Long training is necessary to become an architect, so architects consider that they give the best service. The RIBA recommended percentage fees are about 9% of the estimated construction cost – not the selfbuilder's slimmed-down cost, but a contractors' cost with overheads and profit. Any selfbuilder paying this sort of fee should be getting the services of a Frank Lloyd Wright. (Fortunately, many architects charge less than the recommended rate, sometimes considerably less. Phone around. Ask what their hourly rate is (£30 an hour?). Some architects charge according to floor area (eg, £15 per square metre for design, site supervision and certificate). If you will be requiring site supervision from the architect, it will be cheaper to engage one not too far from the plot.

Of course, money is easily quantified, but what about the quality of their design? This is much more difficult to weigh up. Recommendations may help, or you could ask to see examples of their work. The architect may offer you a design sketch, based on your requirements, without charge or obligation. If you are satisfied with the sketch then you can proceed. The Clients' Advisory Service of the RIBA will be pleased to offer you advice on engaging an architect. (See 'Info centres', Appendix 4 for the locations of their regional offices.)

The relationship with your architect is is one of those ambivalent ones where the servant (the architect) knows a good deal more than the master (the client). There should be a dialogue in which you explain your requirements, and the architect tentatively suggests ways to meet them. The architect will have his own tastes and opinions, of course, but he is there to interpret yours (and perhaps do some guiding!). This can be a long-winded and expensive process. You can help to keep it short by being as clear as possible beforehand just what your needs are. In particular, you ought to have a good idea of the overall size you require for your home, and the money you have to build it.

If you have difficulty choosing a plot, advice from an architect may help.

Architectural designer

Architects are not the only people who offer architectural services. Some surveyors, building inspectors, and the like can design houses. They may well produce as satisfactory work as an architect, at least for a conventional design, and their fees are likely to be less.

Package deal

As already mentioned, there are several companies which offer house 'kits' to standard designs, especially for timber-frame houses. To some extent the designs can be customised. A more individual service is offered by some of the companies. They will produce an individual design to your particular requirements and then supply the materials as part of a package deal.

If you are looking at this option, make sure that you are clear what is included in any particular package, and what is not – packages vary a great deal in their composition. (See 'House kits', Appendix 4 for some addresses.)

Check out in advance how many deliveries will be made for the kit, and at what stage(s) payment will be required. If you have to lay out too much in advance for the kit, before you receive stage payments from the building society, you may have cash flow problems.

Book of plans

There are various books of plans which give the overall layout and appearance of a number of designs. If you select one of these then detailed drawings can be purchased at a low price. This is a very economical way to obtain some drawings, but of course, it depends on some ready-made design being suitable for you. You may prefer just to look through the books to pick up ideas.

(See 'Books', Appendix 4.)

Drawings for another house

This is somewhat similar to the above approach, but depends on you finding another house that you would like to copy. Perhaps its owner or builder will let you have a copy of its plans for a very modest cost? (You should check that you were not infringing copyright.)

With a design drawn up, there are three items which relate to it that can be worked out, if required: a specification, a bill of quantities, and costings. Let's consider each of these in turn:

Specification

A specification relates to a particular design and itemises each component of the building process. It describes in detail the work that is to be done. A small illustration from *Specification 90*:

Plastering on plasterboards: Fill all joints with neat board finish plaster. Reinforce all angles with jute scrim not less than 90 mm wide, embedded in neat board finish plaster.

A specification consists of a long list of such items, arranged in sections for each trade.

For the selfbuilder, the specification is an optional extra. It has two uses:

It can be presented to subcontractors when you ask for quotes, so that they know the methods and standards you require. And for the ownhander, it may be useful as an outline guide to the work that has to be done and the way to do it.

An architect or designer will supply a specification for an extra fee. It can also be obtained with some of the building kits. If you are doing your own drawings, there are useful books on specification in reference libraries. Although there is a general trend in building towards the use of specifications, most selfbuilders manage without one.

Bill of quantities

A bill of quantities is a list of all the work that is to be done to construct a building. It is usually drawn up by a quantity surveyor for putting the job out to tender – it forms the basis of the contract. The work involved is broken down in a prescribed manner with items arranged by trade: the Standard Method of Measurement (SMM). Very few selfbuilders use a bill of quantities. Indeed, most commercial house-building is done on a rather informal basis without one.

However, it's certainly worthwhile producing your own little document of basic quantities involved. Do it once, carefully, and this will save you time and error. For example, the plan area will be needed for calculating the volume of hardcore for the slab, the number of boards for the upper floor, and the area of loft insulation. Otherwise, you'll find yourself doing the same sum on the back of an envelope on different trips to the builders' merchants.

Costings

Once you have a design, you will want some costings for it, both for yourself – can you afford it, and is it worthwhile? – and for your building society.

The simplest and quickest approach is to apply a standard cost figure to the nominal floor area. (For the meaning of 'nominal floor area', see 'General considerations', Chapter 19.) House-building costs per square metre can be found in building price books, such as *Laxton's Building Price Book*. The 1990 edition of Laxton's quotes a building cost of £425 to £600 per square metre of nominal floor area for a private house with central heating. A selfbuilder can expect to be at the bottom of the range or, quite possibly, below it. In fact, Murray Armor, the well-known writer on selfbuild, quotes £30 per square foot as a typical construction cost for selfbuild. There are nearly 11 square feet in one square metre, so this converts to something like £330 per square metre – substantially below Laxton's commercial costs. Another specialist in the field quotes £430 – but subcontracting all the labour.

The price books are pricey to buy, but they are usually available in reference libraries. They allow prices to be worked out with varying degrees of sophistication (though not necessarily with accuracy!).

By far and away the easiest method is to use the rough rule-of-thumb above, using a price per square metre of floor. (Larger houses can be built more cheaply per unit area than small ones, but they tend to have more expensive fittings, which helps to even the cost up.)

A more involved method is to use the section on approximate estimates given in *Spon's Architects' and Builders' Price Book*. This gives, for example, a price per square metre for a floor slab. By taking off basic sizes from your drawings, you can come up with costs for all the basic elements of the construction. Their sum should give you a more precise estimate for the overall building.

This approach can be taken to a much more sophisticated level by using the section 'Prices for measured works – minor works'. (Although you may be building a house, it still only rates as a minor work.) Here, prices are given for every element of construction work (based on the Standard Method of Measurement mentioned previously). So, using the bill of quantities, you can calculate an overall price. But to do all the work yourself, you'd have to be something of a masochist to plough through all the detail. It would take you days.

Though you may take a lot of trouble to work out these figures, how accurate will they be? For many selfbuilders they are too high, often considerably so. To start with, they include 10% extra for your non-existent overheads! Regional variations are allowed for: London building prices (the highest) are a third more than those for the East Midlands (the lowest, except for Northern Ireland).

These price books do have a further use. For each element of work, they give not only the cost but also the time that a tradesperson would take to do the job (per unit area, or whatever). This is useful if you want to get some idea of how long you might take. (Earlier, it was suggested that, if you are a semi-skilled amateur, you might take three times as long as a professional, and that, if you start as a novice, the work may take five times as long.)

Another approach to costings, which is a good deal easier and which will give a realistic figure, is to ask for quotations from subcontractors in all the trades. Let others do the calculating!

Obtaining finance

Building societies have for many years gone some way towards helping the selfbuilder. There are large variations from society to society, but a typical arrangement is as follows:

You show the society your drawings and costings for the project, and your estimate of the value of the finished property. (The society may make their own valuation.) On the basis of the valuation (not the cost) and your income, the society offers a mortgage. The money is released in stages, payments of a quarter of the value of the mortgage being made when:

The foundations are down
The roof is on
The walls are plastered
The house is completed.

For most people this is not a satisfactory arrangement. It means that they have to be able to purchase the plot and build the foundations out of their own pocket. How many would-be selfbuilders have sufficient capital for that? Fortunately, a few building societies and banks have now recognised this and are ready to make an advance for the plot. More may follow, and this will certainly make selfbuild accessible to far more people.

There remains another difficulty. To obtain the mortgage, you need the substantial income of full-time employment. In other words, you are expected to build the house in your spare time! This is feasible if you are mainly subcontracting, but if you wish to do most of the work yourself, it is asking too much. (People in selfbuild groups are usually in full-time jobs, but they have a higher level of expertise and specialisation and so build faster. Moreover, they often subcontract some of the work.)

However, by taking out a mortgage a selfbuilder is not contracting with the building society to stay in his job. The ownhander, once he has an agreement for a mortgage, could leave his job – building societies do not ask for repayments to start until the building is complete. (But some may stipulate that you can take only one, or two, years to build it.)

To satisfy themselves that the house is well built, the society will insist that its construction is inspected by a suitably qualified person (architect or surveyor), usually chosen by yourself. The actual qualifications vary a little from society to society; check that the precise qualifications of your 'inspector' are acceptable. (This might, for example, mean that you choose an architect rather than an architectural designer for the design, because the architect is also acceptable for the inspections.) At the end of the build, your inspector will give you an architects' certificate (or a surveyors') stating that the house has been properly built. (The building society will expect the certificate to be backed up by indemnity insurance so that any large claim can be met.)

Another approach, which should satisfy your building society and any future buyer, is to insure the building directly under the 'Foundation 15' scheme run by Municipal Mutual Insurance Ltd. Under this scheme, your home is covered against structural defects for fifteen years. If you sell, the cover is carried over for the new buyer – subject to the limitation that the defect could not reasonably have been discovered by a survey at the time of sale. (This restriction also applies to the NHBC guarantee.) During construction, an inspector visits both at certain stages and at fortnightly intervals. He should be willing to give advice; in addition, participants in the scheme receive a technical manual.

The cost of a Local Authority inspection is £162-15 (with VAT). The 'Foundation 15' scheme costs about £750 for a spacious house with a floor area of 150 square metres. Architects and surveyors generally charge less for a certificate, though their charges vary greatly. It is unfortunate that building societies do not accept the certificate that Local Authority building inspectors issue. That is why there has to be wasteful and costly dual inspections.

There are wide differences in what building societies offer the selfbuilder – in fact, some offer nothing. If you are contemplating selfbuild, it would seem sensible to put your savings into a society that will help you in the future.

Banks are another source of finance, although they too vary considerably in the provisions offered. In general, they offer a commercial loan during the construction phase, with the expectation that, when the house is finished, a mortgage will be taken out, either through the bank or through a building society. Their procedures seem to be less fixed than building societies, and they leave more to the discretion of the bank managers.

Even if you yourself don't need a mortgage and hence don't have to have an inspection certificate, it may still be wise to obtain one. If you wish to sell within a few years of building, such a certificate would re-assure a prospective purchaser and, more particularly, their building society.

Applying for Planning permission

It is worth having some understanding of the Planning process. As already mentioned, the Structure Plan for a particular area is drawn up by the Local Authority after some liaising with the public. It gives the broad outlines for development within the area; Local Plans detail more specific criteria for each locality. Applications for Planning permission usually need to be compatible with these Plans.

Decisions are made not by the professional Planning officers, but by the Planning Committee of local councillors meeting monthly. (Contrast this with the Building Regulations, where it is the officers themselves who make the decisions.) The Committee obviously takes into account the advice of their Planning officers, and they are also influenced by any local objections submitted. If permission is refused, the Local Authority must give their reasons. If they reject your application, you could modify your plans so as to meet their objections, and submit a fresh application. Or you could appeal to the Ministry of the Environment. This latter process takes from five to ten months, and has statistically an evens chance of success. Otherwise, sell the plot and look elsewhere.

Planning permission is often obtained in two stages. The first stage is Outline Planning permission, which controls the nature and size of development on a piece of land. Usually the permission is granted with some conditions expressed as 'Reserved Matters'. The second stage is to apply for 'Approval of Reserved Matters' for the particular design that you intend.

If you already own land without any Planning permission, then there is a case for dispensing with the Outline permission and going immediately for Full permission. If you were to apply for Outline permission, the Planners may stipulate general conditions that they might not have insisted on in a Full application. For example, Outline permission might be granted for a bungalow only, whereas, if Full permission had been sought directly for a very modest house, it might have been granted. (If you should be confused by Planning matters, the Planning officers freely give advice.)

If you are applying for Planning permission yourself, the form can be obtained from the local Planning office. It is the same form whichever type of application you are putting in: Outline or Full permission, or Approval of Reserved Matters. The cost is the same, too: £76.

Some drawings will be needed. For an Outline Planning application, only a location plan (scale at least 1:2,500) is necessary. The site should be outlined in red, and any neighbouring land that you happen to own in blue. For a Full Planning application, you need additional drawings: a site plan (at least 1:500), and plans, elevations and cross sections (at least 1:100). Four copies of both form and drawings are required.

By law, the decision is supposed to be made within eight weeks of submission, but Local Authorities are usually late. If they are, you can appeal, but that would hardly seem worthwhile.

If a building is erected without Planning consent, the Local Authority has four years in which to serve an enforcement notice to have the building modified or taken down. Otherwise, the building can remain as it is. Local objectors have quite an influence in these matters.

If you are having an architect draw up your plans, it is usual to let him apply both for Planning permission and for Building Regulations approval. This is sensible because he can adjust the design to the Local Authority's requirements. And if he is a local architect, he will probably have a good idea already of what will satisfy them.

Lastly, a note about any trees on your plot: They may have a preservation order on them. In this case you should ask permission before lopping or felling them.

(A practical note: Trees dry out the ground around them, and this can damage foundations. For more about this topic, see Chapter 5: *Foundations*.)

3
PREPARING TO BUILD

☆

☆

☆

☆

☆

☆

☆

Building Regulations approval
Sundry office work
Site layout
Insurances
Certification
Value Added Tax
Subcontractors
Miscellaneous preparations

WITH PLANNING PERMISSION applied for, you might think that you can take it easy while you wait to hear the outcome. Not so! There are many jobs to be done, especially if you want to press on with building as soon as you hear of a favourable decision.

You should by now have some idea of the time span you need for your project, and how this is going to tie in with the seasons. You will soon come to realise that the builder is as vulnerable to the weather as the farmer. Wet ground can cause no end of trouble when you are putting the foundations down. In frosty weather, concreting and bricklaying have to stop. The best time to start is probably the late spring, when the ground is dry and there are several months of good weather ahead. In days gone by, the foundations were sometimes put down in the autumn, when the ground is very dry, and left over the winter; work resumed in the spring. If this approach should suit you, cover the tops of the walls to prevent frost damage. People do start building in midwinter, but this can't be recommended!

Building Regulations approval

A major decision to take is whether or not to apply straight away for Building Regulations approval. This is taking a gamble on your Planning application. (Overall, 15% of applications are turned down.) If your Planning application is rejected, and you make a new application for a modified design, then you will have to apply again for Building Regulations approval. The original fee will have been wasted. Obviously, if you're not in a hurry to start building, the sensible course is to wait for Planning permission before applying for Building Regulations approval.

Applications for Building Regulations approval are processed much more quickly than Planning applications. You should hear the result within a month, but if you don't want to wait you needn't. You can inform the building inspector that you are about to build, and he will come out and inspect your work as it progresses. (You are gambling that your plans, for the foundations at least, do conform with the Regulations.)

If in a quandary about which course to follow, talk it over with your building inspector; he is likely to be helpful. You can phone or visit. (For more information about Building Regulations, see Chapter 19.)

Sundry office work

Paperwork that can be dealt with at this stage is involved in opening various accounts. Open a cheque account, sensibly one that pays interest when you are in credit – some large sums are going to be flowing through the account! And you will want accounts with some builders' merchants. These accounts will not bring much discount, but they will make book-keeping much easier. Invoices handled on site tend to get lost, and that means – unless you obtain a copy invoice – that VAT is lost. Those grubby bits of paper can be worth more than bank notes! (You may be able to negotiate more discount by agreeing beforehand to put all your business through just one builders' merchant. You might not get the best deal on every item, but it could be worthwhile overall. It will certainly save a lot of hassle in chasing round to find who gives the best price on each purchase.)

Another useful account to fix up would be with a tool hire shop. Once again, an account will keep the paperwork tidier, and save the trouble of producing a deposit every time you wish to hire.

Opening these accounts will usually involve references and take a couple of weeks.

Find out the delivery times required for your initial materials. For ready-mixed concrete, cement and sand, it will be a few days at most; but for blocks, and door and window frames, it could be a month; for bricks, as much as six months – it all depends upon whether the construction industry is in a boom or bust phase! It is prudent to get your orders in early. (If building is delayed through a Planning refusal, you can always hold or cancel the orders.) Large quantities of bricks and blocks are delivered straight from the works, but you still have to order through a builders' or brick merchant. It's most economical to purchase a whole lorry-load of bricks, or at least, a whole number of pallets. (Ask the merchant what these quantities are for your particular bricks.) As for the frames, the largest joinery manufacturers have their own showrooms for direct ordering. (You may or may not get discount.) For frames from a smaller manufacturer, order through a builders' merchant. It will be the door frames, of course, that you will need first – as soon as you build up from the dpc.

Site layout

Before receiving any deliveries, you should have sorted out your arrangements for the site. If the vegetation is more than ankle high then cut it down – a hired strimmer is useful for this. (Please try to spare shrubs and trees. They will give your garden an air of maturity while prettier plants develop. Don't be like the professional builders who obliterate nature rather than working with it.) With the site clear, you can think of what is going where. The position of the house, drains and drive is given by the plans! If the access is fair and the ground is dry, it's a good idea to have the big deliveries of bricks and blocks made to the back-garden-to-be; the front becomes cluttered enough later. Arrange to receive these deliveries before excavations (or wet weather) make the back of the plot inaccessible to large lorries.

The spoils from the excavations will also need consideration. Generally, the topsoil from stripping the plan area is kept in a big mound. (This will shrink to halve its size as the vegetation rots and hollows fill up.) It can be in an out-of-the-way part of the site, to be spread around when building is complete. The subsoil from digging out the foundation trenches is not generally so useful, although it can be used for landscaping later – in particular, for levelling off a sloping site. If the site is big enough, the surplus can be left in a mound, away from building activities, until the site is tidied up at the end of the build. By then, there will be other spoil from drain trenches and the like, and it can all be trucked away at the same time. To be rid of it, you will have to hire a lorry to work in collaboration with an excavator. The spoil can be taken to a tip (where a tipping charge will be made). Altogether, this is an expensive job. But if you're lucky, a local farmer will take it for free.

There will be trenches in the front garden for drains and services. Near to the building, you will be needing a mixing area to which cement and sand can be delivered. By the highway, there will be the water stand-pipe. An area will be needed for storing roof trusses. On a small site, forethought is needed to find space for everything without causing obstructions.

Where should the various services enter the house? For gas and electricity, which enter via plastic boxes on an outside wall, appearances are a factor. Even though the boxes can be painted, they are rather ugly, and the house will look better if they are kept off the front elevation. (A side wall of a garage is often suitable.) Remember: the electricity consumer unit is fixed inside, close to the meter box. The supplies to the boxes are laid by the Gas and Electricity Companies themselves, in trenches about a third of a metre deep in straight lines out to the road. The water supply, on the other hand, is your responsibility from the highway edge. Generally, the water enters at the front of the house, eg, via the kitchen or cloakroom. The water pipe needs to be laid quite deep so that it cannot freeze. (Severn Trent Water stipulate 70 cm, for example.) The pipe can be laid on top of drains, if required, but it's considered bad practice to lay a water pipe along the foundations, in case the pipe freezes and bursts.

Lastly, there is the telecom cable. British Telecom will supply you with the cable, leaving you to lay it from the highway edge. The cable is laid about a third of a metre deep, protected by grey conduit (also supplied by British Telecom). This service is the least demanding as to where it enters the house – the cable will simply be buried in the plaster on a route to the phone socket. Entering the building via an opening for the water or drain pipe may be convenient. And if you want to look ahead to the next decade or two, you could put in a draw-string alongside the cable so that you'll be able to pull through an optic fibre, or whatever, in the future.

In this discussion about the layout of the site, we have become way ahead of ourselves. On commercial sites, the services may not be laid until the end of the build. But electricity and a phone are so useful that many selfbuilders like to have them installed much earlier – as soon as there is a wall to take the electric box and the phone socket. (This is presuming reasonable site security, and a temporary earth for the electricity. See 'Temporary supply', Chapter 10.) The convenience of a phone on the site – or, at least, nearby – cannot be over-emphasised. And the local *Yellow Pages* are invaluable. If you don't have a copy, it's very well worth buying one from British Telecom.

Fixing up the temporary water supply will usually be the first real work to happen on site. It is placed by the highway edge, at a convenient position for running the permanent supply to the house later on. It is your responsibility to fix up a stand-pipe with tap, and the Water Company connects this to their main. A fee is charged for 'building water', eg, Severn Trent Water charge £33 plus VAT. It used to be that a stand-pipe was simply a bib tap on some 15 mm copper pipe supported by a stout stake in the ground. You will find that your Water Company is more demanding now. They will probably want an anti-siphonic valve and a stop tap fitted. If, instead, a friendly neighbour will let you run a hose from their garden tap, you will be doing well. There is one sense in which Water Companies are certainly more demanding: Their fees for a new supply have increased enormously since privatisation. For example, Severn Trent Water charge £263 plus Vat for connecting the main. That is much as it used to be. It is the new 'infra-structure' charges which annoy builders. There is a fee of £498 plus VAT for new users of mains water, and £356 plus VAT for sewerage – virtually £1,000 for the right to use mains water and sewerage.

Another item of the site layout to be considered is a lockable shelter for storage of tools and materials. This might be your future garden shed, an old caravan, or a scrap motor van. And if you wish to to live on site, you'll want a comfortable caravan. Planning permission is said by some to be required for this, but it depends on the area of the country how fussy the Local Authorities are about this. What they seem most concerned about is the sanitary arrangements. A chemical toilet (with some arrangements for disposing of its contents) should be satisfactory. But Planning permission may not even be necessary. Construction workers have a right to live on site, though not, presumably, non-building family members. Whether this right extends to selfbuilders is probably an untested area of law. Anyway, some Local Authorities accept it.

Insurances

Another topic that needs your consideration is insurance. Building is a healthy outdoor occupation and you are unlikely to become sick; but, sad to say, you are liable to be injured.

The construction industry is one of the most dangerous, and as a novice in it, you must be at risk. So you may want to consider insurance cover for personal accident.

Then there are other people who come onto your site, whether invited or not, and who may be injured as a result of something that could be construed as negligence on your part. Insurances for Public Liability and Employers' Liability would cover their claims.

And the building itself? Until it is roofed in, the shell is susceptible to storms. Whole walls can be blown over. 'Contract Works' insurance covers such events (and also the theft of tools and materials).

So you may wish to take out insurances. But in the past, it has not been easy for selfbuilders to obtain a builders' policy – some insurers require five years' building experience! Once again, though, institutions are starting to cater for selfbuild. For example, the Norwich Union offers a Self-Build policy that covers Public Liability, Employers' Liability, and Contract Works; the premium is 0·45% of the value of the property on completion. It depends upon your temperament, whether you consider this to be a likely waste of money or a necessary prerequisite for a sound night's sleep!

Certification

If you are taking out a mortgage, the building society will require a certificate from an architect or surveyor, or the Foundation 15 guarantee. (See 'Obtaining finance', Chapter 2.) The construction of your home will be inspected as it progresses. Try to employ somebody who will be helpful to you and who will put in more than two-minute appearances on site. (Some architects and surveyors look upon these inspections as money-spinners.) Are you going to get your money's worth out of them? Some point of building technique that is puzzling or worrying you can often be sorted out easily by a quick phone call to a helpful architect or surveyor. A site visit is even better. If you've had an architect draw up your design, he is obviously the first candidate to consider for a certificate, provided his charges are not too high.

Besides these inspections for a certificate, your building society may want yet another professional (charging yet another professional fee) to come and look over your work. This is a valuer, to check the progress of the build for each stage payment.

Value Added Tax

Although you won't be making out a VAT return until the very end of the build, it's useful to obtain now the VAT leaflet (no. 719) which explains VAT refunds on DIY houses. This can be had by phoning up the VAT department in the nearest Customs and Excise office. Only one claim can be made, when the house has been finished.

If it is your intention to engage tradespeople for some of the work, then there are different bases on which they may wish to be engaged. A 'subcontractor' will do the job for a definite 'supply and fix' price, ie, he will do the work and supply the materials. You should check beforehand that he is VAT-registered, so that he can give you a zero-rated invoice. This means that you do not pay any VAT on the materials he supplies. But if he is not VAT-registered, then materials should be purchased in your name so that you can eventually reclaim the VAT.

Subcontractors

Most selfbuilders employing subcontractors will be happier to be quoted a fixed price for a job. (Get two or three quotes, of course.) But some tradespeople prefer 'day work', ie, charging for time worked. It may well be that these people do the best quality work – and not necessarily charging more than those working to a price. Knowing their reputations and seeing examples of their work will help to choose between the competing claims of different tradespeople. It could be that they would take advantage of your comparative ignorance of building and do shoddy work, but in practice, it is more likely to go the other way, and the unusual and personal nature of the job bring out their best.

The best value in subcontracting is usually offered by the self-employed. Their overheads are minimal, so they can give a keen price. And they need to do good work to maintain a good reputation to bring in more work. If you subcontract to a firm, you could be paying them as much for their overheads and profit as for the labour. That can't be your best deal. The 'cowboy' is, by and large, a mythical figure. If he does take you for a ride – blame your own intuition!

Whether or not your subcontractor is a cowboy, do check the work as it progresses. Don't naively expect that what you ask for is necessarily what you will get. Bricklayers, for example, have a tendency to put window frames in wrong positions, or even to miss them out; the studwork that a carpenter puts up may not accord with the plans; etc. Even though well intentioned and experienced, people can make mistakes. The sooner you spot a mistake, the more easily it can be corrected and the less the aggro.

The first subcontractor to be needed on site is an excavator, and it is useful to locate one in advance. What you want is a 'back-hoe loader', more popularly called a 'JCB'. (J.C. Bamford founded the company that makes them.) They are often operated as one-man businesses. To find one locally, look inside the *Yellow Pages*. (Try 'Contractors' plant and machinery hire', 'Excavation contractors' or 'Groundwork contractors'.) Or just keep a lookout for a JCB working in the neighbourhood. Charges are about £14 an hour for working and half that for travelling. They can do a lot of work in an hour!

Miscellaneous preparations

Although the main items to arrange before building commences have been covered above, there are still many diverse things that can be usefully done while you wait for Planning permission or Building Regulations approval.

Spend some time looking around building sites. Most of the work done on sites is by subcontractors, so if you are intending to use subbies later on, this is an opportunity to contact them and to get some idea of the quality of their work. It is also an opportunity to familiarise yourself with building sites in general, and more particularly, with details of techniques used. But because something is done in one way on one site, don't think that that is the only way. There may, indeed, be better. What you can expect, though, is that the technique must be passably good. Provided that you explain why you're looking around and you don't appear to be a potential thief, you should not be unwelcome.

Knowledge can also be gained from books, magazines, courses, TV programs, and manufacturers' brochures. The best way to get hold of the brochures is through the advertising magazine, *Professional Builder*, available for free at some builders' merchants. And talk with friends, and the man in the pub. Take the opportunity to collect secondhand tools and equipment: a trailer for your car, a cement mixer, builders' trestles, tarpaulins, etc, and perhaps scaffolding. (Auctions are a good source.) Think about clothing. The British approach is to wear any old clothes. That's fine from a recycling point of view; but clothes that were originally designed for fashion aren't very helpful on a building site. The Continental way is better – invest in some purpose-made work clothes. And an apron pouch is particularly useful for holding nails when you are roofing or plasterboarding.

Get yourself a first-aid kit – before you need it!

As a souvenir, are you going to keep a diary of this special time in your life? And you might like to take a photograph of the site before you start – it will never look the same again!

Couples take note: Selfbuild has a reputation for making or breaking relationships!

And last but not least: Prepare body and mind for the task ahead.

So you can see, from all the above, that there is a lot to keep you busy while you wait to hear from the Planning authorities.

Anyway, let us assume now that Planning permission is granted, so that in the next chapter we can set out, at last, to build.

PART TWO

CONSTRUCTING THE SHELL

☆

☆

☆

☆

☆

☆

☆

☆

☆

☆

☆

☆

☆

☆

☆

☆

☆

4

SETTING OUT

☆

☆

☆

☆

☆

☆

☆

Stripping topsoil
Setting out
Levels

INFORM THE BUILDING INSPECTOR that you are about to start building! Even if your plans have not yet been approved by the inspector, it is quite in order to make a start – as long as you are confident about the design of the foundations.

'Setting out' is actually a technical term; it means marking out the plan of the building onto the ground. You may imagine this to be a simple process, but there are a couple of difficulties. How can right angles be accurately constructed on such a large scale? The builder needs to know a little geometry. The other difficulty is that, although you may accurately mark out the positions for the corners with pegs in the ground – what use is that when the excavator just uproots them when digging out the foundation trenches? The use of 'profiles' (as described later) solves this problem in a simple but ingenious manner.

Stripping topsoil

You should have already strimmed the site of excessive vegetation; now, the plan area of the home-to-be needs stripping of its topsoil. (If left, the vegetable matter would decay away, which could cause subsidence of the floor.) So mark out the approximate positions of the corners of the building with wooden pegs. Their positions don't need to be accurate, since it's a good idea to strip away an extra couple of metres from around the perimeter. Using your pegs, the digger driver can strip the area by eye, but you may wish to mark out the boundary more precisely. How do you mark out a line over rough ground? A common method is to take a double handful of sand, preferably dry, and let it trickle down between your hands as you walk along the line to be marked.

The moment when the excavator first trundles onto the site is an exciting one. You are about to make your mark! Actually, stripping is a quick and easy process that can be finished within an hour. The topsoil is best heaped in an out-of-the-way place for use again later. On firm ground, the performance of a JCB is prodigious, but on wet ground the machine can be worse than useless. Not only is it unable to work effectively, but in its struggles it will turn the site into a rutted quagmire. Better be patient and wait for drier conditions – or use a tracked excavator (such as a 'Drott').

Some builders like to strip the topsoil from a much greater area than suggested above – in fact, from the whole area being used for the building operations. The reason for this is that, at the end of the build when this good quality topsoil is levelled off around the garden, the soil will be uncontaminated by all the builders' debris which is invariably strewn around a site.

On a sloping site, you may wish to take off more than topsoil and to strip away some of the higher ground. This will enable the eventual dpc level to be lower. (Remember that the dpc has to be at least 15 cm above the surrounding ground level.) It is usually cheaper to lower the high end of the plan area and cart away subsoil than it is to build up the low end with higher foundation walls and extra hardcore in the floor base. The appearance is affected, too. Do you want a somewhat sunken, sheltered look, or a higher, more exposed and imposing appearance? On very sloping sites, stepped dpc's are used. (For details of this complication, see textbooks.)

Extra excavating is usually needed for the floor of an integral garage; this will be lower than the house floor. And it's a good idea to strip the topsoil of the driveway-to-be at this stage.

Setting out

For setting out, you should allow yourself the best part of a day. It may not take so long, but this is critical work and not a job to be rushed.

Figure 1: Setting out a right angle

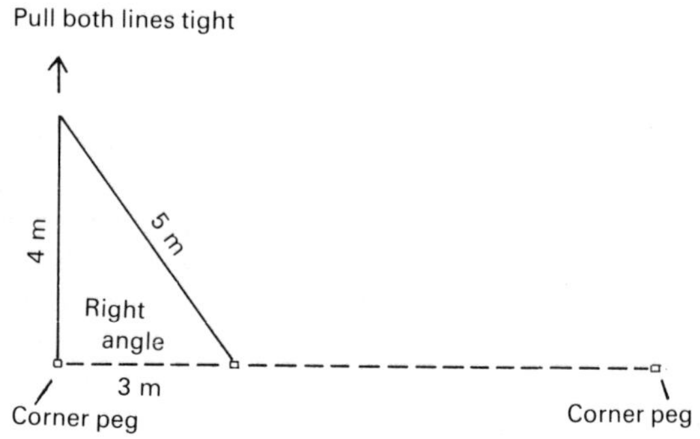

* If the sides of a triangle are in the ratio 3:4:5 then the triangle must contain a right angle.

The positions for the corners of the building need to be accurately located. First of all, mark out the direction for a base line. This will usually be the line of the front wall, though sometimes a side wall may be more appropriate, eg, if it is very close to a boundary.

Use wooden pegs about 5 cm square and 30 cm long. For accurate positioning of the line, knock a nail into the top of each peg, and stretch the line between the nails. When marking out the base line, extend it further than is required, ie, the first step is to mark the direction of the line, but not its length. This direction is obtained by measuring back from the highway, or by lining up by eye with neighbouring property, etc. Then along this line position the first corner, with peg and nail, by measuring the required distance from the adjacent boundary. From this first corner, measure off the required distance for the second corner peg.

With the base line marked out, the slightly tricky part is to mark out a side line at right angles. Sighting along a builders' square can be done, but it is more accurate to use the 3–4–5 triangle. (See 'Squareness', Chapter 27.) So, in the base line, put an extra peg 3 metres from a corner peg. From this corner have a line 4 metres long, and from the extra peg a line 5 metres long. If the two lines are now stretched out together and swung round so that their ends meet, then a right angle will have been formed. (See Fig. 1.)

With a side line marked out, other corners can be located by measuring along the sides of rectangles. Check the squareness by measuring the two diagonals of a large rectangle – they should be equal. If you have a calculator with a square root function, then the length of the diagonal can be calculated direct – there is no need to set out the intermediate 3–4–5 triangle. (For those cases where the plan is not a simple rectangle, it may be necessary to put in an extra peg to make one up.)

How accurate does the squareness have to be? Diagonals equal to within two or three centimetres are fine for timber-frame construction, and double that figure is acceptable for brick-and-block. Does it matter if the building is not exactly square? It does for timber-frame, but for brick-and-block it hardly matters structurally. However, cosmetically, non-squareness may show up in some unexpected ways. On the roof, for example, rectangular tiles will not fit well – though a tiler with his wits about him should be able to compensate satisfactorily. Inside, patterned carpets show up out-of-square rooms. So it is worthwhile achieving squareness even for brick-and-block construction – it's not something that can be rectified later!

What we have done so far is to mark out with pegs the corners for all the external walls and for those internal walls

Figure 2: Profiles with corner peg

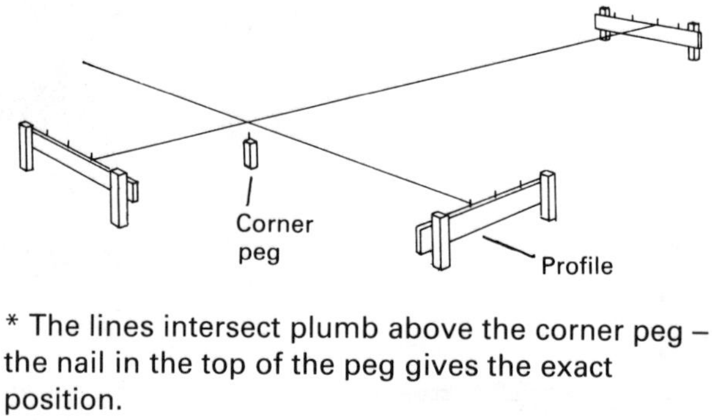

* The lines intersect plumb above the corner peg – the nail in the top of the peg gives the exact position.
* See also Fig. 7, Chapter 5.

which have foundations (including a chimney breast, if any). Don't be disturbed if the house, as marked out on the ground, looks too small. This is a common illusion. As the house is built, the 'dolls house' will seem to expand!

We now come to the use of 'profiles' for fixing the positions of the corners. Profiles are boards used in pairs to mark each end of a line. So, a line through a corner peg is extended out for a metre or so and its position marked on a profile board. The profile must be far enough away to be undisturbed by the digging of the trenches. (See Figs. 2 and 3.)

Figure 3: Positions of profiles

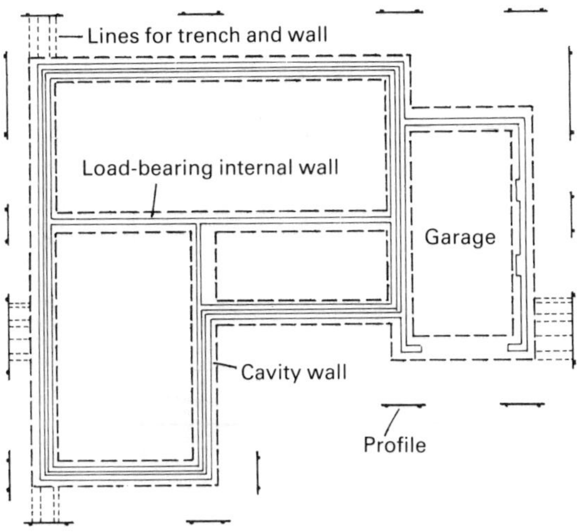

* The profiles fix the positions of all the foundation walls and trenches.

In practical terms the profile consists of a metre length of $2\frac{1}{2} \times 10$ cm timber, nailed at each end to two stout pegs. The direction of the line is marked by knocking a nail into the top of the board. (Some people use a saw cut instead.) From this mark, for the outer face of the wall, we can measure off some other marks: the inner face of the wall (a cavity wall is $22\frac{1}{2}$ cm or 25 cm thick), and the trench sides. In fact, digger drivers often work to a centre line for digging a trench, so this too can be marked.

Set up all the profiles: two at each external corner, and one at a corner with an internal wall. The corner pegs can now be dispensed with. Their positions can always be re-established by the intersections of 'ranging' lines stretched between the profiles.

We are now nearly ready for the digger to return to dig out the trenches. But the reader may have noticed that the selfbuilder is at a disadvantage in the matter of excavations. On a large building site, a digger is available as required. A selfbuilder requires a digger for a short time to strip the site and sends it away. And then a day or two later, he or she wants it back to dig the trenches. Travelling time may be charged at half the usual rate, but unless the digger is local, an unwelcome cost is incurred. There is a way round this that you may like to use: You put the profiles up before the topsoil is stripped. But you put them well away (3 metres or more) from the trench lines, so that the topsoil can be stripped without the profiles causing any obstruction.

You don't have to use an excavator. A few selfbuilders manage without. And the Victorians, and their predecessors, built their houses with muscle power. (The foundations, however, were much more shallow than the modern practice).

Levels

Before excavations are commenced, consideration should be given to levels. An important factor is the slope for the drains. Although this is unlikely to be a problem, the house must be high enough to give an adequate slope on the drains. The lower end is fixed – the sewer that your drains are running into. The minimum slope is generally taken to be 1 in 80, though it is possible to lay drains a little flatter, if necessary. The floor level must be high enough to allow the required slope.

So, after considering the relevant factors – drainage, landscaping, and the choice between building up or excavating away – decide at what level you want the dpc to be. Usually it is 15 cm above the finished ground level. But since, at this stage, 'finished ground level' is a variable factor, it is helpful to establish a datum level. This may be a fixed level already on site (eg, a manhole cover) or a purpose-made datum (eg, a peg set in concrete, out of the way of building operations). Decide the level you want for the dpc relative to this datum. Transfer the level round to each corner, fixing it either with a peg in the ground or by marking a profile. (The levels can be transferred with a level-board or a Cowley level. See 'Levelness', Chapter 27.)

5
FOUNDATIONS

☆
☆
☆
☆
☆
☆
☆

This chapter should be read in conjunction with Chapter 20, 'Mortar and Concrete', and Chapter 21, 'Bricklaying'.

IN SELFBUILD, you have to start with the foundations; you have to plunge into the deep end. And deep water it can be if you're caught out by wet weather. In house-building, the worst comes first. If you've got what it takes to 'get out of the ground', then you can be confident that you can overcome any future hurdles. Even professional builders find the foundations troublesome as they battle with the elements. The DIY enthusiast is not usually called upon to lay foundations; for him (or her), this area is probably unfamiliar, and so is even more difficult. May this book be a good guide!

The purpose of the foundations is to hold up the weight of the walls and the roof, and to provide a level base from which to build. The soil must be firm enough to take the load; and it must not move with the weather. One problem is frost heave, in which water in the ground freezes and pushes upwards as it expands to ice. This is worst with sandy soils. Clay soils present a different problem. In a drought they shrink, and the contractions can crack foundations. Both these weather-induced changes can penetrate to a depth of half a metre. So to reach more stable ground, it is general for foundations to go down nowadays to two-thirds of a metre, or more. (That's the theory. But how is it that so many Victorian houses stand with foundations that go down only through the topsoil? Is much of the concrete that we pour into and over the ground an enormous waste of resources?)

Given below are the two conventional methods for making foundations in firm ground. (On soft ground, a raft of reinforced concrete can be used. See textbooks.)

The 'traditional' method is strip foundations. The trenches are 60 cm wide, and dug to a depth of two-thirds of a metre (or whatever the building inspector deems is suitable for your ground). A level strip of concrete, about 15 cm deep, is poured round the bottom, and on this the cavity walls are built in brick and/or block. (See Fig. 1.)

Figure 1: Strip foundations

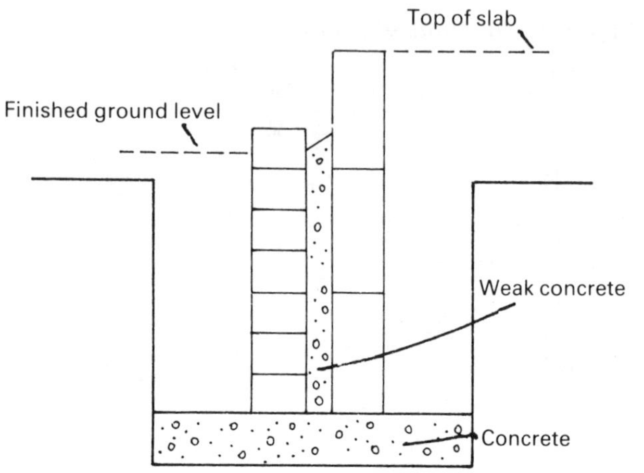

For an ownhander strip foundations are an appropriate method, because they give an opportunity to practise brick and block laying – the results will later be buried out of sight! (A modern alternative dispenses with cavity construction below ground and uses extra-thick blocks – one block being as thick as a cavity wall.)

The method is vulnerable to wet weather. The trenches may flood before the walls can be built. Work is held up, and the sides of the trenches may collapse. (Hiring a pump may allow work to continue.)

A new method is trenchfill foundations – easier and quicker but more costly. The trench is narrower (45 cm), but deeper (about a metre). The whole trench is filled with concrete nearly up to ground level. (See Fig. 2.)

The concrete is supported not only by the bottom of the trench, but also by friction at the sides. The cost of materials is considerably more, but much less labour is required. Because it is narrower, the trench must be dug accurately if the walls are to be central. The big advantage of the method is speed, with less vulnerability to wet weather. The trench can be dug one day and filled the next.

If you are putting in only single glazed windows, then the Building Regulations expect the floor slab to be insulated (U = ·45, or less). Of course, being a sensible selfbuilder you are double glazing, and so there is no requirement about floor insulation. Nonetheless, this is something you may like to attend to – it's very difficult once the house has been built!

With strip foundations, vertical perimeter insulation is easy (though not as effective as whole floor insulation). Just attach polystyrene to the inside face of the foundation walls. And for further insulation, the walls themselves can be built of insulating blocks (suitable for use below ground, of course – eg, standard 'Thermalite' or 'Celcon' blocks). With the trenchfill method, this form of insulation is not possible. (Don't try and attach polystyrene to the side of the trench – remember, the foundation concrete needs the frictional support from the sides of the trench.)

Figure 2: Trenchfill foundations

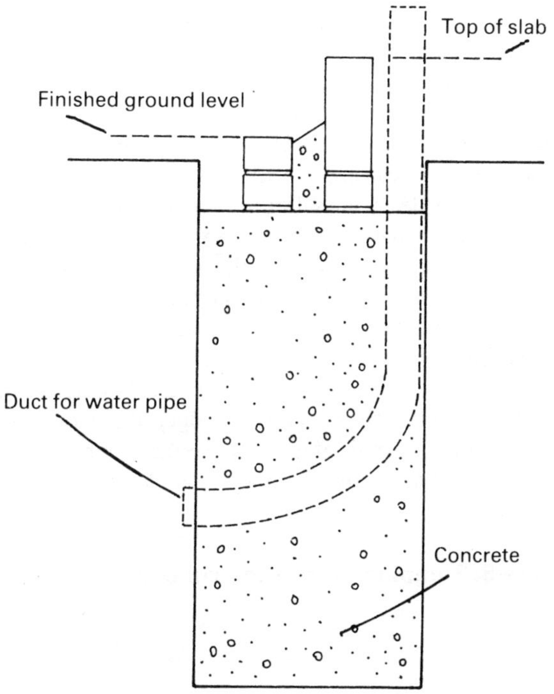

If there are trees near the foundations, they pose a potential hazard; they dry out the ground around them. In a drought, the ground around them will become extra dry, and tend to shrink (particularly clay). This can damage foundations. So if there are trees nearby, the foundations need to be made extra deep. Particularly 'thirsty' trees are elm, oak, popular and willow; allowances must be made for them if they are within some 25 metres of the foundations. (For more information on this subject, see the NHBC's *Registered House-Builder's Handbook*.) If you particularly want trees growing within a few metres of your house, consider the Segal method of construction using concrete pads for foundations.

Don't think that felling a tree will simply solve your foundation problem. Without the tree to dry it out, the ground will gradually become wetter, and so, if it is clay, it will expand. This too can damage foundations. So where a tree has been felled, don't put foundations down for a year or so. This will allow the ground to reach a new equilibrium.

Strip foundations:

Excavating

With ranging lines for the trenches stretched between the profiles, use sand to mark the lines out on the ground. The digger driver will want to use either a centre line or two side lines. Hopefully, there will be no rain to wash the lines away.

When the digger arrives, the driver will work out the order to dig the trenches without impeding himself, ie, without being blocked off by a trench dug too soon. He'll put a 24″ bucket onto the back-hoe and then have a busy couple of hours. The spoil can be heaped up for storage or trucking away. You may want to have some spoil left by the trenches for backfilling them later. (See 'Floor slab', later in this chapter.)

When he starts, the digger will dig down to the depth required (60 cm or more). He can keep the bottom pretty level by eye, but it is prudent to check this by a level-board, boning rods, Cowley level, or whatever, using the datums previously marked at each corner.

If there are to be foundations for 10 cm internal walls, these need not be so deep. (They can also be narrower, although it may not be worthwhile changing the bucket.)

On a sloping site, expensive concrete can be saved by putting in steps. (See Figs. 3 and 4.)

Figure 3: Step in foundation concrete

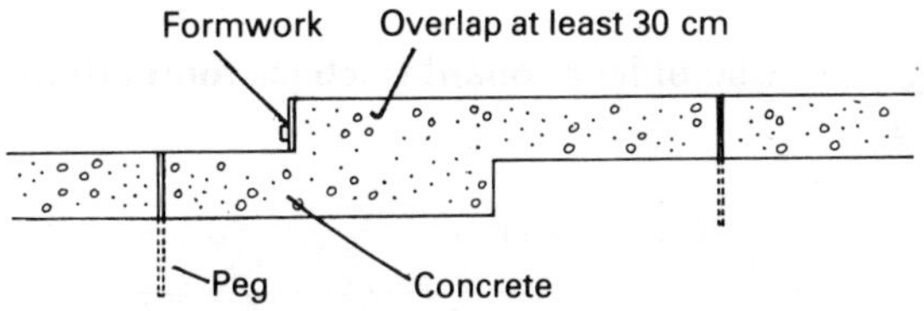

* The height of the step equals a whole number of brick courses ($7\frac{1}{2}$ cm, 15 cm, etc).
* For trenchfill, the overlap should be a metre.
* See also Fig. 4.

The height of the steps should be multiples of $7\frac{1}{2}$ cm, ie, whole brick courses. A good digger driver will leave the trench bottoms clean; otherwise you should shovel out all the loose bits. (The firm 'toothmarks' of the excavator's bucket can be left.)

The garage needs some consideration. Is there a need for foundations under the entrance? Some builders put the foundations in to help tie the side wall in place. Others don't see this as worthwhile. Another point to bear in mind is that the garage floor will be lower than the house floor, so the garage area may need extra excavation.

With the trenches dug, it is time for an inspection. Phone the building inspector, or post him one of the pre-printed stage cards that he will have supplied you with.

Concreting the foundations

No hardcore is used. Steel or timber pegs are used to show

the level required for the top of the concrete. (Pegs can be cut from 1 cm steel reinforcement rod or from 4 x 4 cm timber.) Hammer one peg into the trench bottom so that its top gives

Figure 4: Formwork for a step in foundation concrete

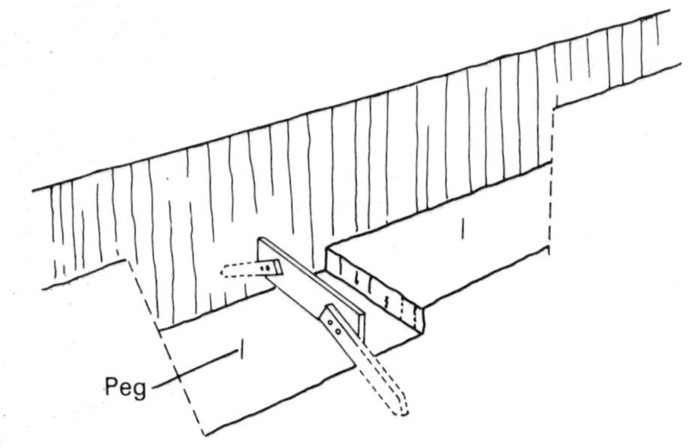

* The tops of the pegs give the levels for the concrete.
* See also Fig. 3.

the required depth of concrete (usually 15 cm). Then work all the way round the trenches knocking in a peg every two or three metres so that its top indicates the required level. To check the level, use a level-board, or Cowley level. (See Fig. 5.)

Figure 5: Use of level-board to check foundation pegs

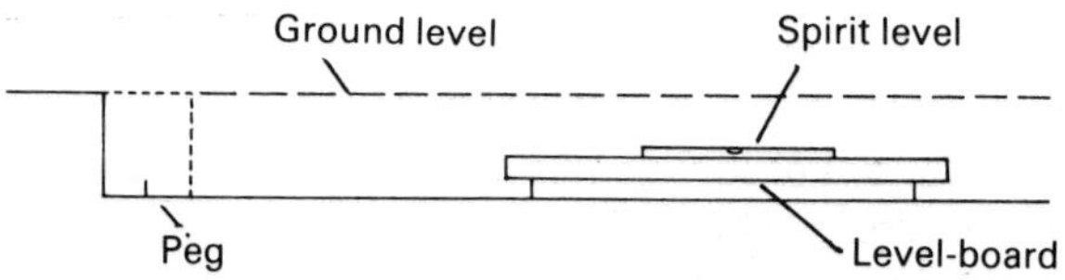

* Board must have parallel edges.

The surface of the concrete should be a whole number of courses below the dpc level. At any step in the concrete, the upper level is a multiple number of courses higher than the lower level. (A step should overlap the concrete below by 30 cm and should not be higher than the thickness of the concrete. If a steeper drop is required, see textbooks.) Some simple formwork is needed to form a step: A board as deep as the step required is jammed into the trench and supported by a couple of pegs. (See Fig. 4.)

The calculation of the volume of concrete required is straightforward. The mix is usually 1:3:6. Ready-mixed concrete comes in lorry loads of 5 or 6 cubic metres. The price for a part load is considerably higher, unless it is delivered in conjunction with a full load. There's no point in mixing such large quantities of concrete yourself; it won't save you money. Get the concrete into the trenches as soon as you can – before they can become waterlogged by heavy rain. (A few puddles at the bottom of the trenches are acceptable – the excess water will float to the top.) For two men this concreting is not an arduous job, so order the loads at, say, half-hour intervals.

You will probably be feeling a funny mixture of excitement and apprehension when the first truckful of concrete appears. Make life easy for yourself by getting the driver to discharge the load at different corners. (If you have stepped trenches, work from the lower to the higher level, of course.) But first the driver may ask you if you want some more water adding to the mix. This seems to be a common site practice to help the workers – with extra water the concrete flows more easily. However, extra water weakens the concrete. Anyway, with the truck's swivelling chute sending the concrete flowing down the trenches, jump in and help it on its way with a shovel. A garden rake is also useful.

But beware! Concrete burns! Wet concrete can burn your skin without you realising it – though later you will certainly feel the pain! At least one selfbuilder has been burnt so badly that he has had to have skin grafts. So wear wellies, and don't allow the the concrete to get over the top of them. Nowadays, suppliers of ready-mixed put a warning on their delivery tickets about the caustic nature of concrete.

Spread the concrete around so that it is level with the tops of the pegs, which can be left in place. A purpose-made tamper is useful: a thick board on edge, about two metres long, with a long handle at each end so that the board can be tamped up and down by a couple of people atop the trench. (See Fig. 6.)

Figure 6: Tamping foundation concrete

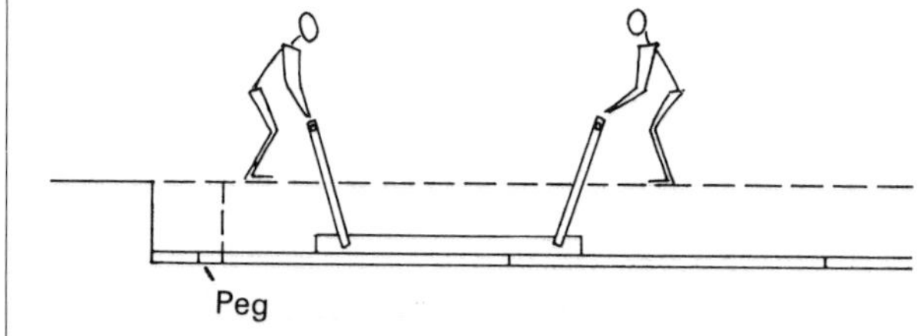

* Pegs can be left in place.

Foundation walls

The following day, when the concrete is firm, start building up the walls. Don't delay lest there should be heavy rain. The walls can be built of bricks – reject facings are cheaper than commons – or blockwork. In either case, make sure the bricks or blocks are suitable for use below ground. Most are. For the ownhander, the foundation walls are an opportunity to practise the laying of bricks and blocks. So in the following paragraphs, the foundation walls are built up as conventional cavity walling: brickwork for the outer skin, and blockwork for the inner. Use a strong mortar below the dpc – 1:4, with plasticiser.

First of all the corners are to be built up off the foundation concrete. To fix their positions, the profiles are used with lines stretched between them.

Figure 7: Use of ranging lines

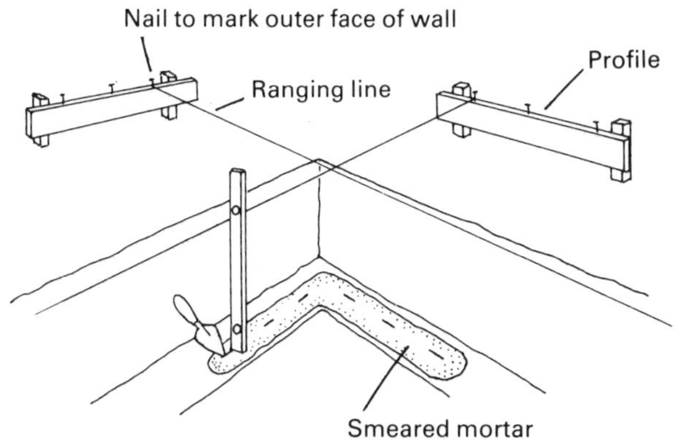

* To transfer intersection of ranging lines onto foundation concrete: Smear some mortar over the concrete and make three marks plumb beneath each line. Score a line through each set of marks to outline the corner.

A corner is given by the intersection of two lines, and its position has to be transferred down onto the concrete in the bottom of the trench. To do this, smear a thin layer of mortar onto the concrete along each arm of the corner. (See Fig. 7.)

Make marks in the wet mortar plumb beneath each ranging line. Use a spirit level, if necessary steadying it with a stick propped against the trench side. Join up the marks to give the line for each wall: the intersection gives the corner.

Mark out all the corners in this manner, and take down the ranging lines out of the way.

Cavity walls are built with the simple stretcher bond. Work the bond out with a dry run. For a particular wall, lay out bricks with a 10 mm gap between them, working from each end towards the centre. (A stick of chalk between bricks gives the right gap.) If you are lucky or, more correctly, if it is a thoughtful design, then the two lines of bricks will meet together maintaining the 10 mm mortar gap. More likely, the gap will be awkward. The gap can be changed by adjusting the cross joints: They can all be thickened or thinned by a millimetre or two. 'Reversing the bond' changes the gap by half a brick length and this may be useful. The bond becomes unsymmetrical. On any particular course, there is a stretcher at one corner and a return header at the other – unnoticeable to most people. (A different method is to keep a strict 10 mm gap, and to 'break the bond' with a cut brick. Usually this is placed beneath the middle of a door or window frame.)

Carry on laying out the bonding for all the foundation walls in this dry manner. Where two walls meet, the bonding obviously has to be consistent, ie, a corner brick appears as a stretcher in one wall and as a header in the return.

With the layout settled, lay the first brick! At a corner, put down a bed of mortar without obliterating the corner lines. Place the corner brick in position, and check that it is bedded level. Ideally the level should be consistent with $7\frac{1}{2}$ cm coursing up to the dpc.

The next step is to transfer the level of this brick round to the other corners. If datum levels were established at each corner when setting out, then these can be used now to fix the level for all the corner bricks. Alternatively, use a level-board from the top of the brick already laid. Step along the foundation concrete every three metres or so, and temporarily bed a brick level with the previous one. Work round the trenches so that bricks are laid at each corner, all on the same level. (Except, of course, that with stepped foundations, some bricks will be some courses higher.) The level of a brick can be adjusted by laying a thicker or thinner bed of mortar. (Stiffen the mix for a thick bed, and add extra water for a thin one.) If the concrete is badly out of level, then don't try to compensate for this totally in the first course. But by the time the wall is out of the ground, the coursing should be level and to the correct gauge ($7\frac{1}{2}$ cm). (There has been a case recorded in which the dpc was not level, and the house started to creep downhill, threatening to topple off its foundations.)

Lay a small corner using the lines already marked on the concrete, and using the level of the corner brick already laid. (See Chapter 21: *Bricklaying*.) Repeat for another corner, and then you can start laying to the line. You have lift-off! The inner leaf of blockwork can be built up in a rather similar fashion, but it is simpler because the appearance of the bond is immaterial. It is common practice to use wall ties, although they would hardly seem necessary below ground.

So, using these methods all the foundation walls can be built up.

Some details as work progresses:

1) Gaps should be left for services to enter.

A drain needs an opening about 15 cm square, with a short lintel above it. (See Fig. 8.)

Figure 8: Foundations with drain

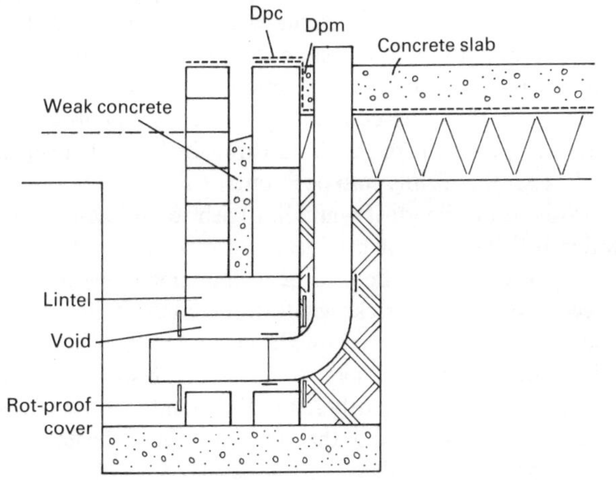

* Void beneath lintel allows differential settlement.
* Dpc and dpm overlap.

Over the course of time, the walls may sink a centimetre or two. The lintel should leave a sufficient gap above the drain for this to happen without the drain being crushed.

The water pipe will enter at a depth of about 70 cm. Flexible land drain is often used as a duct for the water pipe through the foundations, so leave a gap for this. (See Para. 4.)

The electric supply enters through a 'hockey stick' duct about 40 cm below finished ground level; leave a gap for this. (The hockey stick is supplied by the Electricity Company. It comes up inside a cavity wall.)

The gas feed needs no consideration at this stage as the pipe will simply go up the outside of the wall to its box.

2) As the wall is emerging from what will be the finished ground level, change to the good facing bricks. The coursing should, by now, be quite regular. There is no need to tool the joints below ground, but you may wish to do so for the practice.

Temporarily finish the outer leaf a couple of courses below the dpc. The cavity will shortly be filled with concrete up to this level. (See Para. 5.) Leave the outer leaf low until the floor slab has been put down – wet concrete might, by accident, smear the bricks.

3) The inner leaf is carried up to the dpc. If you are using blocks, it may be necessary to finish with a course or two of bricks (or coursing units) to achieve the required level. If your bricks have frogs, the top course should be laid frogs down to give a flat surface for the dpc (even if you are – unnecessarily – laying them frog up elsewhere).

4) There are two ways of dealing with the drains through the foundations. The direct and better way is to put the drains through the foundations at this stage. Have you decided upon the drainage system, clay or plastic? Through the hole left in the foundation walls, position a 'slow', 90° bend. (The manufacturers produce 'rest' bends, but builders seldom use them.) Bring the drain up to the floor level using a coupling and a straight section cut to the required length. (Actually, it should rise about 5 cm above the floor level to allow for connection to the soil-and-vent pipe.) This pipe needs to be about 5 cm from the wall. (The precise distance used to vary with the WC system chosen, but nowadays, with plastic pan connectors, the position of the drain is not so critical.) On the other end of the bend, couple another short section of pipe to take the drain through the wall. Prop the whole assembly firmly into position.

On the other hand, if you don't wish to be involved with drains at this stage, you can just leave a void through the wall and up through the floor slab. (Some small pieces of ply placed around some bricks will form a void through the slab.) The drain can be passed through the void later.

For the water pipe, pass some 8 cm plastic land drain through the hole previously left in the foundation walls. (See Para. 1.) Bend it round so that it reaches above the floor level close to the inside wall.

5) When the drains and ducts through the foundations are in place, fill the cavity with a weak concrete mix (1:12 of cement and ballast). The concrete will strengthen the walls against the sideways pressure of the ground. Finish its top surface with a downward slope to the outside so that any water running down the cavity is shed outwards.

Bricklaying in the trenches is hard work, involving a lot of bending down in a constricted position. You will be glad to get out of the ground.

Modifications for trenchfill

Trenchfill is a speedy method, but more costly in materials than strip foundations. The method is broadly similar to that described above but with some modifications:

The trenches are dug with a narrower, 18″ bucket and dug deeper, typically one metre. (See Fig. 2.) On sloping sites, steps should be used to keep the trench bottom level. The top of the concrete comes up nearly to ground level and should be level – if necessary, it should be stepped, with a metre overlap. To indicate the requires level for the concrete, mark the sides of the trench (eg, knock 15 cm nails into the sides). There is no need to get into the trench to shovel the ready-mixed round; it can all be done from the top. (See Fig. 2.)

Some of the services will need to pass through the concrete. For the water pipe, fix the land drain duct firmly into position in the trench before the concrete is poured. Leave a void, if necessary, for the drains.

The foundation walls can be built up as before, but there are far fewer courses. For trenchfill, the trenches need to be dug more accurately than for strip foundations. The concrete strip is narrower, leaving less margin for error if the walls are to stand centrally.

Foundations for internal walls

Foundations are needed for load-bearing internal walls (ie, those supporting floor joists); but they can be narrower and shallower. (See Fig. 9.)

A bungalow may also use such foundations, even though its internal walls are not load-bearing. The purpose, in this case, is to divide an over-large floor slab into sections.

Other internal walls can be built off a thickened floor slab. (See Fig. 9.)

Foundations for a chimney

A stove (or 'sealed room-heater' in marketing jargon) wastes much less heat than an open fire. So the brief description in this book of the construction of a chimney assumes that it will serve a free-standing stove.

A chimney is a very heavy construction, and foundations for it need to be put down with the wall foundations. Some people use the trenchfill method, putting into the ground a great concrete block of two cubic metres, or more – ugly and costly. The 'strip' method is preferable:

Off a base of concrete, build up two piers, which will support the chimney breast. The piers need to be far enough apart to take a stove and any associated plumbing. If the chimney breast is to be a feature in fair-faced brickwork, then make the piers a whole number of brick lengths apart. (This will already have been settled when setting out.)

Insulation

If the house is to have only single glazing, the Building Regulations expect the floor to be insulated. This can be done by laying polystyrene beneath the floor slab (or beneath a floor screed). Approved Document L of the Regulations gives the necessary thickness of insulation to reach the required U-value of ·45.

Any sensible selfbuilder will be using double glazing, and then there is no obligation to insulate the floor. Nonetheless, you may wish to. Perimeter insulation is nearly as effective as whole-floor insulation, and this can be cheaply and easily done. (See 'Floor insulation', Chapter 26.) Fix polystyrene sheets, $2\frac{1}{2}$ cm thick, on the inside of the foundation walls.

To this end, while the mortar in the walling is still green, insert some nails along one of the upper courses, so that they protrude about three centimetres. Later on, the sheets of polystyrene can simply be pushed onto these nails and so held in place. The sheets are usually 1.8 × ·45 metres. If the tops of the sheets come up to the dpc, they will form some useful ducting in the floor slab around the walls. (By the way, don't put the sheets in place until you're ready to backfill the trenches, else the wind may blow the polystyrene away.)

Figure 9: Foundations for walls

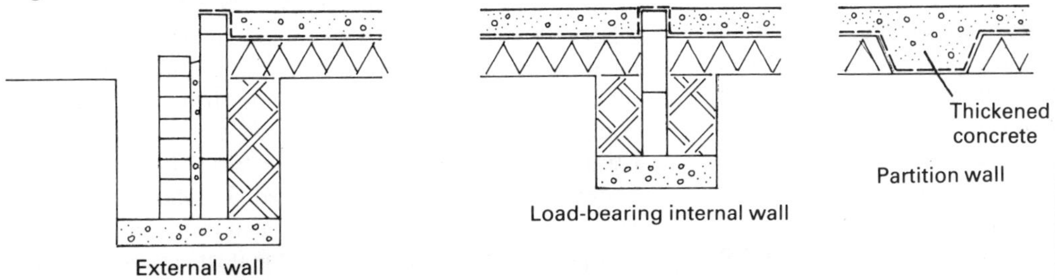

* The foundation wall in the middle diagram has the effect of dividing the floor slab. It may be used for this purpose even with a non-loadbearing partition wall (eg, in the floor slab of a bungalow).

(Note that the floor slab is not fixed to the foundation walls – it just rests in position. Likewise, the house just rests on its foundation walls. It is only its weight which stops the house from being blown away!)

Floor slab

The traditional way of making a solid floor is to cast a rough slab in concrete, and to finish it later with a sand-and-cement screed. A more modern method is to omit the screed and simply to finish the slab itself with a good surface. This is the better method for the selfbuilder. It saves a lot of time and materials, and it makes it unnecessary for the ownhander to learn the technique of screeding. The ownhander can produce a flatter floor by using a tamping board with a good straight edge than by screeding.

But there are two difficulties with this method:

While the concrete is setting, heavy rain can spoil the surface.

And secondly, putting in ducts for pipework requires foresight and is a little tricky.

Nonetheless, finishing the surface of the oversite concrete so that it is both flat and smooth is the easiest way to make a floor, and it is the method described below.

If you have used strip foundations, the trenches need backfilling. You may have left some spoil behind for this purpose. Backfilling inside the foundation walls, ie, under the floor, needs particular care. The backfill needs to be well rammed down, without voids. Check that the building inspector agrees to its use. Otherwise you will have to use hardcore. Backfilling with spoil saves on the cost of materials, but takes more time. Of course, provisions for the services should be in place, as described previously.

The slab is supported on a layer of hardcore at least 15 cm thick. Good quality material for this is 3 cm stone, but cheaper materials may be available. If possible, have the hardcore tipped directly onto the base. If there is an amenable digger driver nearby, get him to come along and spread the hardcore around with the back-hoe. While he's around, he can backfill with spoil the trench outside the foundation walls. Otherwise, get busy with barrow and shovel!

A rake is useful for levelling off the hardcore. The surface should be about 8 cm to 15 cm below the dpc, according to the depth of concrete specified in the drawings. Check this depth with a long board placed on edge across the walls.

If you are building on a sloping site, some of the oversite fill may be quite deep. In the past, there have been problems with poorly compacted fill subsiding; the result has been cracked floors. To get round poor workmanship, the NHBC now stipulates in its *Registered House-Builder's Handbook* that fill should not be deeper than 60 cm (otherwise a suspended floor must be used). You, of course, are not bound by this constraint, but take care. If you are using fairly deep fill, it should be compacted in 25 cm layers with a plate compactor.

In some places, you may want to thicken the concrete slab – where it will support an internal wall, or where its thickness will be reduced by a duct. Leave a trough in the hardcore. (See Fig. 9.)

To compact the hardcore, hire a plate compactor. This is a machine with a vibrating plate at the bottom that compacts materials beneath it. It is easy to use. (Push it; don't pull it.) With three passes, the hardcore might be pushed down a couple of centimetres. Next, the top is blinded with sand to produce a smooth surface that will not puncture the damp proof membrane: Spread some soft sand to a depth of one or two centimetres and compact it.

The damp proof membrane (dpm) is spread on top of the sand. Wide sheets (4 m) of polythene are usually used. The thickness stipulated in the Building Regulations is 1000 gauge (an imperial measure which is just over 250 microns, ie ·25 mm). In fact, many builders use a dpm twice as thick. Where sheets need to be joined, make a generous overlap of a third of a metre. At a wall, the polythene should be carried up to overlap on top with the eventual dpc. The membrane will have to be pierced by the water duct and drain(s). (An extra polythene collar can be cut to neatly fit over these in order to maintain an effective barrier.) Weight the polythene down with loose bricks to prevent it blowing away.

Some builders lay the garage base at the same time as the floor slab; some leave it till later on. Don't forget that the garage base is generally lower than the house floor. A dpm is not a necessity but if you have some surplus, it is sensible to use it here. (Likewise, many people use a dpc in the outside garage wall although it is not obligatory.)

Some people put gas pipework underneath the floor slab. This seems a good idea, not least because the gas pipes would be well protected if the house ever caught fire. Use pre-coated copper pipe and wrap the joints with tape ('Denso') to prevent corrosion from the concrete. Just lay the pipework on the polythene, with a short vertical rise at a wall.

At this stage, the building inspector pays a visit.

Concreting the slab

For the slab, a strong concrete is usually used, equivalent to 1:2:4. If you tell your ready-mixed supplier that you want to have a good finish on the slab, they may send a special mix with extra sand in it. Internal foundation walls divide the floor area into bays. To find the volume required for a bay, estimate the average depth methodically – use a long plank stretched on edge from wall to wall and find the depth in different places. Multiply the average depth by the area to give the volume for the bay. Better order slightly too much than too little.

Are you going to try to do the whole lot in one day? It is possible, but difficult. In order to saw and tamp an adjacent bay, if one bay has just been laid somebody has to balance on the dividing wall – possible, but tricky. It's more prudent to wait until the following day when the concrete in the first bay will be firm. But if you are doing the lot at one time, leave a good hour between deliveries. Even with three people on the job, this is sweatier work than the footings. And the timing of deliveries needs another consideration. In winter, a delivery in the late afternoon will let the slab harden off enough to be floated the following morning. In the summer, delivery early in the morning allows floating in the afternoon. Don't let rain spoil the surface of the slab. If rain looks imminent, postpone the delivery – suppliers of ready-mixed concrete are used to this.

Before the delivery, any puddles on the polythene should be removed. When the truck arrives, ask the driver to shoot the concrete straight into a bay and swing the chute around to distribute it. Step into the concrete (with wellies!), and shovel and rake it around to fill the bay. Work fast. But don't have extra water added to this mix, not least because a wet mix can result in a dusty surface.

Tamp the concrete down. A long scaffold board with a good straight edge can be used. 'Saw' the surface level, using the top of the walls as a guide. This operation needs two people to 'saw' the board, with a third person standing in the concrete in front of the board. This person fills in hollows in the surface, and removes any excess that builds up in front of the board. Give a final light tamp.

Ducts for pipework can be put into the concrete as it is laid. Use smooth timber of the required cross section. (Making this slightly tapered and oiling the surface will help to release the timber later.) Push the timber into the top of the surface. Remove the timber later while the concrete is still green. – That is the quick method. A more deliberate way is to put the lengths of timber into position a day or so before the ready-mixed is laid. Set the timber in dollops of concrete so that its top is level with the dpc.

Leave the floor slab some hours to harden somewhat. Then, when the concrete is firm but still malleable, flatten out the tamp marks with a float. Work from a scaffold board resting on the surface – or support it at each end on a brick on a wall. An alternative is to use a 'skip' float, an item of contractors' plant that can be hired. It consists simply of a wide metal plate that can be skimmed over the surface by a long pole. As you pull and push the float across the surface, raise or lower the handle a little to prevent the leading edge from digging in. If the concrete is becoming too stiff, weight the plate down with a couple of bricks.

A little later go over the concrete with a steel trowel to produce a smooth surface. Don't overwork the concrete at any one time – excessive fine material will come to the surface, leading to a dusty finish. When the concrete has stiffened up some more, trowel it again. That should be sufficient, but for a really fine finish, trowel it once again. Timing and dry weather are important.

(Of course, if you intend to finish the floor with a screed, the tamped finish is all that's required.)

With the foundations completed, you can feel well pleased with yourself. The foundations are only the first stage, but the hardest.

Subcontracting

In some parts of the country (eg, Southern England), there are specialists known as 'groundworkers' who put down foundations and lay drains. In other parts, this work is done by bricklayers.

6
THE WALLS

☆

☆

☆

☆

☆

☆

☆

Bricks
Blocks
Mortar
Wall ties
Insulation
Frames
Lintels
Scaffolding
Subcontracting
Walls from dpc to joist level
Joisting
Strutting
Walls from joists to wall plate
Chimney for a free-standing stove
Weathering
Gables

WITH THE FOUNDATIONS laid, you are ready to spring up with the walls – except that 'spring' is hardly the word for this, the most major of the many daunting tasks in house-building. The walls of a house might take a pair of experienced brickies a couple of months, an inexperienced ownhander many times that. Persevere. Though your output in a day may seem puny, the cumulative change from week to week is impressive. With bricklaying you can at least see the results of your labours – and so will generations to come.

Let us look at what's required to build the walls:

Bricks

The facing bricks should have been ordered months ago, and now be on site. The bricks to be used would have been specified in the Planning application, but let us consider here the choices. Most bricks are made of clay, and come in a variety of appearances, depending on the colour of the clay and the surface treatment of the faces. There is a wide variation in price, but don't presume that expensive bricks are structurally, or even aesthetically, superior to the cheaper ones. If you arȩ doing your own bricklaying, there is an extra criterion to bear in mind: This might be called 'camouflage'. A novice bricklayer has difficulty keeping mortar off the face of brickwork and thereby staining it. Heavily textured faces stain less than smooth ones. And the closer the colour of the face matches the mortar, the less any stain will show. (Actually, mortar stains can be removed with proprietary acid solutions of hydrochloric acid, eg, 'Disclean'. But this is unpleasant time-consuming work which is best avoided in the first place.)

Not all bricks are clay. 'Sand-lime' bricks (made of calcium silicate) have been around for some time. These generally have a smooth surface and for the above reason the ownhander might not choose them. Concrete bricks which look like clay are becoming popular in some areas. They are usually cheaper but heavier than clay.

Some merchants keep 'brick libraries' where bricks can be viewed. Most bricks are of 'ordinary' quality. Bricks of 'special' quality are denser and less porous; they are suitable for very exposed situations like retaining walls. 'Engineering' bricks are even denser.

The standard brick format is $22\frac{1}{2} \times 7\frac{1}{2}$ cm. (See Fig. 1, Chapter 21.) There are virtually 60 bricks per square metre of stretcher bonded brickwork. To work out the number of bricks you require, calculate the wall area from the drawings. (For the triangular gables, remember that the area of the triangle is half of the width × height.) Increase the order quantity by 5% – 10% to allow for wastage.

Brickwork can be easily enlivened by using a secondary brick of contrasting colour. Some possible places for its use are:

- Below dpc – in days gone by, a different, more impervious brick was used here
- Soldier course above window and door openings – a reminiscence of flat, brick arches
- Corbels and gable verges
- Courses around the house at window head and sill height
- One wall, preferably bounded by internal corners so the keying of the brickwork is not obtrusive.

Blocks

The use of the so-called 'aircrete' blocks was pioneered in Sweden, but they are nowadays widely used in Britain ('Thermalite', 'Celcon', etc). They have good insulating properties and are easy to work. The standard blocks have a density of 650 kg/cu m. The lighter blocks (480 kg/cu m) are even better insulators but are weaker. The standard blocks can can be used below ground (where they do have some insulating value), and many people use them throughout the building – foundations, gables, partition walls, and all. As part of of one big order their price will be less than that of dense concrete blocks from a builders' merchant. Many sizes are available, but the common block format is $45 \times 22\frac{1}{2}$ cm. (See Fig. 1, Chapter 21.) One such block is equivalent to six bricks, and so there are ten blocks per square metre of blockwork. (They are often ordered by the square metre.)

Brick-sized blocks, called coursing units, are useful:

- For maintaining the coursing under joists (if the ceiling height is not a whole number of block courses)

For blocking off the cavity at the eaves

Beneath window boards

Over lintels above internal door openings.

You may also want to use 'reveal' blocks for closing off the reveals at the sides of frames. (They are usually made only for 5 cm cavities). Most people manage without them by using cut blocks.

Mortar

Having been ousted almost completely by cement, lime is now making a comeback as an ingredient in mortar. (For the advantages, see 'Mortar', Chapter 20.)

The usual mix is 1:1:6 of cement, lime and sand. Mix the ingredients dry in a mixer, and then add the water. The lime makes the mix workable without the need for plasticiser. Workability is even better if the sand, lime and some water are premixed a day or so beforehand. Alternatively, mortar suppliers (see the *Yellow Pages*) deliver this premixed 'coarse stuff'; it can be kept for weeks or months if covered above and below by polythene. Just mix it with cement as required. (Pigmented mixes can also be supplied.)

To achieve workability with plain sand-and-cement mixes, use masonry cement (1:5) or liquid plasticiser, eg, 'Febmix' (1:6). (The latter mix gives some resistance against frost while the mortar is setting.)

Below ground, a stronger mix should be used, eg, 1:4 with plasticiser.

Wall ties

Ties hold together the inner and outer leaves of a cavity wall. They come in a multitude of shapes and materials, but are all designed to prevent water crossing from outer to inner leaf. (In very wet weather, the outer leaf can become sodden, and water run down its inner surface.)

The cheapest and most common are 'butterfly' ties of galvanized wire – their shape gives them their name. In the past, they have occasionally corroded, leading to tie failure and buckled walls; but the specification has now been improved. Nonetheless, in wet or salty (coastal) regions, you may wish to use ties of plastic, stainless steel, etc.

Special ties are needed for partially filled cavities in order to hold the insulation in place.

Insulation

As originally conceived – and the idea was first used at least a century ago – the cavity of a cavity wall was kept clear to prevent the passage of damp. Nowadays, the 'cavity' can be filled to improve thermal insulation. Mineral wool (ie, rock wool or glass wool), which has been treated to resist the passage of water, is put in the cavity. The width of the cavity is sometimes increased from 5 cm to $7\frac{1}{2}$ cm, to allow more insulation or to keep some cavity clear as an extra precaution against damp. The slabs of insulation, called 'batts', are sized to fit between the wall ties. (See Fig. 1.)

At corners, some types of batt are bent round, whereas others are butted together. (See the manufacturer's leaflet).

An alternative to cavity batts is to have insulation injected through the blockwork prior to plastering. There are several possible materials, but in each case it is a specialised process – use an Agrément Approved installer. With a selection of quotations, some should be below the cost of batts alone (without costing the time to install them). With such a process, it is particularly important to keep the cavities clean. Watch out for mortar that has dropped onto wall ties or the cavity batts, thereby bridging the cavity; it might allow damp across.

Figure 1: Cavity wall with insulation batts

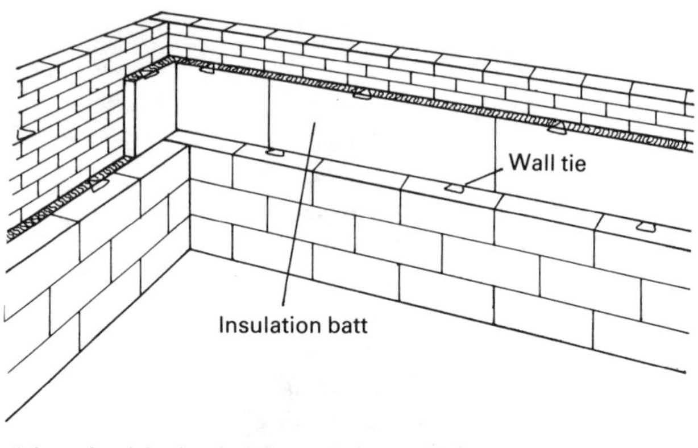

* Lead with the brickwork (usually).
* Keep the cavity clear of mortar droppings.
* At corners, some types of batts are butted together, some are folded round.

In fact, on a wet, exposed site, it is prudent to maintain some cavity and to fill only part of it (with self-supporting cavity batts). This will be less thermally effective, of course.

Frames

The quality of door and window frames has improved enormously over the last couple of decades. There is, however, less choice in design than you might imagine, as the large manufacturers offer similar styles. You want frames with good weather-stripping – the best rubber for this is EPDM or silicon. Study the glossy brochures, and order the frames a month before they are needed on site. (Sealed units come in different thicknesses. Check that the sash rebates are deep enough for the units you have in mind.)

The heights of the frames should fit in with the coursing of the (metric) brickwork. Nowadays, most frames come with their own wooden sill. Be aware that door frames are either outward or inward opening.

Unless for some special reason you want to use obsolescent gloss paint, order frames treated with a 'base coat' rather than primer. When the frames arrive on site, you can take advantage of your flexibility as a selfbuilder by putting on your decorators' hat and painting all the frames with a coat of whatever stain-paint you've chosen. It's easier and faster doing this now, on the ground, and you can reach those parts of the frame that other decorators miss.

(There are several different names for the several types of new paints. Their common feature is that they are micro-porous, ie, they allow water vapour to pass out from the wood, but not wetness into it. In this book, the term 'stain-paint' is used to cover them generally.)

Lintels

These are an unseen item that will cost several hundred pounds altogether. Wooden frames are not strong enough to support the weight of the masonry above. (Though this weight may be less than you think. Because of the effect of bonding, only a triangle of masonry over an opening needs support. See Fig. 2.)

Figure 2: Brickwork needing the support of a lintel

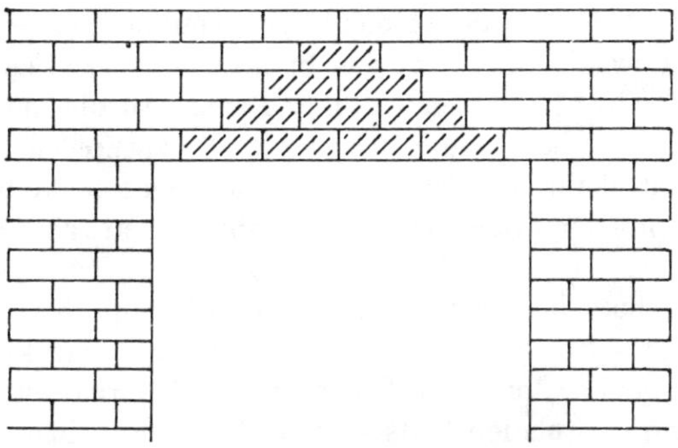

* Only the shaded bricks need support.
* But joists or roof trusses supported above the opening create heavier loads.

Greater loads may be imposed by the floor joists and roof trusses. So 'lintels' (ie, beams) are placed over openings to take the loads. Nowadays, steel lintels, which are relatively light in weight, are very popular. They come in two types:

> Box section (the original 'Catnic' lintel). The box becomes part of the inner leaf of the wall. Before plastering, wooden battens must be clipped to the steel box so that curtain rails in the future can be screwed into place. The first stage of plastering is to 'dub out' the exposed face of the boxes.
>
> 'Top hat' section. This sticks up into the cavity only. This type is preferable, as the inner leaf of blockwork remains uniform. (See Fig. 3.)

Some lintels need a dpm over them in the cavity; some don't. Check with the manufacturer's brochure. This will also show the bewildering variety of shapes and sizes. Some thought is required to select the right type. And don't forget that the lintels must be wider than the openings! Allow at least 15 cm for bedding each side of short lintels; and it's sensible to allow more (23 cm) for long ones.

Figure 3: Lintel detail

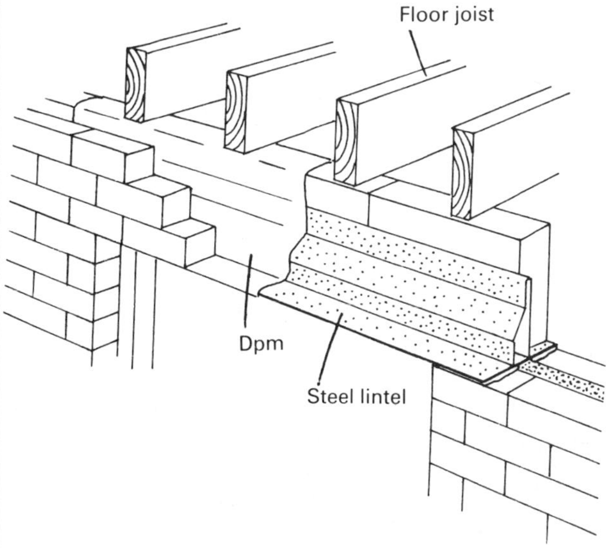

* Some lintels do not require the protection of a dpm.
* The diagram illustrates a 'top hat' type lintel, with the upstand entirely within the cavity.

It may be that, over internal openings, (eg, between lounge and diner), a steel beam will be required to support floor joists. A point to bear in mind about this is that the top of the beam should be at least 1 cm below the top of the joists – to allow for possible shrinkage of the joists, which are supported on the bottom flange.

Scaffolding

A bricklayer can only lay bricks to something like shoulder height. As a house grows, the scaffolding goes up with it. Typically, the scaffolding for a house will involve three 'lifts', or stages, with maybe a fourth for the gables. There may be a preliminary stage which just involves scaffold boards resting on trestles or piers of blocks. (Some people consider this a dangerous practice.)

If you are subcontracting, ask the scaffolder where he will be wanting putlog holes.

(See Chapter 28 for details of scaffolding.)

The ownhander is in a difficult situation with regard to scaffolding. A scaffolder usually gives a price for a limited period, say a couple of months. After that, there is a weekly hire charge to pay. For the long time that an ownhander requires scaffolding, this charge can come to a very hefty sum, maybe thousands of pounds. In this case, you would do much better to buy the scaffolding secondhand and then resell it when finished. You could put the scaffolding up yourself, or you could pay a scaffolder to put up the first lift and learn from him.

If you are subcontracting the brickwork, there is another option: You hire the scaffolding, and the brickies put it up.

Whoever puts the scaffolding up, there is a precaution to take in case of rain. Mortar tends to fall and lie on scaffold boards alongside the walls. If heavy rain falls on this, dirty water can be splashed up and stain the brickwork. To avoid this, if rain is imminent turn the boards by the wall onto their edge away from the wall. Since the weather can't be predicted overnight, do this when leaving the site at the end of the day.

Scaffolding is not essential. In Victorian times, houses in the North of Britain were usually built without it. The bricklayers worked off the floor joists inside. This is still a valid method today, although laying fair-faced brickwork from the inside ('overhand') is slower.

An ownhander can build a bungalow by working off builders' trestles, with perhaps some tower scaffolding at the gables. (See 'Other forms of scaffolding', Chapter 28.)

Subcontracting

Many selfbuilders subcontract the bricklaying as it is the biggest single job in house-building. On the other hand, if you do wish to do it yourself, once you have practised bricklaying with several thousand bricks in the foundations, your bricklaying should look quite satisfactory. But you will still be a lot slower than a professional.

Bricklayers usually work in pairs – it's so much easier to position the line with two people. If they have their own labourer, they are known as a 'two and one' gang. Some prefer being paid by the day, but most will quote a price for the whole job. In this case, it is well to agree beforehand the exact extent of the job. The bulk of it is obvious – the external walls and the internal blockwork. But you need to clarify with the bricklayers:

Is insulation to be built into the cavity?

Are they to erect any scaffolding, or install floor joists or wall plates? Some brickies do some of these.

Are they to rake out joints for flashing?

Are they to fill in the putlog holes after the scaffolding has been stripped?

You should also reach agreement beforehand on how to pay them. They may, for example, wish to be paid each week, on an estimate of the number of bricks laid. But it is important for you to keep back a percentage in hand – a bonus to pay them when the job is complete. Otherwise, they may be busy elsewhere when you want them back to put up the gables.

Walls from the dpc to joist level

Before starting to build the walls, you might like to stack blocks on the floor slab for use later on. It's convenient to do this now, while you have free access to the slab. But don't overload it.

If you are doing your own bricklaying, start with an unobtrusive wall. Make up a gauge rod for the coursing, and mark on it the levels for the tops and bottoms of the frames (with the base of the rod at dpc level). Roll out some dpc for a few metres along the foundation brickwork. (The dpc for this is 10 cm wide, usually in black polythene.) Use loose bricks to keep it in place. Where lengths of dpc are joined, eg, at corners, there should be a 10 cm overlap.

Figure 4: Positions of wall ties

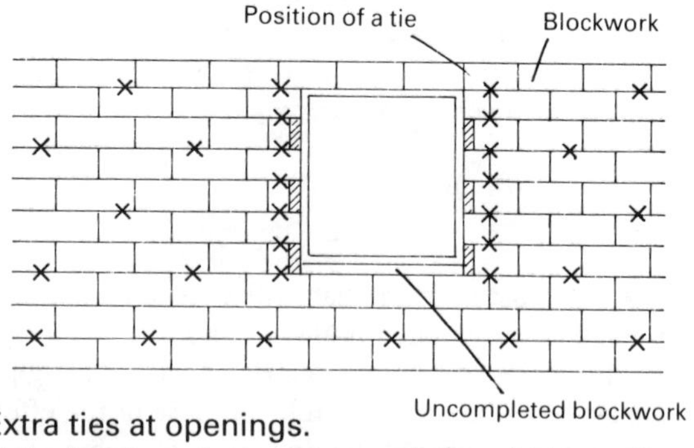

* Extra ties at openings.

* If the blockwork coursing and the window sill are at different levels, the blockwork beneath a window may be left uncompleted and finished later.

Start with an external leaf of brickwork. Build up two corners and then run in the brickwork in between. (See Chapter 21: *Bricklaying*.) Don't forget to put in ties every six courses upwards, and every four bricks along. (See Fig. 4.) The cavity batt size fits in with this. Remove surplus mortar on the inner face of the brickwork. To ensure an even settlement of the foundations, keep the height of the walls fairly even – don't build a wall higher than a metre above the others.

Put a batt into place, and then build up the inner blockwork – two corners as before, and then the blockwork in between. The dpm of the floor slab should overlap with the dpc. (Some insulation batts seem to be thicker than their specification and tend to push out green blockwork. Beware of this. Note too that some batts have a 'grain'; if you are using an off-cut, take care that the grain is kept vertical – to keep the material water-resistant.)

Periodically tool the joints of fair-faced brickwork.

That's the basics, but there are complications:

Building in frames

As supplied, the head of a frame is several centimetres longer each side than seems necessary. These projections, or 'horns', are used to hold the top of the frame in the brickwork. But first, the front of the horn should be cut away: With a panel saw, carefully cut the front of the horn in line with the jamb to about half its depth. Then, with a chisel, snap off the front of the horn. This leaves the back of the horn to be built into the brickwork – treat it with preservative.

Don't remove the temporary diagonal strut on a door frame until the frame has been built in. A few people even add an extra horizontal strut halfway up to stop the pressure of the brickwork from bowing the frame. Use your gauge rod to check the courses on which to bed window frames – it's easy to blithely carry on laying bricks where there should be windows.

At a reveal (ie, a side of a door or window opening), the cavity is closed off by a thickening on the inner leaf. Where the inner and outer leaves meet, the moisture barrier between them is maintained by a vertical strip of dpc, 15 cm or $22\frac{1}{2}$ cm wide. It's convenient to fix the strip to the side of the frame beforehand, usually tacking an edge to the channel that runs down the frame.

The drawings give the positions of the frames in the face of the walls. Take a little licence with the measurements and put the centre of a frame over a cross joint. With this small adjustment, the bonding of the bricks on each side of the frame will be symmetrical. (See Fig. 5.)

Figure 5: Fitting a window frame

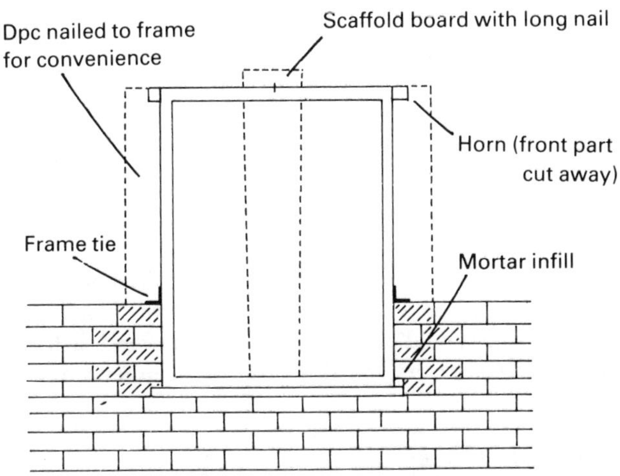

* Cut bricks (shaded) are at least half a brick in length.
* At each end of the sill, a brick can either be cut to shape (as shown on one side) or the gap filled with mortar (as shown on the other).

Figure 6: Supporting a frame

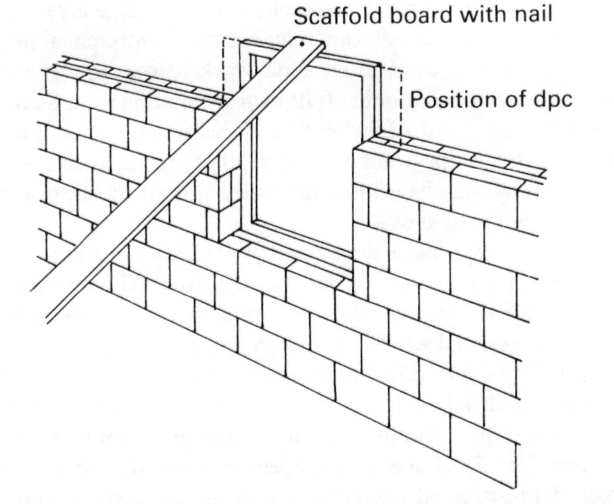

* Steady the foot of the board with some blocks.

To put the frame in position, have ready a long scaffold board with a large nail driven part-way into it near an end. On the outer leaf, spread a bed of mortar. Place the frame on this, and hold it in position with the scaffold board – the head of the frame is gripped between board and nail. (See Fig. 6.)

The other end of the board rests on the ground, stabilised by a couple of blocks.

Adjust the position of the frame to give the required 'depth' in the reveal. Often the inner face of the frame is set flush with the inner face of the brickwork. But with a wide cavity or wide blocks, check that the window board will be wide enough. (See Fig. 7 and 'Window boards', Chapter 11.)

The drip groove under the sill should clear the face of the wall by at least a centimetre; and the head of the frame should be cleared by the lintel above. Check that the frame is plumb in both planes.

Figure 7: Detail at window

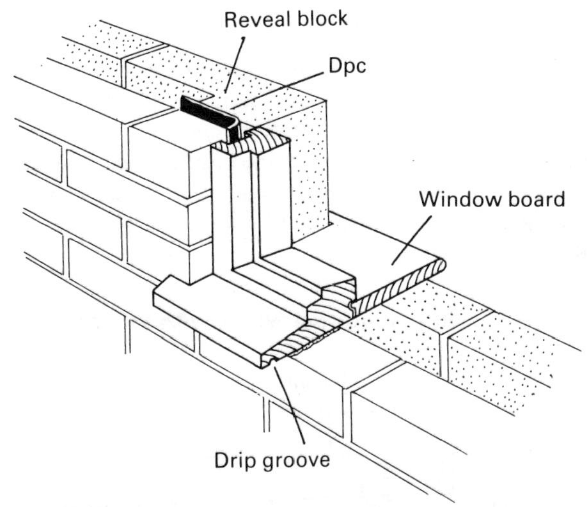

* Vertical dpc separates inner and outer leaf.
* Drip groove well clear of brickwork.
* Instead of a reveal block, the cavity may be blocked off with a piece cut from an ordinary block.

Build up the outer brickwork. There is a small, awkward gap above the sill on each side. Cut a small piece of brick to fit in this, or just fill it with mortar. The bonding on each side of the frame needs some thought. If you carry on laying bricks with a simplistic approach, you will probably find 'quarter bats' (short pieces of brick) next to the frame on alternate courses. Small pieces like this are weak points and look messy. Instead, use a half brick by the frame with a three-quarter bat next to it. (See Fig. 5.) The heights of window frames fit in with the brick format; unfortunately, the widths in general do not. But there are modular windows made, and for these no brick cutting is necessary.

The horns and sill tie in a frame at top and bottom. In addition, the jambs need to be tied into the brickwork every 60 cm or so. Use frame ties (or 'cramps'), screwed to the jamb and held in a mortar bed. A common practice, disapproved of by some, is just to knock a 15 cm nail part-way into the jamb and bed its shank.

At the reveal each side of a frame, the cavity has to be blocked off. This is done by a tiny 'return' of the blockwork.

This should be bonded, of course: You will need to cut some pieces of block, some as wide as the cavity and some wider by 10 cm (the thickness of a block). Alternatively, use purpose-made reveal blocks. As the reveals are put in, build in the plastic dpc that you attached to the frame, so that it forms a moisture barrier between brick and block. (See Fig. 7.)

The blockwork underneath a window may be left a little low at this stage; it will be built up later to the level required for the window board.

Meter boxes

Don't forget to build in the meter boxes. If they are in a cavity wall, they will need a polythene dpm over them, as described for lintels. (See below.) The 'hockey stick' duct for the electric cable should be built into the cavity. (The boxes and hockey stick are supplied 'free' by the Gas and Electricity Companies.)

Keying for internal walls

When the internal walls are built later, they need to be keyed into the blockwork of the external walls. One way to do this is simply to leave an indent, 12 cm or so wide, at each alternate course. So measure off the position for the first gap, and then keep the others vertically above it. When it comes to building the internal wall, blocks are mortared into these indents. (See Fig. 8.)

Figure 8: Tying in internal wall – with indents

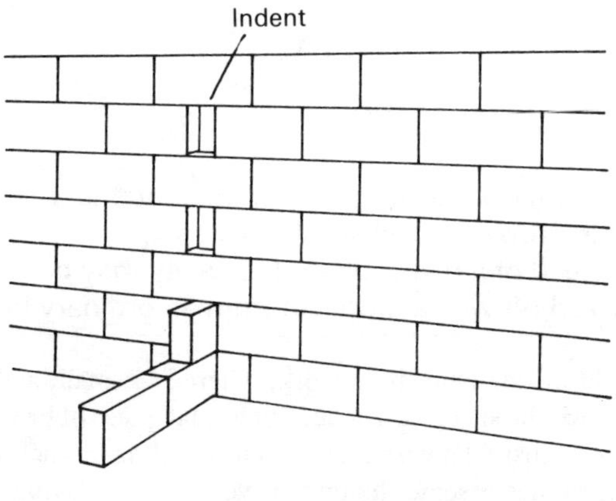

A different method uses expanded metal mesh. From a roll of galvanized mesh, 8 cm wide, cut off 30 cm lengths with tin snips. The inner leaf of blockwork is built with these pieces of mesh embedded into successive courses in a vertical line. To tie in the internal wall, the flaps of mesh are simply bedded into it. (See Fig. 9.)

Lintels

Lintels are placed over the door and widow openings. (See Fig. 3.) Lay the lintels level, bedding them on mortar. If packing has to be used, use a durable material like slate. Lintels should be long enough to allow 15 cm of bedding each side (and preferably 23 cm for long lintels). Use a thin bed of mortar on the flanges when laying bricks or blocks on them.

Figure 9: Tying in internal wall – with metal strip

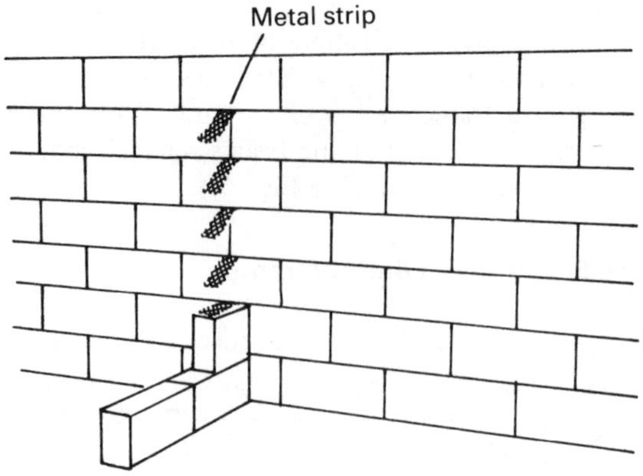

Some lintels need a dpm over them. (See the manufacturer's leaflet.) If a dpm is required, use a piece of polythene sheet. Bed one edge in the brickwork over the lintel; then stretch it upwards and bed the other edge in the blockwork. The polythene should extend about 10 cm beyond each end of the lintel. Check that the 'drip nose' of the lintel clears the frame.

Internal partition walls

On the ground floor, partition walls are generally built in 10 cm blockwork. (For economy, $7\frac{1}{2}$ cm blockwork is sometimes used, but this is more difficult to lay.)

In the case of a bungalow, if you are in a hurry to get the roof on, the internal walls can be left until later. But in the case of a house, the internal walls are needed to support the floor joists, and so they have to be built before joisting. (However, they can still be left until later if the joists are to be supported by hangers. See 'Joisting', later in this chapter.)

To build a partition wall between two existing (external) walls, fix a board vertically to each, so that an edge gives the position of the face of the required wall. Stretch a line between the boards, and lay blockwork to the line. If the partition wall is being built off its own foundation wall, then a dpc will be required. If the partition is being built directly off the floor slab, a dpc is not necessary although it is often used. Partition walls are keyed into the external walls by one of the methods outlined above.

The walls will need door openings. (See 'Door linings', Chapter 11 for the size of opening required. This is a case where some thinking ahead is required: Are the doors to be metric or imperial size?) A common practice is to make up a dummy frame for the openings. Make it a centimetre oversize in width and height to allow clearance for the lining. The frame must be accurately square – use ply gussets at the corners. The lintel over a door opening is usually corrugated steel or pre-stressed concrete. (Often the coursing requires the lintel to be placed a few centimetres above the frame.) The frame can be re-used elsewhere once the opening has been built. The door lining itself will be fixed later.

Build up the external walls to the level required to take the joists for the upper floor (ie, to ceiling height). This will involve a lift or two of scaffolding. (In the case of a bungalow, build up to the wall plate height.) The level required may not coincide with the blockwork coursing, and so it's a common practice to adjust the height of the blockwork with a course or two of bricks. But it's better to keep the inner leaf uniform by using brick-sized blocks (coursing units) instead.

Then build up the internal walls to the same height. Builders' trestles are useful for this.

(If there is to be a landing on the stairs, joists may be needed to support it. Leave indents in the blockwork, or else build in joist hangers.)

With the walls of the ground floor complete, the house is beginning to take shape. The next stage is something completely different – joisting.

Joisting

The building is ready for joisting once the walls have reached ceiling height. Check that you have, indeed, reached the right height. You can delay joisting until after the roof is on by building joist hangers into the external walls. But the usual method is to build the ends of the joists into the inner leaf of the external walls. This is preferable, as it makes for a more rigid structure; it is the method outlined below.

The work is fairly straightforward, and a professional can do the job in half a day. The only difficulty is the hard work of sawing the rather hefty timbers: typically 5 × 20 cm, with thicker ones ($7\frac{1}{2}$ cm) around an opening such as a stairwell. The depth must give enough strength for the longest span involved. (In fact, the drawings show the depth and spacing for the joists.) When ordering, it's a very good idea to ask for the depth to be 'regularised' – the joists are all trimmed to an even depth. (You want both the floor and the ceiling to be flat.) Redwood is the better timber, though white deal is also used.

If you are subcontracting the brickwork, a small point to bear in mind is to keep the break for joisting short. If the brickies go away and become involved in other work, they may not return promptly.

And so to the joisting itself...

Arrange the timbers in similar lengths and check their depths. If they have not been regularised and there are significant discrepancies, you will have to cut the thicker ones down at the ends, or else pack up the thinner ones. The tops of the joists should end up level; the undersides are less important. It is considered bad practice to use timber for packing, lest it rot. But slate, for example, is approved of.

Your drawings will probably show the lie of the joists, which are usually at intervals of 40 cm or 45 cm. (See Fig. 10.)

The interval influences the length of plasterboard you intend to put up for the ceiling. To minimise cutting of plasterboard, a 40 cm interval for the joists is compatible with whole boards 2·4 m in length; that's also the length of flooring chipboard. Whereas a 45 cm interval suits plasterboards 1·8 m in length. (See Chapter 12: *Plastering*.) The interval is assumed to be 40 cm in the following description – adjust the figures accordingly for a 45 cm interval.

Figure 10: Typical layout for joists

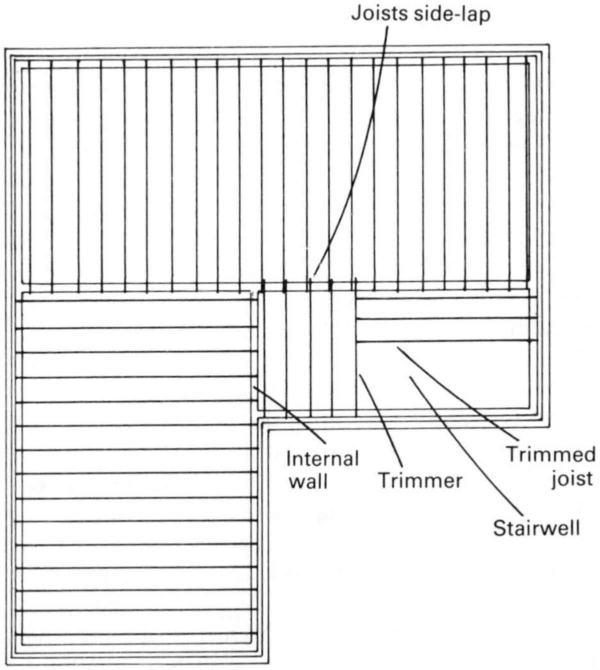

* Usual spacing is 40 cm or 45 cm.
* Trimmer is extra thick ($7\frac{1}{2}$ cm) to support the trimmed joists.

To start the work, get a stack of the joist timbers up aloft. Since the first lift of scaffolding will now be in position, this will not be so difficult, especially with two pairs of hands. The joists can be cut to length either before or after being placed in position. A small bow saw is useful. The first joist, alongside an end wall, should be separated from the inner leaf

Figure 11: Joisting

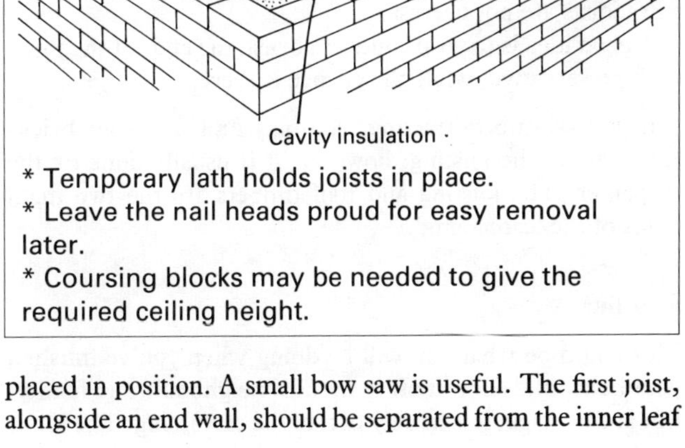

* Temporary lath holds joists in place.
* Leave the nail heads proud for easy removal later.
* Coursing blocks may be needed to give the required ceiling height.

by a 5 cm gap. To be sophisticated, the next joist should be placed with its centre 41 cm from the wall (to leave a centimetre gap between the plasterboard and the wall). Thereafter, space the joists at 40 cm intervals.

As each timber is being positioned, look down its length to see if there is any camber. If there is, place the bow upwards to counteract the natural sagging. Near each end, check the level of the joist relative to its neighbour. (A timber straight-edge to rest across three or four joists is useful.) When a series of joists are resting in position, stabilise them by nailing some roofing batten, or similar, along their tops. A row of batten, about a third of a metre from each end, will keep the joists in place. (The batten is only temporary, so leave the nail heads protruding for easy removal later. See Fig. 11.)

That's all there is to the basics. But a couple of situations need more consideration:

It often happens that a partition wall supports joists on both sides. In this case, side-lap the joists together so that they all have a full bearing on the wall. Don't be tempted to butt end them, which would give too little bearing.

The other situation, around an opening such as a stairwell or chimney, is more complicated. Extra thick joists ($7\frac{1}{2}$ cm) are used around the opening to support the ends of other joists. It used to be that the joists were mortised and tenoned into each other, using elaborate 'tusk tenons'. But once again, technical advances have made life easier for the ownhander (and the professional). The joists can now be supported with joist hangers, and the only skill required is an ability to nail! (See Fig. 12.)

The hangers come in a variety of depths and widths to suit the joist size. Don't confuse the timber-to-timber joist hangers with those for hanging joists from masonry. The designs differ.

(The technique of supporting trimmed joists from a trimmer is also required if a narrow opening has to be made to allow a soil-and-vent pipe to run across the lie of the joists. But it is better if the plumbing can be arranged to avoid this situation.)

To support partition walls upstairs, some extra joists may be required. If the future studwork will lie along a joist, then double that joist up to take the extra weight. (A pair of joists can be secured together by randomly skew nailing through one into the other, or by using some long bolts.) If the studwork will lie between two joists, place one extra joist to support it. (For studwork running across the lie of the joists, extra joists are not necessary.)

A good idea is to go around and brush the ends of the joists with preservative, while the chance is there.

If you are subcontracting, you may find that your bricklayer can do the joisting; however, it is usually done by the carpenter. The joisting and roof timbers are the two main items of the 'carcassing'.

Strutting

This could be what you will be doing when you've finished your house and show it off to friends, neighbours and family. But at this stage, it is merely part of the carcassing. The job is usually left until the roof is on, but as it relates to joisting, this is an appropriate place in the book for it.

Strutting helps to make the floor more rigid and to prevent the joists from warping as they dry out – which could cause cracking of the ceilings below. In good class work, joists with a span more than three metres are reckoned to need a row of strutting down the middle; more than five metres, two rows are needed, dividing the span into three equal parts.

Figure 12: Joist hanger

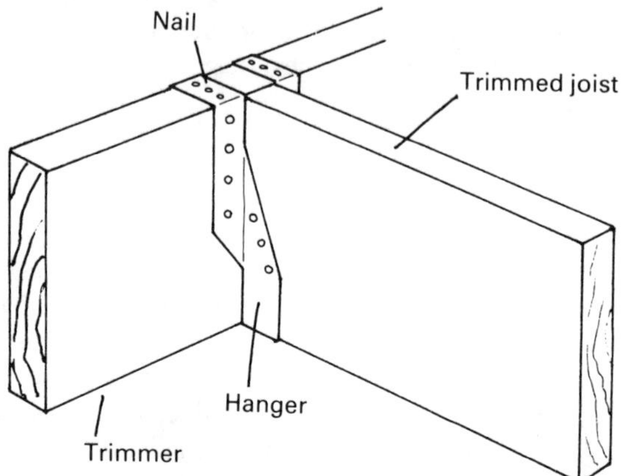

* Put a nail in every hole of the hanger.
* With hangers of somewhat different design, joists can be hung from walls.

Herring-bone strutting is the traditional method: two struts criss-cross between each pair of joists. (See Fig. 13.)

The struts are made from stout timber, say 4 × 4 cm, fixed a centimetre from the top of one joist, and the same distance from the bottom of the next joist. There is a trick for getting the length and bevel for each strut – which can vary slightly from joist to joist. Across the tops of the joists mark the line for the struts (using, for example, a chalk line). Mark another line parallel to this, separated by a distance equal to the depth of the joists less two centimetres. Then, at each pair of joists, place some strutting stuff across and mark the sides of the joists on its underside. These are the lines to cut to, for the right length and bevel for that particular strut. (See Fig. 14.)

A last refinement is to make a saw kerf in each end to help start the nails. (Metal struts are now available, if you don't want to become involved with the above carpentry.)

At each end of a line of struts, the small gap between joist and wall is jammed with a pair of folding wedges to make the whole line tight.

(If some joists are supported by a steel beam – as above an opening – there should be a row of strutting alongside the beam to hold the joists steady. The joist ends should have a shallow housing to fit over the bottom flange of the beam. And as mentioned previously, the top of the beam should be below the top of the joists.)

Walls from joists to wall plate

Once the joists are in position, the walls can be carried on

Figure 13: Herring-bone strutting

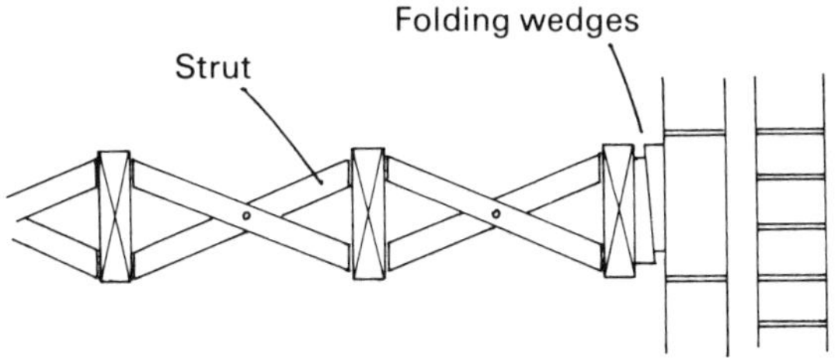

* Prevents joists twisting (which cracks ceilings).
* Stiffens floor.

Figure 14: Marking out a strut

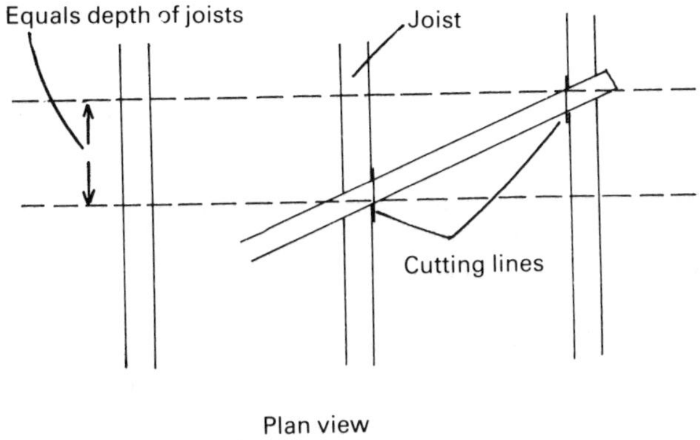

Figure 15: Position of straps

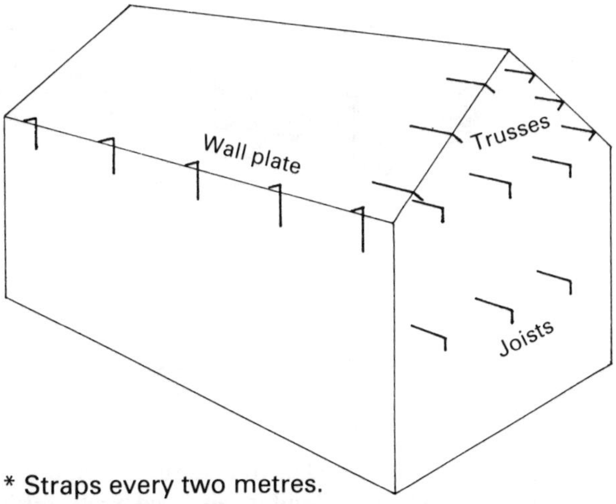

* Straps every two metres.
* See also Figs. 16 and 17.

upwards. When starting the inner leaf, lay blocks between the joist ends to hold them firmly in place.

It is the practice, nowadays, to tie joists to an adjoining wall with restraint straps built into the blockwork every couple of metres. (See Fig. 15.)

The straps are L-shaped strips of galvanized steel with plenty of nail holes punched in them. (See Fig. 16.)

Figure 16: Joist strap

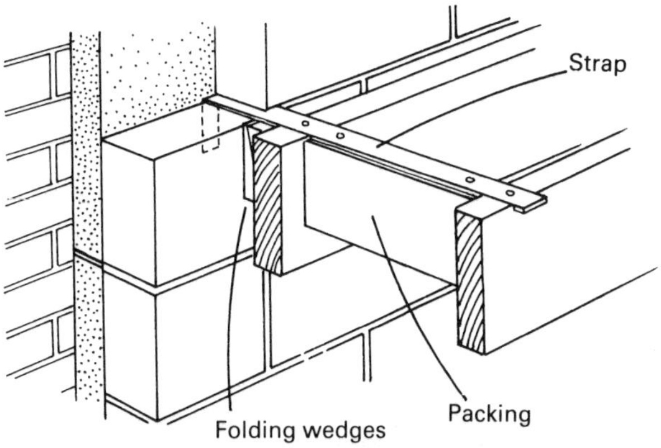

* Notch the strap into the joists (so the floor boarding will not be impeded).
* If the top of the joists is not level with the blockwork coursing, embed a strap with a twist into a cross joint.

(Actually, it's said to be preferable to screw rather than to nail the straps.) A strap lays across the two joists adjacent to the wall and is held within the blockwork. (Some straps have a twist in them; they can be held in a cross joint when the bed joint is not level with the top of the joists.) Make shallow notches in the joists so that the straps will not obstruct the flooring. To make it all solid, fix a nogging between the pair of joists, and some packing at the wall.

Lay scaffold boards on the joists to obtain a working platform for putting up the blockwork. The temporary braces which hold up window frames will also need to be supported off the joists.

If there are to be corbels, don't start building them yet. Instead, leave a rectangular step in the outer leaf of the eaves wall. This should be $21\frac{1}{2}$ cm wide (ie, a brick length), and the appropriate number of courses down. Look at the eaves detail on your drawings to see how to finish the top of the walls – usually, by closing the cavity off. (See Fig. 5, Chapter 7.) Take the gable ends up to eaves height; don't start building up the gables themselves.

Bed the wall plate on top of the eaves walls. (See Fig. 17.)

The plate is stout timber (say $5 \times 7\frac{1}{2}$ cm in cross section) to which the roof trusses can be firmly attached. On a long wall, joint the plate with a half-lap joint nailed together – but don't use short lengths of timber. This is a simple job – even brickies can do it!

In the past, there have been cases of high winds causing roofs to take off like aeroplane wings. So restraint straps are nowadays used to secure the plate to the wall. Use L-shaped galvanized straps, about a metre long. Fix them to the blockwork every couple of metres, or so, with galvanized nails. (The plaster will cover over the straps.)

Figure 17: Wall plate (for a hipped roof)

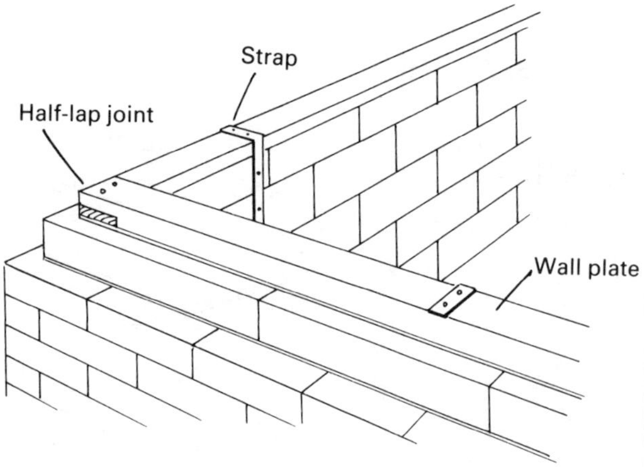

* Plate bedded level on mortar.
* Also use a half-lap joint for straight joints.
* Straps hold plate to blockwork.

Figure 19: Flue liners

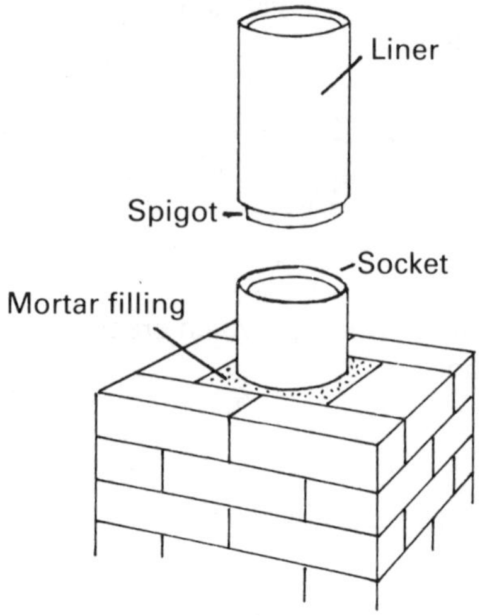

* Socket upwards.

Chimney for a free-standing stove

Two piers have been put down in the foundations to support the chimney breast. The piers have to be carried up to the level of the top of the short section of exposed flue pipe that will be over the stove. (See Fig. 18.)

Figure 18: Brickwork piers for a chimney

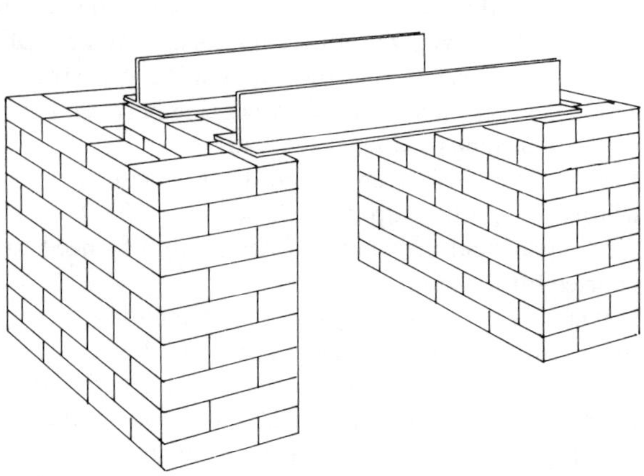

* The bonding of the piers is handed – so they are built of opposite hand.
* Steel sections support the breast and chimney.

At this level, a broad lintel is required to support the chimney breast above. One method is to use a pair of T-section steel beams to support a concrete slab cast *in situ*. Alternatively, it is possible to obtain a precast lintel with a hole in the middle to take a flue liner.

The flue is made up from short sections of clay flue liners. The spigot of each liner faces downwards, so that any tarry residues creeping down the flue can't run out through the joint. Bed the spigot into its socket and clear away surplus mortar to keep the flue smooth. (See Fig. 19.)

A flue is said to draw better if it has a bend or two in it – a chimney breast contains plenty of space for this. The flue is encased in a brickwork 'sleeve', with mortar filling the gap between lining and brickwork.

Figure 20: Chimney detail

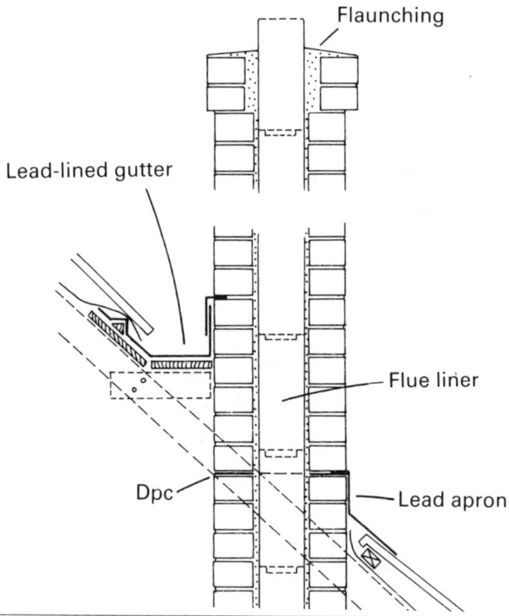

The chimney stack is carried up from the breast. Above the roof, it should, of course, be built in fair-faced brickwork. It is modern practice to build a dpc into the stack as it emerges from the roof. (See Fig. 20.)

The stack needs to be completed before the roof trusses are put up. (There should be a 5 cm gap between the stack and any joists or trusses to prevent the possibility of charring.)

Chimney pots are rarely used these days. Instead, the lining simply sticks out from the top of the stack. (Linings are a relatively recent innovation. Previously, the inside of a brick flue was 'parged', ie, rendered.) At the top of the stack there may be some corbelling; the top itself is flaunched with mortar to shed water.

The above is an outline of what is required. From it, you can see what a cumbersome structure a chimney is. Its construction can be made somewhat easier by using proprietary sections of lightweight concrete.

The completion of a chimney gives a good excuse to hold a topping out ceremony – some compensation for all the extra work involved!

Weathering

Where a roof butts up to brickwork (for example where a roof is pierced by a chimney or where a garage roof butts onto a side wall), some form of weathering is required to cover the joint. Often lead flashing is used. To hold the flashing in position, mortar bed joints have to be raked out to a depth of a couple of centimetres. Physically, this is easily done when the brickwork is green. What is difficult is to work out the position for it. If a loose roof truss is held up against the brickwork, the line of the roof tiles can be estimated, and so a line for the flashing deduced. That sounds simple, and when the flashing is in place, it will look simple. (A lot of building is like that. It looks simple enough – afterwards.) In practice, some people prefer to leave the raking out until the roof is on. With the mortar well set, the job is then physically harder. Use, for example, an angle grinder or a raking-out tool as used for repointing.

If the roof in question is over a habitable space, instead of a garage, then more than just flashing is required. The cavity needs to be blocked off, so that water can't flow down the cavity from the upper, external wall into the lower, internal wall. This is done with 'cavity trays' as the brickwork is built. (See manufacturers' leaflets.)

With the brickwork up to the wall plate all round, and the chimney built, there is now a pause in the bricklaying as the roof trusses are put on. For this, see the next chapter.

Gables

With the trusses in place, it's easy to judge the outline required for the gables. But before building up the gables and thereby blocking off easy access to the loft space, pause for thought. The water tank (for an indirect system) will probably be too big to pass between the trusses. Now is the time to put it into the loft space. It's rather late just to think of it when you get to the plumbing!

There are two basic designs for the gable verges. The fashion of the Eighties – and it looks set to continue into the Nineties – has been a flush verge. The tiles barely overhang the gable. The brickwork involved is trickier, with corbels (usually in brick) and a cleanly cut verge which is often decorative.

The previous fashion had been for an overhanging roof which terminated in a pair of barge boards. In the Sixties and Seventies, these were plain white boards, but in earlier eras they were often cut decoratively.

Both methods are described below:

Flush verges

With the roof trusses in position, and the feet of the rafters cut to the required length, we know the position of the fascia. The rafters give the outline for the gable; but it's useful to nail the sprocket (if any) to the end truss, to give the line for

Figure 21: Corbel and verge

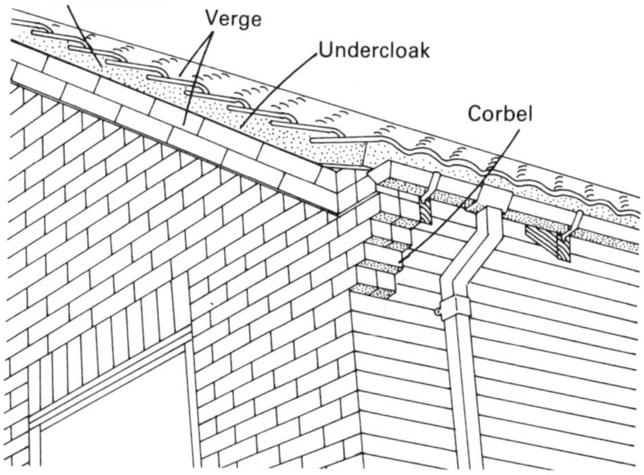

* Corbel bricks overhang by a quarter brick length, at most.
* Decorative 'soldiers' over window.
* Verge may slightly oversail brickwork below.
* Swan-neck in downpipe under eaves.

the bottom of the verge. (See 'Carpentry along the eaves', Chapter 7.) The corbel needs to reach out as far as the outside of the fascia (to protect its end grain). The corbel needs to be a whole brick thick; and it needs to bond with the gable end. (See Fig. 21.)

All this needs careful thought, and some planning out on squared paper is useful. Look at corbels on other houses to see how they work.

With the corbels in place, the gable can be built. The usual order is reversed, and the blockwork raised first. There are no corners to build. Instead, on each course, lay the end blocks into position, making them plumb over the lower ones. Lay to the line in between. At each end, the blocks need to be cut slantwise to match the slope of the rafters. (See Fig. 22.)

As with the floor joists, plenty of restraint straps are used nowadays to hold the gable end and roof trusses together. (See Fig. 15.) Place the straps every couple of metres along the rafters and along the ceiling ties. The straps should be long enough to secure a couple of trusses, again with noggings and packing in between. But this time, do not notch the timber to take the straps.

Insulation is maintained in the gable cavity, although this may seem, at first sight, to be unnecessary. If it were stopped, the top of the insulation would bridge the cavity and that could allow damp to penetrate. Finally, the outer brickwork is built up. A neat way to finish the verge is with a couple of slant courses. To give the required line, use a pair of 'flags'. (See Fig. 23.)

Figure 22: Building a gable wall

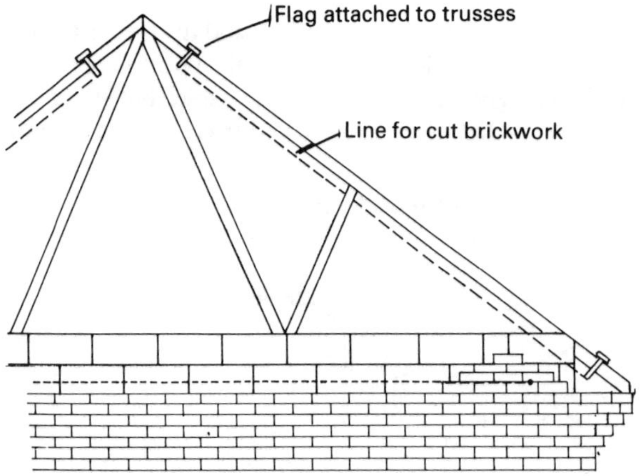

* Lead with blockwork.
* Build up ends of brickwork, then lay to line in between.
* See also Fig. 23.

Figure 23: Gable flag

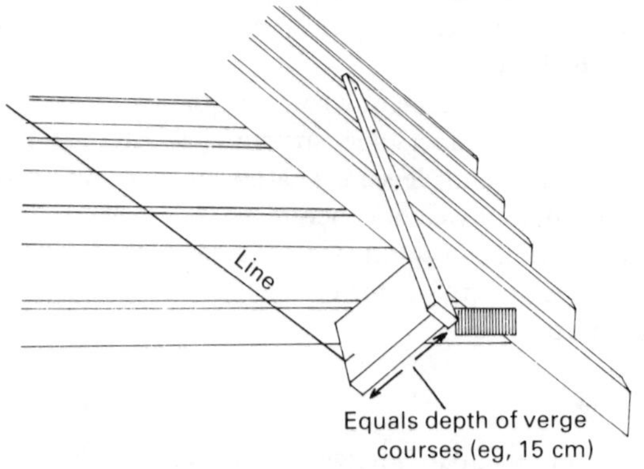

* Plumb upwards to mark face of wall on flag.

The length of the flag is 15 cm (for two courses). Make a mark on each flag plumb above the face of the brickwork. Using these marks, stretch a line from one flag to the other to give the boundary line of the cut edge of the brickwork.

The cut slanted edges need to look neat. If you can't cut the bricks well enough with a bolster or brick hammer, try an angle grinder with a stone cutting disc to score the bricks first.

After that, it is fairly straightforward to lay the last couple of courses on the slant. Oversailing the main brickwork by two or three centimetres looks attractive. Anyhow, the brickwork should finish in line with the rafters.

Overhanging verges

The brickwork for these is easier. (There is more carpentry instead: verge ladders and barge boards.) There are no corbels. The blockwork and brickwork are carried up so that they can support a 'ladder' along each verge. The ladder may be prefabricated by your truss supplier or made by you (either on the ground or *in situ*). A 'ladder' has of a pair of 'stiles' in timber similar to the rafters. The 'rungs' are about a metre apart, and wide enough to give the required overhang. One stile is nailed to the end rafter; the rungs are held by the gable wall; and the other stile will support the barge board. Make sure that the rungs are held firmly by the blockwork and brickwork, though these must not rise proud of the rafters. The slant line of the the brickwork will be hidden by a soffit board, so it can be finished more roughly.

7
THE ROOF

☆

☆

☆

☆

☆

☆

☆

THE TWO SKILLS involved in putting on a roof are carpentry and tiling. They both involve 'know-how' rather than 'knack', and are both amenable to the ownhander willing to take his or her time and think. The roof carpentry has been simplified enormously by the introduction of roof trusses. From being perhaps the most complex skill required in building a house – at least, for a house with a a hipped roof – the carpentry is now almost a labourer's job. As with many aspects of house-building, technology from a factory has replaced skill on site – all to the ownhander's advantage. Nonetheless, hipped roofs are still more difficult, both carpentry- and tiling-wise, so we will assume in this chapter a design involving only gable roofs.

Roof carpentry:

Trusses

The use of prefabricated roof trusses (also called 'trussed rafters') started in the USA in the Fifties, and has now become standard practice in Britain. The triangular-shaped trusses are made up in a factory to the requirements of each individual roof. The members – rafters, ceiling tie and webs – are simply butt jointed together and held by metal plate connectors. (You could make your own using plywood gussets nailed and glued in place as connectors.) The trusses can be put up quickly with little skill; they use less timber than the traditional methods; and they can span from wall to wall unsupported by partition walls, thereby allowing freedom in the layout of the rooms below. Their big disadvantage is that the loft space is wasted – it's a forest of spars. For this reason you may want a traditionally timbered roof. Provided that you stick to a simple gable roof, you should not find this too difficult. But the method given below is for trusses.

Ordering

Allow a couple of months for the manufacturer to make up the trusses from your drawings.

They may also supply the subsidiary timber requirements for the roof: fascia, soffit, sprockets and, for overhanging verges, gable ladders and barge boards with feet. (Some fascinating names!)

Prior to use, the trusses can be stored on site by stacking them on their sides upon bearers on level ground.

Erection

Many hands make light work of this. The trusses are not heavy, but they are cumbersome. With two people on the ground passing the trusses up to two on the scaffold, the work is easy. Keep the plane of the trusses vertical – if held horizontally, they tend to sag and overstrain the joints. Think about the order of erection. Once a truss has been erected, it can be difficult to pass other trusses past it. Let's consider the order of working for a simple roof.

First of all, mark on the wall plates the positions for the trusses. (Use edge marks rather than centres.) The end truss is to be about 5 cm from the gable wall. (But with an overhanging verge, allow for the gable ladder, which is nailed to the end truss.) Most of the trusses should be at 60 cm intervals, not more (and not less if they are to be compatible with plasterboard lengths). At a narrow chimney (two bricks wide) the trusses can pass either side, but they must be at least 5 cm from the brickwork. (For wider chimneys, truss manufacturers produce special items.)

Start erecting at the end away from where you are bringing the trusses up. The first truss to erect should be about as far from the gable end as the rafter is long. (This will allow for some 45° diagonal bracing.) At marks on the wall plates, raise the first truss.

This is a moment of truth. Was the setting out correct? Does the truss fit snugly onto the plates? It's a bit late to find major discrepancies! Assuming all is well, nail the truss to the wall plates; use 10 cm wire nails and skew nail from each side, going through the connector plate if you must. With somebody still holding the truss upright, fix it plumb with a diagonal brace from its apex to the wall plate (on the side away from the gable). (See Fig. 1.)

Now start erecting the adjacent trusses towards the gable. To this end, high on each side of the erected truss, nail a length of temporary batten horizontally out towards the gable. Place the next truss into position between these battens. Nail the truss to the plate, and fix it upright by nailing through the battens. (Make the spacings between the trusses equal at top and bottom; if the first truss is plumb, then so will the second be. A spacing stick is useful.) Proceed; fix trusses along to the gable end, adding more temporary battens if required.

Now for some permanent bracing (all in 10 × $2\frac{1}{2}$ cm sawn). (See Fig. 2.)

Figure 1: Erecting the first truss

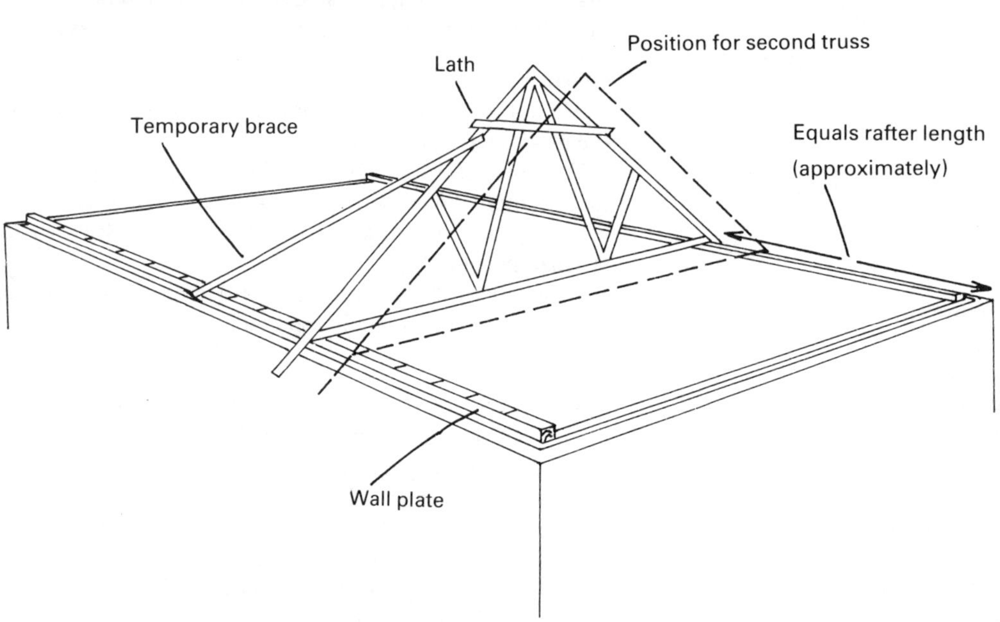

* Truss secured vertically with temporary brace.
* Temporary lath to hold subsequent trusses.

Figure 2: Bracing for trusses

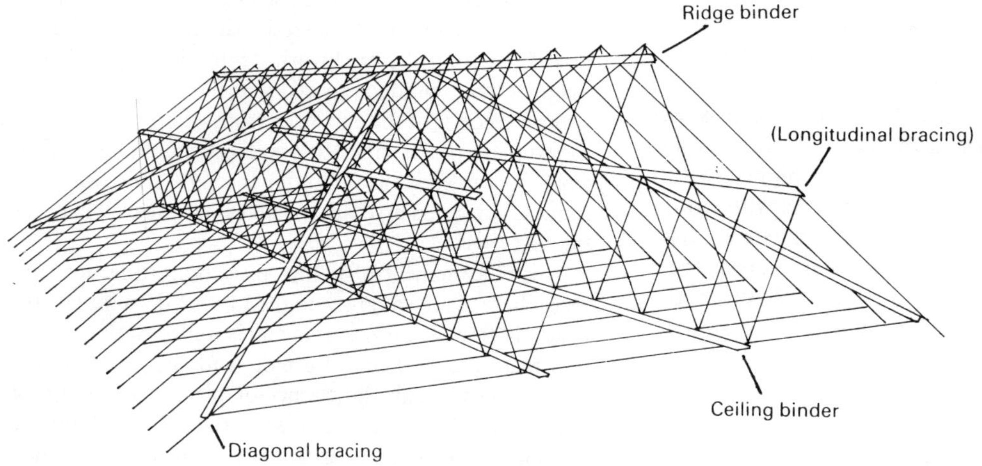

* Longitudinal bracing only necessary if rafters longer than 3 m.
* Butt up binders (and longitudinal bracing) against gable wall.
* Twice-nail diagonal bracing to wall plate.
* Twice-nail every binder and brace to each truss.

The diagonal bracing is threaded up through the trusses so that it can be fixed to the undersides of the rafters. The bottom end is fixed over the outside arris of the wall plate, between the end truss and its neighbour. Getting the bracing into position is a matter of threading it between the right spars by trial and error. Nail it to the plate and to each rafter with a pair of 7 cm nails.

With a half dozen, or whatever, trusses in position, you can now work back in the other direction for the remaining roof. Remove the temporary bracing that held the first truss. Oversail out in the new direction with some temporary battens, as before.

Fix the remaining trusses, and stabilise them with some diagonal bracing as above.

Longitudinal bracing will also be required: a ridge binder, and two ceiling binders. If the rafter slope is more than 3 m, then the rafter/web nodes also need binders. But since all this bracing is required to butt up firmly against the gables, the fixing of it is best left until the gables have been built. (Put the bracing stuff up into the loft space while the gables are open.)

For large roofs, more bracing may be required. If the span is more than 8 m, zigzag bracing is needed along the webs. And if the roof is longer than 9 m, zigzag bracing is needed along the ceiling ties. Check this out with your truss manufacturer.

Adjoining roofs

Complications arise where two roofs meet – invariably at right angles. (See Fig. 3 and, as an example, the author's house on the front cover.)

Where there is no wall plate, the trusses of one roof are supported by an extra-strong truss in the other roof. The face of this truss must be in line with the outside of the wall plate in order to maintain the right span. (See Fig. 4.)

The trusses supported in this fashion require one end to be cut short with a plumb cut. Steel truss shoes (rather similar to joist hangers) are nailed to the extra-strong truss to take these cut ends.

When the trusses for the secondary and the main roof have been put up, there will be an awkward gap between the two roofs. This has to be filled with a set of diminishing valley trusses. Three or so trusses carry the secondary roof onto the slope of the main roof; they become progressively smaller up the slope. To fix the position for them, extend out, from the trusses already in place, a horizontal batten to indicate the ridge line. The valley trusses have the bottom member bevelled to the slope of the main roof. Fit them so that the apexes are along this ridge line. Check that they are plumb.

When the valley trusses are in place, fix them more permanently with a ridge binder. It's a little tricky, but all so much simpler than traditional roof carpentry.

Rafter feet

Trusses are supplied with their ends overlong for cutting to size *in situ*. The eaves detail on your drawings will give the length and type of cut, probably a simple plumb cut: On each end truss, mark off the end of the rafter. Stretch a string between the marks on the two end trusses to mark off for the trusses in between. Set an adjustable bevel and mark the plumb cuts; then saw.

Putting the trusses on takes a day or two. It's satisfying work that makes a big visual impact.

Figure 3: Roofing terms

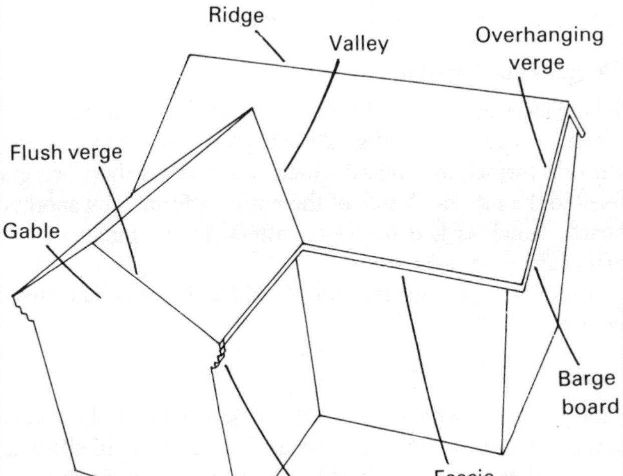

There is now an intermission in the carpentry work as the gables are built up.

With the gables built, the longitudinal bracing can be fixed with the ends butting up against the blockwork. Nail the bracing with a pair of 7 cm nails at each position. Where lengths have to be joined, they should be side-lapped across two trusses.

Note that trusses are engineered products, and they should not be cut or drilled without consulting their manufacturer.

Overhanging verges

For this sort of verge, 'ladders' are used to carry the roof out over the wall. One 'stile' is nailed to the end truss; the other stile will take the barge board. The 'rungs' are held by the gable wall. (See the previous chapter.)

The barge boards meet at the top with a neat plumb cut. At the bottom, barge feet are screwed and glued to the edge of the boards. (The purpose of the feet is to block off the gap beneath the eaves.)

To hide the ragged edge of the gable brickwork, a soffit of say 6 mm ply is fixed to the underside of the ladder. At the barge feet, you'll find that you need to improvise a little.

Carpentry along the eaves

Nail sprockets to the trusses. Nowadays the sprockets are short (wedges of timber about 30 cm long), and their main function is to help the felt lay smoothly over the fascia. (See Fig. 5.)

Figure 4: Typical layout for trusses

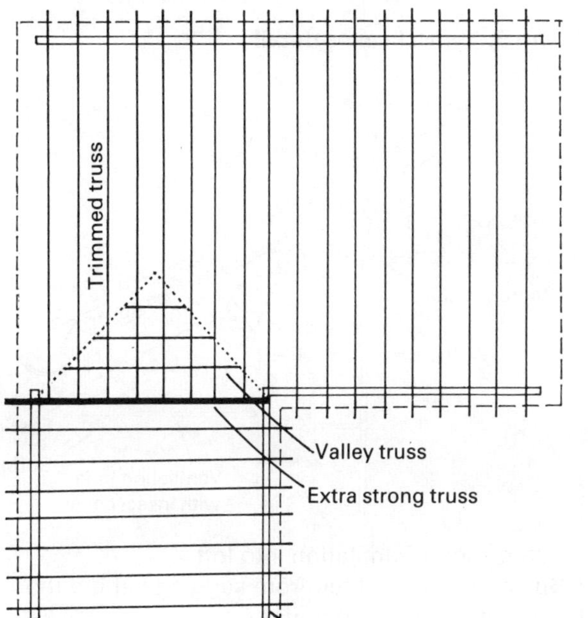

* Valley trusses of diminishing size are attached up the slope of the main roof.
* Trimmed trusses are supported by truss shoes (similar to joist hangers).

The fascia (or 'gutter board') is fixed to the ends of the trusses. (The board can be obtained already grooved to take a soffit.) The top of the fascia should be level with the top of the sprockets. (If there aren't any sprockets, the fascia should have an upstand of two or three centimetres above the rafters.) For finesse, where two lengths of fascia are butted together, the ends should be splay jointed. (See 'Splay joint', Chapter 24.)

The end of the fascia is butted up to the barge board or to the corbel, as the case may be.

The soffit is often made from 6 mm WBP ply. One edge can be supported in the groove in the fascia. The other edge can be pinned to a fillet fixed along the wall. (There are other popular methods.)

The loft needs to be well ventilated to disperse the humid air that comes up through the ceilings. To this end, the eaves need to be ventilated along their length. Proprietary grills with mesh to keep out insects are available for fitting into soffit board. Or just leave a centimetre gap between soffit and wall. (In this case, any fillet holding the soffit must be held off the wall by spacers.) To prevent the eaves ventilation being blocked off by loft insulation, plastic guards can be nailed along the top of the trusses. Many books show an eaves detail with the insulation as in Fig. 5.

In practice, that is fanciful – working in the loft near the eaves is very difficult, and it's unlikely the insulation will be draped over the wall plate as the diagram shows. However, it is easy to fix polystyrene to the wall plate, and this both insulates the plate and preserves a ventilation channel. (See Fig. 6.)

Figure 5: Typical eaves detail

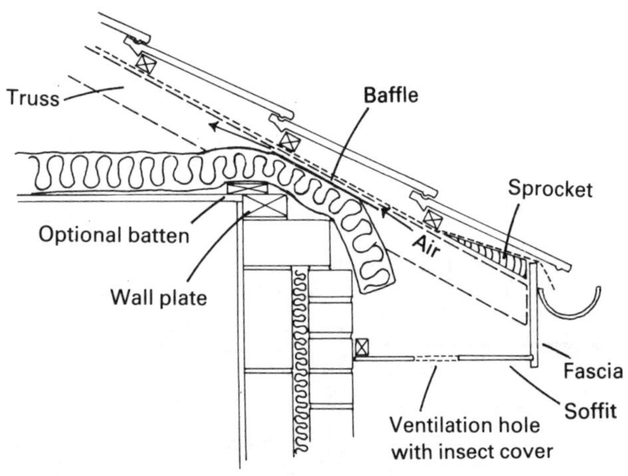

* Baffle allows ventilation into loft.
* Sprockets prevent felt from sagging behind the fascia. Felt hangs into gutter.
* Optional batten to support ceiling board.

Later, the loft insulation can be butted up to the polystyrene.

A rustic effect can be had by dispensing with both fascia and soffit, leaving the rafter feet exposed. The gutter fixes direct to the rafter ends. (Block off the top of the wall plate with expanded metal mesh to stop birds nesting on it.)

(All these variations will already have been settled at the design stage.)

In anticipation of fixing the plasterboard ceiling later, an optional job is to fix some support for it along the wall. (See Fig. 5 and 'Boarding ceilings', Chapter 12.) While the roof is open, it is easy to nail short strips of timber along the top of the wall plate so that they overhang it.

Figure 6: Wall plate insulation

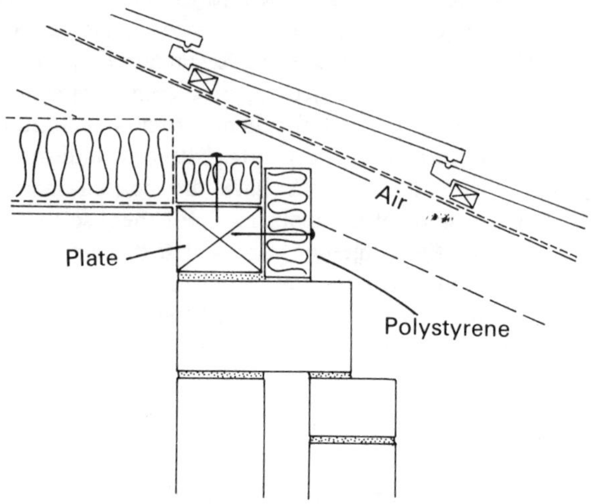

* Ventilation to loft assured.

Another optional job, for low-pitched roofs, is to fix a ply underlay along the eaves. This will support the felt and so prevent puddles forming where the felt runs over the fascia. The ply needs to be about 30 cm wide, and nailed to the top of the sprockets,

With this ancillary timber work in place it's a good idea for the selfbuilder to give it all a coat of stain-paint, while it is easily accessible before tiling and guttering.

Chimney stack gutter

Where the slope of a roof runs down onto a chimney stack, a gutter is needed. (See Fig. 20, Chapter 6.) The base of the gutter is formed by a board which is laid across short bearers fixed to the rafters. A side of the gutter is formed by another board, which is laid onto the rafters. (The chimney itself makes the other side.)

If the stack goes up through the ridge, there is, of course, no gutter.

Tiling:

Tiling is a job with some mathematical content. It is very amenable to the ownhander because it requires an intellectual grasp rather than a physical knack acquired by much practice. But it's not all intellect – as you may come to realise as you carry tonnes of tiles up onto a roof on a hot summer's day!

Although the work is so suitable for the ownhander, it may not be economic to do it. Roofing specialists can obtain their tiles very cheaply, and their prices might be so low that subcontracting the work is irresistible. Nonetheless, the work is described below.

Types of tile

Plain tiles are small flat tiles in clay or concrete; they give a pleasing, traditional finish. But they have to be laid with a double lap: at least two thicknesses of tile everywhere, and twice as many battens as single lap tiles. The result is a heavy, costly roof covering. Laying plain tiles, although not dissimilar to the method described below for single lap tiles, is a little more complex. Slates are laid in a rather similar manner to plain tiles. Natural slate has become very expensive, but effective imitations are available.

Single lap concrete tiles are widespread. They are economical, and available in a wide variety of shapes and shades. Interlocking corrugations around the edges check the passage of water and allow the tile to be used in a single thickness. The more expensive through-coloured tile keeps its colour better, though the fading of surface-coloured tiles is not necessarily unattractive. Clay tiles are said to look best, but they are more expensive.

Most interlocking tiles are profiled, but a flat design is available. This is easy to walk on at low pitches, so it may appeal to the ownhander. But if flat tiles butt onto a wall (or chimney), the weathering is more complicated because water can be blown sideways along the tile. (See 'Weathering', Chapter 8.)

The minimum slope for the tiles to be weathertight varies with their design (22° or more). So if your roof has a low pitch, check from the manufacturer's technical leaflet that the tiles you have in mind are suitable. The leaflet will give a lot of useful information about laying that particular tile.

Ordering

The area to be tiled can be calculated from the drawings. (Use the elevations to find the distance up the slope.) The manufacturer's leaflet will specify how many tiles cover a square metre. Hence you can calculate your order quantity – but add an extra 8% for wastage. (If you do find yourself short later on and have to order extra, disperse the new ones amongst the others, else a colour variation may well be obvious. This advice applies to bricks, too.)

Note that interlocking tiles, unlike plain ones, are handed. The right edge overlaps a left edge. This means that ordinary tiles can be used for the right-hand verge (since the right edge has a proper top surface). But for the other verge, order special left-hand verge tiles. (Alternatively, ordinary tiles with the left lip cut off can be used.) Don't forget to order the ridge tiles too.

Allow about a month for delivery, although in times of shortages it can take longer.

Proprietary dry-fixing systems for the ridge and verge have become available. But described below is the traditional method of bedding in mortar; there is nothing very difficult in it.

Felting and battening

The felt is the second line of defence should water get past the tiles. The water runs down the felt to be discharged into the gutter. Cheap slaters' felt will do the job, although more expensive and stronger polythene felt is available. The felt comes in rolls a metre wide.

The roofing battens for rafters at 60 cm spacings are 25 × 38 mm – imperial lives! Sensibly, they should come preservative-treated. To work out how much battening you'll need, you will need to know the gauge for your tiles. The 'gauge' is the spacing of the battens; it equals the exposed 'margin' of the tile. (See Fig. 7.)

Figure 7: Gauge and lap of a tile

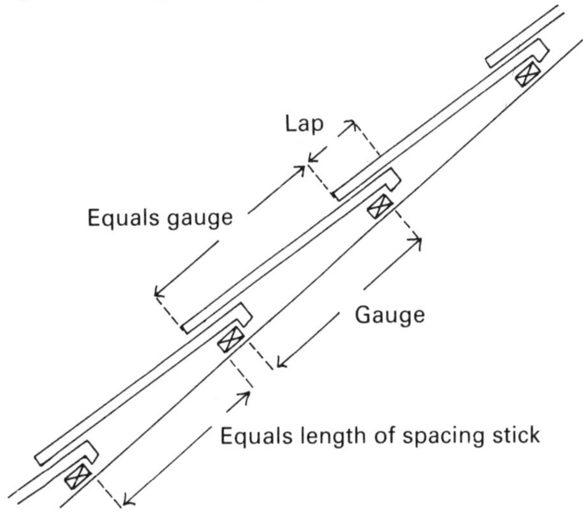

* Gauge + lap = length of tile.

The manufacturer's leaflet will give the maximum gauge for your tile. From the length of the roof, you can calculate the (minimum) running length of battens that you will require.

If there is no fascia, there is an extra little job to do before felting. Nail a line of battens along the foot of the rafters (or sprockets). The felt will lay over the these battens and protect them from the weather. Their purpose is to support the bottom row of tiles – normally done by the fascia.

To get into the swing of felting, start the work on a simple slope without a valley. And hope that it will not be windy!

First mark the trusses to guide the laying of the felt:

The lowest strip of felt will run over the top of the fascia into the gutter. Allow about 10 cm for this, and so mark 90 cm up the rafter next to a verge. Successive strips up the slope will overlap by 15 cm. So continue with marks up the rafter every 85 cm. The top strip should fold over the ridge onto the slope on the other side. (Adjust the 15 cm overlaps if necessary.) With one rafter marked out, transfer the marks to other rafters at two or three metre intervals.

A basic principle of roof covering is to start at the bottom and work upwards.

Put a roll of felt at the bottom of the verge, and check the top edge against your mark on the rafter. Tack the top of the felt to the rafter with a short clout nail. Now unroll the felt along the roof, tacking every few metres to keep it up to the marks. Cut the roll at the far verge with a Stanley knife. (Or hack down it with a slaters' axe).

With the first strip of felt in place, it can be battened.

The lowest course of tiles will extend over to the middle of the gutter – ie, 4 cm or 5 cm out from the fascia. This determines the position for the lowest line of battens. This line can be marked on the felt with a chalk line.

(Chalk line reels are sold as a tool. But plain chalk lines are also sold – rub a stick of chalk along the line. Actually, for roof work, red cement colour is preferred as this shows up better on battens.)

Mark the position for the battens at each end of the roof, hold the chalk line tight between the marks (you need a helper!), stretch with your free arm to pull the twine back like a bow string and let it twang onto the felt. Using this line, nail on the bottom row of battens, as described below.

The next step is to work out the precise gauge for the battens. (You have already found out the maximum gauge specified by the manufacturer.) At a verge, find the position for the very top batten. This should allow the top tile to be well covered – 7 cm or more – by the ridge tile. Yet the tile should not clash with the top tile on the opposing slope. Measure the distance between top and bottom batten. (See Fig. 8.)

Figure 8: Calculation of tile gauge

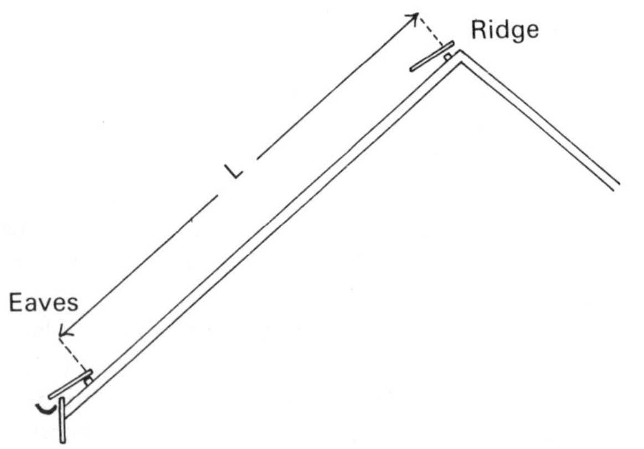

* Divide L by the maximum tile gauge and round the answer upwards to the nearest whole number. This is the number of courses required (in addition to the eaves course) and divided into L it gives the actual gauge.

Hence calculate the gauge – not larger than the maximum – which covers the slope in a whole number of tiles.

(Check that the slope at the other end of the roof is pretty much the same length. It ought to be! If not, you will have to adjust the gauge, varying it imperceptibly along the roof.)

With the gauge worked out, you can now fix battens up the slope from the bottom row. The next row is fixed at the gauge distance from the row below – for convenience, make a couple of spacing sticks. (See Fig. 9.)

Nail the battens using 8 cm galvanized wire nails. Where lengths of batten have to be joined, butt joint them on top of a rafter. (Saw the fixed batten *in situ*, forcing an off-cut of batten between it and the rafter to protect the felt.) Battens give stiffness to a roof. But a joint is a point of weakness, so make sure that not more than one in every four battens are jointed on any particular rafter. And battens should be long enough to span at least three rafters. Finish the battens more or less flush with the verge. At this stage, don't nail the battens to the end rafter – you will want to prise the battens up a little later.

Figure 9: Felting and battening

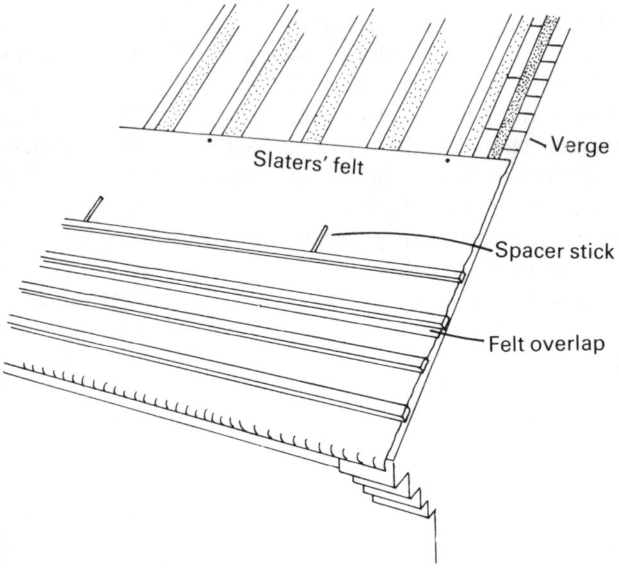

* Enough felt at bottom to run into gutter.
* Overlap layers of felt by 15 cm.
* Rest next batten on spacing sticks for required spacing.

So, fix battens up the first strip of felt. At the top of the felt, allow for a 15 cm overlap and tack on the next strip. In this manner, proceed up the slope, felting and battening. To walk on the slope, step on the battens at a rafter. (And if you should step through the felt, this will have to be patched. Remember, the patch must under-lap felt above it. Prise up battens on each side to fix the patch.)

Join up lengths of felt at a rafter, overlapping the lengths by several centimetres on each side. And at the ridge, lap the felt over onto the other slope. Where the felt comes to an abutment (eg, a chimney stack), cut it slightly overlong so that it curls up against the brickwork. Between the trusses, let the felt sag slightly (ie, don't pull it taut).

Valleys

Valleys occur where two adjoining roofs meet, invariably at right angles. They need special treatment.

With plain tiles, the traditional method has been to 'lace' the tiles continuously from one slope to the other. This is attractive but requires much skill. For single lap tiles, a gutter can be formed with special valley tiles or with lead. Nowadays however, a fibreglass valley trough is usually used. Fixing this is quick and easy. The troughs are flexible to suit roofs of any slope; they come in lengths of about three metres. They are the obvious choice for the ownhander.

The valleys are, in fact, the first part of a roof to be felted. Run a length of felt down a valley, with the middle of the felt along the crease of the valley. Overlap it, at the top, with the felt from the neighbouring valley, cutting the felt if necessary.

As the adjoining slopes are felted, overlap the ends of the felt nearly to the crease of the valley. Leave the battens overlong at this stage and not nailed near the valley.

When the whole roof has been felted and battened, temporarily lay the plastic trough in the valley and mark the line of its outer edges onto the felt. Nail a counter batten down each side of the valley to support the sides of the trough. The actual position for the counter battens depends on the design of trough. In the original design, the counter battens support the ends of the tile battens (with the edge of the trough sandwiched in between). The difficulty of this is that the tile battens have to bend up to accommodate the thickness of the counter batten. To disguise this, the tile battens should be progressively packed up for two or three rafters. Well, that's the theory. In practice, the tile battens are usually cut short of the counter batten, leaving their ends unsupported. An improved design (Marley) is profiled so that the outer lip of the trough supports the tile battens in their normal plane.

With the counter battens in place, nail on the trough. (Drill holes through the plastic.) The bottom of the trough should run out over the gutter. Since this runs round a corner, cut the bottom of the trough to shape with a fine saw.

Once you've got started, felting and battening can proceed quickly. It might take you a couple of days – for another transformation of the house.

Laying the tiles

You've already worked out the gauge of the tiles up the roof. Now, in a rather similar way, you need to work out the spacing across it. Along the eaves, measure the width of the roof, including the overhang that you require at the verges (typically about 4 cm). The cover-width of the tile can be varied by a few millimetres from the nominal one given be the manufacturer. Work out what yours needs to be for a whole number of tiles along the roof. (If need be, the overhang can be altered a little.) Lay a trial course out along the eaves. To get a suitable overhang at both verges, shunt tiles sideways as required – changing the cover-width slightly. (Check that the width of the roof is the same along the ridge. If there is any appreciable discrepancy, the cover-width of the tiles will have to be changed gradually up the slope.)

Guidelines for the tile spacing need to be marked every couple of metres or so along the roof, dividing it into sections. The lines go up the slope and mark the position for the left-hand edge of tiles. So, from the tiles laid out along the eaves, mark off for the sections along battens near the top and bottom of the slope. Join the marks with chalk lines up the slope, marking the tops of the battens. (Or simply use a batten as a straight-edge instead of the chalk line.)

So far, work has been light, as much brain as brawn. But the next stage is sweaty, especially on a hot day: carrying the tiles up onto the roof. A professional carries half a dozen at a time, on edge on his shoulder. (It's more comfortable with a cloth pad on the shoulder!) Having carried some tiles up, how do you stack them on a sloping roof? There is a little trick for this – use one tile to prop up the others. (See Fig. 10.)

Figure 10: Stacking tiles on a roof

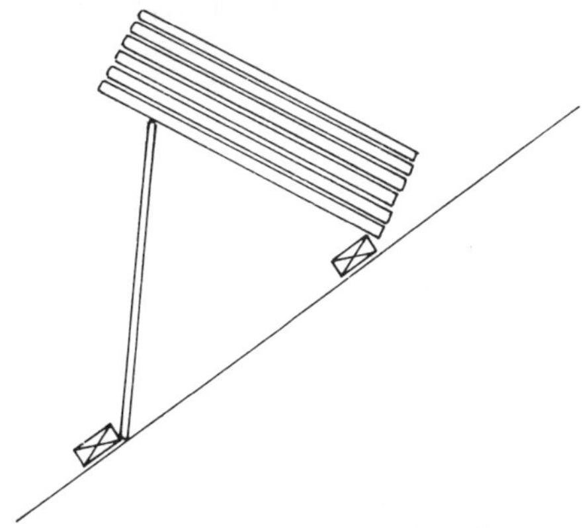

Make a lattice of little stacks all over the slope. It's worth being clever about this and spacing the stacks according to the area they will cover.

Lay the tiles in sections, corresponding to the guidelines previously marked. Work from right to left, and from bottom to top.

The first section involves the right-hand verge. To give an overhang of about 4 cm, an undercloak is used – commonly a 15 cm soffit strip of fibre-cement board. The board is slipped down from the top in between the felt and brickwork (or barge ladder), and held by the battens. Now is the time to nail the battens to the end rafter. (If the rafters have sprockets, use a separate short piece of undercloak at the bottom for the different slope.) The undercloak supports a thick bed of mortar. The preferred mixture for this is 1:1:5 of cement, lime and sand. Dollop it on generously; it will cover the batten ends. Bed a verge tile onto it, and nail. (For good adhesion, wet the tile first). The edge of the tile should be plumb above the edge of the undercloak. Proceed in this manner, laying tiles up the verge. Fill the gap between undercloak and tiles with mortar, and strike it off to give a clean finish. (Some people like to use a coloured mortar for this.)

With the right-hand verge in place, start laying the first section of tiles from the bottom. If you are using high profile tiles, nail plastic eaves fillers of matching profiles to the top of the fascia (to prevent small birds getting under the tiles). Nail on the first couple of courses at the eaves. Carry on laying tiles up the section, adjusting the cover width to keep the edge of the section to the guideline previously marked. Nail alternate courses and the top course.

If you are building to last a century, use alloy nails for securing tiles; to last the usual target life of 60 years for a house, galvanized nails will suffice (typically, 4 cm long). Only alternate courses need to be nailed, with one nail per tile. The other tiles just hang from the battens by their nibs. (This has a beneficial side effect later. If you push up each alternate loose tile so that the heads of the fixed tiles can be stepped on, you obtain an instant 'roof ladder'.) However, around the perimeter all the tiles need to be nailed: tiles down the verges, two courses along the eaves, and the top course along the ridge. These tiles are vulnerable in high winds. (In very exposed locations, you may want to use special clips to hold the perimeter tiles even more securely.)

Work along the roof to the left-hand verge, laying the tiles section by section. For the left-hand verge, special tiles are used. (If these are not available, cut off the underlip of ordinary tiles.) Bed this verge in a similar fashion to the right-hand verge.

Figure 11: Ridge detail

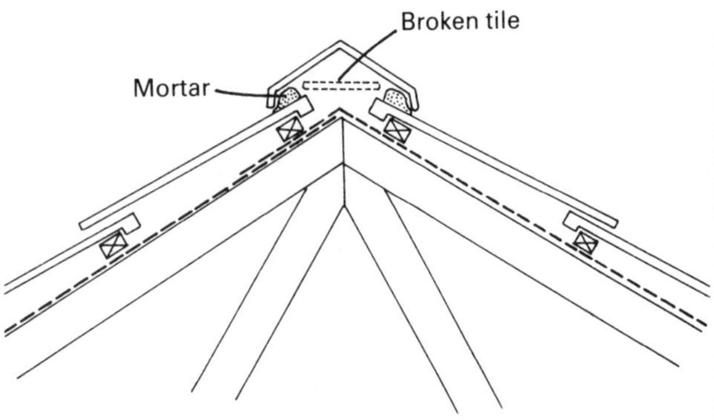

* Felt laps over ridge.
* Edges of ridge tiles bedded in mortar.
* Broken tile at joints supports mortar to seal the joints between ridge tiles.

And also in a rather similar fashion, the valley 'verges' can be dealt with. A fibreglass valley trough is smooth in the middle to allow an easy flow of water, but it is roughened elsewhere to give good adhesion to the mortar. A lot of unpleasant tile cutting is involved. Tiles need to be cut individually with a slanted cut to give a straight line up the valley. A disc cutter can be hired. Besides being very unpleasant tools to use, they are potentially dangerous. Take care. (For cutting just a few tiles, you can use an angle grinder with a stone-cutting disc: Score down a tile and then snap it. Or else use a tungsten-carbide rod saw fitted to a hacksaw frame.) Cut tiles may need an extra nail hole – drill this with a masonry bit.

Lastly, the ridge tiles are put on. These are laid with a gap of about a centimetre or so between them. To match the length of the ridge, this gap can be adjusted. (Or else a ridge tile can be cut shorter. But don't put the shortened tile at the end where it will be particularly vulnerable in high winds.) A ridge tile needs to be solidly bedded in mortar at both its ends. Use a 1:1:5 mix as for the verges, and wet the tiles. There's a trick to save mortar. Balance a flat piece of tile on the heads of the two tiles that meet at the ridge, and put your mound of mortar on this. (See Fig. 11.)

In addition, the ridges should be bedded along their edges. With high profile tiles, it's a fashionable practice to insert 'dentile slips' into this bed – easily done if you want to.

With the roof on, you have some reason for congratulations. However, if you think that you are virtually home and dry, think again. The building may now be dry, but it is still a long way from being home! You have, however, done the hardest half.

8
COMPLETING THE SHELL

☆

☆

☆

☆

☆

☆

☆

Weathering
Guttering
Stripping scaffolding
Glazing:
Ordering
Fixing
Sealing frames

Weathering

Where roof tiles meet masonry, a weathertight joint is required that is flexible, since there is a lot of thermal movement in a roof. So lead, a malleable and lasting material, is widely used. It can be easily worked – by an expert – into complex shapes. Creasing it along a line is simple enough, but forming it into a box corner is not – at least, for the amateur. It's said to be a matter of 'gaining' or 'losing' lead by hitting it with a bossing mallet to make the lead 'move'. Anyway, it needs a lot of practice. Traditionally, this is the work of the plumber – indeed, his name comes from the Latin word for lead, 'plumbum'. But nowadays, some roofers do the work also – which is sensible. The weathering is achieved by forming the lead into flashing, soakers, aprons, gutters, etc.

If you want to do it yourself, then below is described the simple case of cover flashing for a roof butting up to a wall. The weathering for a chimney is a good deal more complex, and you will have to consult elsewhere. (Briefly, it consists of a gutter along the top, flashing down the sides, and an apron on the outer face of the chimney. See Fig. 20, Chapter 6.) Fortunately, it's possible for the ownhander to purchase ready-made kits to fit most chimneys.

Cover flashing is used with profile tiles. The lead is simply dressed over the top of the tiles. With plain tiles and slates this would not be effective enough, because wind could blow water along the flat surface underneath the flashing. In such cases, 'soakers' are used. These are small sheets of lead made with an upturn to go against the side of the chimney. They are interleaved with the tiles as these are laid, and then a stepped flashing is dressed down over the upturns. (See textbooks for more details.) With flat interlocking tiles, cover flashing is again unsuitable, but in this case, it's not possible to use soakers. There are three possible solutions: a secret gutter, proprietary flashing units, or a cover flashing with special clips. (See manufacturers' brochures.)

Lead comes in various thicknesses and widths. The cover flashing for profiled tiles should extend over the tiles about 15 cm, and up the wall for a couple of courses. It should be installed with individual strips no longer than $1\frac{1}{2}$ metres. Typically, a width of 30 cm would be required, with a thickness given by BS Code 4. (For interest, this is 1·8 mm thick, and weighs 20 kg per sq m. This thickness is suitable for most leadwork on roofs, except that soakers can be made from the thinner Code 3.) If the roof slopes down the wall, then the flashing has to be stepped to follow the slope. (See Fig. 1.)

Figure 1: Stepped flashing

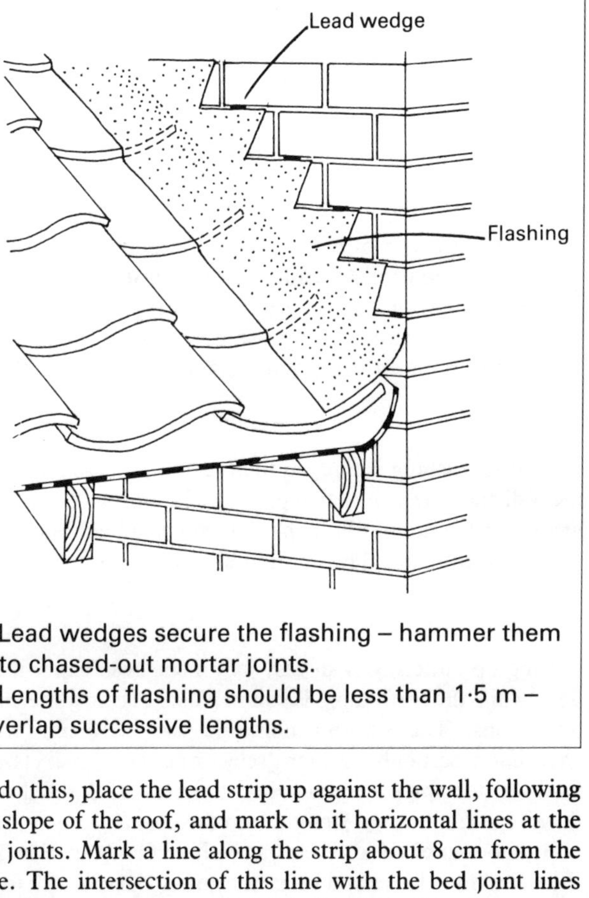

* Lead wedges secure the flashing – hammer them into chased-out mortar joints.
* Lengths of flashing should be less than 1·5 m – overlap successive lengths.

To do this, place the lead strip up against the wall, following the slope of the roof, and mark on it horizontal lines at the bed joints. Mark a line along the strip about 8 cm from the edge. The intersection of this line with the bed joint lines determines where to cut the lead. (See Fig. 2.)

(Lead is an expensive material to make mistakes with. A tip suggested for amateurs is to cut a piece of unwanted wall-paper to the required shape; when satisfied, transfer the shape of the paper to the lead.)

Whether flashing is straight (horizontal) or stepped (sloping), the top of it is let into the brickwork. The bed joint needs to be raked out to a depth of about two centimetres to receive the flashing. With clever foresight, this will have been done when the mortar was green. But that is more easily said than done. Even professional brickies find difficulty in working out where the flashing will be fitted. No matter – if the job has been left until now, the hard mortar can be chased out with an angle grinder or raking out tool. Crease the top edge of the upstand so that it fits into the chasing. The flashing is to be held in position every metre or so by small wedges of lead. So take a little piece of lead a couple of centimetres wide, and roll it into a tiny cylinder. Flatten this into a wedge shape, and push, or hammer, it into the chasing so that the flashing is wedged tight. Dress the flashing down the wall and over one or two profiles of the tiles. (Use a small mallet, or whatever.) Wet the joint for good adhesion, and repoint, using a small hawk and pointing trowel.

Figure 2: Cutting steps in flashing

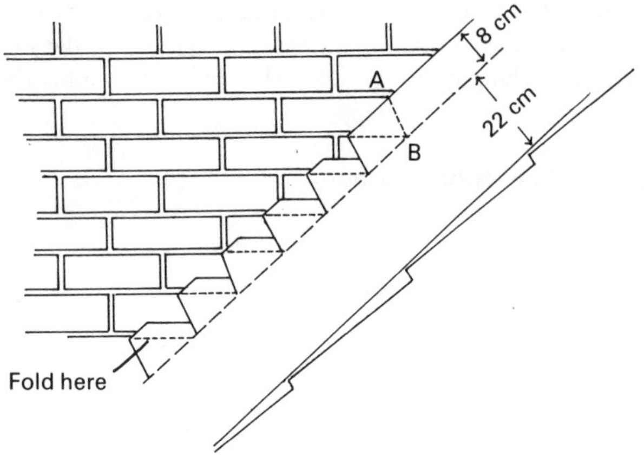

* Mark a margin of 8 cm. The intersections of the edge and the margin with the bed joint of the brickwork gives the line AB for cutting.
* With soakers (inserted between slates) use a narrower flashing that overlaps the upstand of the soakers.

Guttering

Putting up guttering is an easy job, made even easier if it is done while the scaffolding is still in place. Plastic guttering is ubiquitous. The size for domestic use is 10 cm. When choosing a particular system, select one with brackets that hold the downpipe a couple of centimetres off the wall – the downpipe can then go straight into the drain.

Gutters can be fixed level, but with a fall (about 1 in 500) the water flows faster and keeps the gutter clean. Don't forget that the roofing felt should drain off into the gutter.

Mark the position for the lowest gutter bracket, near the downpipe, and for the highest bracket, at the far end of the run. Stretch a line between these two positions to give the levels of the intervening brackets. These should be spaced at a metre, or less. Fix the brackets to the fascia (or the rafter feet) with non-rusting round-head screws ($2\frac{1}{2}$ cm, gauge 10). Pull the ends of a bracket out and down to slip in the gutter. That's easy enough – it's a lot harder on the fingers if, for any reason, you want to take the guttering out. Join lengths of guttering with unions. (Leave room for expansion by aligning it with the manufacturer's marks.) Cut guttering with a tenon or hack saw. As a guide for a square cut, some people wrap a rectangular sheet of paper round the guttering. Fit a 'stop end' to block off the end of a gutter.

The gutter runs into an outlet, which discharges into the downpipe. Fix the downpipe from the bottom upwards. To reach outwards to the gutter from under the eaves, make up a 'swan-neck' from a short section of pipe and a couple of offset bends.

To hold the downpipe to the wall, use pipe brackets at intervals of $1\frac{1}{2}$ metres. Drill and plug the walls to secure the brackets. It's all pretty simple. Check for leaks by pouring some water into the gutter.

The gutters discharge into the surface-water drains. When these are installed, the job can be finished off. If the downpipes are held off the wall a little, they can run straight into the drains. For this, stand-off pipe brackets are needed, but if they are not available you could improvise spacers by cutting off short sections of plastic tubing.

The top of the drain should be sealed, most simply with mortar. (To stop wet mortar from falling down the drain, jam something like polystyrene between the pipe and the inside of the drain.)

Stripping scaffolding

If you have subcontracted the scaffolding, the scaffolder will strip it. It's a small job that creates an impression of a big step forward.

Unless you've used independent scaffolding, the putlog holes will have to be pointed up. This is a simple job, though it is not so easy to keep mortar smears off the bricks. (See 'Jointing', Chapter 21.)

External doors

The doors are hung as described in Chapter 15: *Second Fix Carpentry*.

Glazing:

Some spec builders are still building houses with only single glazing. Amazing! Double glazing – while the house is being built – makes not only economic and environmental sense, it also makes for a more comfortable living space.

The simplest way to double glaze is with sealed units. There is a popular belief that these are filled with gas. This is true only for expensive units – most contain dry air. The units generally come with a five or ten year guarantee. And why not fifty? After all, some building blocks and tiles are guaranteed for a century. The answer is that the seals tend to break down and condensation occurs inside the units. The manufacturers blame the installers (they would, wouldn't they?!); they say that, with badly installed units, the seals become wet and so can eventually break down. It's difficult to find out the likely life of well installed units. Those who know keep sealed lips, as well as sealed units. Perhaps 30 years?

So, sealed units with the present technology are not ideal, but they are commonly used, and their fitting is described below. They are more effective if their inner pane is made of low-emissive glass. This is glass with a virtually invisible metallic coating; only a very slight blue or gold bloom is apparent from the outside. Though the coating is transparent to light, it reflects low-frequency, infra-red radiation. So radiant heat from a room is reflected back inside. Sealed units halve the heat loss compared to single glazing. The use of low-emissive glass halves it again, making the units as effective as triple glazing.

Ordering

Get several quotes for sealed units as prices vary a lot. The technology used also varies somewhat, though basically it is simple enough. Two sheets of glass are kept apart by a spacer strip around the perimeter. The strip is hollow and contains a desiccant, which dries out the air inside. Around the edge is a seal, which holds the whole thing together, and which is, or ought to be, air-tight. A typical unit consist of two sheets of 4 mm glass, with a 6 mm gap. (See Fig. 3.)

Figure 3: Detail of sealed unit in sash

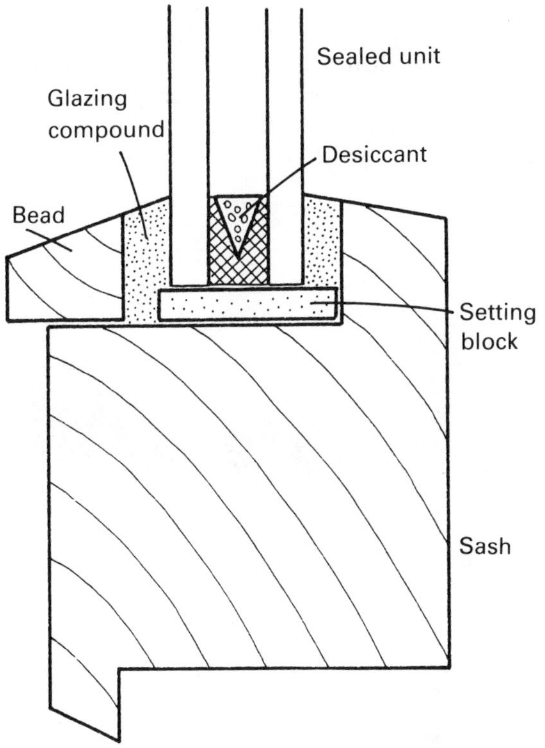

A wider, 10 mm gap gives a little better insulation; but check that the rebate of the frames will accommodate it.

(Most units have flush edges, but there are also stepped units; these are designed for use in narrow rebates and can be fixed like single glazing. With this design, the seal is well away from any rainwater. However, the units don't look so neat, because the seal is exposed within the sight line. And they cost a little more.)

Prices are even more variable for low-emissive (low-e) units. Some firms seem to base their prices on the exorbitant, double-glazing replacement market. A high price may well mean that you are paying for a marketing strategy, not for better quality. When obtaining a price for the supply of units, ask also for the extra cost of fitting them. Professionals glaze so fast that the extra is likely to be small. You could expect the firm to do a good job of glazing its own units. And if the seals break down, they can't blame poor installation!

Glazing is a trade in which metric does prevail. Order your sizes in millimetres, but remember, the glass size needs to be less than the rebate size. Sealed units need 3 mm clearance at each edge. (5 mm for units over 3 sq m, and 2 mm for single glazing.) Be clear, when ordering, that you are giving the glass size, not the 'tight' size (of the rebate).

For bathrooms, front doors and the like, you may want an obscure glass. And the glass for doors should be made stronger by tempering, ie, heat treatment. Not only does this glass become tougher, but also, if it does break, it breaks into harmless, small pieces.

Allow about a month for delivery of the units.

Some joinery firms supply their own sealed units for their windows and doors. At least, you'll know that you're getting the right sizes!

Fixing

The usual method of fixing sealed units is with wooden 'beads' – not objects for threading on necklaces, but narrow timber strips. (They are usually supplied with the frame.) The units are bedded in butyl compound (eg, Arborflex 500). A 10 kg tub will glaze about 30 m of perimeter. You will also need some plastic blocks to support the units. In the past, these have been difficult for the amateur to get hold of. If need be, improvise from nylon, oak, lead, etc. Two sorts of block are required:

1) Setting and location blocks

These blocks hold the unit away from the bed of the rebate and stop it moving about. Technically, the setting blocks support the bottom of the unit, and the location blocks hold the sides in position. In practice, there's little difference between them. They should be about 3 cm long, 3 mm thick and 3 mm wider than the thickness of the unit.

For fixed and side-hung sashes, the positions of the blocks are shown in Fig. 4.

For pivoting and sliding sashes – and for a fuller account generally – see the leaflet produced by the Glass and Glazing Federation. (See 'Books', Appendix 4.)

2) Thickness blocks

These 3 mm blocks are used in pairs, squeezed between the back of the rebate and the glazing bead, with the sealed unit sandwiched between them. Place them about 5 cm in from corners and at intervals of 30 cm or so.

The blocks support the unit, allowing movement in the timber without stressing the glass. First of all, try a dry run to check that the unit with blocks fits the rebate. Remove the unit, and seal the rebate and inside faces of the beads with two coats of rapid-drying sealer. (This can usually be purchased with the glazing compound.)

Figure 4: Positions of glazing blocks

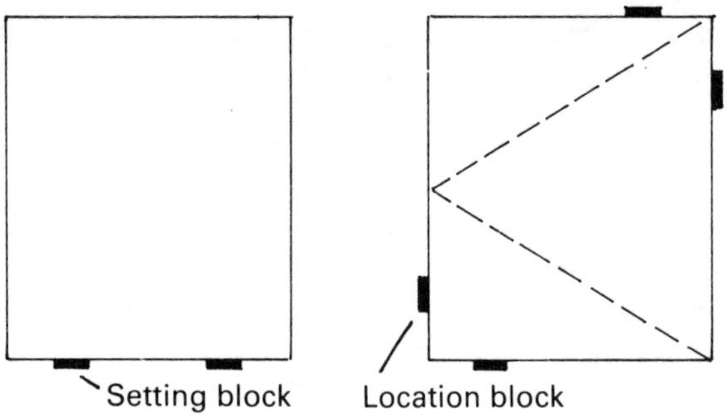

* Blocks should be located at positions indicated (as a minimum requirement).
* Note that the dashed line points to the hinged side of a sash.

Apply the glazing compound into the rebate. The knack for this, to do it quickly and well, takes considerable practice. Here is an outline of the method, though it is better to watch a glazier actually do it:

Take a ball of the butyl compound (enough to hold easily in one hand), and knead it to make it pliable. Holding the ball in one hand, push your thumb across its surface to scrape a 'thumbful' of the compound into the rebate. Move your hand a little further along the rebate, and turn the ball to present a fresh surface to the thumb. Repeat the procedure, progressively pushing in compound along the rebate. For the amateur, this is all more easily said than done. A professional makes it look easy.

Push the blocks into position and then insert the unit. Press strongly around the sides to push the unit back against the thickness blocks, squeezing the sealant out at the back. Apply more sealant against the glass and rebate, and push in thickness blocks opposite those already in use. Push on the beads, squeezing sealant up against the glass and also a little between the bead and frame to bed it. Secure the beads with long pins opposite the thickness blocks. (To avoid hitting the glass, slide the hammer head along it.)

A professional can glaze a house in a day. An amateur may take several.

Sealing frames

There is no hurry for this, but it is considered beneficial to seal the joint between brickwork and frames with mastic. Frame sealant is widely available in tubes. Cut the nozzle of the tube at 45° to give a fairly wide hole. 'Push' the gun along the crack, rather than pulling it. If the mastic doesn't stick everywhere, you're moving the gun along too fast. On the other hand, if it forms wiggley piles, you're moving it too slowly.

PART THREE
FITTING OUT

☆

☆

☆

☆

☆

☆

☆

☆

☆

☆

☆

☆

☆

☆

☆

☆

☆

9
FIRST FIX PLUMBING

☆

☆

☆

☆

☆

☆

☆

Brain-work
Radiator sizing
Marking out
Boiler
Cold supply
Storage tank
Hot supply
Primary circuit
Radiator circuits
Practicalities
Gas
Discharge pipework

This chapter should be read in conjunction with Chapter 22: 'Plumbing and Heating'. The heating system described in detail in that chapter is assumed in this chapter. It will be followed up by Chapter 13: 'Second Fix Plumbing'. There are many possible variations for wet heating systems, but the simple and effective system described in these chapters will give the reader an understanding of the basics.

WHY THE TERM 'first fix'? The answer is that the plumbing, like the electrical and carpentry work, is done in two stages, before and after plastering – the first and second fix.

If you are subcontracting, make it clear with your plumber who is supplying what. It is common for the builder to supply the sanitaryware and boiler. You might like to supply the radiators as well – liaising with the plumber for the sizes required. For supplying materials, plumbers commonly charge an extra 10% – 25%. On the other hand, they may have access to better discounts than you can get.

The brain-work

Before the ownhander can get his or her hands dirty, there is a lot of brain-work to do in working out the sizes and positions of equipment, and the layout of the pipes. With a well designed house (eg, with the bathroom over the kitchen), the pipe runs will be reasonably short.

The drawings will show the positions of the sanitaryware and of the 'stack' (as the soil-and-vent pipe is commonly

Figure 1: Cold water supply

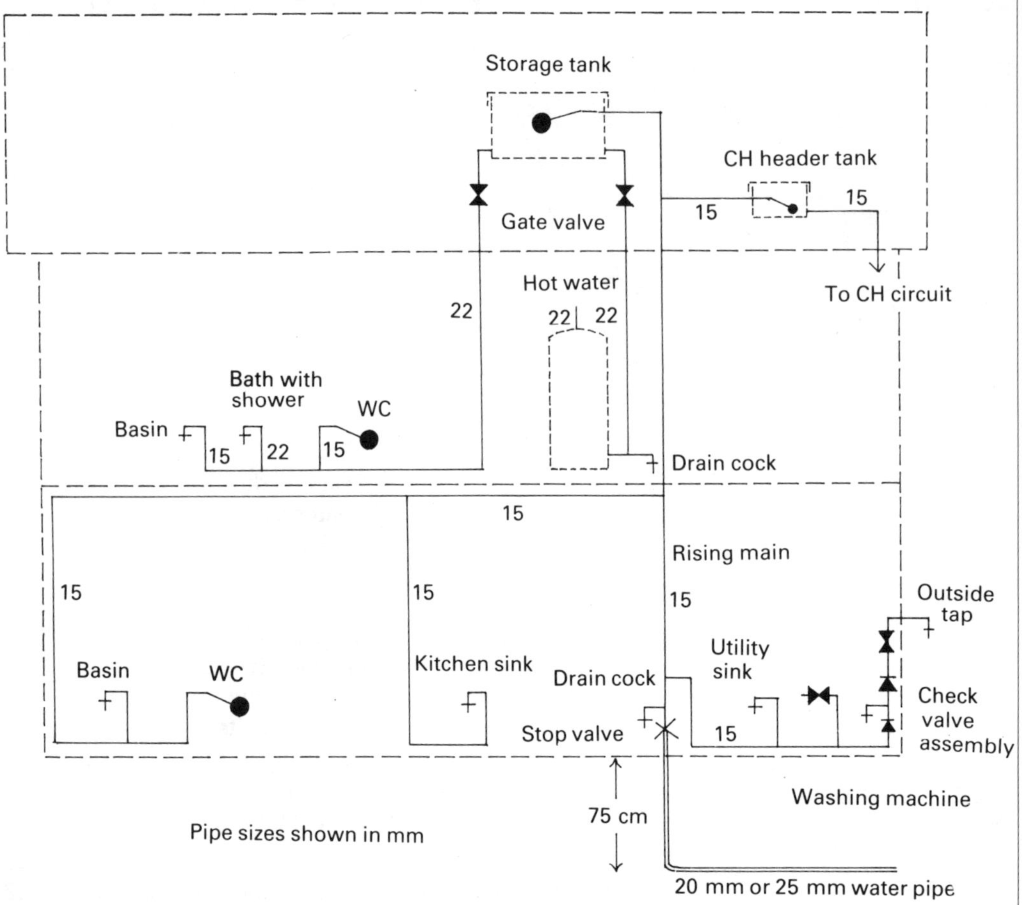

* An indirect supply is shown to the bathroom (with a shower), and a direct supply on the ground floor.
* Gate valves are used on the low pressure supply. Stop valves are used on the mains supply.

known). The position of the stack deserves some consideration. Simplest is to run it up an external wall, but this and the exposed waste pipes are generally unsightly. Most modern houses have it inside. The 11 cm pipe can run within the upper floor space, but only in the direction of the joists. It can't go through a joist! (Though if need be, joists could have been trimmed. See 'Joisting', Chapter 6.) Vertically, the stack will generally need to be boxed in; taking it up through the airing cupboard is a good idea. Waste flowing down it is noisy, so it is not sensible to take the stack through the lounge or dining room, even though boxed in.

The position of the cylinder is important in minimising the runs to frequently used hot taps. Favourite places for the airing cupboard are in the bathroom or on the landing. A (balanced-flue) gas boiler is usually placed in the utility room, kitchen, garage, or cloakroom.

There are also the radiators to consider. You will need to know their sizes. (See below). As for position, there are several points to bear in mind. In the days of single glazing, their position was automatic: The radiators went below the cold windows. With weather-stripped, double glazed windows, this is now a poor option – the radiators are interfered with by curtains, and need long pipe runs. Consider other positions, especially internal walls requiring short runs. A couple of radiators might be fitted back-to-back, one on each side of a wall. Think also about the placing of furniture, especially of beds for which there might be little choice of position. Radiators should not interfere with the furniture, nor with the passage of traffic (eg, in a hallway). In kitchens, it's difficult to find a stretch of bare wall free from cupboards and appliances. In bathrooms, a good position for a low radiator is beneath a towel rail.

Some heating suppliers will design a heating system for a modest fee, so saving you a lot of brainwork. (See 'Heating designs', Appendix 4.)

Radiator sizing

The ideal is to fit each room with a radiator with sufficient output to keep the room warm in the coldest weather, ie, the radiator can emit heat as fast as the room loses it. Heating engineers use complex formulae to calculate precise figures for the outputs required. However, there are many arbitrary assumptions in their formulae, so the figures have only rough validity. Working figures out to a great degree of precision doesn't necessarily make them any more accurate! But if you do want to work out fairly accurate figures for heat losses, then you can go through the calculations given in Appendix 2: *Thermal Sums*. In practice, the following rough and ready formula is good enough for radiator sizing.

For a particular room:

1) Multiply the length of external wall (in metres) by 40.

2) Multiply the floor area (in square metres) by:

17 – for the upper floor of a house
22 – for the ground floor of a house
28 – for a bungalow.

Figure 2: Hot water supply

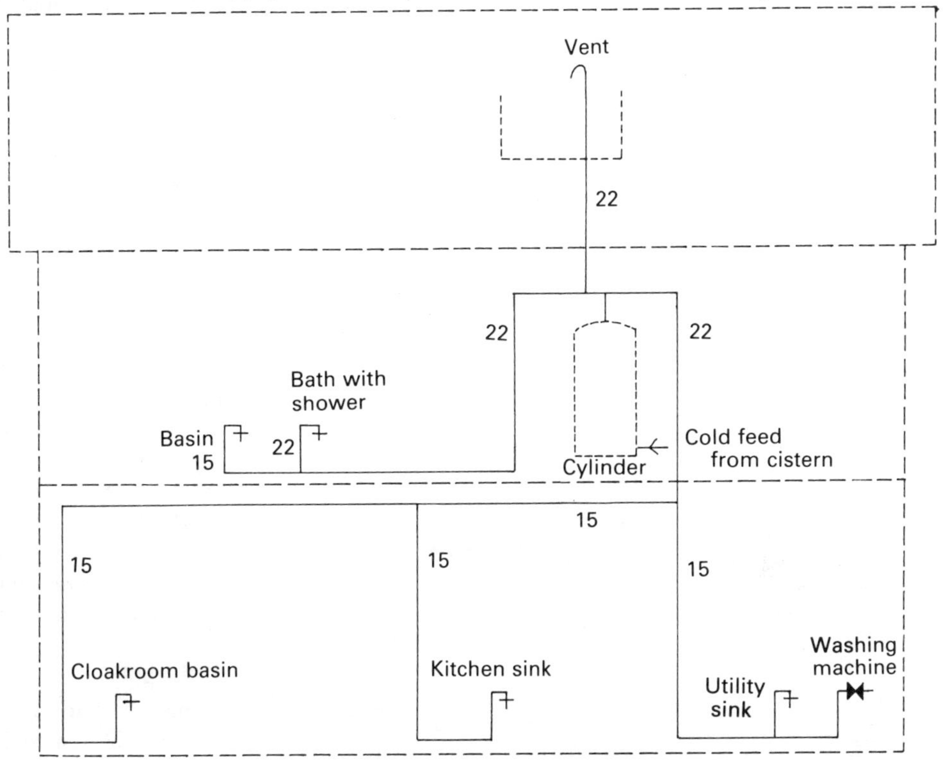

Typical pipe sizes shown in mm

* Cloakroom basin needs a long run – it may be better to use an instantaneous electric heater.

3) Add the two results together to give the maximum rate of heat loss in watts, ie, the output required,

These figures assume the target U-values of the Building Regulations, with double glazing in addition. Other assumptions are:

Temperature difference between inside and outside: 25°C
Ratio of windows to wall area: ·1
Ceiling height: 2·3 m
Air changes per hour: 0·5.

The figures are only arough guide. Use discretion: Eg, increase the output for a bathroom (without an airing cupboard) or a room with extra glazing; decrease it for the hall and landing, which can be cooler.

(You may come across other rules-of-thumb which yield much higher outputs – they invariably assume a poorly insulated house.)

Marking out

With the radiator sizes worked out, it's a good idea to draw a layout for the radiators, appliances, and pipes on the plans. All the circuits need to be planned, even though, for the first fix, only parts of them will be installed – in particular, the pipework in the floor void, and the pipework that will be buried beneath plaster. Particular aspects of the circuits are detailed below.

With a clear conception of the circuits, start marking out the positions of the pipework and appliances.

With chalk or crayon, mark the positions for the hot and cold supplies to the taps, and the flow and return to the boiler. Mark out the layout for the pipework in the cylinder cupboard – this can be quite complex. (Mark the positions for any vertical runs on the walls.) Mark the positions for the flow and return pipes at the radiators. (Don't forget to make an allowance on the widths of the radiators for their valves.)

Then turn your attention to the waste, in particular, the stack and any long waste runs. Again, roughly mark out all the runs.

It's better to recognise difficulties at this stage, rather than halfway through an installation.

Boiler

The output required from the boiler must be at least as great as the sum of the radiator outputs. Often, extra is added (eg, 10%) for the heat emitted by the pipework. (Though in fact, except from pipework in the loft, this heat is not really lost.) What about the output for the hot water? A family typically uses 200 litres of hot water a day. If the water is heated through 50°C, then this requires 200 × 50 × 4,200 joules, ie, 42,000 kjoules of heat. (The specific heat of water is 4,200 joules per litre per °C). Now one joule is the amount of heat that can be produced by one watt in a second. So the heat required for a day's hot water can be expressed as 42,000 kwatt seconds, ie, 11·7 kwatt hours $\left(\frac{42,000}{60 \times 60}\right)$.

Typically, the boiler will have an output of 8 kwatts. So producing the heat for the hot water takes such a boiler about $1\frac{1}{2}$ hours (11·7 ÷ 8). This, of course, is spread intermittently over the day. Anyway, there is a plentiful $22\frac{1}{2}$ hours for central heating. (Though it's a common practice to add again 10% extra to the required boiler output, as an allowance for the domestic hot water.)

Balanced-flue boilers (also called 'room sealed') are the most popular boilers as they don't require a flue to be built

Figure 3: Heating circuit

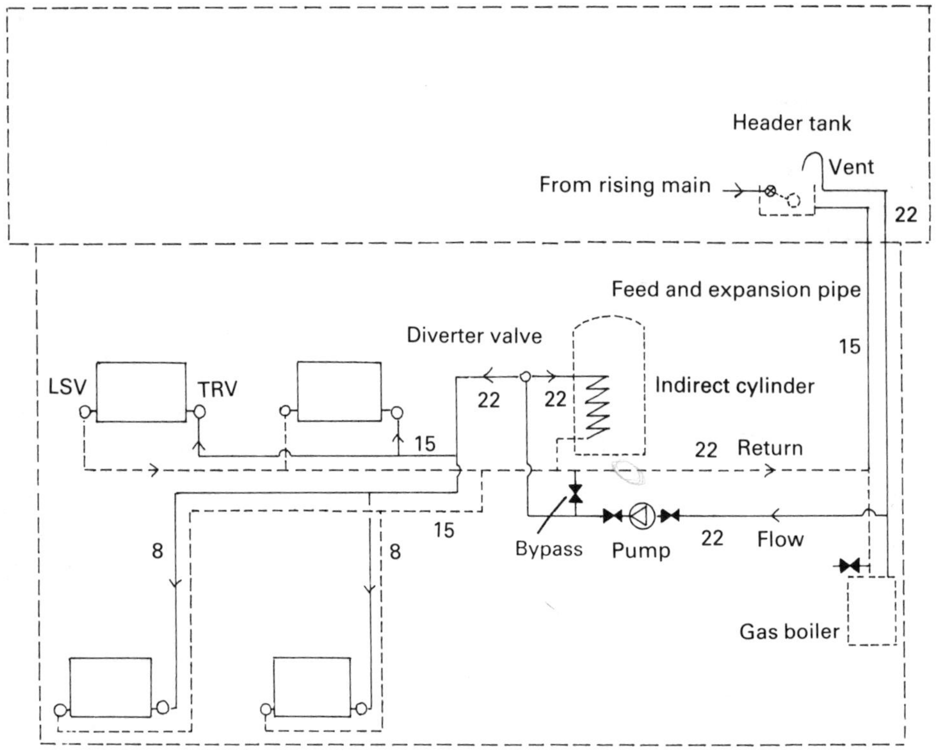

Typical pipe sizes shown in mm

* Fully pumped system – the circulation through the cylinder heat exchanger is by pump, not convection.
* Note the relative positions: Boiler → vent tee → pump → radiators/cylinder → feed-and-expansion tee → boiler.
* Thermostatic radiator valves (TRV's) in flow; lockshield valves (LSV's) in return.

and they can be fitted on any external wall. The effect of wind on their flue is balanced out since it blows equally on inlet and outlet. However, turbulence can interfere with this, so keep the flue at least 60 cm from corners. It should also be at least 30 cm below the eaves or a window sill, and at least 10 cm from rainwater pipes.

Cold supply

Start where the rising main enters the building. (See Fig. 1.)

Fit a special compression coupling to the end of the blue polyethylene pipe (a tube insert fits into the bore to stiffen the plastic). Connect 15 mm copper pipe via a reducer; fit a stop tap and drain cock.

For a direct supply, the pipework runs to the taps and WC's direct from the mains. And a pipe runs up to the storage and header tanks in the loft.

Assuming a direct system, run the supply to the cold taps.

Storage tank

A large tank holding 250 litres, or more, is required for an indirect cold supply; for a direct system, a tank about half this size is sufficient. The tank is invariably in the loft: Over the cylinder is a good position.

If a large tank is required, this should have been put into the loft space before the gables were built. (However, if this wasn't done, two smaller tanks can be connected in series by a pipe low down. Fit the ball valve in one tank and the outlets in the other, so water flushes through the system.)

To get a good head, the tank needs to be raised on a platform. This is especially important if there is to be a shower – a head of two metres, or more, is needed between the shower rose and the water level in the tank.

Hot supply

From the storage tank above, a 22 mm cold feed runs to the bottom of the cylinder. (Just before this enters the cylinder, fit a drain cock, so that the cylinder can be emptied if required.) From the top of the cylinder, a 22 mm hot supply goes to the bath tap, with other hot supplies being tee'd off. (See Fig. 2.)

Also tee'd off, near the cylinder is the 22 mm vent pipe, which rises up to bend over the storage tank – it should rise 40 cm above the water level. Note that this pipe should not rise straight up from the cylinder, because wasteful convection currents might be set up in the pipe. This possibility is prevented by including a short horizontal run in the vent pipe (conveniently, to reach a nearby wall).

Primary circuit

The flow and return to the boiler are in 22 mm pipework. (See Fig. 3.)

You will need to have a good idea at this stage how you are going to connect up to the boiler, in order to put the pipework in the right position. The flow goes to the cylinder via a three-port valve (for the typical system described in Chapter 22).

The pump will be placed in the flow between the boiler and this valve. The airing cupboard is often a good place for the pump. Anyway, it should not be at the bottom of the system, where sludge tends to collect.

The flow enters the heat exchanger half-way up the cylinder. The return exits from the bottom of the cylinder, and returns to the boiler.

Figure 4: Discharge pipework

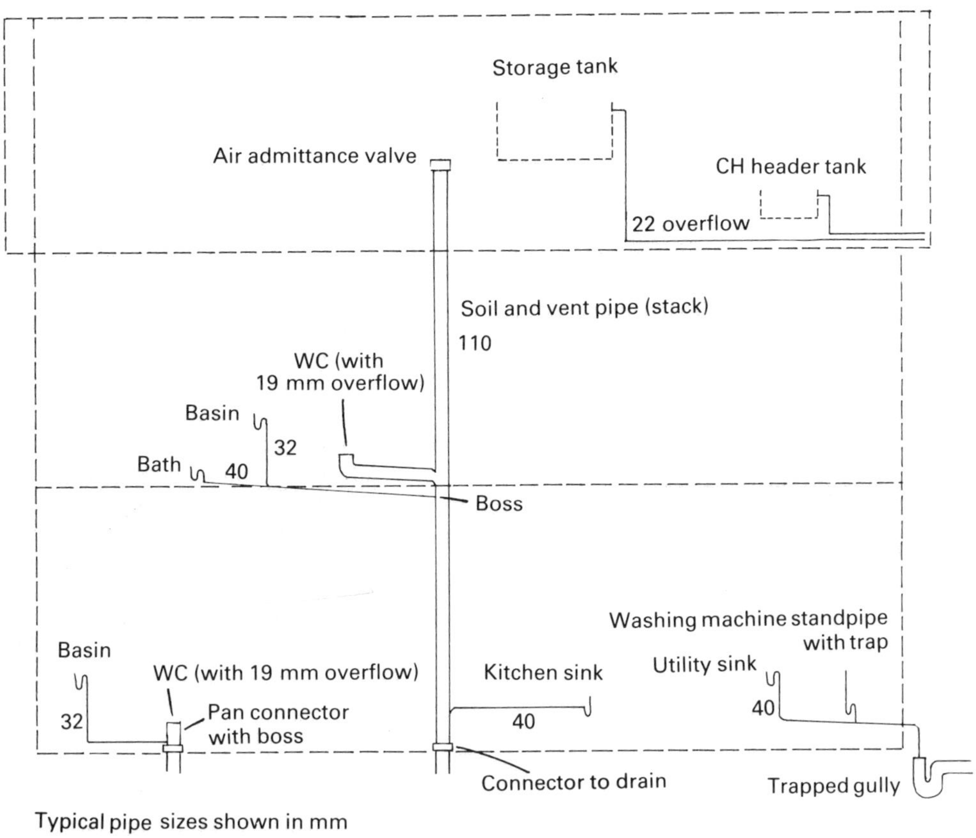

* Comprised of soil-and-vent pipe (the stack), waste pipes, and overflow pipes.

Most of the pipework at this stage is in the ceiling/floor void. Pipework running in the direction of the joists can be clipped to them. Carrying water, the pipes will be heavy, so clip them every 2 m for 22 mm, and 1·2 m for 15 mm pipe. (Vertically, on a wall, the clip spacing can be doubled.) Where pipes cross the joists, care is needed not to weaken the joists too much – particularly long joists. This is no problem with microbore. Drill a hole half-way up the depth of the joist; this leaves its strength virtually intact. (See 'Beams', Chapter 27.) The pipe can just be threaded through the hole like cable. (As a point of interest, it is acceptable to drill fairly large holes, up to a quarter of the depth of the joist, provided that they are in the middle of the depth. The holes are best located about a quarter of the way along the span.) Rigid pipe needs a notch in the top of the joist, preferably near an end (not more than a quarter of the span from the end). The notch should not be deeper than a sixth of the depth of the joist.

An unfortunate tendency of wet systems is for them to creak annoyingly as the pipework expands and contracts across joists. To prevent this now rather than later, when it is too late, put a sleeve of felt (obtainable from plumbers' merchants) round every pipe where it lies in a notch.

Two more points about pipework in the floor void:

Don't lay pipework along a line where studwork will have to be nailed later.

Insulate hot pipes, both to save heat in the summertime and to give a quicker hot response at the tap.

Microbore running down the walls can usually be accommodated in the thickness of the plaster. To prevent the corrosion of the copper by cement in the wall, place a strip of dpc between the pipe and the wall. And to protect the outer side of the pipe, fix galvanized steel channelling over it, with galvanized nails. (Some people use plastic channelling instead, but that would hardly seem effective protection.)

Wider pipes needs chasing into the wall. Cut the chasing out with bolster and club hammer – much easier with aircrete blocks than dense concrete ones! These pipes can be protected from corrosion by wrapping 'Denso' tape around them

Radiator circuits

The 22 mm flow to the radiators leads off from the three-port valve previously mentioned. It often splits into separate circuits for upper and lower floor. The size of the pipe may be reduced where it splits off and carries a smaller flow. All the pipework on the upper floor can be in 15 mm. For the ground floor radiators, it is convenient to keep the circuit in 15 mm within the ceiling void, and to drop down the walls to the radiators in microbore. Alternatively, the ground floor circuit can be buried in ducts in the floor slab.

Alongside the flows, there will, in general, be parallel returns.

Practicalities

The positions of the pipes as they reach the appliances have already been marked. Where pipes are to emerge from the floor, leave a sufficient gap for plaster and skirting board. And where pipes stick out from a wall (eg, for radiators) keep them higher than the (10 cm) skirting. Leave the pipes somewhat longer than required, and knock the ends flat to prevent dirt from entering.

Be methodical, and the job will then seem less confusing. Take each circuit in turn, starting with the larger pipework. It's a good idea to label pipes with masking tape – it's easy to get flows and returns mixed up.

– a messy business. Again, it should be protected by channelling. ('Denso' tape is sometimes used to protect pipes buried in concrete or screeds. It not only protects against corrosion but it also allows for some thermal movement. However, water pipes should be in ducts, anyway.)

Where a pipe passes through a wall, it should be sleeved: Use pipe the next size up. The sleeve should be long enough to pass through the plaster also, else the plaster may be cracked as the pipe expands.

Gas

The gas runs are simple, perhaps in 22 mm copper pipe from the meter, teeing off to 15 mm to the appliances. Use soldered joints, not compression fittings.

Discharge Pipework

Most waste pipes run into the stack, which discharges into a drain. (See Fig. 4.)

Some wastes on the ground floor (eg, from a sink) can be taken outside to discharge into a gully. And a WC downstairs may discharge into a separate drain without any stack.

The whole system needs to be visualised, but at this stage it is only the pipes in the floor void that need to be laid. Finish these pipes about floor level, so that when the floor is laid the chipboard can be accurately cut to go round the pipes. To prevent debris getting in, block the ends of the pipes with paper, or whatever.

There are three common sizes of waste pipe:

32 mm for basins (with a short run, less than 2 metres)

40 mm for baths, sinks, showers, etc, and basins with a long run

50 mm for combined flows.

The stack size (soil pipe) is 110 mm. The pipework should, in general, have slight falls, between 2 cm and 7 cm per metre. Strong gradients tend to induce siphonage. (Anti-siphonic valves can be used if this is likely to be a problem.) Waste pipes needs supporting every half metre, and the soil pipe every metre. Clip the pipe to the side of a joist, or rest it on bridges nailed between the joists. (On vertical runs, the support spacings can be doubled.)

Plumbers have to deal with a bewildering variety of fittings. To find out what is available, get hold of product catalogues for waste and copper fittings.

10

FIRST FIX ELECTRICS

☆

☆

☆

☆

☆

☆

☆

Physical installation
Ring circuits
Light circuits
Other circuits
Bonding
Non-mains wiring
Temporary supply

This chapter should be read in conjunction with Chapter 23: 'Electrics'. It will be followed up by Chapter 14: 'Second Fix Electrics'.

THE FIRST FIX ELECTRICS is a fairly straightforward job that would take a competent electrician about half a week. If you are subcontracting, it can be going on at the same time as the plumbing work.

You need to be clear what your requirements are. What is to go where? If in doubt, it's better to over-provide. Most rooms need three or four double sockets – single sockets are usually a false economy. In general, the sockets should be fixed about knee height. In the kitchen, some will need to be above the worktops: About 1·2 metres is a good height. Don't forget sockets for particular appliances: fridge, freezer, clothes and dish washers, gas cooker (!), etc. And some in the garage, especially if part of it is to be used as a workshop. None in bathrooms or WC's.

For the central heating system, power is taken from a 3 amp fused spur off a ring circuit. The time controller, boiler, pump, motorised valve, and thermostat all have to be connected together, which is best done through a special junction box or wiring centre. Circuit diagrams come with the appliances, but since these allow for all sorts of variations, working out the circuit for your particular configuration is confusing. It's simpler to keep to controls all made by the same company and then to use one of their recommended circuits.

When thinking about the lights, your mind will have to jump ahead a little. On which side are you going to hang the doors? (This is probably indicated in the plans; if not, see 'Doors', Chapter 19.) The light switch should be by the latch jamb, easily accessible. Then think about the position of pendants and wall lights. Do you want fluorescents in the kitchen or garage? A light in the loft is useful, and perhaps one outside, as well. Remember two-way switching for the hall/landing, and maybe elsewhere. These are all standard considerations, without getting into the multitude of special effects that are possible with lighting. (And a shaver socket can be taken off from a lighting circuit.)

The cooker, if electric, needs its own circuit. The heavy and expensive cable runs to a control switch at the side of the cooker. From there it drops to the cooker outlet terminal, at which the cooker will be connected.

The immersion heater is another fixed appliance with its own circuit; include a time control and dipole switch. An electric shower may need its own circuit, too.

A clock, and a bell with transformer are fixed appliances that can be connected, via fused spurs, to either lighting or power circuits.

The consumer unit is generally kept close to the meter box.

Lastly, there are the non-mains electrical circuits to consider: telecom, bell, TV and radio. (See 'Non-mains wiring' later in this chapter.)

Altogether, quite a lot of planning is required, and it is well to mark it all out on the plans. Otherwise it's easy to end up with a socket behind a cupboard or radiator!

Physical installation

If you have been able to work out the theoretical circuits, then you will doubtless find their actual physical installation easy and straightforward. There are fewer physical limitations than with plumbing. It is easy enough to take cables through a joist. (As mentioned in 'Beams', Chapter 27, a hole half-way up a joist hardly affects its strength; and the cable will be out of reach of nails, later.)

Work out an economical route for each circuit. Sometimes it saves cable to reach a distant socket with a spur; take it from a ring circuit either from a socket or a 30 amp junction box. Similarly, in a lighting circuit, a spur from a 5 amp junction box might be useful to reach a remote light.

Upstairs, the walls are likely to be studwork rather than blockwork. If so, the boxes will not be fitted until the second fix – special plasterboard boxes simply fit into rectangular holes in the plasterboard.

For the present, lead the cable to approximately the position required, via holes drilled through the studwork. Be generous with the amount of cable you leave hanging around – better to find later that it's too long rather than too short.

Quite a lot of wiring will be in the loft. Clip it to the sides of trusses, or run it along the longitudinal binders. Later, there will be insulation between the trusses. Keep the cabling above this level, so that it is visible and less prone to overheat.

Keep cable away from hot pipes. On walls it should run vertically and/or horizontally, not on a slant. (When the cable is hidden by plaster, its whereabouts can then be intelligently guessed at, if need be.)

Cable can be cut with side cutters.

Ring circuits

A ring circuit, in 2·5 mm two-core-and-earth cable, starts

and returns to a single 30 amp fuseway in the consumer unit.

The first job is to fix the steel boxes for the sockets. A box, double or single, needs to be set into the blockwork a little, so that it is a centimetre proud of the surface (ie, so that it will be flush with the floating coat of plaster). A suitable recess can be cut out with an electricians' bolster and club hammer. Try to keep the back of the recess even or else you will have to use packing to get the box out to the right depth all round. (It's helpful to first drill out a lot of holes using a drill fitted with a depth stop.) Normally, a 35 mm deep box is suitable. But a 50 mm box is necessary for a dipole switch, and it is helpful for the extra cabling of a spur.

Prise out one of the 'knock-outs' to make a hole for the cable. A rubber grommet is supposed to be fitted round this to protect the cable. Chase out a short, shallow channel for cable to enter the hole. Fix the box in place with a couple of screws (or nails) so that the top is pretty level. (The blockwork coursing is a useful guide.) Leave a generous loop of cable hanging out from a box, for connecting later on. At a spur, there will be an extra cable entering the box. (Or the spur could be taken from a 30 amp junction box, hidden, for example, in the ceiling void.)

Fix cable tightly to blockwork with cable clips of the appropriate size. A sloppy cable will interfere with plastering later, and clipping every 30 cm is recommended.

Some people cover cable with PVC channelling. This seems to be an evolution from the metal conduit that was formerly used to contain wiring. That had two purposes: to protect the wiring, and to allow it to be easily replaced in a rewire. However, plastic channelling gives little protection to the cable from nails or drills; real protection is given by the RCD. And modern cable is expected to last the life of the house, so rewiring should be unnecessary. In other words, the cable can be simply buried as it is in the plaster. The only exception to this might be cabling not protected by an RCD, eg, to a freezer. In this case, do the job properly and protect the cable with galvanized steel channelling.

For safety reasons, don't put sockets in the bathroom, and in the kitchen keep them well away from the sink. The theory is that, with arms outstretched, you should not be able to touch both a socket and a tap (or a metal sink).

Light circuits

These are run in 1·0 mm^2 cable (or sometimes 1·5 mm^2 if the circuit will have a heavy load or if the cable will be buried under insulation). The cable simply runs from one light rose to the next, though for some lights a spur might be convenient. The easiest position to fix a rose is to a joist (or ceiling tie of a truss). If this position is unacceptable, fix it to a bridge between two joists (or ties).

At most light roses, there will be three cables, one of them being a 1·0 mm^2 two-core-and-earth dropping to the switch. (To prevent possible confusion later, it's a good idea to tag this with tape.) The box for the light switch is quite shallow, only 'plaster depth', ie, 10 mm. The box is simply screwed straight onto the blockwork. The same box is used whether the switch is to be 1, 2 or 3 gang (operating 1, 2 or 3 separate lights). Don't forget, a pair of two-way switches need to have a strap between them, a three-core-and-earth.

In a bathroom, a corded ceiling switch is used for safety.

For wall lights, take a spur from either a junction box or a light rose, leaving a short length of cable hanging out from the wall.

The cheaper fluorescent and spot lights don't have a connection block for loop-in wiring: Use the junction box method of wiring instead.

Other circuits

The circuits for a cooker, immersion heater, and electric shower are straightforward.

Each circuit needs a 50 mm box for a dipole switch. In the case of a cooker, this will be the cooker control unit (at shoulder height, to one side of the cooker). Cable drops down from this to the cable outlet box about knee height behind the cooker.

For a separate hob and oven, one switch is sufficient provided it is within 2 m of both appliances. In that case, the hob and oven can share one outlet, or each have their own.

For an electric shower, the isolating switch should be outside the shower room. If this is not convenient, use a 30 amp dipole ceiling switch with a neon indicator.

The circuit for the central heating is certainly not straightforward. You will have to integrate the circuit diagrams that come with each of the electrical components. The power to all the devices is taken by a fused spur off a ring main. Use 1·5 mm^2 cable. For a simple system, the devices can be connected directly to each other. (See Fig. 8, Chapter 23.) But a special junction box simplifies the connections, especially as it comes with instructions for connecting all permutations of popular devices. (See Fig. 1; and Fig. 9, Chapter 23.)

Figure 1: Typical first fix cabling for central heating

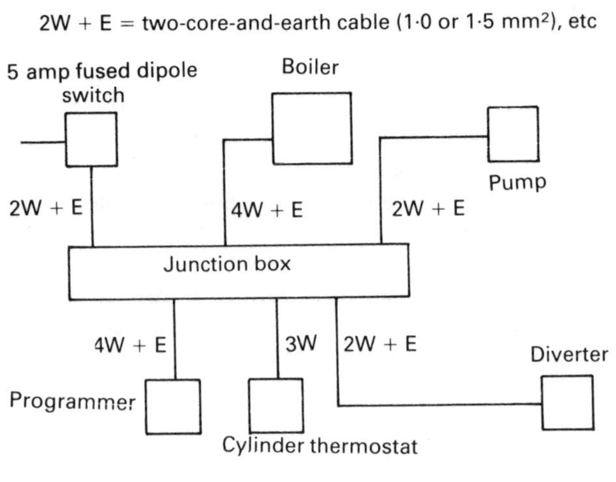

A wiring centre makes getting the right connections even simpler.

One group of devices will probably be in the airing cupboard: the cylinder thermostat, the diverter, and the pump. Elsewhere, there will be the boiler and programmer.

Note that, with a low water content boiler, the pump must continue to work for a short while after the boiler has shut down, to dissipate heat. Consequently, the pump must be powered from the boiler (which incorporates the time delay), and the boiler must have a permanent power supply. (See Figs. 8 and 9, Chapter 23.)

Some door bells are mains powered, in particular ones with an illuminated bell-push. They use a low voltage from a transformer. This can be connected, via a 3 amp fused connection unit, into either a lighting or power circuit.

Bonding

The main earthing terminal is usually taken to be the earth block by the meter. (Alternatively, the consumer unit's earth block may be used, in which case a 16 mm^2 earth 'tail' will later be needed to connect this into the meter cupboard.) Main bonding is taken from the main earthing terminal in 10 mm^2 earth cable. One cable earths the consumer unit. Another earths the rising main near its entry into the house. Gas pipework is earthed near the gas meter. (These two can be bonded in series if that saves cable.)

In the bathroom (and shower-room), some 4 mm^2 or 6 mm^2 earth cable for supplementary bonding can be put in. How the bonding will be earthed is the main consideration at this stage. There are three methods:

1) By cross-bonding from the rising main (which is earthed elsewhere by main bonding).

2) By taking the bonding cable to a socket on a ring main in an adjacent room. In the second fix, it can be connected to the earth terminal in the socket.

3) By taking the bonding cable back to an earthing terminal in the consumer unit or meter box.

Non-mains wiring

Bell: Thin, two-core bell wire is available for wiring between the bell and bell-push.

TV and FM sockets: Coaxial cable can be run from a box in the lounge up to the loft. (Leave plenty spare there to connect later to the aerials.) With a 'diplexer', it's possible to combine the TV and radio signals so that they can both run in the one cable. And to be even more sophisticated, a mains-powered amplifier enables the signals to be distributed round to several rooms in the house.

Telecom: Several TV extension sockets may be a bit of a luxury – or an irrelevance – but in the near future, having several telecom sockets will be quite basic. Spec builders rarely put them in, because they only build for what enough people want. As a selfbuilder, you don't have to follow any trend. You can be ahead of it – or just go your own way. In the future, telecom sockets will be not only for telephoning, but also for all sorts of electronic communication.

Where you want a telecom socket, fix a one-gang box (the same as for a power socket). The telecom cable from the outside world terminates at the 'master' socket. The other, 'slave' sockets are connected to this either in a single line or a branch circuit – it makes no difference which. The wiring is thin four-core cable, available from telephone suppliers. (But if you really want to look ahead, you'll put in eight-core so that you can have a separate line for a fax, or whatever other communication devices appear in the future.)

Temporary supply

Putting in a temporary electrical supply is not really part of the first fix, but this is as good a place as any in the book to mention it. An electrical supply is not part of the traditional way of building, but it is very useful. It is particularly welcome if you live on site.

You might be able to wait for a temporary supply until you have the meter box fixed in position on a (partly built) outside wall. In this case, the service cable will only have to be installed once, and there will be a cost saving. Before connecting up, the Electricity Company will require the apparatus to contain an isolating switch, a RCD, and an effective earth.

If you are intending to install a consumer unit with a RCD, then you can utilise this also for the temporary supply, using only a single 30 amp fuseway. Leave a couple of 16 mm^2 tails to connect the unit to the meter; and also some 10 mm^2 earth cable.

For a temporary earth, you will need a copper earth spike, say a metre long. (Specialist electrical suppliers sell them for a few pounds.) Bang the spike into the ground near the consumer unit, and connect the two with 10 mm^2 earth wire. But before the Electricity Company connects the supply, the earthing will need to be tested. For this you will probably need a professional electrician with special equipment.

11
FIRST FIX CARPENTRY

☆

☆

☆

☆

☆

☆

☆

The stairs
Fitting stairs
Flooring
Studwork
Door linings
Window boards
Hatchway
Temporary protection

This chapter should be read in conjunction with Chapter 24: 'Carpentry'. It will be followed up by Chapter 15: 'Second Fix Carpentry'.

The stairs

The stairs need some thought and action long before the time comes for fitting them. A simple staircase can be assembled from standard parts produced by joinery manufacturers, and these may be supplied within a couple of weeks. But a custom-made staircase may take a couple of months. There's a great deal of skill in making such stairs. The geometry involved, particularly with the winders for turning a corner, is very difficult. If the stairs are being made up from the architect's drawings, make sure that the drawings reflect the reality, ie, they accord with what has actually been built. In particular, the distance from finished floor level to finished floor level (the total rise) is critical. Measure this. Allow for the boarding of the upper floor, and for any screed on the ground floor. At the top, the part tread, which rests on the trimmer joist, is usually 22 mm thick. If 18 mm chipboard is to butt up to this, the easiest way to get a flush joint is to pack up the chipboard slightly. (This point is mentioned here because it needs to be born in mind when calculating the total rise.) If the staircase will be tightly confined by the stairwell, then the horizontal distances must also be checked. Don't make any mistake. Stairs either fit or they don't.

The most popular and economical stairs have closed (uncut) strings. The 'strings' are the long, wide boards at each side which support the steps. A step consists of a 'tread' and a 'riser'. (See Fig. 1.)

A more spacious effect is obtained if the strings are cut to the shape of the steps.

Another variation is the open-riser stair. The risers do not completely fill the gap between the treads, and this gives a lighter appearance. Since these treads are difficult to carpet, they are usually left bare, in high-grade timber.

Figure 1: Parts of staircase

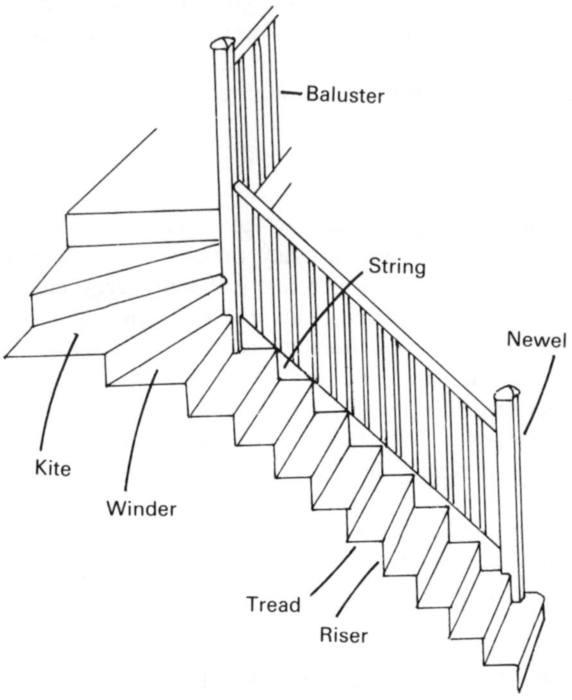

Here are some other technical terms you will need to become familiar with:

Newel: the stout vertical post at each end of a string, which supports the string, the handrail, and sometimes winders. Until recently, newels were made in one piece of timber. But now there are DIY kits available for newels, handrails and balusters, and with these, the newel is in two parts. A base contains the housings to take the string and step(s). On top of this, fits the ornate newel post which supports the handrail.

From a landing, a newel may extend all the way down to the ground floor, thereby helping to carry the load of the stair. But often it finishes with a decorative flourish a short distance beneath the ceiling (a 'newel drop').

Balusters: These are the numerous vertical bars that prevent people and things from falling off the stairs or landing. The Building Regulations expect them to be close enough to prevent a ball of 10 cm diameter from passing through.

Bullnose step: The bottom step often projects in front of the newel to give easier access from the side. If the step curves from the front of the newel, it is called a bullnose step. A half-round, or 'D', step has a grand sweep round from the outside of the newel.

Rise: the vertical distance between successive treads. The rise multiplied by the number of steps gives the total rise of the stairs. (See Fig. 2.)

Going: the horizontal distance between successive risers. On a straight flight, the going multiplied by one less than the number of steps gives the total going. (The tread of the top step is effectively the upper floor.)

Landings: A quarter-landing turns a staircase through a right angle; a half-landing turns it through 180° – a 'dog-leg'. A small quarter-landing may be incorporated as part of the staircase, but a larger one is built separately. Besides effecting a turn, a landing makes the ascent less demanding.

Figure 2: The rise and going of stairs

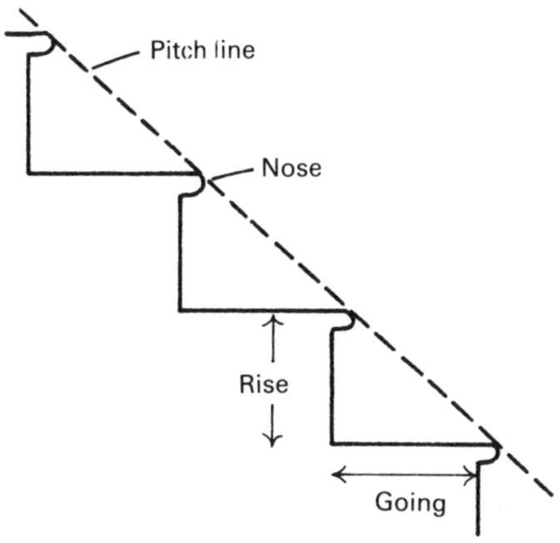

* The going excludes the nose.

Winders: If space is limited, then winders are used for a turn, instead of a landing. The tread of a winder is triangular, or sometimes kite-shaped. (See Fig. 1.)

Fitting stairs

Do order your stairs early, particularly if they are a 'special'. If the stairs are late and have to be fitted after the walls are plastered, it is difficult to make a neat job.

Anyway, once the parts of the staircase – flight(s), newel bases, and possibly loose steps – are on site, they can be assembled. It may be tedious, but it is best to do a dry run without glue. Assemble the whole structure, as outlined below, and then put it into place to check that it fits.

A string is fitted to a newel with a double mortise-and-tenon joint. An 'off the peg' flight and newel base will require the joint to be made, but this may be beyond the capabilities of many ownhanders. The supplier may do this for you as a special; otherwise you will have to get a carpenter in to help you. (If the newels come complete, rather than as a base and separate post, then the handrail may have to be fitted at this stage too.)

Both ends of a wall string will need to be cut. The top of the string has to be cut to fit over the trimmer joist. It is finished at the top with a level cut to suit the skirting on the landing. At the bottom, it is cut to the floor line, and finished with a plumb cut, again to suit the adjoining skirting.

The stairs may come with a box of bits and pieces, some of which are wedges. Any loose steps are fixed into the strings by these wedges and plenty of glue. For the dry run (ie, no glue), don't knock the wedges in hard, or they won't come out later. Put the wedge for the riser in first – this will force the nosing (the front of the tread) into its housing. Then insert the wedge for the tread. (Cut off the tail of the first wedge if it is in the way.) With loose steps, screw the riser to the back of the tread below.

So having dry-assembled as much as is practicable, think about fitting it. A small quarter-landing may be an integral part of the staircase, but a larger one is constructed separately with its own joists. Typically, a stout trimmer, $7\frac{1}{2} \times 17\frac{1}{2}$ cm, supports 5×10 cm landing joists. These can be housed into the trimmer, and the trimmer supported by joist hangers at the walls. It is desirable to house a newel to be a tight fit over its supporting trimmer – for this, cut out a $1\frac{1}{2}$ cm deep housing in readiness. It is also desirable that the bottom newel is fixed to the ground floor. On a timber floor, skew-nailing is sufficient. On a concrete floor, a metal dowel will do the job; bore a hole in the newel to receive the dowel.

Prepare to fit the staircase. In a confined stairwell, this can be tricky. The top riser should fit against the trimmer with its part-tread (loosely called a nosing) resting on top. The newel should be housed over the trimmer. If this is not possible for some reason, nail a stout bearer to the side of the trimmer to support the stair. (Note that, when fitted, the stairs should be supported by the newels and strings rather than by the part-tread.) If there is a gap between trimmer and riser, packing will have to be nailed to the trimmer. Check that the treads are level.

If all is well, take down the staircase, dismantle it, and make any alterations necessary. Then reassemble it, using liberal amounts of PVA glue. In addition to the wedges, there may be triangular blocks to glue and screw beneath some treads.

Also, the strings should now be draw-pinned into the newel bases with dowels of 1 cm diameter. (See 'Draw-pinning', Chapter 24.) After leaving the glue to dry, once again fit the assembled staircase into place. This time it is to be secured in place. Fix the string(s) to the wall, either with large cut nails or with large screws and plugs. (Use the technique described in 'Fixing to walls', Chapter 24.) If there is a gap between string and wall, pack it where it is to be nailed (or screwed). Nail the top part-tread (nosing) to the joist.

As you can see from the above, fitting stairs can be complex and difficult work. As with roofs, the ownhander is advised to keep the work simple by choosing a simple design in the first place.

Flooring

This work is much more straightforward. Tongued-and-grooved chipboard is the usual stuff to use – it's easy to use and relatively cheap at about £6 per square metre. It does look better covered with carpet. If you like bare wooden floors, you may find that tongued-and-grooved floorboards at £9 per sq m are both more attractive and cheaper overall.

However, chipboard is more common – 18 mm is a suitable thickness for joists 45 cm apart. (To cover wider spans, up to 60 cm, use the 22 mm thickness – though some people use this anyway.) Lay the boards with their length across the joists, and the correct way up. (See Fig. 3.)

The advantage of tongued-and-grooved board is that the long joints along the sides don't need support. The head joints, however, are said to need support. One way is to fix a nogging between the joists to help support the end of the board. Another way is to shorten the end so that it can be butt jointed on a joist. But some people don't bother with extra support, especially if they are using adhesive.

In the bathroom and kitchen, and any other area where water may be splashed around, moisture-resistant board should be used. It may be of interest that the NHBC now expects all chipboard used in a house to be moisture resistant. (This board costs about a quarter more; it can be recognised by its greenish tinge.) Store boards flat on top of each other.

Figure 3: Tongued-and-grooved chipboard flooring

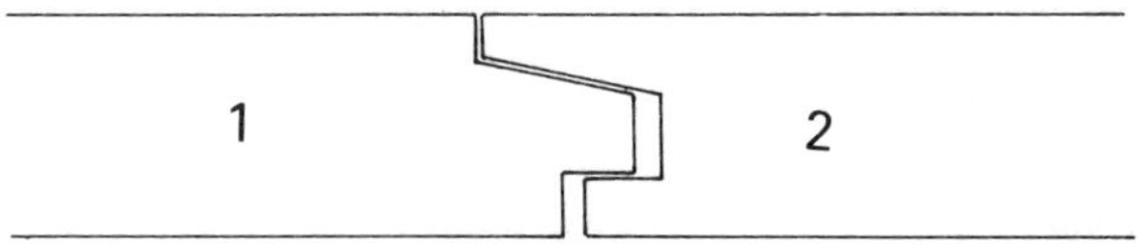

* Lay the board the right way up – the joint is tight only at the top.
* For extra stiffness apply PVA adhesive along the tongue before fixing.

Before boarding, there is a little job that may need to be done.

Figure 4: Laying chipboard flooring

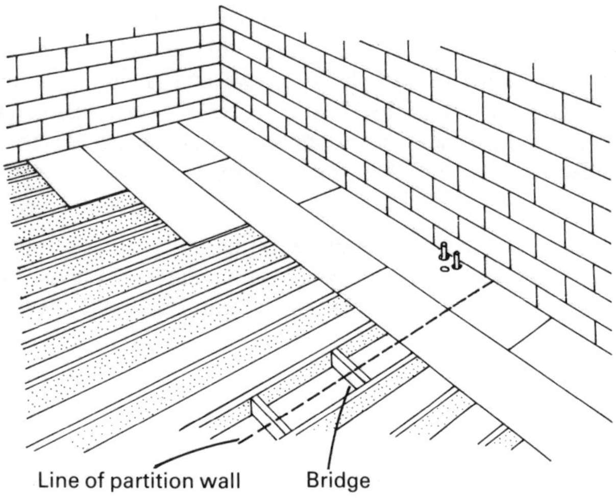

* End joints staggered.
* Bridges to support partition wall – but it would have been better to put in an extra joist when joisting.
* Plumbing supplies poke through floor.

Where there are to be stud walls running in the direction of the joists, extra joists should have been built in. (See 'Joisting', Chapter 6.) If this wasn't done, you can make do now with some bridges between the joists. (See Fig. 4.)

As you board them over, mark their positions on the floor, for later reference. In fact, it's a good idea generally to mark the positions of joists and pipe runs on the boards. What seems obvious before boarding becomes a matter of conjecture afterwards.

Start boarding in a corner, laying a row of boards along a long wall. The first board should be orientated so that the two tongued edges are into the room. If this isn't possible with the board the right way up, try another corner. It is said that a centimetre gap should be left between boards and wall to allow for possible movement. Fix the board down with ring-shank nails (or 5 cm lost head nails, or countersunk screws) about 30 cm apart.

Continue along for the first row. For the adjacent row, the head joints should be staggered; so start with about half a board.

Where pipework comes up through the floor, holes will have to be accurately cut in the board to fit. Before nailing, make the joint with the neighbouring board a tight fit: Take a narrow piece of grooved off-cut, slip this over the board's tongue to protect it, and hit the off-cut with a mallet to tighten the joint. (An option is to spread PVA adhesive along the tongues before fixing.)

Mains electricity is much appreciated for this work. Straight cuts can easily be made with a circular saw, using a batten as a guide. Or a jigsaw can be used. (This is invaluable for cutting the larger holes.) Note that if two cut edges are butted together, they should be supported on a joist.

How is the floor on the landing to be finished around the stairwell? (The faces of the joists around a stairwell used to be finished with painted timber boards, an 'apron'. But nowadays, they are often finished with plasterboard.) A simple answer at this stage is to board up to the edge of the joists. And at the top of the stairs, butt the board up to the part-tread of the stairs, making the surfaces flush with a little packing if necessary.

Studwork

Roof trusses don't need any support from partition walls below, so they leave the upper floor clear to be divided up as required by studwork walls. No great skill is needed to make these, but a little know-how helps.

Studwork is usually made from $5 \times 7\frac{1}{2}$ cm timber (though with very high ceilings 5×10 cm is better). (See Fig. 5.)

A novice would probably try to make up the studwork *in situ*, but it is better to construct each section flat on the floor, and then to fit it all into place. Unlike in some old houses, your floors will be level and your walls plumb. Anyway, the studwork is made square. At each side, leave a centimetre clearance for fitting. For the top, you have to decide about the ceiling boards. Some people like to fly over the studwork with continuous sheets, but others cut the board to fit each side. If you are aiming to fly over, leave about 3 cm clearance; otherwise, half of that.

The spacing for the studs is 60 cm for 12 mm plasterboard, (but only 45 cm for 9 mm board). Consider using double thicknesses of board for sound insulation. The simplest way to reduce sound is with mass; twice as much plasterboard makes for a significant reduction in sound transmission. (The NHBC expects commercial builders to use a double thickness

Figure 5: Studwork

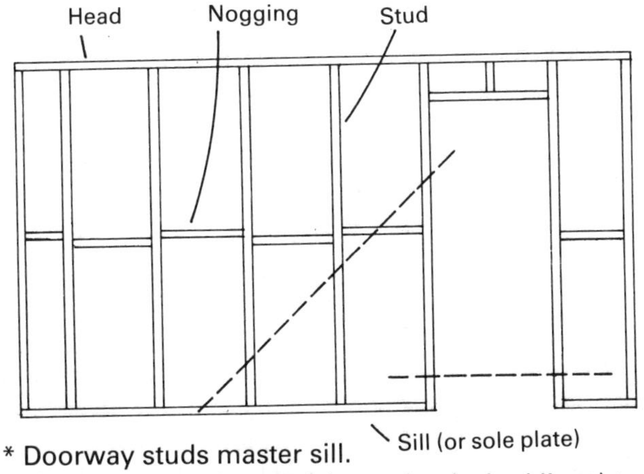

* Doorway studs master sill.
* Use temporary braces (shown by dashed lines) to keep studwork stiff and square until fixed in place.

of plasterboard on both sides of studwork around a WC – or a $2\frac{1}{2}$ cm thick quilt of mineral wool inside the studwork, with its edges turned and nailed to the studs. The selfbuilder may well want sound insulation for all the studwork.) Space the studs to minimise the cutting of board. (So the second stud centre might be 60 cm from the wall rather than that distance from the first stud centre.)

Figure 6: Stud walling

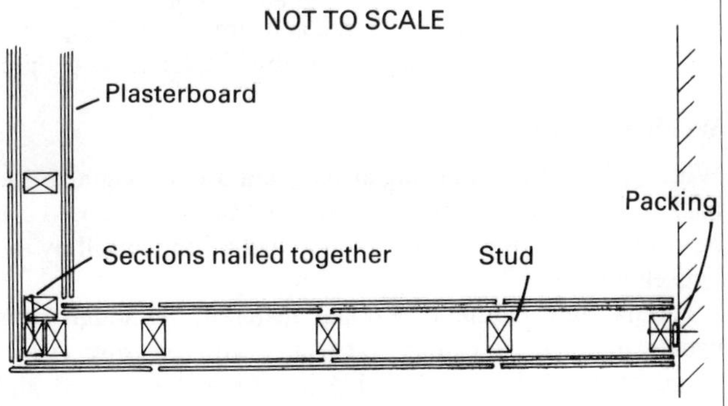

* Double thickness plasterboard is used for extra sound insulation. Stagger the plasterboard joints.
* At corners, extra studs are needed so that every board edge can be nailed.
* Make up studwork in sections and nail them into place; use packing where necessary.
* Where possible, space the studs so that the plasterboards need not be cut.

Two other points:

At doorways, it is better for the stud to master the sill so that the stud will be firm when the door lining is nailed on.

Noggings are needed to stiffen the structure; usually, a row half-way up is sufficient. They may be in line, which will involve some skew nailing, or staggered.

Now let's look at the method of construction:

The first thing to do is to mark out on the floor the position of all the studwork. Mark the positions for the studs. Leave a centimetre clearance at the end studs, and half of that at door openings. At corners, extra studs are needed, so that every edge of plasterboard has a stud behind it to which it can be nailed. This may become quite involved. (See Fig. 6.)

With a clear plan in your mind and a clear area on the floor, start making up a length of studwork.

Figure 7: Rebated door lining (elevation)

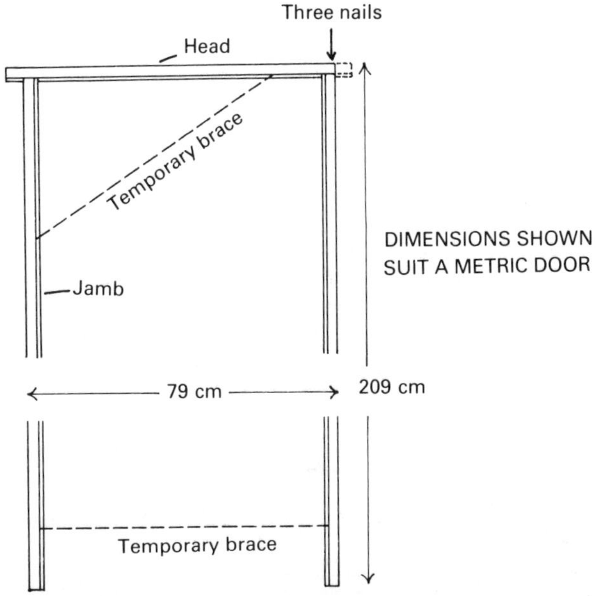

* The opening is 210 × 80 cm, to allow 1 cm clearance each way for fitting the lining.
* Fix temporary bracing to keep square.
* Remove horns after nailing head on (not before).
* For an imperial door, overall dimensions of the lining are 6′ $7\frac{1}{16}$″ × 2′ $8\frac{1}{4}$″ (203·5 × 81·6 cm).
* The simple joint shown will suffice – make a housing to the depth of the rebate. (British Standards suggest a more elaborate joint.)

From the layout marked on the floor, mark out the head with side marks for each stud. Then place the sill alongside this, and transfer the marks over. (See 'Marking out', Chapter 24.) (Don't forget that the sill will be cut short at the door studs.) Onto another piece of timber, mark out lengths for the noggings. Mark out a length for a stud, and transfer this over onto other timbers. (Don't forget that door studs are longer.) Now cut all the timbers nice and square – easy with a circular saw. Some people cut housings in the sill and head, but this isn't really necessary. Just nail it all together, using a couple of long wire nails at each joint. You can use your masonry walls as a stop while nailing, and a corner should keep the framework square. (The studwork is on the floor.)

When the framework is assembled, nail a temporary batten across the bottom of any door opening. Make the framework accurately square by equalising the diagonals, and fix it square by nailing a temporary batten diagonally accross. (See Fig. 5.)

If the studwork is to run across the lie of the roof trusses, then the head will be simply nailed to them. If it is to run between trusses, bridges should be nailed across them to which the head can be fixed.

Move the frame into position – it's helpful to have two people for this. Nail the plate to the floor, preferably to joists not pipes! Keeping the studwork plumb, nail the head. (If you wish later to fly over with the ceiling board, drive the nails only part way, so that they can be withdrawn later to pass the boards over.) Nail the end studs plumb to the wall, with packing if needed.

Door linings

Door linings, or 'casings' as they are also called, are used at internal door openings both to support the door hinges and to give a pleasing finish to the opening. (Door frames are used for external doors.)

Linings come in two types: one made of rebated stuff, and the other of flat timber with loose 'door stops' – these are for nailing on after the door has been hung. Rebated linings have a better appearance, and their fitting is described below. (Plain linings are more common in Southern England.) (See Figs. 7 and 8.)

Figure 8: Door lining (plan)

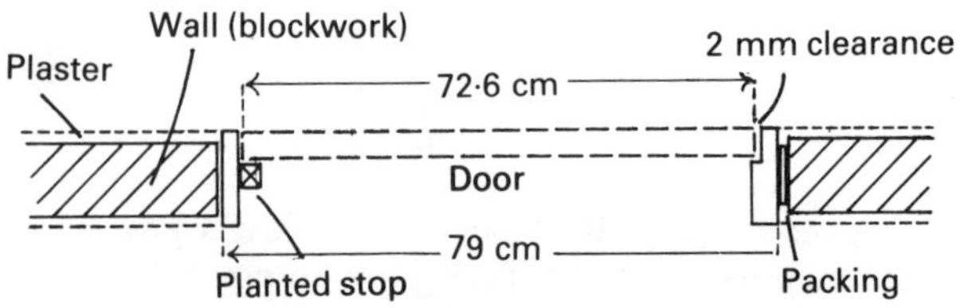

* Select a depth of lining to suit the final wall thickness.
* For illustration only, one side shows a rebated lining, and the other a plain lining with planted stop.
* Dimensions shown are for an internal metric door (72·6 × 204 × 4 cm). An imperial door is 6′ 6″ × 2′ 6″ × $1\frac{3}{8}$″ (198·1 × 76·2 × 3·5 cm).
* Other door widths are available.

The size must obviously suit the door to be fitted, which is usually 6′ 6″ × 2′ 6″ (198·1 × 76·2 cm) for imperial doors, and 204 × 72·6 or 82·6 cm for metric doors. For internal use, imperial doors are usually $3\frac{1}{2}$ cm thick, and metric doors 4 cm. The metrication of door sizes has not been successful, and imperial doors are much more widely available. To allow for clearance, the lining is 3 mm or 4 mm wider than the door and 2 cm higher (for a carpet strip).

Linings come in two common board widths, $10\frac{1}{2}$ cm and 13 cm (approx), or 'ex $4\frac{1}{2}$″' and 'ex $5\frac{1}{2}$″' as they are unhelpfully described. The first is suitable for $7\frac{1}{2}$ cm studwork with single sheets of plasterboard each side. The second is suitable both for studwork with double thickness plasterboard each side, and for 10 cm blockwork plastered both sides. The point is that the width should match the finished thickness of the wall – though some discrepancy can be accommodated by tapering the plaster thickness.

Linings can be bought as sets of two jambs and a head to suit a particular door size. Or they can easily be made up from running lengths of the rebated stuff. (At each side of the head cut a housing in the thick section to take the jambs.)

Assemble a lining on the floor, and nail the head to the jambs. Fix a temporary brace near the bottom to keep the jambs the right distance apart. Equalise the diagonals to make the lining square, and nail a diagonal brace to a jamb and the head. Now cut off the horns of the head so that it will fit the opening.

Offer the lining up to the opening. If there is to be a screed on the floor (despite advice elsewhere in the book to the contrary), pack up the bottom of the jambs to allow for it. Temporarily wedge the jambs tight with folding wedges beneath the lintel. Adjust the lining in the depth of the opening so that it will be flush both sides with the finished wall surface. Check that the jambs are plumb both ways and that the head is level. Between jamb and wall, insert packing pieces or thin folding wedges. Fix the jambs securely. (In blockwork, use cut nails, or screws and plugs.) Check that the jambs are still plumb. If not, a wrecking bar is useful for adjustments.

An alternative approach, which might appeal to the ownhander, is the use of door sets. These are a recent innovation available from some manufacturers, for both internal and external doors. The doors come with linings (or frames) and hinges, and sometimes even with architrave – all ready for fitting. Making up linings is easy enough, but hanging doors is tricky and time consuming. Although the sets are expensive, they may be worthwhile for some people.

Window Boards

Window board has a nosing at the front and a tongue at the back to fit into the groove in a window frame. The board can be cut to length as required. (It is called a window sill by the householder.)

Parana pine is the traditional material. Although it is usually painted, it can be varnished with pleasing effect. Window board is also available in common softwood and MDF (Medium Density Fibreboard).

Most window board is $22\frac{1}{2}$ cm wide; this typically gives a 5 cm overhang over a standard cavity wall. 25 cm board can be found, which is useful over wider cavities or wider blocks. (The width required is also influenced by the position of the frames within the thickness of the wall. See 'Building in frames', Chapter 6.)

Cut the board some 10 cm longer than the width of the window opening – it is usual for the board to run past the reveals a little way.

In inferior work, the ends are left square; but it's not difficult for the ownhander to put a nosing on each end to match the front. (See Fig. 9.)

Figure 9: Window board

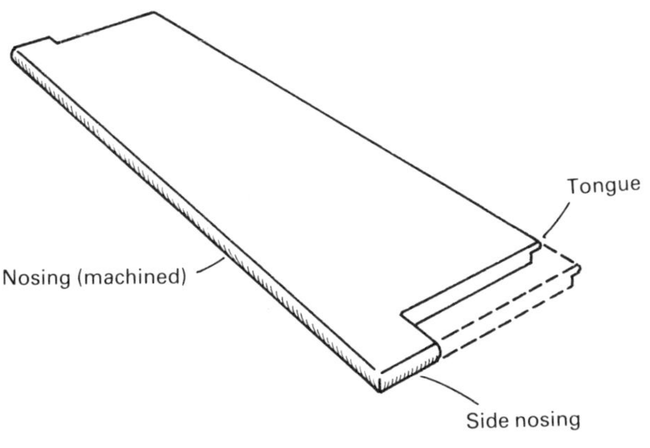

* Make side nosing with a plane.
* Tongue inserted into groove in window frame.

This can be done better if a nose is put across the whole width, even though most of it will then be cut away:

Mark guidelines across the top and bottom faces at each end to give margins equal to half the thickness of the board; and mark down the centre of the end grain. Start planing off across an end at a 45° angle. Then vary the angle, keeping between the guide lines – a quadrant section will appear. Repeat on the underside to complete the nosing. (Remember to plane inwards from the front edge so that it cannot split off.) Sand the nosing, and you will be surprised at the neat result.

Figure 10: Fixing a window board

* Pack up board to make level.
* Fix wires to underside of board so that they will be buried in the plaster.

But now cut most of the nosing off so that the board fits between the reveals. Since there is $1\frac{1}{4}$ cm of plaster to be applied later, the board can be cut to a loose fit. Fit the board with the tongue uppermost into the groove. Pack up underneath the board from the blockwork. (The blockwork may need building up with coursing units.) Check that the board is level both ways.

The method in common use for fixing the board is to nail through it from the top. But the old-fashioned way, which is not difficult to do, leaves an unblemished top surface for varnishing:

The method uses short lengths of wire, which are freely available by stripping some off-cuts of electric cable. Fix a wire at each quarter point to the underside of the board flush with the wall surface. (A long board needs a third wire in the centre.) Drop the wire down the wall for 20 cm and nail it to the wall. Now pull the wire to one side, like a bow string, and nail it taut. (See Fig. 10.)

It's simple enough. (The wires will eventually be buried in the plaster.)

The method allows the board some movement. Otherwise, if a wide board is fixed rigidly, it may split.

Hatchway

If you were to forget about the loft hatchway and board the whole ceiling over, you would not be the first to do so!

The hatch is usually placed above the landing. The hatchway cannot be very wide, since it must be contained within a pair of trusses (at 60 cm intervals). (Note that a truss acts as an integral whole, so it must not be cut to make a wider opening. If a wider hatchway were essential, it could have been designed in by the truss manufacturer.) Keep the hatch away from the eaves to allow sufficient headroom.

Figure 11: Loft hatchway

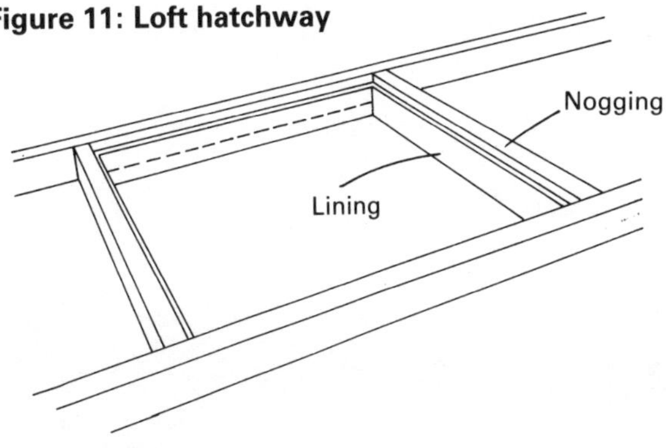

* First make up a square lining (slightly undersize), then nail it into place using packing if necessary.
* The lining may finish below the ceiling, or flush with it (the joint masked with architrave).
* The lining can be used as a stop for the hatch (as shown), or it can finish above the joists (for a hinged hatch).

For the hatchway frame, nail some stout timber – of the same depth as the trusses – between the two trusses. A lining to the frame can be made up from some $2\frac{1}{2}$ cm PAR. The depth of the lining depends on the design of the hatchway. Sometimes the lining is finished flush with the ceiling board, and the joint concealed with architrave. Sometimes it is dropped a centimetre of so below the ceiling – simpler and less obtrusive.

If the trap will simply be a loose board, then the lining can be used as a stop – fix it some way below the top of the frame. (See Fig. 11.)

But if the trap will be hinged, finish the lining somewhat higher than the surround – the trap can then be hinged to fold right back when it is opened.

Make up the lining to allow a little clearance at the frame. (Nailed butt joints are sufficient.) Brace it to make it square, and then nail it in position using packing pieces.

In the loft itself, it's a good idea to board the route from the hatch to the water tanks, and to lay boards around the tanks (for future maintenance).

Temporary protection

It is prudent to give some temporary protection to vulnerable woodwork. Door linings are too easily scraped by a wheel-barrow – tack hardboard on them. Some people tack board onto stair treads. Some even cover floors with building paper.

12
PLASTERING

☆

☆

☆

☆

☆

☆

☆

This chapter should be read in conjunction with Chapter 25: 'The Basics of Plastering'.

PLASTERING is one craft that most DIY enthusiasts leave alone. It is a skill not easily learnt from books. The main difficulty that the ownhander faces is the very limited time in which gypsum plaster stays workable. Another is the hard work – plasterers are usually quite muscular. Nonetheless, it is possible to do satisfactory work, even without prior experience. The use of timber battens as screeds makes it easy to get the floating coat flat. Getting a blemish-free skim coat is more difficult. Some selfbuilders get in a plasterer to show them the methods while he plasters one room. Anyway, keep to small areas until you start to get the knack. Since you are working against time, it is very beneficial to have a 'labourer' (your spouse?) to do the mixing. When plastering does go well, it is very satisfying work. The plaster transforms a rough and gloomy building into something light and nearly civilised.

When the job is subcontracted to plasterers, it normally includes the plasterboarding as well. However, this is quite straightforward work for the ownhander, and you may well wish to do it yourself – especially if you have a helper to hold up ceiling boards. A professional could board and plaster an average house in about three weeks single-handed. If you are doing it yourself, you must expect to take considerably longer.

There are some options to consider. For the blockwork walls, there is a choice for the floating coat of lightweight gypsum or a harder cement/lime/sand render ('harder' when it has set, not necessarily harder to apply). There is also available a lightweight, cement-based plaster (eg, 'Limelite'), but this is used mostly for remedial work. The choice for the ceilings is between skimming and texturing. Subcontracted, the prices will not be very different. If you are doing the work yourself, you could consider dry lining – sticking plasterboard onto blockwork and filling the joints. Using this method, even novices can produce professional-looking results – flat and smooth.

(There is another method, which is practised in Scandinavia but seems unknown in Britain, and which is well suited to the amateur. The blockwork has to be built truly flat and neat – not so difficult with aircrete blocks. A very thin, cement-based render is then worked onto it with a large two-handed float. The large face of the float gives a flat result, and little skill is required. No skimming is necessary. However, since this is a book of conventional techniques in Britain, only these are dealt with below.)

In general, board and plaster the upstairs first; then move downstairs (where the plastering materials are stacked).

Boarding ceilings

Usually square-edged board is used, though round-edged lath, which saves scrimming, is a possibility.

The maximum span for 9·5 mm (ie, $\frac{3}{8}''$) board is reckoned to be 45 cm, but 40 cm is preferable. This latter joist spacing will fit with 240 cm wallboards – definitely two-person boards to put up. ('Wallboards' are often used on ceilings, despite their name.) The maximum span for 12·5 mm (ie, $\frac{1}{2}''$) board is 60 cm, so this should be used on roof trusses. (In fact, you may prefer to use the thicker board for all ceilings, as it will help to reduce sound transmission through the ceilings. This is significant, even in a bungalow. Sound can bypass a masonry wall between two rooms by travelling through the ceilings and loft space. In a house, if you are really concerned about the transmission of sound through a floor/ceiling, consider the old practice of 'pugging' – a 5 cm layer of weak sand-and-cement laid on top of the ceiling. The new types of reinforced board that are available – strong and moisture-resistant – may make this feasible again.)

Large boards reduce the number of joints in a ceiling – joints involve more work, and are liable to crack. From this point of view, the 240 × 120 cm wallboards are fine, but smaller boards are easier to handle. (Positioning large boards above your head is not easy.) A popular choice is 180 × 90 cm board.

With difficulty these can be put up single-handed. A professional does it by sticking a few nails into the board in readiness, balancing the board on one hand to put it in place, and then hammering the nails home. With the board supported, he can finish off the nailing more comfortably. The job is quite demanding! Most single-handed amateurs would want to use a 'dead man' to help them. This is a T-shaped prop (easily made up) that reaches from the floor (or working platform) to jam the board up against the joists. Much better, though, is a live man.

A different approach for the single-handed is to use Gyproc Laths which are much smaller boards and easily handled. They have round edges which need not be scrimmed. Instead, a gap of $\frac{1}{4}$ cm is left between them, and plaster is forced in to hold them together. There are a lot of joints, though, to be treated in this way.

In the best class of work, ceiling boards are supported at all edges. In ascending order of quality:

1) No support at free edges. The ends of boards are nailed to the joists, but the sides are free. (However, if the nearest joist to a wall is more than 15 cm away, the end of the board must be supported at the wall by clips or a nogging, as below.)

2) Metal retaining clips support the board at the walls, midway between each pair of joists (or trusses). The special clips are nailed to the walls and covered over by plaster.

3) The more traditional way is to fix noggings at the walls. Where trusses (rather than joists) are supporting the board, the easiest method is to nail short boards to overlap the top of the wall plate – before the roof is covered in. (See Fig. 5, Chapter 7.)

4) Noggings between joists (or trusses) to support all plasterboard edges, not just those at the walls. The extra noggings are not really necessary if the board will be skimmed, but they are said to be necessary for texturing. However, quite a lot of extra work is involved, and it is not always done.

The noggings around the walls help to keep a good line at the angle and to prevent cracking. (This is irrelevant if you are later putting up coving.)

Plasterboard may come with a grey face on one side, which is for skimming, and white on the other, which is for texturing, painting or papering.

Figure 1: Fixing ceiling boards

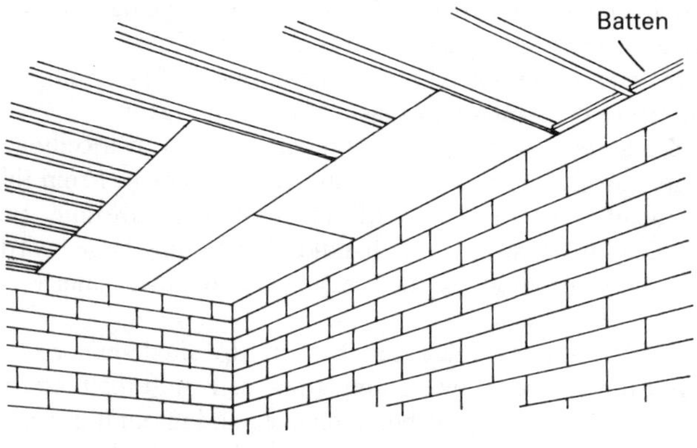

* Stagger head joints.
* Optional batten nailed to wall plate (before roof felted), or a nogging nailed between joists.

In preparation for boarding, take the boards into the room to be worked on and stack them upright against a wall. (Normally, plasterboards are stacked level.) Then build a platform of scaffold boards. (See 'Tools', Chapter 25.) (Once the platform is in position it is difficult to bring in more boards.) Mark the positions of the joists on the wall so that you know where to nail when a board hides the joists.

Fix the boards across the joists. Start with a board in a corner, and cut it to length so that one end fits to the centre of a joist.

Add another board at the end of the first, leaving a gap of 3 mm or so; work along the row. (See Fig. 1.)

Start the adjacent row with a shorter board, so that the head joints are staggered. (This lessens the likelihood of the joints cracking.) However, don't use a very short board fixed to only two joists – it will tend to sag. If the ceilings are to be skimmed, leave the same gap (3 mm) at the sides of the boards. But if they are to be textured, butt joint the paper-bound sides. (It may be worth making a rod, cut to the length of the boards. Offer it up to the joists and mark on it the length of board required.)

Upstairs, you may have decided to make the studwork slightly lower so that you can sail through with the ceiling. In this case, retract the nails holding the head in position, as required to let the boards pass over. Hammer the nails finally home as the boards are fixed.

Reaching up above a stairwell is tricky. Place a ladder against one of the walls of the stairwell, and use one of its rungs to support the end of a scaffold plank. The other end can be supported from the landing, at the required height off the floor. (Double up this arrangement for a more spacious platform.)

And lastly, a word of warning – once the ceilings are boarded, don't delay too long in skimming (or texturing) them. The plasterboard relies on the skim coat to hold it taut. If you leave the skimming for more than a fortnight, the boards may start to sag, especially in damp weather.

Boarding studwork

Boarding studwork is less strenuous than ceilings. Otherwise, it is fairly similar work. Usually boards 2·4 m long are used, stretching from floor to ceiling.

If a double thickness of plasterboard is being applied for sound insulation, fix the outer layer with 5 cm nails. Try to arrange that the joints in the two layers don't coincide. (Note: The thickness of the board(s) will already have been determined when the door linings were fixed.)

At a corner, a board can be scribed to fit:

Temporarily pin a fresh board over the last whole board, and scribe down it with a nail stuck through a batten to mark off a plasterboard width. (See Fig. 2.)

Remember the electrical wiring. The cabling will already be loosely in place in the studwork. Cut rectangular holes in the plasterboard for the boxes (which can be slipped into place later). If the other side of the studwork is still unboarded, pass the cable through the holes. Otherwise, it will have to be fished for.

Figure 2: Scribing plasterboard

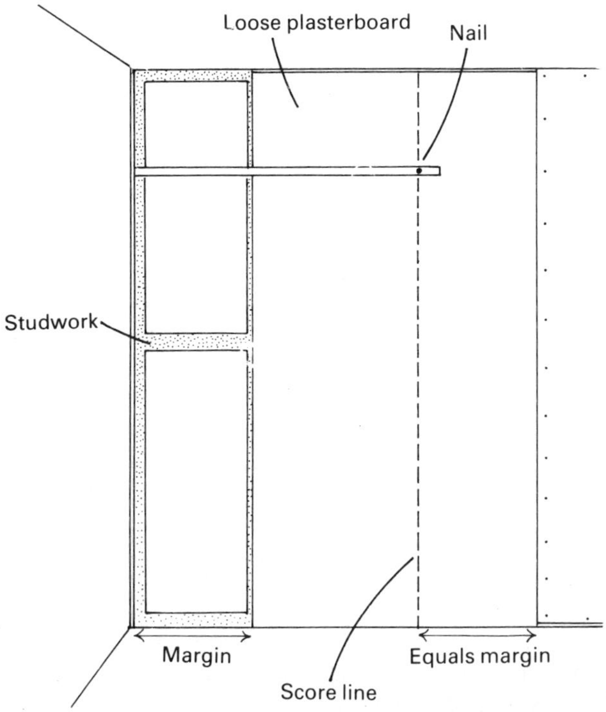

* Fix nail in batten to mark off the width of a plasterboard.
* Place a loose plasterboard over the penultimate board, and mark down it as shown – the offcut exactly fits the margin.
* Compare Fig. 7, Chapter 27.

Plastering:

Ceilings

The ceilings are skimmed before the walls are plastered. (But texturing is done afterwards.)

To gain experience, start with a small ceiling! Build a platform of scaffold boards to work off.

Most commonly, square-edged board will have been used, and all the joints of this will have to be scrimmed to prevent the joints cracking in the future: The scrim is embedded in a thin layer of plaster. Rolls of jute or cotton scrim are available. Jute is preferable, though more expensive and bulky. (Cotton is more popular, though weaker and liable to allow the joint to crack.)

As a preliminary to this, cut off lengths of scrim for all the joints. (Tuck a length temporarily into its joint so you can remember where it belongs.) Cut the long lengths first. Nowhere should scrim overlap; that would give a high spot.

Prepare a bucketful of Thistle Board Finish, and put it onto the spot board. Lay on a thin band of plaster, about 15 cm wide, along the joint. Insert one end of the scrim into the plaster so that it bridges the joint. Then pull the scrim out along the joint with one hand, drawing the trowel along behind it to press the scrim into place. Lay a little more plaster over it and flatten it all together. At the ceiling/wall angle, apply the scrim to the ceiling first, then to the wall. Since the blockwork will have a high suction, it may be necessary to dampen it first.

(For the joints between boards, some people make the job easier by using the self-adhesive scrim originally intended for dry-wall jointing. There is no need to embed it in plaster.)

Thus prepared, the ceiling can be skimmed with a 5 mm coat of Thistle Board Finish. (See 'Skim coat', Chapter 25.) Work from the perimeter to the centre. When the second coat has been applied, check for flatness – in particular, at the angle with the wall. The straightness, or otherwise, of the line here will be quite noticeable. Test with a feather-edge rule. Where there are hollows, apply more material and feather it out with the rule. (At least, that's what you do if you're trying for a top class job.) When looking for blemishes, etc, in the ceiling, look towards the light, ie, the window.

Skimming ceilings is tricky. If you try and fail, you could always texture the ceiling afterwards!

Blockwork

Walls are plastered nowadays with a two-coat system: a 1 cm 'floating' coat, covered with a 2 mm 'skim' (or 'finish', or 'setting') coat.

The most commonly used material for the floating coat is Carlite Browning. Material-wise, this is more expensive than cement render, but professional plasterers like it because it can be skimmed after a few hours, allowing rapid progress. This benefit is not likely to be significant with the ownhander, but there are other advantages:

> The lightness of the material makes the plaster more likely to stick to the wall rather than fall to the floor
>
> Less physical effort is needed
>
> The floating coat can be skimmed while it is still damp, and this makes skimming easier.

A cheaper option is to use a 1:1:6 mix of cement, lime and plastering sand, mixed in a cement mixer. This gives a harder floating coat which is sometimes thought to be desirable. Because of its heaviness, a thick coat may not stick to the wall. (This can be overcome by applying two thin coats in succession.) A cement-based plaster gives the ownhander more time in which to apply and work the material. However, such a plaster contracts on setting (unlike a gypsum plaster which tends to expand). So before it is skimmed, the floating coat must be left for several days to allow any shrinkage and subsequent cracking to occur.

A slight disadvantage results in that the dry render has greater suction, and this may make skimming more difficult. So dampen the wall before skimming.

(Don't be tempted to mix together both cement and gypsum plaster – they react chemically together with undesirable results.)

Preparation of walls

There is quite a lot of preparation to do before the plastering of walls can begin.

First of all, knock off any 'claggs' – mortar which has been squeezed out of the joints in the blockwork, and which would be proud of the plaster. 'Dubbing out' is the process of filling in any large hollows in the blockwork – for example, around badly fitting door linings. Dub out with a sand-and-cement mix, or gypsum plaster. Scratch the surface to give good adhesion for the floating coat. (If, despite earlier advice to the contrary, you have used box lintels, these will need to be dubbed out. But first, some provision must be made for fixing curtain rails: Attach a horizontal length of lath to the back of each lintel, using special clips hooked into the holes in the lintels.)

In some places, a wall surface may change, eg, from blockwork to timber. If the interface is left untreated, the plaster is liable to crack. So the joint should be covered with jute scrim, galvanized mesh, or even a strip of thin plasterboard. (In practice, this precaution is unnecessary at the wall plate.)

Any bare steel embedded in the plaster (eg, nails) will rust, and the stain will penetrate through the plaster and paintwork. So make sure that any nails present are non-rusting.

The external angles, eg, at window reveals, are usually beaded to give a strong, straight and plumb arris. The metal plaster bead comes in 2·4 m lengths and can easily be cut with tin snips or a hacksaw.

The bead can be stuck in place with plaster dabs – conveniently using up plaster left over from skimming the ceiling. Put dabs at half-metre intervals down both sides of the angle. Then press the bead into them, and check that it is plumb and straight. (See Fig. 3.)

Figure 3: Preparing window reveals for plastering

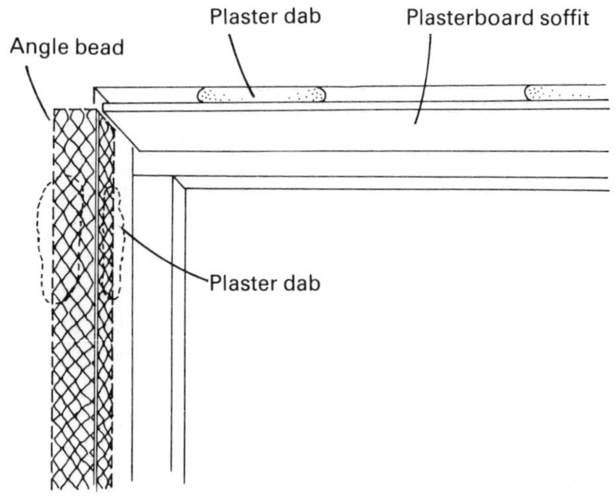

* Dabs of plaster hold the angle bead and plasterboard soffit. (Or use galvanized nails.)

At window reveals, use your eye for this: Stand back from the window and line the bead up with the jamb of the frame. Similarly, for the top bead, stand on a crate, or whatever, and line the bead up with the head of the frame. Check also that the margin is even all the way round the reveal (ie, the distance from the bead to the frame is uniform).

Smooth away the plaster dabs so they are not proud.

(Alternatively, instead of plaster dabs, galvanized nails can be used to fix the bead. Some people find this easier.)

Plastering the soffits of window openings is not too easy – the plaster tends to fall off. Instead, you can use plasterboard cut to size, sticking it up with plaster dabs.

Floating coat

The purpose of the floating coat is primarily to make the surface flat. But how flat? The British Standard Code of Practice requires plastering to be true to within 1 in 600 (eg, 3 mm in 1·8 m). That almost seems like craft for craft's sake. If you put a 1·8 m straight-edge up against many apparently flat walls, you may well find discrepancies double the figure suggested. Does this matter? Hardly – neither from a utilitarian nor an aesthetic point of view. However, in an angle (ie, a corner), an out-of-true surface does show up – as a wavy corner line. So do take care to get the floating coat flat at the corners. (If you are dissatisfied with the wall/ceiling angle, it can always be covered later with coving.)

(Methods of obtaining differing degrees of flatness for the floating coat are given in 'Floating coat', Chapter 25.)

Start on a small wall to gain experience. To reach the top of the wall, you'll need a scaffold board on some supports (bottle crates are useful). Dampen the wall beforehand if the blocks are too dry. Some people use diluted PVA (1:5) as it doesn't dry as fast as water. Don't forget to use a scratch float on the floating coat before it sets hard.

Do the window reveals after the main wall. Keep the reveals square and flat. This is easier said than done! (A new plastic gadget, called a 'Squangle', may help.) If there are windows without window boards, eg, in the bathroom or kitchen, then plaster the shelf as well. A piece of plasterboard cut to size can be used for this (as for the soffit).

Plaster should finish flush with the door linings, so graduate the thickness of the floating coat, if necessary.

Reaching the top of the walls at a stairwell can be tricky. To make a platform, stretch a scaffold board across the well onto a rung of a ladder, as suggested earlier.

Skim coat

Carlite Finish is the plaster to use on top of Carlite Browning. It can be applied only a few hours after the Browning, but if it is left for several days, the floating coat may have to be dampened. Once again, you might find it more effective to use diluted PVA.

A cement-based render should be left for several days to dry out and to allow any shrinkage to take place. It may then have excessive suction for skimming. To test this, brush some water on. If it is sucked straight in, then the plaster needs to be dampened: Flick water on with a brush, spray it on, or, if necessary, throw it on by the cupful. Or use diluted PVA. The wall should be damp all over, but not wet. Use Thistle Multi-Finish.

Apply the skim coat as two thin coats to attain a final thickness of 2 mm. If a wall is too large for you, as a novice, to finish in one go, do part of it first. Then cut a line down the edge of the skim coat, and scrape away the margin. This should leave a neat, cut edge from which to start with the second go. (Well, that's the theory.)

Studwork

If square-edged plasterboard has been used, it is skimmed all over:

First, scrim the joints, as for the ceilings.

If there are any external corners, they need protecting with plasterboard bead. This is somewhat different from the ordinary angle bead – it can be buried in the thin skim coat. Fix the bead with galvanized nails.

Use Thistle Board Finish or, possibly, Thistle Multi-Finish for a slower set. (See 'Skim coat', Chapter 25.)

For a completely different approach which avoids skimming, see 'Dry lining' later in this chapter.

Options:

Texturing the ceiling

This technique is often called by the name of the leading brand, 'Artex', although there are, in fact, several brands to choose from. The more economical ones come as a powder to which water is added. Some need warm water, which may not be convenient on a site. And only some mixes are suitable for ceilings in steamy bathrooms and kitchens.

It is easier to texture a ceiling than to skim it. The material costs are higher, but bear in mind that a skimmed ceiling also needs to be painted. A textured ceiling can be left as it is. (However, some people paint the ceiling with a silk finish to enhance the texture.)

Lots of patterns are possible. The special stippling pad gives:

The ubiquitous stipple – slightly twist the pad between dabs so that no distinct pattern is formed

The popular circular swirl – just rotate your wrist (alternately in opposite directions)

The scroll – move the pad with figure-of-eight swirls keeping it on the surface all the time

A 'broken leather' effect – put a plastic bag over the pad and swirl it around in a figure-of-eight.

If you really like these effects, you can texture the walls too! Profiled rollers and combs give more patterns.

Unlike with skimming, the plasterboard should preferably show its white surface, and the ceiling rose should already be fixed in position. The walls should have been plastered and dried out.

The texturing is done in two stages, the first of which is to caulk the joints:

Make up a stiff mix of the compound, according to the manufacturer's instructions. Special paper tape is to be embedded in the compound to strengthen the joints. Tear off some lengths of paper as long as the joints; immerse them briefly in water; shake off the excess; and leave them for five minutes. The paper becomes supple. With a flat-ended stripping knife, load a dollop of the compound onto a caulker. (This is a simple tool with a broad plastic blade.) Draw the caulker along a joint, pressing the compound into the crack. As the compound gets squeezed down the blade of the caulker, scoop it off with the stripping knife, scrap it back onto the front end and continue. So fill the crack, and spread a band of compound about 8 cm wide across the joint. The paper tape is bedded into this. Play out the tape with one hand, and press it into the compound with the caulker in the other. Go over the tape again with the caulker, squeezing it tight against the board and removing the excess compound. (The process is somewhat similar to applying scrim for plaster.) Then fill in over nail heads. Leave a smooth surface. (Clean up any splashes on the floor, while they are easy to remove.)

The following day, apply a wider band of a thick mix over the tape. Feather this out at the edges. And cover nail heads again.

In a fairly short time, the compound will be firm but not dry, and the decorative coat can be applied. (However, a better method is to let the compound dry out completely and then roll on a sealer. This improves the wet-edge time, the workability, and the coverage of the decorative coat. The sealer takes a few hours to dry.) So with damp but firm joints (or with a dry sealer over the whole ceiling), the decorative coat can be applied:

Mix the compound to its required thickness. 1 kg of powder covers 1 to 2 square metres, with a mix from 1:10 to 1:20.

You can make up a day's supply at a time, as the compound doesn't set until applied to the ceiling (unlike plaster, of course). A suitable brush for applying the compound is a broom with bristles of medium stiffness. The tub containing the compound must be wide enough for the broom head (eg, a small plastic dustbin). The thickness of the compound depends somewhat on the pattern to be used. Make it thicker for a deeper texture.

A good system is to have two people working together, one laying on and the other texturing. The texturer has to be fast enough to keep a 'wet edge'. So work across the room in bands about half a metre wide. Immerse the broom into the compound, but only up to half the bristle depth. (Don't overload the bristles.) Brush the compound onto the ceiling in a small patch. Restrain yourself from brushing it out too much, which will give too thin a texture. After every few applications, squeeze the compound out from the stock of the broom; otherwise it will start splashing onto the floor.

Applying the pattern is not difficult. Try it out on a piece of spare plasterboard first. Decide beforehand whether the pattern is to be random or regular. Don't apply more than a square metre, or so, before texturing it. And at the wall angle and ceiling roses, after texturing the area, make a margin by drawing along a damp paint brush, 1 cm or 2 cm wide.

Clean up the floor and the tools.

Beamed ceilings

A different look for ceilings can be obtained by exposing the bottom of the joists below the level of the ceiling, so showing the beams. It's easier than trying for the conventional flat, smooth ceiling. Break the flatness up with the joists, and go for a rough plaster finish – simple and effective.

Before plasterboarding, nail battens along the sides of the joists about 5 cm up from the bottom. Cut the 12·5 mm plasterboard to fit between the joists, and nail it to the battens. (See Fig. 4.)

Figure 4: Beamed ceiling

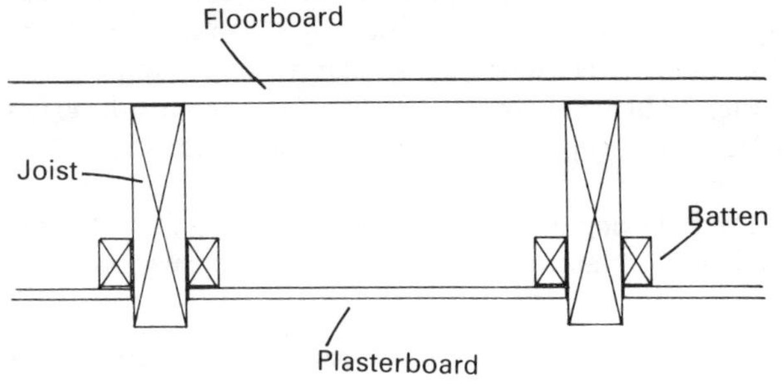

(At joints, noggings are advisable.) With a trowel, lay on a thin coat of finish plaster onto a small area, say 1 m^2. Give it a rustic finish with a polythene bag containing a cloth. Swirl the crumpled bag over the wet plaster in a loose figure-of-eight to give a 'broken leather' texture.

It's an effect to use as a feature – easy, cheap, and different. (You can save yourself time overall by stain-painting the bottom of the joists before boarding them – while there is no cutting in.)

Dry lining

Since so many people find the knack of plastering elusive, the ownhander may well find dry lining a good option – it eliminates plastering. Even a professional plasterer can get a flatter wall by this method. A little disadvantage is that the surface is not so solid.

Tapered-edge board, either 9·5 mm or 12·5 mm thick, is used with the white side showing. It can be nailed to trued up battens on the wall, but a cheaper way is to use the direct bonding method outlined below. (This simple technique has replaced the 'dot and dab' method.)

The board is to be stuck to the blockwork with bonding compound. (Don't confuse this with bonding plaster for use on concrete.) Start boarding from an internal angle, fixing one board at a time. Use boards 120 cm wide, cut a couple of centimetres less than the height of the room. A ribbon of the bonding compound is needed around the perimeter: at the top, bottom and sides of the wall, and arround any door or window frames. (See Fig. 5.) Where a board is to be fixed, apply a row of dabs at the sides. The dabs should be applied vertically with a trowel at every second course of blockwork. Keep them about 3 cm from the joints so that these are not bridged. Apply a third row of dabs midway between the outer ones. (For 9·5 mm board, apply two rows equally spaced between the outer ones.) Push the board onto the dabs and flatten it in place with a straight-edge. The eventual contact area of the dabs with the boards should be at least 20%. Raise the board to the ceiling with a foot-lift, and wedge it to keep it there. (See Fig. 6.)

Figure 5: Drylining a blockwork wall

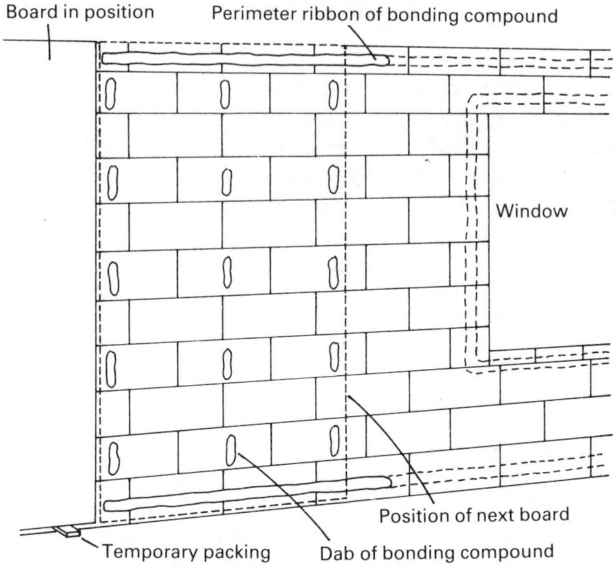

* Direct bonding method.
* Continuous ribbon of compound around perimeter of wall (including frames).
* Dabs shown take a 120 cm wide sheet of 12·5 mm thick plasterboard.

Check that the edge is plumb. Cut edges should be placed at an internal corner, and masked by a bound edge on the adjacent wall. At window reveals, make sure that a bound edge always masters a cut edge. The flattened dabs are about 1 cm thick, so there is space behind the board for electric cable. Cut out apertures in the board beforehand so that the boxes can be inserted later.

Jointing for dry lining

Special materials and tools are needed for jointing tapered-edge board. The process is rather long-winded but needs little skill. Use Gyproc Jointex. Instructions for it can be obtained from British Gypsum. (Redland's 'Fast Set' is an alternative.) The process is somewhat similar to the treatment of joints for texturing. Briefly:

Any gaps greater than 3 mm should be filled with a stiff mix of Jointex.

Apply a thin band of Jointex along the joint with a caulker. Press in a length of joint tape, going over it with a stripping knife to embed it. Leave for five minutes.

Apply another band of Jointex, 20 cm wide and flush with the board. Feather out the edges with a special jointing sponge, rinsing the sponge occasionally. Leave to set.

Fill any depressions and sand down proud spots. Leave to set.

Apply a thin band of Jointex, 30 cm wide, and feather out the edges. Leave to set.

Lightly sand to remove imperfections. An orbital sander is useful. (By the way, an orbital sander attachment with a pivoting head is a far superior tool to the simple type.) A dust mask is recommended.

Sometimes cut edges do occur and these will not have a tapered depression. Sandpaper the edges to remove any burrs, and proceed as above using thin coats.

Spot over nail heads twice.

At internal angles, fold the jointing tape and apply it in a similar way to the above.

At many external corners, eg, window reveals, special corner tape can be used. This has two metal bands fixed along the tape. For more strength at exposed corners, use plasterboard angle bead. Again, bed either of these in a rather similar way to the above.

Figure 6: Foot-lifter

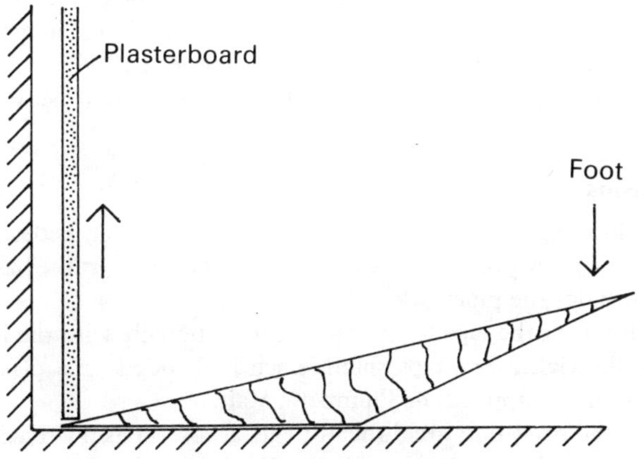

* Press down on the timber foot-lifter to raise the top of the plasterboard to the ceiling.

Finally, apply some Gyproc Topcoat over the whole surface to give a homogeneous surface for painting. If the wall is to be papered instead, Topcoat should still be used – to protect the plasterboard when the paper is wet-stripped at a later date.

Plasterboard plugs can be used for attaching small fittings to dry linings. For heavy fittings, the fixing should go through to the blockwork or into the studwork.

Skirting and architrave can be nailed on, as usual, or stuck on.

Brush plaster

The author knows a teacher of music who says "If you play a bum note – just play it with conviction!". Brush plastering shows a similar attitude. If you can't skim the walls smooth, then make them rough!

For brush plastering, make up a wetter than usual mix of finish plaster, so that it is like a slurry. Apply it to the wall with a large brush (or a trowel if you can). Finish it by dragging a stiff brush lightly down the walls to leave a vertically textured surface. (A decorators' paste brush is suitable.) Again, the process is easy, and the result effective as a feature.

One Coat plaster

British Gypsum suggest that their Thistle Universal one-coat plaster is the most suitable plaster for amateurs.

The usual thickness of plaster can be laid on and ruled off for a flat surface in the normal way. Then swirl it with a sponge float, and finish with a trowel for a smooth surface.

The idea of using one plaster instead of two may appeal, but it's not necessarily easier. With the two coat system, there is only one objective with each coat: flatness with the floating coat, and smoothness with the skim coat. Achieving both of these in the same process can be more difficult. But give it a try if you want to find out for yourself.

13

SECOND FIX PLUMBING

☆

☆

☆

☆

☆

☆

☆

PLASTERING has given the house a civilised feel. Now to add the convenience!

Most sanitary and heating ware is available from plumbers' merchants within a few days, but it's prudent to order a couple of weeks beforehand. There is a small point to bear in mind: If the plaster is dry, paint it where radiators and other appliances will be fitted. Take advantage of your flexibility as a selfbuilder – the job is easier now than later.

Sanitaryware

This is a realm of consumerism, or at least that's how the manufacturers promote it. Fashion colours come and go; the avocado of yesteryear gives way to the pale ivory of the ever shifting present. And if you wish to indulge your vulgarity – no better chance. You can show off to the world, or at least, to those of it who come into the intimacies of your home, your taste in indulgent opulence and the depth of your purse.

The best WC's – ones that always work, look good, and use less water – come from Sweden. (The makers, Ifo, have recently started selling them in Britain.) As the compulsory metering of water becomes widespread, the volume of water used for a flush becomes financially significant.

On a practical note, three materials are generally useful:

PTFE tape, for wrapping (clockwise) round threads to give a watertight joint.

Plumbers' putty, eg 'Plumber's Mait', for giving a watertight seal under a flange.

Boss White, for smearing sparingly on olives to give a good seal in compression joints.

Actually, in addition to Boss White, there is now Boss Blue. Unlike Boss White, this cannot support bacterial growth, and Water Companies are insisting that this is used in direct cold supplies. And they are also insisting that lead-free solder (based on tin) is used in this pipework. (Lead-free Yorkshire fittings are available.) The Water Companies seem to want perfection in new installations. Too bad that, in many places, the water they supply is far from perfect.

Anyway, where the text mentions Boss White, use Boss Blue if it's appropriate.

Basins

Wall hung and vanity basins are available, though pedestals are the more popular. The pedestal helps to support the basin and hides the pipework.

First, fit the taps to the basin, conventionally with the hot on the right. The taps should each be bedded on a plastic washer (if supplied) or Plumber's Mait.

If the back-nuts are difficult to get at, use a basin wrench – they are cheap enough to buy. (Don't overtighten nuts on pottery ware, because the ware is easily cracked.) The waste outlet should similarly be bedded on a sealing gasket (if supplied) or Plumber's Mait. Fit a trap with a $7\frac{1}{2}$ cm seal. The easiest way to connect up the taps is with flexible tap connectors, so fit these to the underside of the taps. (Though it is cheaper to make the required bends in ordinary pipe fitted to swivelling tap connectors.)

To fix the basin, stand it on the pedestal, check that the top is level, and mark the positions for the holes in the wall. Drill and plug the wall, then secure the basin with screws and rubber washers. The pedestal also needs to be screwed at the base.

Connect up the pipework.

Bath

Plastic baths are popular – no need to break your back carrying a cast iron one upstairs! They have a reputation for flimsiness, so check on the thickness before you buy. They are now available a centimetre thick, double what was formerly used.

If you will want to fix a shelf alongside the bath, fix a bearer to the wall before installing the bath.

The taps, or mixer unit, can be fitted as above for a basin. And fit a combination waste/overflow – baths, unlike basins, don't have an have an integral overflow.

The bath comes with a cradle that needs to be screwed to the floor. Put the bath into position and mark for screw holes. As you try to reach the further ones, you might come to realise that you need to be something of a contortionist to fit a bath! And you might also foresee a problem: too little space for a trap. Generally, traps have a 'deep seal' ($7\frac{1}{2}$ cm), but shallower traps are made for baths. Even so, you may have to cut a hole in the floor to make room. Screw the detachable feet into position. Prepare the pipework. (Again, it will be easier with flexible tap connectors.) The bath waste is usually in 40 mm pipework.

Drop the bath and cradle onto the feet, and adjust them so that the bath rim is level (in both directions). By design, the bath will then drain satisfactorily. Connect up the pipework.

(An alternative method, which could save cutting a hole in the floor, is to raise the bath up by screwing the feet to a couple of short timber bearers. But they shouldn't be too thick – you will still want the bath panels to fit.) To support the panels, some plumbers make up a light stud framework (eg, out of roofing lath), but it is not absolutely necessary.

Shower

A mixer unit is usually attached to a wall, with the hot and cold supplies chased into the wall. They turn straight out of the wall into the mixer, so they must be the right distance apart.

Fitting up the waste and trap is similar to the method for a bath. (Again, there may be a problem fitting a deep seal trap – a 5 cm trap will suffice, as a shower is most unlikely to lead to siphonage problems.) Some shower trays have a panel in the front for easy access to the trap.

The size of most shower trays (75 cm square) is rather mean. It's a good idea to increase the area of the cubicle by putting a shelf (to be tiled later) around the edge of the tray. Or search for a larger tray.

Water closets

The simplest and cheapest pan is a washdown, in which a torrent of water washes out the pan.

Siphonic pans use a different principle: Flowing water sucks air along with it, reducing the air pressure. This reduced pressure is used to suck out the contents of the pan. Siphonic pans are quieter in operation, but the design is more complex and has a tendency to block. There are two types, single and double siphonic, the double chamber design being more effective but more expensive.

(To identify the type of a pan in use, compare the water level, as it flushes, with the standing level:

The level is higher for the whole flush: washdown

The level initially rises but is then lower: single siphonic

The level is lower throughout the flush: double siphonic.)

The cistern is usually attached to the pan (ie, 'close coupled'), though separate low level cisterns attached to the wall can be used with washdown pans. These cisterns are cheaper but are considered less attractive. Bottom entry, rather than side entry, makes for neater plumbing of the supply and overflow.

The pan contains its own trap, so it is connected directly to the soil pipe. Plastics technology makes this a simple matter, with a selection of straight and bent connectors to join pan to pipe. The distance of the pan from the wall is determined by the (close-coupled) cistern. Check that the pan is level, and screw it to the floor with non-rusting screws. Don't over-tighten – the pan may crack. (On solid floors, it's common practice to bed the pan on mortar before screwing it.)

Prepare the cistern, fitting the overflow and ball valve. The valve comes with two jets, one for connection to a high pressure (direct) system, the other to a low pressure (indirect) system. Attach the cistern to the pan with the thick rubber seal and nuts provided; and screw it to the wall using thick plastic washers. For the 22 mm overflow, you will have to drill through the wall. Stick the pipe out 10 cm, or more.

The 15 mm cold feed is attached to the ball valve via a tap connector. Optionally, a stop or gate valve (depending on high or low pressure) can be put in the feed.

Sink

A variety of designs are available in stainless steel: single, double, or one-and-a-half bowls; drainers, right and/or left hand; one hole for a mixer, or two for separate taps; square or roll fronts, or else the fashionable inset fitting. The one you want may not be in stock! Taps and mixers, too, come in quite a variety.

Fit the taps, using a 'top hat' back-nut. Fit the combination waste/overflow and a $7\frac{1}{2}$ cm trap. With double sinks, run 40 mm pipe from each trap into one pipe via a swept tee. Or join the pipes before a single trap.

To fix a sink (square or roll front) to a sink cupboard, push pieces of wood over the bottom flange of the sink; screw into these to fix the sink to corner connectors at the top of the cupboard.

Washing machine

An integral trap with upstand is available that takes the flexible waste pipe from a washer. (This device allows air to be sucked into the waste and so prevents any chance of siphonage emptying the machine.) Run the waste away with 40 mm pipe. If the machine is a long way from the stack, remember that there is the option of running the waste to a separate drain outside, via a yard gully.

Terminate the hot and cold supplies with washing machine taps. Later, the flexible hoses of the machine can be screwed onto these.

A dish washer is connected in a similar manner (though usually only a cold supply is required).

Outside tap

A 'bib' tap is designed to be fixed to a wall. You probably want one with a hose connection.

On the inside of the house, there should be a stop valve so that the tap and its pipework can be emptied in wintertime.

There should also be a check valve in the pipe. But if – as is quite likely – a garden hose may be connected, the Water Supply Byelaws now require more than this; they require a 'double check valve assembly'. Until a more elegant device is developed, this consists of a pair of check valves with a drain cock in between them for testing purposes. (A check valve allows only one-way flow.) The assembly seems excessive, unless the end of the hose might be stuck in a garden pool – from which back flow could just conceivably contaminate the supply.

The discharge system

The stack needs completing. Just emerging from the floor slab is the drain, and the stack runs into this. (Soil pipe fits directly onto a plastic drain. A clay drain, however, has a different external diameter, so manufacturers produce adapters to fit soil pipe.) Waste pipes run into the stack via 'bosses'. Patch bosses can conveniently be stuck on the stack wherever required; or else branches with preformed bosses can be incorporated into the stack.

If the stack is inside the building, the noise of waste running away can be obtrusive. To quieten it, wrap 5 cm insulation around the pipe. Then box it all in with board $2\frac{1}{2}$ cm thick (eg, two layers of plasterboard).

In the past, the stack was taken up through the roof and left open at the top. It's a popular belief that this is to let obnoxious gases escape; in fact, it is to allow air to be sucked into the pipe as the wastes run down it. Nowadays, installation can be made easier by topping the stack with an air admittance valve. This device lets air in, but not out. With it, the stack can be terminated just a little higher than the washbasin. Perhaps more prudently, just in case the valve isn't perfect, you will wish to carry the stack up and terminate it in the loft. Anyway, you will have saved yourself the trouble of breaking through the roof tiles.

If the stack is fixed to the outside of the building, it can be simply terminated at eaves height with a balloon grating (a plastic or wire cage) to stop birds nesting.

Storage tank

For an indirect cold supply, a large tank (about 250 litres) is needed, and this should have been left in the loft before the roof was covered. With a direct supply, a tank half this size will suffice to feed the hot water cylinder.

The first thing to do is to construct a platform for the tank. A good location is above the hot cylinder. For a reasonable shower, the platform needs to be at least a metre and a half above the shower head. The platform must be strong – 250 litres of water weigh 250 kilos, a hefty weight!

The British Standard method (BS 5268, part 3) requires the weight to be supported close to the nodes of the trusses (ie, where web members are connected to the ceiling tie). The maximum load at a node is ·45 kN. Since a force of 1 N equals the weight of ·1 kg (approximately), the maximum weight to be supported at a node is 45 kg. Each truss can support 90 kg, so the weight of the tank needs to be spread over three, or preferably four, trusses.

As bearers, use a couple of stout boards on edge to span the three (or four) trusses. Tuck each board in as close as possible to the nodes. Span across these two bearers with further boards on edge (lying in the direction of the trusses). Use these to support a platform – a piece of water-resistant chipboard is fine. However, this platform will not be very high. If you want to increase the water pressure, you will have to raise the platform higher by supporting it on posts nailed to the boards. Altogether, it will be a cumbersome structure.

Instead of the approved method, described above, some people simply fix bearers at the required height to four trusses. On each truss, nail a bearer across its four web members. Lay cross bearers on them to support the boarding.

Prepare the connections into the storage tank. Holes can be cut with a hole saw in a drill, or with a tank cutter in a brace. For a clean cut, press waste timber against the back side of the plastic.

And what holes are needed? Obviously, a cold feed in to the ball valve, about 5 cm from the top of the tank. (See Fig. 1.)

Figure 1: Storage tank

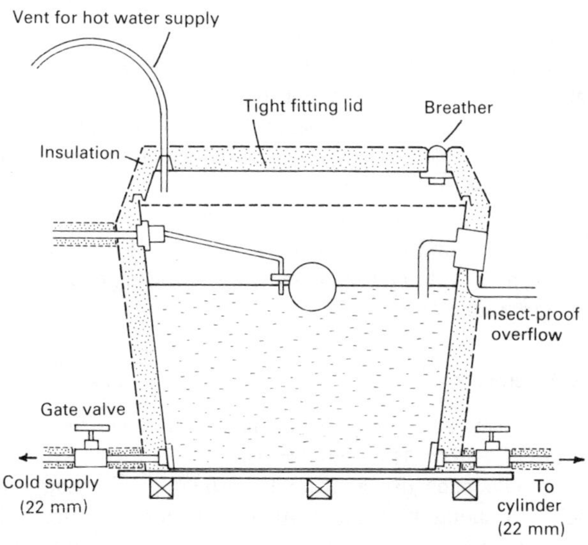

* Complies with Byelaw 30.
* An extra 15 mm supply to a shower will give a steady flow.

And a hole is needed about 8 cm from the top for the 22 mm overflow pipe – to run to the outside where a dripping pipe will be noticed. The supplies are taken off from the bottom of the tank – traditionally 5 cm up from the bottom to be clear of debris. (However, since storage tanks are now kept almost clinically clean, this seems excessive.) One 22 mm supply runs to the cylinder, and another to cold taps and WC's (in an indirect supply). Preferably, a shower should have its own separate supply (15 mm) so that its pressure is independent of the usage of other taps.

With the holes cut, connections can be made to the tank. Use the plastic washers provided with the connectors, not mastic. A special, elbowed tank connector is available for the overflow. This enables a short piece of pipe to go down 5 cm below the usual water level, thus preventing icy draughts blowing in along the pipe.

Attach the ball valve – which should be suitable for high (mains) pressure.

Attach suitably sized tank connectors at the bottom. These can be straight or bent to suit your pipework.

Place the tank in position, fit an insulation jacket, and connect up the pipework as follows:

Connect the copper pipework with swivel connectors (use PTFE tape). It's a good idea to have gate valves on the pipes for future maintenance. (The one to the cylinder is usually put in the airing cupboard.)

The vent from the cylinder curves over the top of the tank, to go down through the lid. It should stay clear of the water level, and rise 40 cm above it.

Fit the plastic overflow pipe. It should have a continuous fall and be supported.

The Water Byelaws now require the tank to be insect-proof. The lid must fit tightly and have a filtered breather to let in air but not insects. The vent pipe needs a grommet around it, where it goes through the lid. And to prevent insects getting in through the overflow pipe, this needs a mesh in it. The Byelaws are also concerned about insulation. The insulation jacket should be put on the tank before connecting up the pipework. This way, small holes can be made in the jacket to let the pipes through. 'Byelaw 30' kits can be obtained for complying with these regulations.

Cylinder

Common sizes for indirect hot water cylinders are 120 litres (90 cm high) and 144 litres (105 cm high). As a matter of passing interest, a bath uses about 100 litres of water, and a shower about a third of that. It's quite sensible, in summer-time, to heat the water with cheap night electricity, and in that case select the larger size. Fit a 'high recovery' cylinder, which enables the water to be heated up in half an hour. This is not only a matter of convenience. Such a cylinder can absorb more of the output from a boiler, and so inefficient cycling of the boiler is reduced. Factory-applied jackets give more effective insulation than ones fitted later. But they are usually made of polyurethane, which is not the world's friendliest plastic.

(If you are using solely Economy 7 water heating, you will need a bigger cylinder (210 litres), which is considerably more expensive. Because it is 150 cm high, the shelves in the airing cupboard will be inconveniently high.)

A cylinder with water is heavy. The common practice is to stand it slightly off a timber floor. Lay three 5 × 5 cm bearers on the floor (across the joists), and stand the cylinder on some board on the bearers.

The connections to the cylinder are best all fitted before it is put in place.,(See Fig. 2.)

Use plenty of PTFE tape, but don't overtighten the fittings as the copper walls are weak. Try to arrange the pipework in the cupboard so that all is accessible. (The cupboard needs to be at least 80 cm wide.)

Figure 2: Hot water cylinder

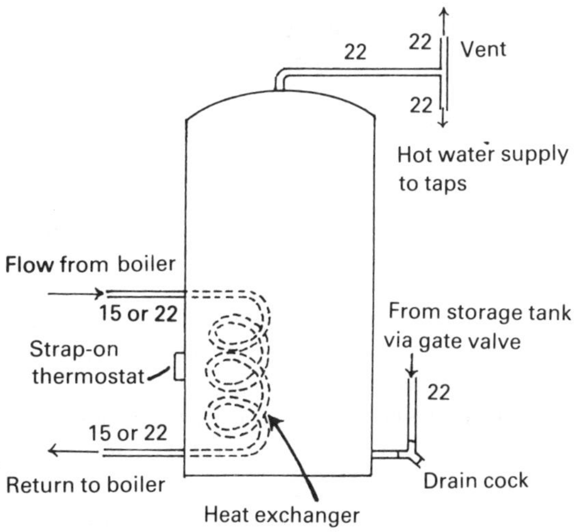

* Indirect cylinder – the hot water supply is separate from the central heating system.
* To prevent convection inside the pipe, the vent does not rise directly from the cylinder.

The 22 mm feed from the storage tank goes into the 1″ female iron tapping at the bottom of the cylinder. ('Iron' refers to the type of thread: BSP – British Standard Pipe thread.) For this, you need a copper-to-male-iron coupling. There should be a gate valve in this pipework, and a drain cock at the bottom. (Connect the latter via a short length of pipe, if necessary, to put it into an accessible position.)

The 22 mm flow from the boiler goes into the higher 1″ male tapping, and the return to the lower one. Connect via copper-to-female-iron couplings. Fit an air vent in the flow by the cylinder if this is a high spot, but not, for example, if the pump is above the cylinder. (If the system uses gravity, not pumped circulation, the pipework will be 28 mm or 32 mm. Cylinders with larger, $1\frac{1}{4}''$ BSP studs are available.)

The draw-off at the crown of the cylinder is usually a bend (copper-to-male-iron), which takes the 22 mm pipe. This rises slightly – so that air is not trapped – to a tee at the wall. From there, the feed goes downwards to the taps, and the vent goes upwards to the tank.

Insert a long immersion heater from the top (or possibly a shorter one from the side). Some of the insulation may need cutting away. You will have to borrow, hire or buy (£4) the special spanner to tighten the very large nut. The heater is sealed by a fibre washer, but it's prudent to wrap some PTFE tape around the thread as well. If it's not already fitted, you need a 'dry-pocket' thermostat to slip into the heater. Set the thermostat to the required temperature, eg, 60°C.

Cylinder thermostat

This is strapped to the side of the cylinder, about a third of the way up. Cut away the insulation to obtain metal-to-metal contact. This thermostat controls the motorised valve.

Central heating header tank

This is a small tank with a water capacity of 45 litres. It is usually located in the loft, above the cylinder. Support it on a board across a pair of ceiling ties. It must be at least 1·2 m above the pump and radiators – which is usually no problem. Connections are made into this tank as into the storage tank. It needs a ball valve, with a 15 mm feed tee'd off from the rising main. (See Fig. 3.)

Note that the cold water level should be only about 10 cm deep. (As the water in the system warms up, the water level in the tank needs space to rise.) The 15 mm feed-and-expansion pipe is connected a little above the tank bottom; its other end makes the last connection into the return to the boiler. The 22 mm vent pipe is tee'd into the flow as the first connection from the boiler. It runs up to the tank and curves over it to finish inside the lid. The top of the curve should be about 40 cm above the water level.

This tank, too, needs an overflow, fitted a little below the ball valve inlet; and an insulation jacket.

Figure 3: CH header tank

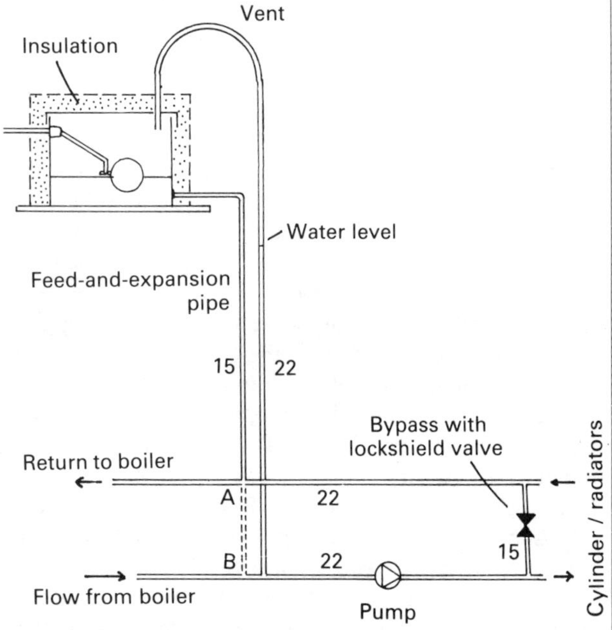

* Position 'A' is the most reliable for the connection of the feed-and-expansion pipe. Position 'B' – 15 cm from the vent – is also used.
* The by-pass is necessary to maintain a circulation if all the radiators can be closed off.
* The water level in the vent is lowered by the suction of the pump.

Pump

This is fitted in the 22 mm flow between the tee for the vent and the three-port valve. A good position is in the airing cupboard. It should be easily accessible, possibly above the top of the cylinder. Support the pump only by its pipework; in particular, it should not rest on the floor. Fit it with its arrow in the direction of flow and with isolating valves each side.

But for now, temporarily remove the pump, and complete the circuit with some hose or a piece of pipe with suitable fittings at each end. (See 'Commissioning the heating system', later in the chapter.)

Diverter

This three-port motorised valve, for switching the flow between cylinder and radiators, is also usually in the airing cupboard.

The valve can be operated manually for filling or draining the system.

Bypass

If there are thermostatic radiator valves on all the radiators, it is possible that they would all be shut at the same time. This would stop any flow through the heating circuit, and so, if there was no flow to the cylinder either, the pump would be wearing out. To prevent this, a bypass is connected between the flow and return, in 15 mm pipe. A restricting valve is incorporated so that, under normal conditions, water does not flow through the bypass. This valve should be of a lockshield or screw-adjusted type so that it cannot be accidentally turned. It will be set to have a higher resistance to flow than the radiator or cylinder circuits. Tee it into the flow between pump and diverter. (See Fig. 3, Chapter 9.)

The bypass is unnecessary if a flow through one radiator is always certain.

Boiler

Installation instructions come with the boiler. A balanced-flue boiler requires a rectangular aperture through the wall. To make this, mark the shape on the wall with the template supplied. (Match the position with the brick coursing to make the job easier.) To mark the corners, drill squarely through both leaves of the wall with a long, thin bit. In each leaf, chain drill the rectangle with lines of thin holes, and cut it out with a hammer and bolster.

Connect up the 22 mm flow and return, and the 15 mm gas supply using jointing compound.

Radiators

Fix the valves to the bottom tappings, using PTFE tape: a TRV ('Thermostatic Radiator Valve') on the flow, and a lockshield valve on the return. If the pipework is microbore, either use valves that accept it or use reducers.

Put the mounting brackets into the back of the radiator, and measure their distance apart. Transfer this spacing onto the wall, and draw two plumb lines for the brackets. (With studwork, the brackets must obviously be secured to the studs – which is easier if the stud positions were prudently marked on the floor earlier. If there are no studs at the required positions, fix two horizontal bearers across the studs, and secure the brackets to these. For a neater job, recess the bearers into the plasterboard by cutting out strips of board with a Stanley knife.) The radiators should be 15 cm, or more, off the floor and level (or with a slight rise to the air vent).

Fix the brackets securely because a radiator with water is heavy. Long radiators may need three brackets.

Hang the radiators and connect up the pipework.

Have you already painted the wall behind?

The pipework

Fit a drain cock at the lowest point of the system and at any down loops. And if the pipework rises and then falls, fit an air vent at the top of the loop. (Don't forget that the radiators and pump contain vents.)

Pipework in the loft needs to be insulated. Water Byelaw 49 requires pipe insulation (of $\lambda = \cdot 04$) to be 32 mm thick – or even 38 mm if the ventilated loft space is regarded as 'outdoors'. (Is such a thickness really necessary?) Elsewhere, hot pipes also need insulation, including the two vents.

When all the plumbing installations have been completed, check the pipework methodically:

First check the cold supply. Tie up the ball valve in the CH header tank to close it off, and close the gate valve to the cylinder. Open the cold taps to prevent air-locks forming, and then open the main stop valve. Check that there are no leaks. Compression joints may be cured simply by tightening the nuts. With capillary joints, the pipework will have to be drained and the fitting replaced or re-soldered (feed solder in at an end).

Then check the hot supply. Open the hot taps, and then the gate valve to the cylinder.

Commissioning the heating system

Open the radiator valves, and close the air vents and drain cock. Attach a hose to the drain cock and lead it outside – you may want to drain the system down in a hurry! As mentioned earlier, the pump has been temporarily replaced by a piece of pipe so that it can't become clogged.

Let water into the header tank and fill the system up, switching the diverter valve manually. Search for leaks. If you fail to find any, be pleased. Let air out at all the vents. (You will need a radiator key for the radiator vents and a screwdriver for the pump vent.) Open the drain cock to flush water through the system for ten minutes – in at the tank and out at the drain cock. Empty the system, replace the pump, and then refill,

When gas and electricity have been connected, the system can be tested. Run the system for half an hour. If the pump stops, it may be clogged by debris: Clear it by rotating the spindle with a screwdriver. Then drain the system down again, while warm. Refill, this time adding the appropriate 'Fernox' corrosion inhibitor to the header tank, and re-vent.

The pump bypass needs adjusting. Set the pump to the required speed, probable the minimum (see below). Close the bypass. Put the boiler on full load by turning up its thermostat and opening all radiator valves. After a while, switch to minimum load (ie, the cylinder only) by turning off the radiators. Gradually open the bypass until the boiler operates quietly at all flow temperatures. (The usual operating temperature is 80°C.)

The system is now nearly up and running, but lastly it needs balancing. This is not easy to do on a warm day. If your radiator sizing was correct, then the system will be balanced when there are equal drops in temperature at all the radiators. You can check this crudely by testing whether they feel equally hot to the touch! For more sophistication, hire a couple of radiator thermometers:

Open all the radiator valves, and select the lowest pump speed. Start testing at the radiator nearest to the boiler and progress to the furthest one. Clip the thermometers to the flow and return pipes. The temperature fall should be 10°C at each radiator. (The textbooks specify 11°C, but this precise figure is another imperial remnant – 20°F.) If the fall across a radiator is insufficient, impede the flow through it by screwing down the lockshield valve a little. (This, of course, reduces the heat emitted by the radiator.)

If the required temperature fall can't be reached at every radiator, increase the pump speed and check them all again.

(Some boilers allow the operating gas pressure to be reduced, thereby reducing the heat output. A boiler will operate more efficiently if its rated output matches the design output of the radiators.)

Gas fire

A recent innovation is the balanced-flue gas fire. This is easy to install (no chimney!) and passably efficient (about 70%).

Chain drill an aperture for the flue, as described previously for the boiler.

Take the gas supply to the fire in 15 mm copper pipe (no plastic pipe here!). Where the pipework is exposed as it enters the fire, use better looking 8 mm chromium-plated pipe.

Commissioning the gas supply

Leaks in the system are tested for at the meter. This has a special connection to allow a glass U-tube containing water to be connected to the gas supply. The difference in water level in the two tubes gives the gas pressure. The test pressure is equal to the pressure of a 30 cm column of water. Allow a minute for temperature settlement. There should be no loss of pressure over the next two minutes.

The ownhander is unlikely to have this equipment. Leave the test either to British Gas when they connect the supply, or to an obliging gas fitter.

The pipework needs to be purged of the initial air/gas mixture that is formed when gas is first let into the pipework – the mixture could be explosive. Open windows, extinguish lights, and don't operate an electric switch (which might spark). Turn on the gas appliance furthest from the meter and let plenty of gas escape. When the air has cleared, test that the flame is normal.

14

SECOND FIX ELECTRICS

☆

☆

☆

☆

☆

☆

☆

THIS IS STRAIGHTFORWARD work and requires little skill. The brain-work has already been done, and now it's just a matter of making the connections. Having said that, sometimes there are a lot of wires to be crammed into a small space, and the work can be fiddly.

It should hardly be necessary to mention, but in a two-core-and-earth cable, the red wire is taken as the live, the black as the neutral, and the bare wire is the earth. Wherever earth wire is exposed, as happens inside sockets, roses, etc, it is good practice to slip a green/yellow plastic sleeve over it. (Lengths of this can be purchased.)

In the first fix, the boxes for sockets and switches were installed on the blockwork walls, but this was not possible on the studwork. Instead, with the plasterboard in place, it can be done now. At the required positions, simply cut rectangular holes in the plasterboard (if this wasn't done whilst boarding). Use plasterboard boxes. These have sprung lugs to hold them to the board. If you haven't used foresight, you may have to fish around to find the cable within the studwork.

For making the connections in a box, the outer PVC sheath of the cable needs to be stripped back to leave wires of suitable length. (There is a trick for doing this. With a Stanley knife, cut a short way down the end of the cable to expose the earth wire. Grip this with pliers and pull it back down the cable, thereby cutting through the sheathing.) The ends of the wires can be bared with wire strippers, of which there are many designs. The length of insulation to strip off needs care – enough to make sure that the terminal screw grips copper and not plastic, but not so much that bare wire is left exposed.

Power circuits

Connecting the face plates in a ring circuit is simple. At most sockets there will be just a pair of cables. Connect the two red live wires to the 'L' terminal, the two black neutrals to the 'N' terminal and the two earths to the 'E'. That's easy enough. At a spur from a box, there will be three cables, and then the physical manipulation of the cable becomes more trying, unless a deeper box has been fitted.

Screw the plates into the lugs in the box. One of the lugs is movable to allow the plate to be fixed level. (If the plaster is rather thick, the bolts might not be long enough; extra-long ones are obtainable.)

Switched sockets are more convenient than unswitched, and little more expensive. Neon indicators are useful when it's not immediately apparent whether an appliance is working or not.

Light circuits

At first sight, connections at a light rose seem bewildering. But a little thought can soon bring order. Typically, there are three cables into the rose: one bringing the power in, one looping onto the next rose, and the third going off to a switch.

To start with, all the earths can go to the earth terminal. It is important to realise that, though an earth connection in a plastic rose may seem ineffective, the connections should be made to maintain a continuous earth – other lights in the circuit may use metal fittings.

All the red wires can be connected at the 'loop' connection block, which has three terminals: one for the live wire looping in, one for the live wire looping on to the next rose (if any), and one for the live wire running to the switch.

The two black wires of the looping cables go into the neutral block. The third black wire, which returns a switched live from the switch, goes to the switch block, with just two terminals. Some people flag this wire with red tape.

The flex to the lamp-holder is two-core 0·5 mm² flex. Connect its brown wire to the switch block, and the blue to the neutral block. There are two lugs over which the wires should be twisted to support the weight of the lamp.

At a rose where the circuit branches, there will be another cable; some terminals will have to take a pair of wires.

For wall lights, there will be cables sticking out from the wall. Insulate their ends if the lights are not yet being fitted.

Most light switches are one-way switches. But for two-way switching you will need two-way switches! These have three terminals: The common terminal is switched to either terminal 1 or 2. The strap connects corresponding terminals at the two switches. (See Fig. 6, Chapter 23.)

Two-gang switches, for operating two separate lights, are always made as two-way. For one-way use, just ignore the L1 terminals.

Other circuits

Fixing the cooker control switch is straightforward provided that you have put in a deep enough box. At the cooker outlet below, the cooker itself can be connected if it is on site.

From the immersion heater switch (double-pole, with 20 amp fuse and neon indicator), a special, heat-resistant 2·5 mm^2 flex runs to the immersion heater. The live, in fact, goes to the thermostat (which acts as a switch), and then on to the heating element. You will probably want a time controller in the circuit.

If there is a shaving socket to be connected, note that the expensive ones contain a transformer and are for use in bathrooms. Cheaper ones can only be used elsewhere.

Making all the right connections for the central heating system is tricky. A ten-way junction box with associated instructions makes the job simpler, and a wiring centre even easier. But if, when you come to test the system, you find that it is not functioning properly – check your wiring before suspecting a faulty component.

If the consumer unit is not already in place, fix it now. Leave a pair of 16 mm^2 tails and a length of 10 mm^2 earth cable for the Electricity Company to connect at the meter box. (If need be, these cables can run inside the cavity wall, but no other cables or pipes should do so.) The fuseways will need fuses or MCB's rated according to the type of circuit connected.

Earth bonding

The earth conductors are connected to pipes with earth clamps. (Clean the pipes first with wire wool.) The main conductors (10 mm^2) are connected at the earth block in the meter box (or possibly in the consumer unit).

In the bathroom, all the metal parts must be connected together with supplementary bonding (use 4 mm^2 or 6 mm^2 earth cable). This involves the pipework for the hot and cold taps and the radiator, etc.

(See 'Bonding', Chapter 10, for methods of earthing.)

In the kitchen you may also want to cross-bond the hot pipework and the sink to the rising main (which is earthed by main bonding).

Testing

Before the Electricity Company will connect their supply, your circuits need to be tested by a competent electrician; the Company require a signed test certificate.

However, the ownhander can do some preliminary testing with a piece of inexpensive equipment: a universal test meter, of the sort that is sold in motorists stores for a few pounds. (The leads will need to be considerably extended.)

Continuity test

Working round each circuit, check that there is zero resistance between the live terminals of pairs of sockets around the circuit, ie, the terminals are connected together. Include the consumer unit in the test, and repeat the procedure for the neutral terminals. Make sure that single-pole switches break the live phase, not the neutral.

Polarity test

This involves checking that the live and neutral have been connected the right way round in the sockets. It is checked whilst doing the above test.

Earth test

The resistance in the earth circuit between any socket and the earth block in the consumer unit should be less than one ohm. Check that this is so, especially for sockets remote from the consumer unit.

Insulation test

Between live and earth:

Disconnect the neutral at the consumer unit. Measure the resistance between the live and earth at the unit. It should be more than 1 Mohm (ie, a million ohms).

Between live and neutral:

Remove any appliances or lamps in the circuit, and turn switches to 'on'. Measure the resistance between the live and neutral at the consumer unit. Again, it should be greater than 1 Mohm.

It must be stressed that these are only crude, preliminary tests. Proper testing uses 500 volts from a 'Megger' insulation and continuity tester, whereas a universal meter is only using 1·5 volts. At the higher voltage, the resistances may break down – which is what could happen when the mains voltage is applied.

Nonetheless, the preliminary testing may indicate faults. To locate these, examine a section of the circuit at a time. (Disconnect the rest of the circuit).

Connection of supply

The Electricity Company require a signed test certificate, as mentioned above. They will then put in a supply in two stages. First, a team lays the service cable to your meter box, and then, several days later, the meter is connected. With the paperwork, it takes a few weeks to get a supply installed.

Telecom extensions

British Telecom's cable terminates at the master socket. So that the company can test their line if a fault arises, they require that any extensions can be disconnected at this socket. (They sell a master socket that allows this to be done.) Elsewhere, connect slave sockets.

There's a plastic gadget (sold for 50p) for making the connections. Use it to push a wire into its terminal so that the insulation is cut and the wire is gripped. At corresponding terminals, the wires should be the same colour, eg: 2 – orange; 3 – green; 4 – black; 5 – white; (1 and 6 not in use).

15

SECOND FIX CARPENTRY

Architrave
Skirting
Doors
Sizes
Hanging
External doors
Door furniture
Stair and landing banisters
Cladding
Miscellaneous

Architrave

Architrave is the moulding which is fixed round a door lining to hide the joint with the plaster. With architrave and skirting, the selfbuilder can save time overall by painting it in long lengths with one or two coats before cutting and fixing it. A lot of mitres will have to be cut, and for this you need a mitre box. (See Fig. 8, Chapter 24.)

Firstly, mark a margin (say 4 mm wide) round the lining, to give the position of the inner edge of the architrave. (It's worth making up a little template for doing this.) Start fixing the architrave with an upright. Mark its 'short' length to suit the margin at the head. (In case you've never noticed before – the thick edge of the architrave goes on the outside to butt up to the skirting.) Cut the mitre with care; then nail the upright in position with small ovals.

The head is next. First cut a mitre to fit to the upright. Then mark and cut a mitre on the other end. When cutting mitres, great care is needed to get them the right way round. And even with care, you'll find that some come out wrong! Fix the head, and then finish with the second upright.

Skirting

Is skirting necessary? In days of old, walls were panelled to keep out draughts blowing through the crude walls. Over the course of time, panelling was reduced to wainscoting; then to the high, kick-proof skirting of Victorian times; and then to the minimal skirting prevalent today. Its main function nowadays seems to be to protect walls from vacuum cleaners – the wall/floor joint is covered by fitted carpet. (If you do wish to do without skirting, this must be allowed for when plastering – make a good finish right down to the floor.)

Anyway, here is how to fix skirting:

Mitres are again involved, but this time across the thickness of the timber, not its width as with architrave. An ownhander can cut the mitres accurately with a circular saw. Some board ends are mitred, some cut square, and some are scribed. (See 'Mitring' and 'Scribing', Chapter 24.)

If there are any external corners, the skirting boards are simply mitred.

At internal corners, one board is butted up to the wall, and the other is scribed over it. Which board to put over which? In general, when viewing from the doorway, the eye should not see into a joint. (See Fig. 1.)

Figure 1: Joints for skirting board

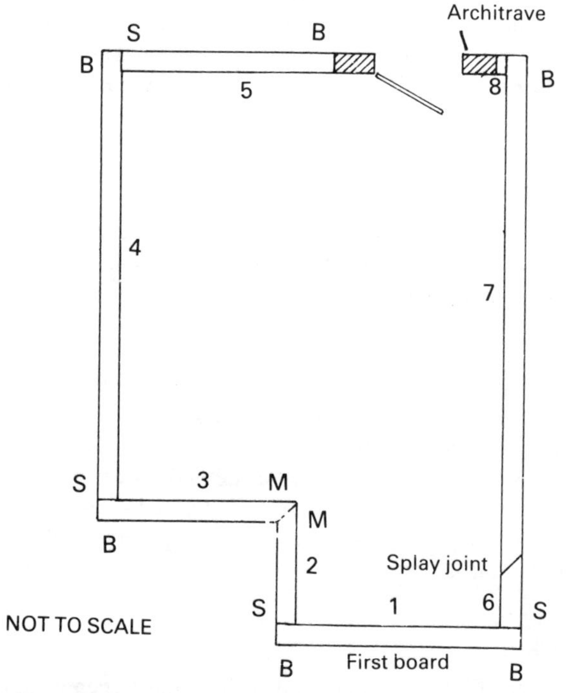

Joints: B - butt S - scribed M - mitred

* Start opposite doorway – with board (1) butt jointed at both ends.
* Progress round to doorway in order shown.
* Use a splay joint if boards are not long enough.

Another advice is that any board should be scribed at one end only, not both. (Scribe it first, and then cut the other end to length.) Where lengths need to be joined, use a splay joint. (See 'Splay joint', Chapter 24.)

The first piece of skirting should be fixed opposite the doorway. Then work round the room, as in the example in Figure 1.

When fixing the skirting to the wall, use a kneeling board to force a tight fit to the floor – rest a short board from the top of the skirting to the floor and kneel on it. (In fact, for a quality job, the skirting should be scribed to the floor. However, a small gap is acceptable if it will be hidden later by the floor covering.) Skew nail the skirting board with cut nails (to blockwork) or ovals (to studwork).

Doors

Sizes

Metric external doors: In a new house, invariably metric doors and frames are fitted (to suit the metric brick coursing). The common size for the door is 80·6 × 199·4 cm (and 4·4 cm thick). The format size for the frame is 90 × 210 cm, but its actual size is $\frac{1}{2}$ cm less both in height and width to allow for building in. British Standards allow a clearance between the door and frame of only $1\frac{1}{2}$ mm all the way round. When fitting the door, plane it down to double this clearance – to allow for swelling in damp weather.

Metric internal doors: These are unpopular, supposedly on the grounds that they are too high, leaving only a mean margin of wall above the door opening.

The door is narrower than the imperial size (though wider ones are available at 10 cm increments): 72·6 × 204 cm (and 4 cm thick). The format size for the opening is 80 × 210 cm, but the actual size of the lining is 1 cm less both in height and width. (See Figs. 7 and 8, Chapter 11.) A clearance of 2 mm is allowed at each side and the top; and at the bottom 18 mm is allowed for the carpet or threshold strip. (The latter is a strip of wood, as wide as the lining, fixed to the floor beneath the door.)

Imperial internal doors: These are more popular and more widely available. The usual door size is 2′ 6″ × 6′ 6″, and $1\frac{3}{8}$″ thick (76·2 × 198·1 × 3·5 cm). The actual size of the lining is 2′ $8\frac{1}{2}$″ × 6′ $7\frac{7}{8}$″ (82·5 × 202·9 cm). This allows a clearance of $\frac{1}{16}$″ ($1\frac{1}{2}$ mm) at the head of the door and each side, and $\frac{3}{4}$″ (19 mm) at the bottom.

Note that, for good looks, the clearances are the same at the head and at each side of the door.

Hanging

How simple a door hanging on a pair of hinges seems! Yet as the ownhander may discover, there are so many little ways in which the hanging of a door can go wrong. At this stage, we are dealing with internal doors. The sizes are as indicated above, but for cloakrooms, airing cupboards, etc, narrower doors are available.

Internal doors are usually light in weight – which is not good for sound insulation. They are often a veneered panel on a flimsy framework. There may be a wooden block to take the latch on one side only. This fact can't be seen, but if it is the case, the penny-pinching manufacturer will have marked the edge in some way – for example, 'H' (hinge) stamped on one edge, and 'L' (latch) on the other. Note these marks before you plane them off!

The hanging jamb will have been determined already, before the light switches were put in. (See 'Doors', Chapter 19.)

Firstly, the door has to be made to fit the opening. If the door has projecting horns, cut these off carefully with a square cut. Check the hanging edge by placing it up against its jamb. With good fortune, the jamb will be straight and no planing will be necessary. But it's quite possible that you will have to scribe the door edge to the profile of the jamb. (See 'Scribing', Chapter 24.) To support the door for planing, a Workmate is useful: Balance the door on edge on the floor and grip one end of it in the jaws of the Workmate.

Next, at the top and bottom and at a couple of intermediate heights, measure the width(s) of the opening. Reduce by 4 mm, and transfer the distances across to the closing edge of the door. Join up the marks with the line to which to plane. (Note that the edge lippings on a modern door are not very thick, about 1 cm. If more than this has to come off, then some of the width should be reduced on the hinged edge instead.)

The door should fit into the opening with an even 2 mm gap each side. When satisfied with this, plane down the leading edge with a very slight bevel so that the edge will clear the jamb when opened. When you are satisfied with each edge, lightly plane off the arrises.

Figure 2: Marking out hinge recess in rebated lining

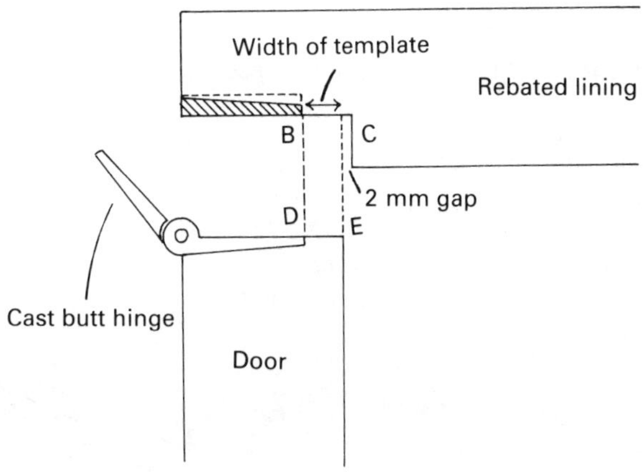

* Diagram shows a cast hinge – the leaves are tapered. The centre of the pin is in line with the face of the door.
* For the lining, make a template of width BC, where BC = DE + 2 mm. Use the template to mark out the recess.
* The recess may be either uniform in depth (easier) or tapered (neater).

Place the door in the opening and check the fit at the head – lift the door up on a couple of wedges. Again, there should be an even 2 mm gap (the thickness of a twopenny piece). If not, scribe and plane accordingly. (This is awkward. Straddle the door at an end and plane downwards; then turn the door over for the other half.) The gap at the bottom of the door needs to be $1\frac{1}{2}$ cm to 2 cm to allow for the floor covering. Cut as required. A circular saw may be useful, but keep a straight line – imperfections will be visible. Wedge the door into the opening to check the final fit.

Now to fit the hinges. Stand the door in the Workmate, and on the hanging edge mark the positions for the hinges, eg, 15 cm down from the top and 22 cm up from the bottom. (The different distances are said to look optically equal.)

There are two sorts of butt hinges: pressed steel and cast brass. Cast hinges, which have slightly tapered leaves, look neater as half the knuckle is hidden in the joint. (The cheaper pressed hinges have to be fixed with all the knuckle exposed.) For internal doors, a pair of $7\frac{1}{2}$ cm cast hinges will suffice.

The following description assumes cast hinges and a rebated door lining:

To mark the housings for the hinges on the door, hold a hinge in position on the door and mark its ends. Set a marking gauge to the width of the hinge leaf (to the centre of the knuckle), and mark the width of the housing. (See Fig. 2.)

Cut this line quite deep, either with the marking gauge, or with a chisel held against a steel rule. (Try not to overshoot!) Then set the gauge to the radius of the knuckle less half the clearance gap (eg, 4 – 2/2 = 3 mm), and mark the depth of the housing.

To cut out the housing, use a $2\frac{1}{2}$ cm chisel. Make square cuts at each end, then a series of slanted cuts. (See Fig. 3).

Figure 3: Chopping out hinge recess

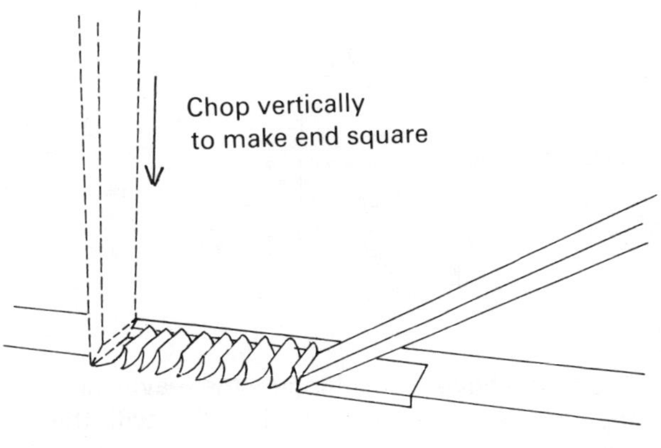

The waste can be pared out, working from the face of the door. Note that the seat of the housing can be squared off (easier) or inclined (so that the tapered hinge leaf finishes flush at the surface).

Screw the hinges into the housings.

Now wedge the door back into the opening, with some 2 mm packing at the head. Transfer the positions of the hinges from the door across to the jamb.

The depth of the housing on the jamb is marked as for the door. Marking the width is more involved. The aim is to achieve a clearance of 2 mm between the back of the door and the rebate. On the edge of the door, measure the margin at the side of a hinge. Add 2 mm and cut out a small template (eg, in ply) to this width. (See Fig. 2.) Holding the template against the side of the rebate, mark the line for the housing with a chisel. (Keep the template for hanging other doors.)

Cut out the housings on the jamb, and offer the door up, holding it square to the opening. Hopefully, the hinges will fit into the housings; secure them with just one screw each. Does the door still fit nicely into the opening? If the housings are too deep, they can be packed out up with cardboard – not a first class job but it does work. Check that the door hangs neutrally. If it tends to swing outwards, the upper hinge is forward of the lower, and *vice versa*. If the door resists closing, it may be binding against the rebate. Altogether, there are many points to watch out for, and adjustments may be necessary. Which is why the hinges have been secured with only one screw each. When satisfied, you can screw in the full complement.

A professional hangs an internal door in about an hour. Your first one may take half a day. Or perhaps you have chosen the easy way and used pre-hung door sets?

External doors

External doors are liable to swell if they becomes damp, so they need a larger clearance gap, 3 mm, at the top and sides. They are also liable to warp; prevent this with a third hinge half-way up. (By the way, some people also use a third hinge on airing cupboard doors.) Hang the door in the normal way, and then add the extra hinge. The doors are thicker and heavier than internal ones, so use 10 cm hinges.

For inward opening doors, a metal water bar is set across the bottom of the frame. To accommodate this, the bottom of the door needs to be rebated; a circular saw is ideal for this.

Doors in an exposed position need a weather bar along the bottom edge to prevent water being blown inside. (A weather bar is also called a 'weather board' or 'door drip'.) The moulded bar can be purchased from a timber merchant cut to your required length. Three stout screws will fix it; but to reduce their length, counterbore wide holes for their heads. Just before fixing, paint the back face of the bar with varnish, or smear mastic along its top edge. This will keep the joint watertight.

Garage doors are invariably proprietary, up-and-over doors. Fitting instructions come with them, but it is a fiddly job that can take several hours.

Door Furniture

Internal doors are generally held shut with mortise latches operated by lever handles or knobs. (With knobs, longer latches should be used if people are not to catch their knuckles on the door lining.) The usual position is halfway up the stile. The latch can be fitted *in situ* by jamming the door steady with wedges. Or the door can be taken down (again!) and held in a Workmate. A tubular latch fits into a deep mortise in the stile. Mark the position for this on the edge, and with brace and bit, bore some deep holes to take out most of the wood. Then chop the mortise out with chisel and mallet. Cut out a shallow recess for the plate. On the face and back of the door, mark the position for the spindle, and drill through from each side. Fit the latch, (re-hang the door,) and transfer the position of the bolt over onto the jamb. Chop out a hole to receive the bolt. Fitting the striking plate is straightforward.

A back door usually has a mortise lock, fitted in a similar way to a mortise latch. A front door usually has a cylinder rim latch – though this is sometimes called a lock. Is there a difference between a lock and a latch? The terminology is a little fuzzy, but it goes something like this:

A latch has a sprung bolt. The bolt is automatically engaged by the spring; it may be retracted by a handle or a key. In the later case, the latch is sometimes called a lock, as a lock has a bolt which is worked by a key. Latches are commonly used for internal doors.

Most locks have a dead bolt – this needs a key to both engage and retract it. The better types of cylinder rim latches can be deadlocked both from the inside and the outside – the bolt cannot be forced back against the spring. Some locks contain both sorts of bolts: a latch for convenience and a deadlock for security (eg, a typical mortise lock for a back door).

Both latches and locks may be of the mortise variety (fitting inside a mortise within the stile of a door), or of the rim type (fitting on the face of the door, eg, a 'Yale' lock).

Most people want to be able to lock the door of a WC or bathroom. In an emergency, it may be necessary to open the door from the outside – Continental-style knob sets allow this to be done. (There's a hole in the knob through which a knitting needle can be pushed to releases the locking mechanism.)

The front door will need a rim latch (lock), preferably one that can be deadlocked by the key. Such a lock is simple to fit if you have a hole saw for an electric drill. (Instructions come with the lock.)

The letter flap is also simple enough:

Mark a rectangle for the slot. At each corner, drill a fairly wide hole to touch the rectangle along two lines. Cut along the lines between the holes with a jig or pad saw.

Take care that the holes and saw cuts are square to the door surface.

Stair and landing banisters

'Banisters' is a householder's word for balusters and handrail. It has a connection, believe it or not, with wild pomegranates. 'Banister' is a corruption of 'baluster', which came come from the French 'balustre'; which came from the Italian 'balausta', which came from the Latin 'balaustium', which came from the Greek 'balaustion' – meaning a wild pomegranate flower. The connection lies in the shape of the calyx tube of the flower, which, like a classical baluster, is pear-shaped at the bottom with a slender stem above.

Anyway, banisters now come in DIY kit form. Instructions for assembly come with the kit. (It is quicker overall to stain and varnish the pieces before assembly.) Briefly:

The newel bases will already be in position as integral parts of the staircase. A newel post is fitted into its base by forcing it onto an upright dowel inside a large socket in the base. The handrail is fixed to the newel with a special metal bracket. More traditionally, a draw-pinned mortise and tenon joint is used. (See 'Draw-pinning', Chapter 24.)

The balusters (or 'spindles') are contained by grooves in the handrail and base rail. Their positions are fixed at regular intervals by fillets pinned between them in the grooves. Centralise the spindles in the run by making the first and last gaps equal.

For the balustrade on the landing, the base rail may need support – screw a bearer to the side of the joist. The end of a balustrade is finished with a half-newel (ie, a newel sliced down its length) screwed to the wall.

Nice as a balustrade looks to many eyes, all the turned wood is expensive. But you don't have to use spindles. The space can be simply and cheaply blocked in. This may not be in fashion at the moment, but it was, and doubtless will be again.

(For example, the author knows some banisters that have had an interesting history. The house was built in the 1930's, when softwood could only be painted over – it was considered too inferior to be varnished. So the balusters were painted white. But in the 1950's, streamlining came into vogue. The dust-catching balusters were boxed in with hardboard. Then, in the 1980's, 'pine' became fashionable. The hardboard was removed, the white paint laboriously stripped, and the balusters stained and varnished. They do look attractive, but what will another generation do to them?)

Where a staircase is enclosed between two walls, a separate handrail should be fitted – 90 cm above the pitch line through the nosing of the steps.

Cladding

Walls can be covered very pleasingly with timber cladding (eg, V-jointed matching in knotty pine). And it saves plastering the walls.

It's a fairly simple job. Nail some rows of horizontal battening (eg, 2 × 3 cm) to the blockwork – a row near the top and the bottom, and a couple in between. For a neat job, make sure the battens are plumb over each other, especially at the corners – use packing if necessary.

A suitable thickness is 13 mm. Don't naively start the cladding with a whole board in one corner – you may end up with a silly thin strip at the other. Rather, think of the two positions for symmetry, and choose the one with a wide board at each corner. (See 'Symmetry', Chapter 27.) (Remember, the effective width of the board does not include the tongue.) If there is a doorway or window, consider also how the boards will fit round this.

Rip the first board down to the required width, removing the groove. Fix the board in the corner, plumb, with panel pins skew through the tongue. (A pin-push is a great help.) The first board may need pins down its other side, as well. Then carry on fixing additional boards; occasionally check their plumbness. If necessaary, to tighten a joint put a grooved off-cut over the tongue and hit with a mallet.

(External corners are a little trickier – see DIY books for techniques.)

Miscellaneous

There is a variety of miscellaneous work for the carpenter: shelves for an airing cupboard, and fitted cupboards for the kitchen, utility room and, perhaps, bedroom. ('Cupboard' hardly seems an appropriate word for a bedroom fitting, but 'unit' is a very overworked word.)

The standard height for the top of a kitchen worktop is 90 cm. This is level with cooker hobs, and allows other appliances to fit underneath. Adjacent cupboards are best set on one continuous plinth (not several) to keep them all in line.

16
DECORATING

☆

☆

☆

☆

☆

☆

☆

Exterior painting
Interior painting:
Ceiling and walls
Interior woodwork
Decoration
Rag rolling
Stippling
Spattering
Stencilling
Carpet printing
Colour mixing

DECORATING is the most popular of DIY activities, and the one where most selfbuilders feel most confident. So little space is taken in this book to explain the basics.

However, no less skill is required for decorating than for the other trades. As much know-how is required to paint as to plaster. The main reason that most people can do the one and not the other is that redecorating is required much more frequently than replastering. Homeowners get plenty of practice at it. This throws an encouraging light on the other skills: They present the ownhander with no more inherent difficulty than decorating. (Or is that over-stating the case?)

Exterior painting

Timber is a most useful material, but it is has one particular weakness. It has a tendency to rot – especially in the British climate. Some sort of surface treatment is required to keep out damp. Traditionally, a gloss paint has been used – a mixture of pigment, resin binder, and solvent. When the paint is applied, the solvent evaporates, and the resin binder oxidises with the air to give a solid film. This keeps water out. Unfortunately, it also keeps water in, should cracks in old paintwork allow the timber to become damp. So modern technology has produced permeable paints, ('microporous' in the jargon). These allow the timber to 'breathe'.

Besides dampness, timber is susceptible to another, very different, foe: sunlight. The ultra-violet of sunlight attacks and decomposes wood. To protect against this, a paint needs to be pigmented. The ultra-violet is then absorbed at the surface, without penetrating the wood. The result of some fresh thinking from Scandinavia is a host of new 'paints', or wood finishes, incorporating the two features mentioned above. There's a bewildering variety of types, and a confusion of names. It will be interesting to see how the language settles down, but at present, the terminology is in a state of flux. Some people, for example, might consider a microporous, pigmented preservative to be a 'paint', others might not. We shall see. Anyway, in this book, the term 'stain-paint' refers to the new paints, and the word 'paint' is used in a very broad sense.

You should take the opportunity with new joinery to use the new permeable paints, rather than the old sealer, or gloss, paints. They are much quicker and easier to put on, and the timber should suffer less if the paintwork is neglected in future years. The stain-paints are mostly available in shades of brown, but black, red, green, blue, and even white are also available.

If you followed advice earlier in the book, you will have ordered door and window frames pre-treated with a base coat; and before installing them you will have given them one or two coats of stain-paint. Now they should have one or two coats more.

Most garage doors are pressed steel and are usually painted in conventional gloss. 'Hammerite' metal paint is quicker, lasts longer, and the mottled colours are more subtle. The big expanse of the door can easily be broken up by first painting any indented ribbing in another colour.

Interior painting:
Ceiling and walls

Plastered walls are dry enough to paint when their colour has turned from pink (or grey) to something like white. This may take a week or fortnight, depending upon the weather. Plastered blockwork takes half a year, or more, to really dry out: It should not be papered during this time.

Textured ceilings don't need painting, but some people like a silk emulsion to show off the texturing. (If a ceiling is to be painted, it should, of course, be painted before the walls – even professionals cause some drips.)

Don't waste time with silly 7″ rollers from DIY stores. Going up to 9″ makes all the difference. Indeed, some people use 12″, but these are more for outdoor work. An adjustable, extending handle is very useful. Use a short-pile mohair roller – long piles are for heavily textured surfaces. Washing out a roller at the end of the day is a messy business. Instead, it can be kept overnight by simply wrapping it up in a plastic carrier bag. (Paint brushes, too, can be conveniently kept overnight in a similar way, wrapping a plastic bag around the bristles.)

The first coat of paint on plaster can be very dilute (2:1 of paint and water) – to seal it rather than colour it. Then apply two coats of good quality emulsion. 'Bargain Offers' of cheap paint will probably waste your time, their poor covering power necessitating an extra coat. Buy your paint where the professionals do, from decorators' merchants. But don't use the very top quality emulsions. These produce a rather impermeable plastic film, which impedes the drying out process and which might eventually lift off.

Painting over the stairwell can be a little tricky. (It's easier to do this before the balusters are put in place.) It's probably a matter of supporting a plank on the rung of a ladder, as described under 'Boarding ceilings', Chapter 12.

As a matter of interest, in emulsion paints the binder is not dissolved in a solvent, but is emulsified in water. As the water evaporates, the globules coalesce to form a film. The type of binder used, which sticks the pigments together and to the surface, is often given as a description of the paint eg, 'vinyl' or 'acrylic'. ('Alkyd' or 'polyurethane' are binders for solvent paints.) Fillers such as chalk are used in emulsions. An excessive amount may be used in cheap emulsions, resulting in poor covering power. Some paints have additives to produce particular qualities, eg, easy brushing. Lastly, while we're looking at the composition of paints, the surface appearance of the finish – matt, silk or gloss – depends upon the ratio of pigment to binder. Matt paints have more pigment, and so tend to have more covering power. Gloss paints have more resin binder, and so are stronger.

Interior woodwork

In the past, hardwoods were often varnished, but the appearance of softwoods was considered to be inferior, and so they were painted. Now the fashion has changed, and at the time of writing, at least, stripped pine is 'in'. If this is your preference, then window frames, for example, can be varnished rather than painted. Varnishing may not only look better – it is quicker and easier.

Whether it is to be varnished or painted, woodwork needs to be prepared. Punch nail heads below the surface, and fill the holes with stopper. (If to be varnished, match the colour of the wood.) Sand down if necessary.

To varnish, first apply a sealing coat of polyurethane diluted with 10% white spirit. Loose fibres in the surface swell, so sand smooth when dry. Then apply a couple more coats of polyurethane, sanding in between. The smoothest finish can be obtained by rubbing the polyurethane in with a cloth, rather than with a brush.

The traditional gloss treatment uses primer, undercoat and topcoat, but some new paint types dispense with this and just use one paint – very convenient. Selfbuilders can make life easier for themselves by painting architrave and skirting with one or two coats while it is still in long lengths (ie, before fitting it). This is quickly and easily done.

Decoration

Outside, the main purpose of paint is to protect timber. Inside, it is to produce a smooth surface for cleanliness, and to reflect light. But there's also a whole complex of psychological effects, involving colours, patterns, fashion, and the like.

Several old, almost extinct painting techniques have been rediscovered and popularised. They can be used to produce the visual richness we seem to want around us. They are highly suitable for the selfbuilder. The materials cost little, the 'tools' even less; no great skills are required, just some creative imagination. Details of the methods can be found in many books. Here are brief outlines of some of the techniques. They are generally used for decorating walls, but they can also be used on doors, cupboards, etc.

The techniques are all applied to a dry base coat. (It's best to practise first on a spare surface.)

Rag rolling

Except that it's messy on the hands, this is an ideal DIY technique. Paint is cheap, rags are free, and the skill can be learnt in minutes. Yet the effects are most pleasing, and capable of wide variations.

Select a rag – the type of cloth will govern the effect. (A square metre of an old sheet is fine.) Dip the rag lightly into a tray of paint (whose colour compliments or contrasts with the base colour). Crumple up the rag, and form it into a 'sausage' held in both hands. Starting at the bottom of the wall, roll this up to the ceiling. The imprint of the creases will be left on the wall. Re-shape the sausage and roll up another band alongside the first. Let the bands weave about, rather than be straight. Recharge the rag with paint as needed. And if the rag becomes too limp, change to a fresh one.

You'll be delighted with the effect.

Rag rolling can also be done in an inverse way. Apply a band of wet paint to the wall, and then roll up it a fresh rag. This time, the rag sausage takes the paint off. Re-make the sausage for each band, and again, take a new rag occasionally. This is a good job to do in pairs, one person applying paint just ahead of another rolling it off.

Stippling

A subtle stipple can be obtained with a sea sponge. First, moisten it with water, then charge it with a paint darker than the background. Remove the excess paint by dabbing onto scrap paper. Then lightly dab the sponge onto the wall to give a mottled effect.

A more pronounced stipple is obtained with a rag. Crumple up a rag into a ball; charge it with paint and remove the surplus; then lightly dab onto the wall. Shield the ceiling above the wall with a piece of stiff card.

As with rag rolling, stippling can also be done by removing paint. Use a dark emulsion paint, diluted with an equal amount of water. Paint on a band about half a metre wide, and stipple it with a plastic bag containing some rag. Overlap the dabs to give a crinkled effect. Wipe the surplus off the bag as required. This technique is sometimes called 'bag graining'.

Spattering

This is an effect similar to that sometimes found in public lavatories. Don't let that put you off!

Slightly dilute an oil paint with white spirit. Use a brush with stiff bristles, such as a banister brush. Dip the tips of the bristles into the paint, hold the brush about 10 cm from the wall, and draw a ruler back across the bristles. As the bristles are released, droplets of paint are flicked onto the wall. This can be done with either an even or a haphazard coverage.

The rolling, stippling and spattering effects can all be made richer by adding further colours (once the previous colour has dried, of course).

Stencilling

Stencilling can be used to give repetitive patterns or individual motifs. It is not a new idea to stencil walls: It was done in Europe a couple of centuries ago, and in Egypt in ancient times.

The spacing of the patterns can be adjusted to fit the dimensions of the wall. This is preferable to the way that wallpaper patterns are arbitrarily cut off at a corner.

Precut stencils can be purchased; or you can cut out your own in stencil paper from an artists' shop.

To position the stencil, lightly mark out the wall with grid points to suit the pattern. Position the stencil on the wall with pieces of masking tape. The paint is stippled on with a stencil brush (which has short bristles). Dip the tips of the bristles in a little pool of paint on a board, and remove the excess by dabbing onto waste paper. Then stipple the stencil, working from the edge inwards. The colour can be varied from one stencil position to the next, from one cut-out to another, or even shaded within a single cut-out.

The possibilities are enormous. Try some out.

Carpet printing

Carpet printing is akin to the potato printing that children do. (The author had thought he'd invented the technique until a friend from Canada told him that it was practised there. Once again – nothing new under the sun?)

The technique produces a simpler pattern than stencilling, but the texture of the carpet pile gives a lively result.

Cut out a shape from some waste carpet, and stick it onto a flat backing – a small piece of ply with a handle at the back is ideal. (See Fig. 1.)

Figure 1: Carpet die

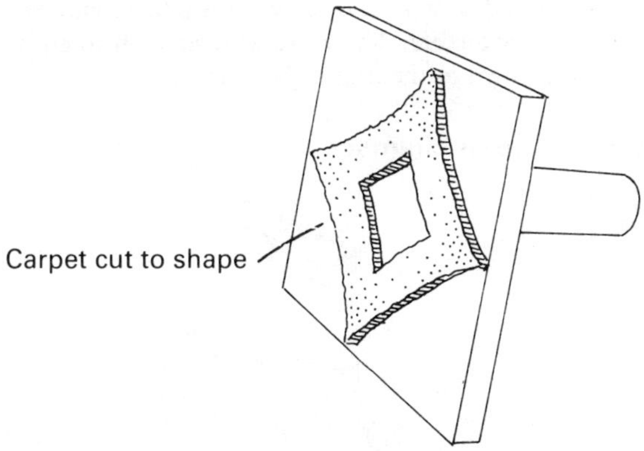

* The texture of the carpet affects the print.

Mark out a guide grid on the wall, as for stencilling. (You don't need a mark for every position of the pattern. Filling in some positions by eye is quicker and it produces a lively, spontaneous result.) Take the carpet 'die' and dab it into a pool of paint. Remove the surplus and lightly dab it onto the wall. (See Fig. 2.)

Once again, you don't have to stick to one colour. Nor to one die – a complex pattern can be built up from a few dies. Once the dies are made, large areas can be patterned quickly.

Figure 2: Carpet printing

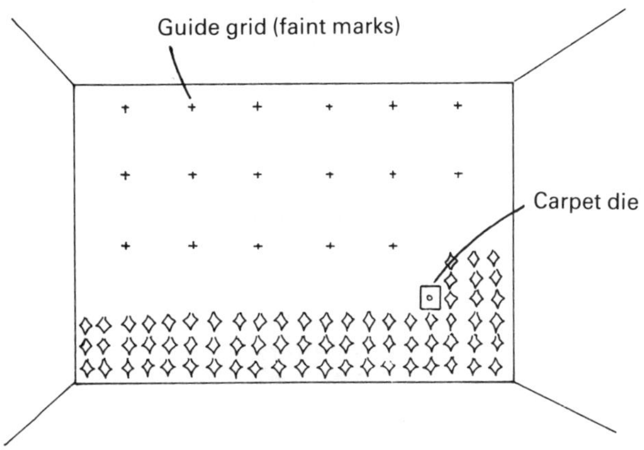

* Wet the carpet die with paint and press it onto the wall.
* Colour of the paint can be varied.
* Use two or more dies for elaborate patterns.

Colour mixing

A couple of generations ago, painters mixed up their own colours. And before that, people made up their own paints – 'Suffolk Pink', the traditional finish for houses in that county, was made from buttermilk and pigs' blood! Nowadays, of course, paints come straight from the tin. But it is cheaper and more fun to make your own pastel shades of emulsion. White and magnolia (the latter for mellower colours) can be obtained cheaply in large quantities. Colour them with a stainer from a decorators' merchant, or a strongly coloured emulsion. (For future colour matching, keep a small jar of the liquid paint. With a liquid paint you can get a perfect match, but this is difficult once the paint has dried – it becomes darker. And don't let artistic inclinations lead you to add a second stainer – matching then becomes very difficult.)

Lastly, here is one other offbeat idea. Usually, radiators and the like are painted in gloss paint. Instead, paint them in emulsion – matching the walls, for example. Then, to give a hard finish, paint them over with clear polyurethane.

17

DRAINS

☆

☆

☆

☆

☆

☆

☆

Design
Laying
Clay pipes
Plastic pipes
Inspection chambers
Manholes
Testing drains
Soakaways
Septic tank
Cesspool

USUALLY THE DRAINS are laid after the shell has been completed, though they can be laid at an earlier stage – even as early as the foundations. There is a good deal of latitude in the timing: Choose a time when the weather and the flow of work make it convenient. The main point is to put them in when there is no longer a call for heavy lorries to cross the site. The weight of a lorry could damage a drain; or its wheels could sink into the soft backfill of the trench and the lorry be trapped. On the other hand, you may not want to leave installation too long – with the drains in place you can connect a WC. Anyway, once started, hurry the work along. As with the foundations, open trenches tend to fill with water and may even collapse.

There is no great skill or special know-how required for this work. Although most selfbuilders will not have done any drain laying, they should find it easy enough. Modern drains, whether clay or plastic, simply fit together with push-fit couplings. The manufacturers produce well-illustrated technical brochures which are very helpful.

Design

The layout for the drainage system will already have been submitted for Building Regulations approval. The layout will depend upon the availability, or not, of main sewers. There may be a sewer to take foul waste, and perhaps another to take surface water. In an old residential area, there may be a single combined sewer. In rural areas, there may be neither. Fortunately, there are alternatives:

Surface water can be disposed of simply enough (in suitable subsoils) with soakaways. These are basically pits in the ground that can be covered over with soil. They need to be big enough to store the run off from the heaviest rainfall until it can seep away.

Foul waste can be treated in a septic tank, provided there is a waterway or spare land nearby to take the clarified effluent. If not, a cesspool will have to be used, where all the sewage is stored. At frequent intervals, say bimonthly, the sewage is sucked up into a tanker and trucked away, a smelly and expensive business. If you have chosen a plot where a cesspool is necessary, there must be some outstanding attraction about it!

Designing a layout for the drains is not particularly difficult. The manufacturers of drainage systems will be pleased to send you catalogues which show the many components that can be assembled together, and which give technical information on layouts. (Some manufacturers offer a free design service.)

Domestic drains are usually in 10 cm clay pipe (internal diameter), or in the equivalent 11 cm plastic pipe (external diameter). For surface water, the cheaper 8·2 cm plastic pipe is occasionally used.

The main requirement is, of course, that the drains should everywhere be running downhill. The minimum slope for foul drains is about 1 in 60 for clay, and 1 in 100 for plastic. The surface water drains are more accommodating, and the minimum slope can be half that for the foul. (By the way, if the sewer is uphill, there is still hope – with a ready-made pump chamber.) Try to keep drains away from tree roots. A drain can run under a driveway, but it should be encased in concrete if it is less than 60 cm deep.

To keep a steady flow, drains should run in straight lines joined by the minimum number of bends. Branch connections should join obliquely in the direction of flow. If surface water and foul drains are required to cross each other, they must, of course, be at different levels. Bear this in mind when considering the levels.

Another requirement is that a drain should be roddable along its entire length, so that any blockages can be freed. To this end, access is required at different parts into the pipe. The form of the access depends on the depth of the pipe below the ground. For shallow pipes, down to 60 cm, 'access chambers' are available. These are wide enough to allow an arm to reach down to the drain. (See Fig. 1.)

Figure 1: Access chamber

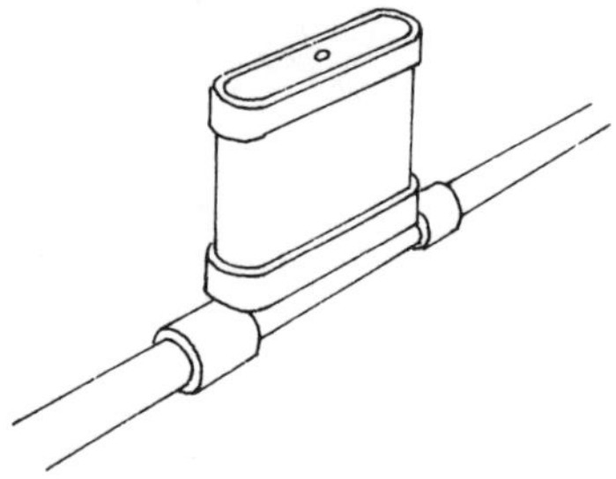

* For access to a shallow pipe.

For deeper pipes, down to a metre, 'inspection chambers' are used. (See Fig. 2.)

Figure 2: Plastic inspection chamber

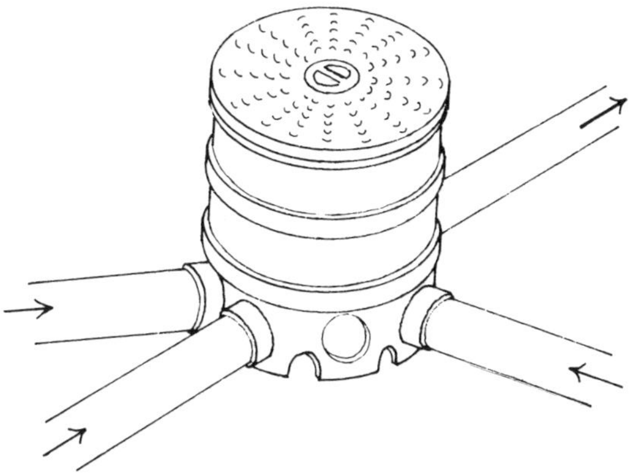

* According to its design, a chamber can either be built up or cut down to the required depth.

Figure 3: Rodding eye

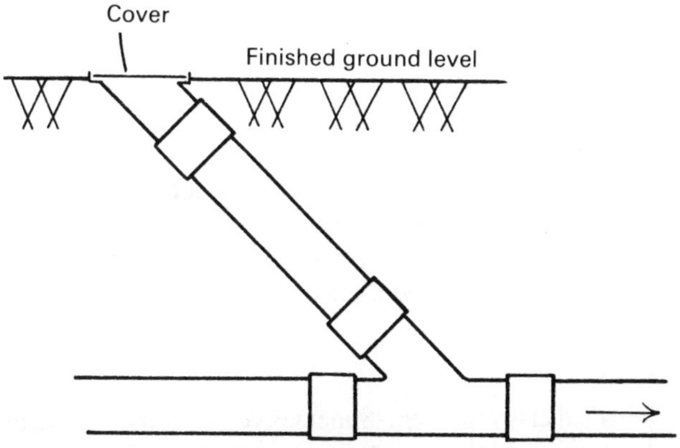

* Gives rodding access to drain.

These are wider, so that the upper part of the body, with outstretched arm, can be stuck down. Nowadays, inspection chambers are made in plastic – a little expensive, but saving a great deal of time. At their base, they have the provision for branch drains to join. Inspection chambers are yet another example of technology in the factory replacing skill on site – to the ownhander's advantage.

For yet deeper pipes, 'manholes' are necessary. These must be wide enough for a person to be able to squat down in them, albeit, with little comfort! As yet, there are no plastic versions, and they are usually built of brick. (See Fig. 8, and textbooks.)

There are two other forms of access into drains:

'Back inlet gullies' can be obtained in roddable versions. These gullies, which contain a water trap, can be used to receive a waste pipe. For example, it might be easier to run a waste from a utility sink outside to a gully, rather than inside to the stack. (Note that the waste pipe should finish below the cover of the gully.)

'Rodding eyes' are a cheap, versatile and unobtrusive form of access. An 'eye' is merely a pipe, with a removable cover at ground level, which runs down into the drain. (See Fig. 3.)

To clear a blockage, rods can be pushed down the eye into the drain. The drainlayer makes up an eye as required, using a 45° junction, some straight pipe, and a small, ready-made cover. Remember, the direction of rodding is downhill.

Where is rodding access into the drains required? –

1) Where a drain leaves the house – there should be no need to go into the building to rod.

2) At, or near, pronounced bends.

3) In very long runs. (See Approved Document H of the Building Regulations.)

(See Fig. 4 for a typical layout for foul drains.)

Figure 4: Typical foul drainage layout

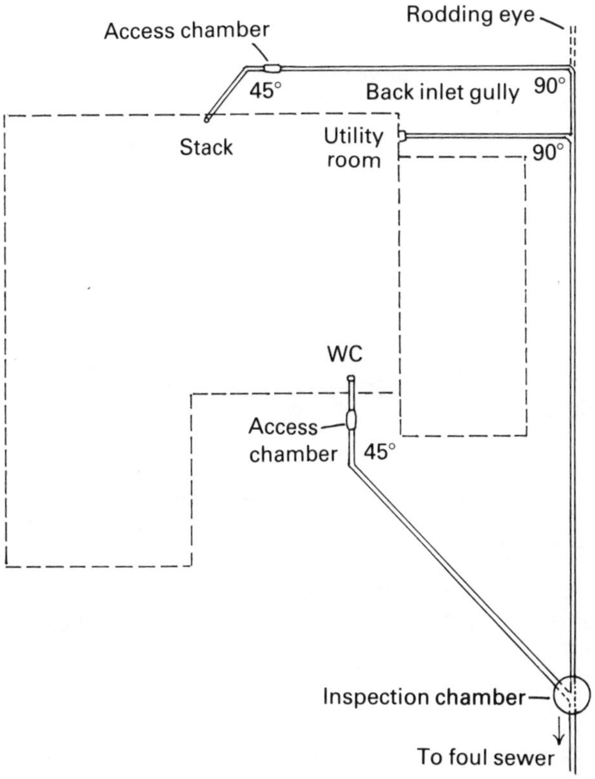

It's easier to lay shallow drains than deep ones. A 'back-drop' enables shallow drains to be run into a deep manhole. (See Fig. 5.)

Figure 5: Backdrop to manhole

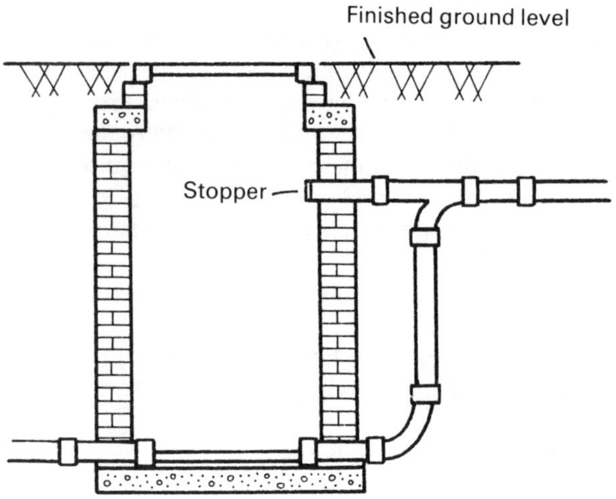

* Enables an economical shallow drain to flow into a manhole.
* Remove stopper for rodding.

And the innovatory marscar bowl receives shallow drains, from any direction, and feeds them into a deeper one. (See Fig. 6.)

Figure 6: Marscar bowl

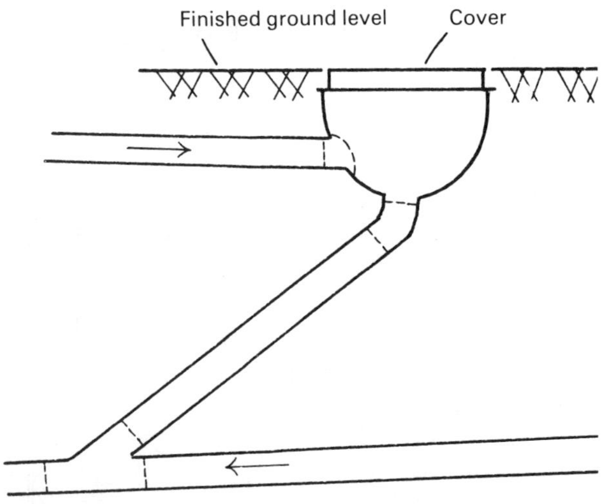

* Can receive several shallow drains from any direction and discharge them into a deeper one.

The head of the drain needs to be ventilated, via the stack. Note that a branch drain from a ground floor WC need not be ventilated.

A couple of points about surface water drains:

Where a drain receives the downpipe from guttering, a gully is optional – there is no real need for one.

But if surface water drains run into an old-fashioned combined sewer, then the drain should contain an interceptor trap to prevent foul air passing back along the pipe.

(See Fig. 7 for a typical layout for surface drainage.)

Figure 7: Typical drainage layout for surface water

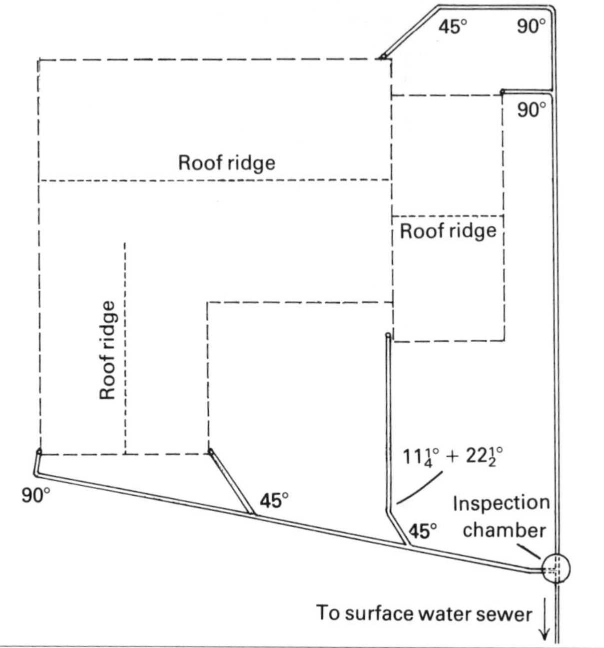

Laying

First of all, a choice has to be made between clay or plastic pipes. Both have their strong supporters. But both are widely used, which shows that neither has any overwhelming advantage over the other. However, if the gradients are very slight, the decision is made for you: plastic.

Clay pipes

The vitrified clay pipes (eg, 'Supersleeve') are very strong. In most ground, they can be laid directly onto the trench bottom (but not in very soft or rocky ground). The days of jointing clay pipes with tarred twine and mortar are gone. These pipes are simply joined with push-fit plastic couplings. The pipes are rigid and rather short, 1·6 metres. The couplings allow for a little movement to accommodate any settlement. A fall of about 1 in 40 is fine, though it can be flatter (1 in 60) if necessary.

To cut clay pipe, hire a pipe cutter. Wrap its chain around the pipe, and squeeze the handles together. If the cutting discs are sharp, the pipe will snap apart with a clean break. The outside arris of the cut needs to be chamfered to ease the fitting of a coupling. (There is a special tool for this, but it can be done well enough with a file.) Smear the end with the special lubricant before pushing on the coupling.

An advantage of clay pipe is that it can normally be laid directly onto the trench bottom. It is then covered to a depth of 15 cm with 'selected backfill'. This is merely soil that can be distributed with a shovel – it excludes large stones and the like. The upper part of the trench can then be backfilled mechanically – if there is an excavator available. A shallow pipe, with less than 30 cm of cover above it, needs to be surrounded by concrete for protection.

Plastic pipes

Light plastic pipes come in longer lengths than clay – three or six metres. Some systems use plain pipes with separate couplers, others use socketed pipes with integral couplers. An advantage of plastic pipe is that it can be cut with a handsaw. (A tip here is to wrap a rectangular sheet of paper around the pipe – use the edge of the paper to guide a square cut.) With some systems, there is no need to chamfer the cut afterwards. Another advantage is that because of the smoother bore and fewer joints, the pipes can be laid to a slighter fall. 1 in 70 is fine. 1 in 100 is normally the minimum, though it is said that with special care 1 in 130 is satisfactory. A disadvantage is that, because the pipes are weaker, they cannot be laid directly onto the trench bottom. The trenches must be overdug and bedding material put down. For some pipes, this can simply be 10 cm of selected backfill. But more usually, a gravel such as pea shingle is used to a depth of 5 cm. The same material is used to cover the pipes to a depth of 10 cm, and then another 30 cm of selected backfill is added. After that, you can finish backfilling with a JCB if you want to. The bedding helps to absorb any deformation in the ground (eg, if a lorry runs over them). Even so, plastic pipes need more protection than clay, and pipes down to 60 cm are said to need a concrete surround.

When making cost comparisons between clay and plastic, don't just compare the cost per metre of pipe. Include pea gravel, if any, and couplings, junctions, bends, inspection chambers, and the like. Clay is likely to be slightly cheaper.

It is usually worthwhile to get in a JCB to dig out the trenches for drains, though sometimes a spade or graft is more appropriate. (A 'graft' is a form of spade with a long narrow blade, specially made for digging graves, trenches and the like – the origin of 'hard graft'?)

To guide the JCB, mark out a centre line for the trenches with sand. Narrow trenches help to protect pipes from subsequent heavy loads. On the other hand, you need room to work in the trench, so ask for an 18″ bucket on the JCB. An experienced digger driver can judge the gradients well by eye, but use a level-board, boning rods, or optical level to get them right. (For example, if there is to be a 1 in 40 fall, with a three-metre level-board there should be a drop of $7\frac{1}{2}$ cm from one end of the board to the other.) If the pipes are to be bedded in pea shingle, the excavator can put this around in the trenches for you. (And if a trench has mistakenly been dug too deeply, its bottom should be raised with pea shingle, not with backfill.)

The laying of the pipes is simple and quick. To make a joint, lubricate the end of the pipe and push it home past the rubber sealing rings. With some systems, the pipe needs to be retracted a little to allow an expansion gap. (It's a good idea to make a distance mark near the end of the pipe beforehand, so that, at any time, the retraction of the pipe within the coupling can be checked.) Getting the required angles at bends and junctions is sometimes a little tricky. It can help to lay these pipes out loosely on a trial run to see how they fit. A different difficulty is fitting the very last coupling in a run – there is too little space between the pipes. A special sliding coupling solves the problem.

Note that the bend at the bottom of the soil-and-vent pipe, connecting the stack to the drain, should be a 'slow' bend (ie, of gentle curvature). The manufacturers produce 'rest bends' that prop in position, but most builders use 'long radius bends' (or perhaps two 45° bends joined together). The bend usually passes through an opening in the foundation wall. To allow for differential movement, there should be a lintel with clearance above the pipe, and a coupling in the drain just outside the foundations. (The coupling allows a slight movement of the pipes.)

Inspection chambers

Putting in plastic inspection chambers is easy enough. Depending on the type, they can either be cut down to give the required depth, or built up with extra sections. The heaviest flow should preferably be along the straight channel. Saw off the blank ends for the side channels required. The usual backfill should be placed around the chamber, which is topped by a cover in a frame. (If the chamber is in a driveway, a load-bearing cover should be used, and its frame supported in concrete.)

If you are short on money but long on time, you can build your own inspection chamber, in a similar way to the manhole below. The internal dimensions should be about 75 × 70 cm, and the brickwork may be 10 cm thick, preferably in engineering bricks. Or render it on the outside to keep out ground water.

Manholes

Manholes need to be of double brick thickness and larger inside (120 × 75 cm). (See Fig. 8.)

First of all, dig a hole big enough for the manhole with space around it to work. Cast a concrete base, and build up the brickwork just a few courses. Put in the channelling, which can be purchased either straight or bent from a builders' merchant.

Place the main, straight-through channel on the concrete base, and hold it in position with fine concrete. The ends of the branch channels rest on the main channel so that the sewage drops down into it. (Though plastic channel junctions are on one level.) Then take the concrete benching up nearly vertically from the sides of the channels, as high as the crown of the exit pipe. Slope it away to the sides of the chamber, keeping everywhere a slight slope towards the channels. (If there is a temporary overflow, the sewage should be able to drop back into the channels, not be left high and dry.) Finish the surface with a smooth coat of 1:2 mortar.

After this, the brickwork can be completed. Some inward corbelling may be necessary near the top to reduce the cross section to that of the manhole cover to be fitted. The cover might be made of steel or, more attractively, of reinforced concrete. (In a driveway, an extra-strong cover should be used.) In a deep manhole, step irons can be built into the brickwork.

Figure 8: Manhole

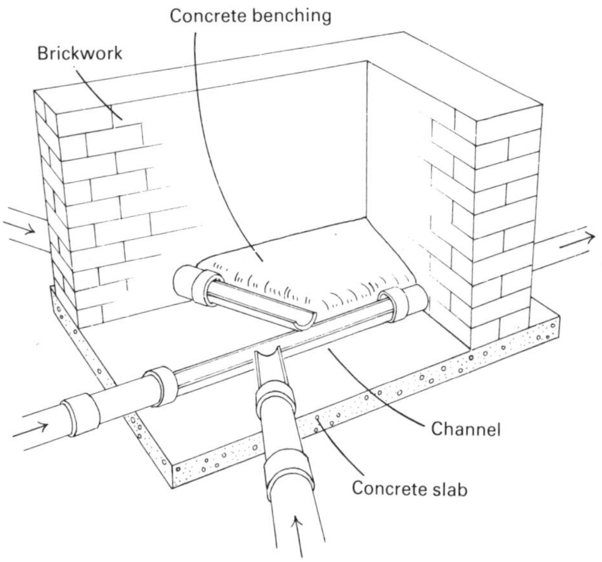

* The benching is as high as the crown of the exit pipe.
* Preferably the main channel takes the heaviest flow.
* Side channels drop into the main channel. Alternatively, pre-formed branches (in plastic) allow for entries at the same level and save having to cut the ends of channels.
* Preferably each pipe has a coupling just outside the manhole (to allow for differential movement due to settlement of the manhole).

However, you probably won't have to build a manhole.

Testing drains

Before the drains are covered over, the building inspector will want to see them. He or she will also inspect them after they've been backfilled and may want to test them. With the more reliable jointing methods used nowadays, inspectors are not as strict about testing as they used to be. Even so, you may want to test the drains yourself, for your own peace of mind. It's better to do this before backfilling – any leaks can be more easily located and rectified. (To be totally thorough, you would test them again after backfilling.)

The simplest test is to roll a tennis ball down the drain, to make sure there are no obstructions.

To test for leaks, first of all check that all the pipes are properly inserted into the couplings. (Look for the shoulder marks that you made earlier.) Then do a water test:

At an inspection chamber near the bottom of the drain, block off the entry into the chamber with a drain stopper. (This device for blocking a pipe can be hired or purchased.) At the top of the drain, intercept the pipe with a bend and a short vertical pipe to get a good head of water. Use this to fill the drain and create a head of water about half a metre high. Check that the level stays reasonably static for about half an hour. (It should lose less than ·05 litres per metre run of pipe.) If water is being lost, look for the leaks.

When the test is finished, the water can be released through a valve in the stopper. It does happen that occasionally the pressure of water sweeps the stopper away. As a precaution, tie some twine to the stopper beforehand.

And of course, you can't release the water if the drain has not already been connected to the sewer. This is done by cutting a hole in the top of the sewer and fixing a 'saddle' on top to which the new drain can be connected. If this involves digging a road up, the work is probably best subcontracted.

Options

With many of the Water Companies, it is compulsory to have a water meter installed on new property – they may install the meter themselves, by their stop tap in the highway. A meter measures the volume of water supplied, of course, but this is also taken to be a measure of the sewage disposed of. (The assumption is that what goes in must come out!) For Severn Trent Water the charges in 1990 are:

Water: 42 pence / cu m
Sewerage: 28 pence / cu m
Surface water: A flat rate of £51 per annum.
(1 cu m = 1,000 litres.)

The average consumption of water per household depends on the number in the household:

No. of persons in household	1	2	3	4	5	6
Ave. water consumption (cu m / annum)	55	100	145	165	180	200

(Extravagant households may use 50% more.)

As a point of interest, the (cold) water for a bath (100 litres) with its disposal costs 7p.

Those are the running costs. But on new installations, there are also 'infra-structure' charges which come as something of a shock to many people. As mentioned in Chapter 3, Severn Trent Water, as a typical example, charge £572 for allowing a new water service, and £409 for sewerage.

Anyway, bear the above figures in mind when looking at the costs of options below.

Soakaways

In the past, soakaways were used mainly in rural areas for disposing of surface water. They are now being encouraged by the Water Companies who are worried by falling water tables, and that is reflected in the high charge above (£51 p.a.). Even if a surface water sewer is available, you may well prefer not to use it. You'll be saving money, and you'll be putting clean water into the ground, uncontaminated by agricultural nasties. (But it takes a generation, or so, for the water to work its way through the ground to the water supply.)

To make a soakaway, a pit is dug, say a $1\frac{1}{2}$ m cube. The actual size required depends on the type of soil – the building inspector may advice you. (If you break into gravel or stratified rock, this will aid drainage.) The pit is nearly filled with brick and block rubble, which is covered with polythene and some 30 cm of soil. A slight disadvantage of a soakaway is that this soil quickly dries out in a drought, resulting, for example, in a yellow patch of lawn.

Place a soakaway 5 metres or more from the house. Two of them will probably suffice: one for the front roof, and the other for the back.

Septic tank

A septic tank needs to be 15 metres, or more, from the house. The further, the better – it may give off an aroma! Occasionally, the sludge that accumulates has to be emptied out by suction into a tanker. This requirement affects the position of the septic tank. The hose from a tanker may be as long as 40 metres, but there should not be a steep rise from tank to tanker, as the latter can only suck against a head of five metres. Emptying the tank at yearly intervals is usually recommended, though people do leave it a lot longer. (A typical price for de-sludging might be £40.)

Again, plastic has replaced brick. Prefabricated tanks in GRP (Glass Reinforced Plastic) are available at modest cost, say £350 for a 3,000 litre tank. (See Fig. 9.)

Such a tank is about two metres high, and the same in diameter. The size of the tank depends upon the anticipated throughput from the house. (A rule of thumb: 2,000 litres plus 200 litres/person.)

Excavate a big hole for the tank, put $\frac{1}{4}$ cu m of concrete onto the middle of the floor, and lower the tank onto it. (To lift the tank, tie it to the end of the excavator's arm.) Backfill with sand or gravel, consolidating well. In wet or heavy clay soils, it's advisable to surround the tank with concrete. In this case, as the concrete is built up, the tank must be filled with water to an equal level, to prevent it floating upwards. (See manufacturers' brochures for more details.)

An easy way to dispose of the effluent is into a waterway. (Check with the Water Company first). But it is more likely that you'll have to use land drains – if the soil is suitable. Use perforated plastic pipe (as used for land drainage), at a depth of half a metre and surround it with gravel. A total length of about 40 metres is required, but this can be arranged in a herring-bone pattern for compactness. A fall of 1 in 200 is suitable. (Again, see brochures for more details.)

Figure 9: Septic tank

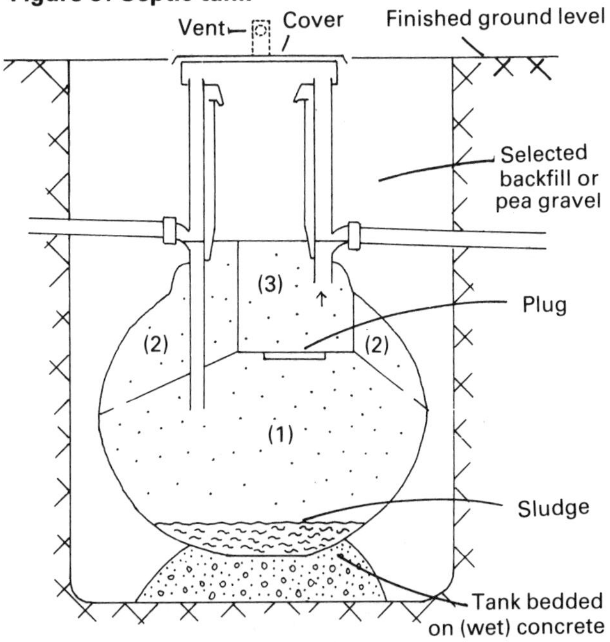

* Effluent enters chamber 1 where solids are deposited. It passes into chamber 2 where fine sediment settles out. The clarified effluent passes over a weir into chamber 3, from where it is discharged.
* For de-sludging, the plug can be removed.

Cesspool

A septic tank uses bacteria to decompose organic sewage, but a cesspool merely stores it. A cesspool requires a large storage tank, of at least 18 cubic metres capacity. Plastic tanks are available. Emptying charges are in the range £40 to £200.

Hopefully, you will not need one. But if you do, consider whether you really need a WC, which will be a prolific producer of sewage. (A fifth of the national water supply is flushed down lavatories.) There is an alternative – a dry biological toilet. These run on electricity (about $1\frac{1}{2}$ units a day), and convert faeces into sterile garden compost. Not uncommon in Sweden, these 'bio-loos' can be obtained in Britain.

18
GARDEN WORKS

☆

☆

☆

☆

☆

☆

☆

The works of a person that builds begin immediately to decay; while those of him who plants begin directly to improve. In this, planting promises a more lasting pleasure than building – William Shenstone, 'Unconnected Thoughts on Gardening', 1764.

WITH THE HOUSE complete (and starting to decay!), you can rather more leisurely turn your mind to the garden. If you are so inclined, here is great scope for creative imagination. The ugly building site can be transformed, with some help from Nature, into beauty. You are loosed from the dull restrictions of Planning and Building Regulations. Make the most of it. The creative opportunities are enormous, the possible variations of form and texture endless. Skills used in housebuilding – the manipulation of brick, concrete and timber – can be be put to good use.

Before you commit yourself to any 'hardware' in the form of paths, walls or the like, it is best to make a plan for the garden; this can be conveniently done on squared paper. (Consider, amongst many other factors, the shadow areas at different times of the day.) When you have come up with a plan, it's a good idea to mark it out on the ground with lines and pegs. Leave it for a few days and see if it still feels right. There are those who say that you should experience a garden for a complete year before changing it – by now, you have probably known your site for that long! Consult gardening books about design, but here are a couple of general observations:

Firstly, let the garden be more formal near to the house. Use straight lines, bricks, and regular levels to complement the formality of the house. Further away, be more rustic, with curved lines, local stone, and undulating levels.

Secondly, do use the opportunity to vary the levels for a prettier, more interesting garden. Commercial builders usually leave a bland, level garden. You have the resources, though, to do more. When you have an excavator on site, you can modify contours as you wish – perhaps to enhance the natural contours, rather than flattening them. Or, instead of trucking loads of spoil away, you might like to use it to creative effect.

The efficient usage of an excavator needs some forethought, unless you are fortunate enough to have a local one readily available. The sort of work that needs to be done in the garden includes:

Stripping away topsoil for the drive, patio and paths, and levelling these areas

Digging shallow foundation trenches for walls

Levelling or contouring the garden

Trucking away spoil

Redistributing topsoil.

The first priority will be to lay the driveway and paths, especially if winter is imminent. The house can then be occupied comfortably, and the other garden work carried out at a leisurely pace. Don't make the drive too narrow – it needs to be wide enough to give easy access from both sides of a car.

The areas for the drive, patio and paths need to be cleared of topsoil and flattened. In fact, they need a fall of 1:50 for drainage. Next to the house they must be at least 15 cm below the dpc. Usually a sub-base is needed, both to strengthen the construction and to regulate the levels. For small areas use up hardcore from the building process: broken bricks, blocks and tiles. For more material buy in whatever is locally available: crushed stone, quarry waste, hoggin, etc. A useful material from a quarry might be described as '20 mm down to dust'. This is a mixture of aggregate, from 2 cm stones down to fine material (the latter giving a blinded surface). The depth of the sub-base depends upon the likely loads (lorry or wheelbarrow?) and the stability of the subsoil. For a light construction, a sub-base may be unnecessary.

Driveway

The material most commonly used for drives is tarmac – a term loosely taken to cover both bitumen and tar macadams, as well as the more expensive asphalt. These materials give a stable but flexible surface. A cheaper alternative is concrete. This must be laid well if it is not to crack; and it must be kept clean and oil-free if it is to stay smart. Comparing the two materials: Concrete consists of stones stuck rigidly together by a cement paste, whereas tarmac consists of stones bound flexibly together by tar or bitumen.

Widely used on the Continent and becoming more popular here are paviors, or 'pavers', as the name is becoming anglicised to. These clay or concrete 'bricks' give an attractive finish. But they are expensive.

A cheap, distinctive, but somewhat old-fashioned finish can be obtained with gravel.

We will assume that, at some stage, the driveway has had its topsoil removed and it has been levelled as required. Note that, if a drive runs down towards a garage, it should nonetheless slope away from the entrance to avoid any chance of flooding in wet weather. Mark out the boundaries for the drive with string and pegs. These boundaries don't have to be straight lines!

Tarmac

The word 'tarmacadam', which has become shortened to 'tarmac', was derived from 'tar' plus 'MacAdam'. At the beginning of the last century, a Scot, John McAdam, invented an effective type of road construction based on layers of interlocking broken stone. It became even more effective when tar was added to help bind the stone together.

The terminology involved with tarmac can be confusing. Crude tar is a distillation from coal (or earlier, from wood). This is refined, giving off various oils, such as carbolic oil, and leaving behind base tar – also called pitch. Road tar is obtained by recombining the base tar with some of the distilled oils to obtain some particular viscosity (thickness). With the demise of town gas, there is not enough tar available nowadays. It has largely been replaced by bitumen, an equivalent product derived from crude petroleum. When this is refined, petrol, and diesel and other oils are distilled off, leaving behind bitumen. This can be used as it is, or remixed with volatile oils to make it less viscous.

Bitumen also occurs naturally – in asphalt. Most natural asphalt is imported from a 'lake' of the material in Trinidad; it contains bitumen mixed with very fine aggregate. However, most asphalt nowadays is obtained not from the natural material, but from bitumen mixed with sand and mineral dust. When asphalt is mixed with stone, it yields 'hot rolled asphalt' – on a stable base, this gives a first-class road surface. The largish stones (2 cm) are held firmly in place by the bituminous 'mortar' – it can all be likened to currents in a pudding. There is about 10% of binder which fills the voids and gives an impervious surface.

What the lay person loosely calls 'tarmac' includes both the 'hot rolled asphalt' outlined above and 'coated macadam'. The latter is stone coated with bitumen and/or tar. It is mainly the interlocking of the stones that gives strength to this material, not the bitumen. Coated macadams have about 5% of bitumen binder, leaving a significant volume of open space between the stones – about 25% for base course. The material is porous, though the wearing course, with smaller stones, is less so. The bituminous binder is hard at normal temperatures but it can be heated to become semi-liquid.

This is the material to use for a DIY driveway. Technically, the binder of tarmacadam is tar, and of bitumen macadam it is bitumen; but this book goes along with popular usage and uses 'tarmac' for both materials. Nowadays, bitumen is much more widely available than tar.

An adhesive material occasionally required is bitumen emulsion – a suspension of tiny globules of bitumen in water. 'Tack coat 30%' means that the bitumen content is 30%. There are two basic types: Class A (anionic) uses evaporation of the water to form a film, and class K (cationic) relies on chemical coagulation – in the damp British climate this is the more useful. A tack coat is said to 'break' when it turns from a liquid to a sticky film – the colour changes from brown to black.

(In case you read an American book: 'asphalt' [American] = 'bitumen' [English].)

Laying tarmac

Tarmac needs firm edging to constrain it, otherwise it starts to creep and crack up at the edge. Precast concrete edging is usually used, set firmly in weak concrete. (See Fig. 1.)

Figure 1: Section of tarmac drive

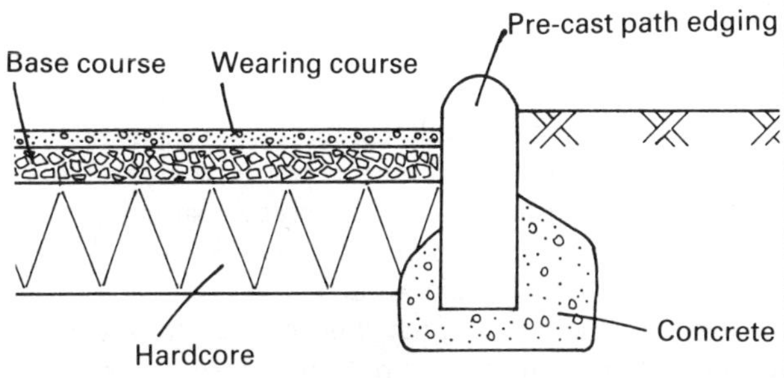

* Base course for strength.
* Wearing course for a weatherproof surface.
* Firm edge required to prevent the surface from breaking up.

(The precast edging costs about £1-60 for a metre length. Casting it *in situ* is much cheaper.) The top of the edging should end up a centimetre or two above the tarmac surface.

Unlike concrete, tarmac is easily broken up by plant roots, so it's prudent to treat the area beforehand with weedkiller. The tarmac – bitumen macadam – needs to be laid on a firm base, 10 cm to 15 cm of compacted hardcore. The tarmac will be applied on top of this in two layers: a thick base course containing large stones, and a thinner wearing course with small stones.

For a base course 4 cm thick, order material with 2 cm (and smaller) stone. This will be satisfactory for most domestic driveways. But if heavier loads are anticipated, put down a thicker base course (with the maximum stone size half the thickness).

With hardcore and edging strips in place, prepare for a delivery of base course. Light a fire with scraps of wood and have this ready to heat up a shovel and rake. Warm tools make it easier to work the tarmac. This is delivered warm and needs to be put in place before it cools. As with concreting, you are working against time – it's a job for two or three people.

Have the base course tipped halfway down the drive and cover it with a tarpaulin to keep the heat in. This is even more important if it rains, as this quickly cools the tarmac. Shovel or barrow the base course to the area being worked on, rake it out level, and compact it. Once the material has been taken from the warm heap, it cools rapidly, and so needs to be worked on promptly. Camber the base for good drainage. The base course can be compacted by about six passes of a roller (hire a powered single-wheel roller) or with a plate compactor. Clean the tools off in the fire at the end of the session.

The wearing course can be put down within a few hours; it should not be left longer than a fortnight if it is to bind well with the lower layer. The wearing course has 6 mm stones (maximum), and should be laid to a thickness of $1\frac{1}{2}$ cm. But put down $\frac{1}{2}$ cm more than this to allow for compression as it is rolled. Note that this course should be rolled rather than whacked. Water the wheel of the roller to keep it clean.

It may be advisable to dust the surface with sealing grit. Scatter the grit on, and brush it in with a stiff brush. (This prevents debris from accumulating in cracks and seeds germinating. As these take root, they can break up the tarmac.)

For a variation, a coloured wearing course (usually red) can be put down. This looks well, except that oil stains show up badly. And it costs about twice as much. A more modest variation is to sprinkle white chippings sparingly onto a wearing course of fine cold asphalt and roll them in. (Despite its name, cold asphalt is laid warm!)

Altogether, there is no great skill required for this work. But if you do want to give yourself more time, you can have extra 'cut back' (eg, creosote) put into the tarmac to slow it going off. (Though if an excess is used, it can take weeks for the tarmac to become firm.)

Bituminised macadams cost about £40 per tonne collected, and there are about 2 tonnes to the cubic metre. If you wish to subcontract this work, prices for laying drives are something like £15 per square metre.

Concrete drive

The selfbuilder who has laid floor slabs will already have acquired the techniques required for concrete drives; he or she may well wish to stick to this familiar material.

Figure 2: Section of concrete drive

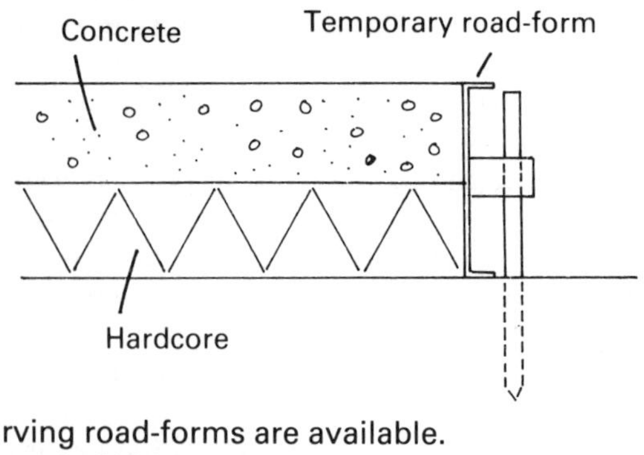

* Curving road-forms are available.
* Instead of hiring road-forms, timber formwork can be used.

Firstly, fix the formwork. Use stout timber, or hire steel road-forms from a plant hire firm. Road-forms are 10 cm or more in depth; flexible ones are available for curves. (See Fig. 2.)

To help drainage, allow a cross-fall of 1 in 50. Every three or four metres, there should be a break in the concrete to allow it to contract in cold weather. To this end, a strip of hardboard or wood can be used to divide the concrete. (Long drives will also require an occasional expansion joint; bitumen-impregnated fibreboard is the material to use for this.) Hold the strip in place with supporting formwork. After the slab has been cast and the formwork removed, keep the contraction strip in place and cast the adjacent bay.

The usual thickness of concrete is 10 cm. It can be laid directly onto firm ground, but on soft or clayey ground, hardcore is necessary (10 cm deep). A strong mix is required, 1:2:4. If ready-mixed is being used, ask for it to have an air-entraining agent – the microscopic bubbles of air make the drive more resistant to frost damage.

The slight ripple effect of a 'sawn' finish will give a surface with some traction, but a neater finish is obtained with a wood float. (See 'Finishing', Chapter 20.) If the drive has a steep slope, the deep corrugations of a tamped finish help traction. By the way, when laying on a slope, use a stiffer mix and start at the bottom. Even so, the wet concrete will tend to slide down, and you may have to carry the surplus from the bottom back up to the top.

While the concrete is fresh, protect it from weather extremes: frost, rapid drying, or heavy rain. Preferably don't lay concrete with such weather imminent.

Paved drive

Pavers give a flexible and attractive surface which is becoming popular. The pavers are thick blocks of concrete or clay, butted together. The load on one block is spread to its neighbours by the friction of sand in the joints.

The method of laying is fairly simple.

If the ground is stable, the drive can be laid directly onto it, but if the ground is soft or clayey, put down a 10 cm sub-base of compacted hardcore. At the boundaries, some edging is necessary. This may be concrete edging, as for a tarmac drive, or it may be formwork held in place with pegs every metre. Have the top of the formwork at the required finished level. A cross-fall of 1 in 50 is advisable. Put down sharp sand to a depth of 6 cm. (Compaction will later reduce this by a centimetre or so.) Use a straight board to screed the sand flat. (To get the required level, nail bearers to the board so that it can be supported at each end from the edging. Or cut the ends of the board.) (See Fig. 3.)

Having smoothed off a couple of metres of sand, start laying the blocks. Various patterns are possible. The herringbone gives the most resistance to lateral forces. It can be laid in two ways:

The simple way is to lay blocks parallel and perpendicular to a long edge. The other way is to lay them at 45°; this is very suitable for irregularly shaped areas.

For the edges, blocks will have to be cut. Hire a stone splitter. (You will also need to hire a plate compactor, ideally one with a rubber sole plate to protect the surface of the pavers.) When a section of blocks has been laid, bed them into place with the compactor. (Keep the compactor away from an edge, which is liable to become displaced.) Compaction forces sand up into the joints between the blocks. Similarly, spread a thin layer of sand on top of the blocks, and vibrate it down into the joints. (This may be difficult with damp sand – in which case, water the sand in with a watering can and rose.)

Figure 3: Laying pavers

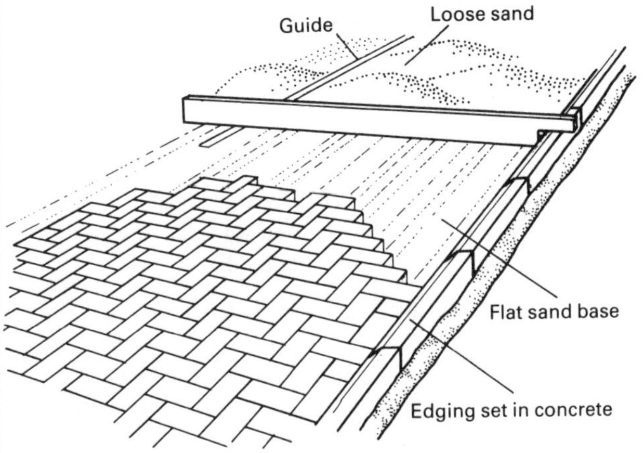

* Herring-bone pattern has no continuous joints, and so resists lateral displacement.
* For a drive of irregular shape, lay the herring-bone pattern at 45° to the pattern above. Hire a block splitter to cut the irregular pieces at the edges.
* Screed rail produces a flat base of sand. Two methods are shown above for guiding it.
* Instead of using edging, the edge pavers can be set with concrete.

The edges need to be fixed permanently, either with concrete edging, as mentioned above, or by bedding the perimeter pavers in sand with cement.

A more traditional method in Britain is to use rigidly jointed paving. This uses thinner pavers, about $3\frac{1}{2}$ cm thick; they are bedded in mortar with pointed joints. For a driveway, this all needs to be laid on concrete, so it hardly seems worthwhile.

Gravel drive

Gravel is a fairly cheap way of making a long drive.

First edge the drive, to stop the stones spreading. (Treated timber is sometimes used for edging rather than concrete.) The ground must be firm. Apply bituminous emulsion from a watering can with a rose, at the rate of five litres per square metre. This has a triple effect. It stabilises the ground, deters weeds, and binds the stones. (The American, Ken Kern, in his fascinating classic *The Owner Built Home* says that he wouldn't begin a construction project without bituminous emulsion being on site – he considers it so useful and versatile.)

Cover the drive with stone chippings and roll them in. Roll them again the following day. A fortnight later, apply some more emulsion, this time at only two litres per square metre. Spread pea shingle and roll it in. Roll again a few times over the following week. (Keep the wheel of the roller wet to stop it picking up gravel.)

The above procedure gives a good firm surface. But for the more traditional 'scrunchy' feel, apply another layer of pea shingle (without the emulsion) and roll it.

Paths

Paths can be made in the same way as drives, but because of the lighter loads, the construction can be slighter.

It is common practice to put a concrete path around most of a house. This is required to be at least 15 cm (two brick courses) below the dpc. A good width is 90 cm, with a cross-fall of 1 in 50. The foundation trenches will have been backfilled with spoil, but as this is not particularly stable, make a base of hardcore. (In fact, the path and driveway are good places to dump broken bricks and blocks when you tidy up while the walls are being built.)

Use a 1:2:4 concrete mix, laid to a depth of 5 cm. With a small depth like this, use small stones, up to $1\frac{1}{4}$ cm. At the wall, there is no formwork from which to strike off a level surface. A remedy is to form a concrete screed alongside the wall at the required level. (The brick coursing gives a guide.) If the mix was fairly dry, after a short interval the screed will be firm enough to work off: After tamping the concrete, 'saw' it flat across the path.

For popular finishes, use a wood float or a stiff brush. (See 'Finishing', Chapter 20.) Take care not to stain the brickwork with the wet concrete. (Though if you do, a proprietary mortar cleaner such as 'Disclean' will remove the stains.)

At each corner, and at every six metres, break the concrete with a contraction joint – ie, a piece of timber, hardboard, or bituminised fibreboard placed across the path to divide the concrete.

Patio

Precast concrete slabs are the favoured material for patios. They usually come in boring squares, though hexagons are also available. For more interesting patterns, use a couple of different shapes or sizes. (Hydraulically pressed slabs are stronger than moulded ones; they can be recognised by the gridwork of indentations on one face. These slabs should particularly be used on a driveway.)

The area for the patio should have been cleared of topsoil (sensibly, when you had an excavator on site). On soft or clayey ground, a sub-base of hardcore is necessary; but on stable ground, the slabs can be laid direct. Mark out the boundaries for the patio with string lines, and knock in levelling pegs around the perimeter to give the required surface level. (Allow for a fall.) Make up the sub-base to the required level – allow 2 cm or 3 cm for the mortar bedding, in addition to the thickness of the slabs.

Use a 1:4 mix of cement and sharp sand, with little water. Bed each slab with a dab of mortar at each corner, and a dab in the middle. This gives a reasonably firm bed, while allowing the level to be easily adjusted. Use a straight-edge to level the slab from the levelling pegs or adjacent slabs. The slabs may simply be butt jointed. For mortared joints, use wooden spacers a centimetre thick for a regular spacing. Fill the joints with a dry, crumbly mortar, ramming it down with the edge of some ply; finish it a centimetre below the surface to facilitate drainage.

The slabs can be cut with a stone splitter. Alternatively, score them on both sides with a sharp bolster or a stone-cutting disc; split the slab by giving a sharp blow to a bolster held on the scored line.

Making your own concrete slabs is both economic and satisfying. You can make more interesting shapes and finishes than are commercially available. It's easy enough:

A straightforward method is to cast a slab of mortar on a flat surface, and then to cut it into smaller slabs. The garage floor might form a suitable base. Lay on it some formwork 4 cm deep, to cover an area of several square metres. Spread some damp sand on the floor inside the formwork, and then cast the slab with a 1:3 mix of cement and sharp sand. For a decorative, non-slip finish, embed some stone chippings in the surface. An hour or two after casting the slab, use a trowel and straight-edge to cut the slab into smaller slabs of the size and shape required. Leave them for several days to cure before moving them.

Slabs are often coloured. In the words of the British Cement Association, 'cement colours all soften and mellow with the passing of time'. In other words, they fade. So avoid cement colours if you can (though adding lime is said to make the colours more fast). Instead, make variety by using differently coloured sand and stone, with grey or white cement.

A further variation is to lay a slab of plain concrete for the patio and then to decorate it by casting thin mortar 'slabs' onto it, *in situ*. Use a mould for the 'slabs', a mere centimetre deep. Cast the slabs while the concrete is still green, so that the mortar and concrete bind together. Cast alternate slabs in a regular pattern, and then, when these have hardened somewhat, fill in between them with a different mortar mix. Interesting effects can be obtained. For example, with an octagonal mould, a pattern of octagonal and square slabs results.

Garden walls

A brick wall can be used to mark a front boundary with distinction. Piers can support fine gates. (But if the wall is to be particularly high, you'll need Planning permission – higher than 1 m next to a highway, or 2 m elsewhere.) Other walls may be needed for terracing, raised flower beds, and the like. The simplest wall is a single brick-width thick, in stretcher bond. It needs reinforcing every three metres with piers.

If you are building a pair of piers for gates, and the bonding of the piers is handed, remember to make them mirror images of each other. (See 'Handedness', Chapter 27.) Build in the hinge pins for the gates as you proceed. The hollow centres of piers can be filled with concrete for strength.

If you are being more ambitious and going for a stronger, double width wall, then you will have to become involved with traditional brickwork bonding. This is where brick-laying becomes more tricky and more interesting. Any textbook on the subject will have a substantial part devoted to bonding, so consult one of these.

Even a humble garden wall needs foundations. Dig out a trench, a third of a metre deep, with a width equal to twice the thickness of the wall. Peg out the concrete level in the bottom of the trench for a depth of 10 cm (as for the house foundations). Tamp in some weak concrete to the tops of the pegs. Building a garden wall off this should be a doddle for anyone who has already built a house.

The only new factor is 'coping' – some form of cover along the top of the wall to stop rainwater seeping into the bricks and causing frost damage. A simple and neat method is to lay the top course in engineering bricks. If these are used at the bottom also, then they will act as a dpc, which some people consider desirable even on a garden wall. An alternative is to top the wall with precast concrete copings.

Open screen walling can be built from pierced concrete blocks. (But so few patterns are commonly available, out of the endless and fascinating possibilities!) This type of walling is not particularly strong, so it is not very suitable for boundary walls. Use it as a visual screen or as a partial wind-break.

Screen walling is not built directly off the foundation concrete. Instead, a brickwork or blockwork foundation wall is built off the concrete to emerge above ground level. (Blockwork can be rendered to make it more attractive.) The screen walling is built up off this.

Every two or three metres piers are needed for support. These can be built of bricks, in which case the screen blocks are tied in with wall ties. Alternatively, they can be built with purpose-made block pilasters, which have vertical recesses to hold the screen blocks. (Put reinforcing rod and mortar down the centre of the pilasters.) It's usual, but not necessary in this case, to top the wall with a coping.

With white blocks, white cement is recommended.

Types of fencing

Fencing marks your boundaries; keeps out casual intruders; provides a wind-break; puts a frame around your pretty garden; and, if high enough, permits some privacy. Look at your deeds to find out which boundaries are your responsibility. Keep the fence posts on your side of the boundary.

Very basic fencing can be made from wire or chain-link mesh, stretched between concrete posts. A fuller fence, suitable for a rustic environment, is made from palings of cleft chestnut held by twisted wire. On some estates, a ranch-type post and rail fence is used – simple enough. It might even be in white plastic.

A close-boarded fence is better quality. This is supported by concrete or wooden posts at two or three metre intervals. (See the next section for how to erect the posts.) The posts are mortised at top and bottom to receive horizontal arris rails. (An arris rail is triangular in cross section, and is fixed with its long face vertical.) High fences need a third rail in the middle. Feather-edged boards are nailed vertically to the arris rails, with an overlap of a centimetre or more. Arrange this overlap so that whole boards fit between the posts without leaving a gap. (Use a spacer block, the width of a board less the overlap, to rapidly position the next board relative to the previous one.) Check every few boards for plumbness. Use galvanized nails.

Panel fencing

Timber panels supported by timber or concrete posts are popular. The timber used is often waney-edged, resulting in a panel of low price and limited durability. (A 'waney' edge of a board is an uncut edge from the outside of the tree trunk, ie, next to the bark.)

Stretch a line to show the boundary, and mark off the positions for the posts (at intervals of a panel width plus a post thickness). A modern way to support a post is with a metal post socket driven into the ground. This holds the post out of the ground, where it would be liable to rot. A cheaper way is to support the post with concrete in a hole in the ground. Dig the hole to a depth of one-third of the height of the panel. (For several holes, it's worth hiring a post-hole borer.) Put a half brick at the bottom of the hole to keep the end grain off the wet soil, and wedge the post upright in the hole with pieces of brick. Fill the hole with weak concrete and pieces of hardcore. Finish the concrete just above the ground with a slope to shed water. (Use temporary struts to support the post, if necessary.)

The panels can be fixed to the posts either as they are erected, or later on (eg, if it's windy), provided that the posts are accurately positioned. Panels can be nailed to wooden posts. With concrete posts, the panels either fit into a recess, or are held by clips. On a sloping site, arrange that the panels step down in a regular manner. If there is a large gap beneath a panel, fill it with a 'gravel board'. (This is a board which is next to the ground, and so is liable to rot. The idea is that it can be easily replaced.) When the concrete in the holes has set, saw off the tops of the posts to the required height, eg, 5 cm above the panels. To protect the end grain, either slope the cut, or, better still, fit a cap.

If the site slopes steeply across the fence, you may have to hold the ground back with a retaining wall or paving slabs set upright in concrete. Don't expect a wooden fence to do this.

Lawn

Lawns are everywhere. A European survey of 'national smells' came up with 'cut grass' as the characteristic smell of Britain. Commercial builders invariably lay a lawn to civilise the site. And so, although planting a garden is outside the scope of this book, it may be worthwhile giving some space to the laying of lawns.

Commercial builders use turf as they don't have the time to let seeds sprout. If you too want fast results, meadow turf can be obtained for something like 60p a square metre, and cultivated turf for somewhat more. (Look under 'Turf Supplies' in the *Yellow Pages*.) Ask to see a sample of the turf before you accept a quote. The turf should be about 4 cm thick and weed free. Laying the turf doesn't involve much expertise, just hard work. The ground needs to be levelled, or sloped as required, and well rotavated. (If you're building in the country, a farmer might do this with a tractor-driven rotavator and so save you a lot of effort.) Rake the soil flat, removing all the building debris. Lay the turf with staggered joints, green side up! Water it, and then roll it. (But if the ground is very wet, delay the rolling.)

You can, of course, have the turf laid, at about double the cost.

The cheapest option is to grow your own. You may need to get in extra top soil. Ask around to find some, or if desperate, try landscape gardeners. The soil needs to be rotavated to a fine tilth. After the first rotavation, let the soil dry out for a day or so, and then rotavate again. (When rotavating, the soil should be neither too wet nor too dry.) Patiently rake the soil flat to a fine tilth, removing debris, large stones, etc. Apply a fertiliser, if required, and a mixed grass seed at the rate of 1 kg per 20 square metres. Broadcast the seed by hand in a methodical fashion. Lightly rake it in; and lightly roll it if the soil is dry. Keep the grass watered once it has sprouted.

PART FOUR

TECHNIQUES

☆

☆

☆

☆

☆

☆

☆

☆

☆

☆

☆

☆

☆

☆

☆

☆

☆

☆

☆

☆

19

DESIGN

☆

☆

☆

☆

☆

☆

☆

Houses are built to live in and not to look on: therefore let use be preferred before uniformity, except where both may be had – Francis Bacon (1561 – 1626).

DESIGN is the crucial first step in the building process. No matter how fine the subsequent craftsmanship, if the design is poor, the finished building will be unsatisfactory. It is possible to make minor adjustments and improvements as you build – subject to the approval of the building inspector – but it is better to get the design right in the first place. Good design – to update Francis Bacon's words – combines function with pleasing appearance.

Most people have an intuitive feel for what they like or dislike about a house. But if you want to get involved in the design process, this intuitive understanding has to become conscious, rational knowledge. There are houses all around. Start looking at them in a more thoughtful way, both as a whole and in detail. What works and what doesn't? If you see a house you particularly like, what makes is so attractive? And when you are inside houses, think about their layout. Look at mundane details such as the staircase, or the grouping of rooms that require plumbing services. The intention is not so much that you should be able to design a house yourself, which is ambitious, but rather that you can make informed decisions about what you want, and communicate them to your architect.

For most prospective house-owners, there are two main criteria for consideration in a house. How well does it fit their needs, and how much does it cost? For the selfbuilder there is an extra factor – how easy is it to build? This is especially relevant for the ownhander. To this end, he or she should have one over-riding principle: simplicity. Complexities may be fine when put together by a craftsman, but they absorb an inordinate amount of effort from the ownhander. Let simplicity be next to godliness!

General considerations

A house design is required to satisfy your housing needs, within the constraints of your budget, the site, and the restrictions that the State imposes in the form of Planning and Building Regulations.

Most people, at the outset anyway, have no idea of building costs; it's an unknown area to them. They know the limits of their budget, but they don't know how much house can be built for that, neither on a contracted out, nor on a selfbuild basis. But you will come across rough rules-of-thumb quoted. Building price books, for example, quote building costs per square metre of floor area. (See 'Costings', Chapter 2.) Such figures should be taken only as a very rough guide, but they do give something to work on. (By the way, the nominal floor area used in these figures is calculated from the inner surface of the external walls. It includes the area of the stairwell, internal walls, etc. It is a quickly calculated, very useful measure of the size of a house. Use it, for example, when comparing designs.) Building a large house is generally cheaper, per unit area, than a small one; but large houses often have costlier fittings, which evens up the cost per square metre.

To help the reader relate floor area to house size, here are some representative figures:

80 sq m – 2-bedroomed bungalow
110 sq m – 4-bedroomed bungalow, 3-bedroomed house
140 sq m – spacious, 4-bedroomed house
180 sq m – grand, 4-bedroomed house.

Do take the cost estimates with a pinch of salt. From bricks through to kitchen fitments, the components of a house can vary in price by factors of two or three.

Spon's price book also has a section on comparative prices, which may help you to make some design decisions. For example, it shows that the traditionally timbered roof is about 15% more costly than one using trussed rafters. Could the space gained under a traditional roof compensate for the higher cost and greater difficulty of construction?

The starting point for a design is the plot itself. Make yourself familiar with it.

A steeply sloping site necessitates a design that is either dug into the hillside or raised up from it. If possible, avoid such complexities by finding a level site.

Consider the sun's orientation. Bedrooms facing east let the sun prompt the sleeper out of bed in the mornings. A lounge that faces south-west is warmed by the sun for most of the day, and is a sunny room in the evenings, when it is most used. An opposing requirement, perhaps, is to let the lounge face the road, as part of the public facade. Bathroom, WC, and, perhaps, kitchen are hidden away at the back or side. And for further consideration, what views do all the rooms have? In short, design is a matter of compromise between a host of differing requirements.

Bear in mind the neighbouring properties. Does your design complement them? The Planning authorities invariably forbid a contrast. You can harmonise by using similar materials for roof and walls, and by imitating particular details, eg, roof pitch. On the other hand, if you want to make the house look more imposing, build a high, steep roof; and a grand entrance porch can impress.

Another influence on appearances is the positioning of the window and door frames in the elevations. Architects like them to line up, one over the other, for an orderly appearance – even though, from a consideration of their positions inside the rooms, they might be arranged differently. (Francis Bacon would have arranged them differently!)

Before you purchased the plot, you probably had in mind whether you wanted a house or a bungalow. Bungalows (which were rare before the 1920's) need a plot with a wider frontage; this costs money. (On a narrow plot, a bungalow or house can be built 'sideways on', with the gable end towards the road. But this is generally unattractive and unimpressive.) For the ownhander, a bungalow is easier to build. There is no upper floor to joist and board, nor any staircase to fit. And the lower height is reassuring to anyone not used to heights. It can even be built without normal scaffolding: Use builders' trestles or tower scaffolding – either on the outside or on the inside. (See 'Other forms of scaffolding', Chapter 28.) But a bungalow needs a larger floor slab and more roofing. Some people like living on one level, others don't. Much comes down to personal preference. The overall building costs of bungalow and house are much the same.

Choices:

Layout

Let's look at some particular choices concerning the layout:

Lounge and dining room: Separate, combined in open plan, or a compromise with a room divider?

Kitchen: A small, efficient kitchen just for cooking, or large enough for eating in and looking after toddlers?

Ancillary rooms: Study, cloakroom, utility, etc ?

Bedrooms: How many double, and how many single? *En suite* facilities? Built-in cupboards?

Bathroom and WC: Together, or separate (both can be in use at the same time)? Shower?

Hallway: Spacious, or just a passageway?

Stairs: Straight flight (easy construction) or with turns (more interesting, less daunting)? Headroom needs to be 2 metres at least.

Garage: Integral (cheaper, and usually better looking), or separate (may allow more flexibility in design). Space for workshop? One car or two?

Basement: Out of fashion in Britain this century, but there's much to be said for one. On the Continent, basements with high windows are widely used for utility room, store room, workshop, playroom, guest room, etc.

Conservatory: Coming back into fashion. A simple way to use passive solar gain.

Position

Is the front or the back garden to be the larger? Is the house to be aligned with its neighbours? If the Local Authority have fixed a 'building line', no part of the house can be in front of it.

The whereabouts of drains can influence the position and even the design of a house.

Shape

There's no doubt that a simple rectangular plan makes for the easiest building – for professionals and selfbuilders alike. Even an L-shape, which is hardly complex, brings difficulties to the ownhander, especially in the construction of the roof. When your head is already stuffed full of things to think about, extra is not welcome!

Strip or trenchfill foundations?

Strip foundations are still used by many builders. They are certainly cheaper on materials, but they take longer to build and so are vulnerable to bad weather.

For the ownhander, they have the big advantage of allowing him to practise bricklaying without the results showing. (A modern version, though, uses solid wide blocks instead of cavity construction.)

Trenchfill – the filling of the foundation trenches with concrete – is fast and easy. It is particularly attractive in wet weather when trenches may flood.

An ecological analysis of house-building methods is overdue, but from that perspective, the use of so much concrete can hardly be right.

Concrete or timber floor?

There is a belief that timber floors are warmer than concrete. They do feel warmer to a hand or foot, but they let as much heat escape from the room as a concrete floor. Although wood is a much better insulator than concrete, there is only two or three centimetres of it between the room and the cold air below. Heat passing through a concrete floor (via the ground) has a much greater distance to travel to the outside air. As it happens, the overall effect is that the U-values of timber and concrete floors are much the same.

There are differences, though.

A concrete floor acts as a heat reservoir, helping to stabilise the room temperature. The floor gives up heat if the room temperature drops, but cools the room on a hot day. It is cheaper and easier to put in than a timber floor – especially as Approved Document C of the Building Regulation expects 5 cm of concrete (and a dpm) to be put under a timber floor anyway.

A timber floor does have some advantages. The space beneath can be used for plumbing pipes and electric cable. (With an unscreeded concrete floor, ducts have to be put in as the slab is laid, or else all the pipes and cables dropped down the walls.) Some people prefer the spring of a timber floor. And of course, if the floor is boarded with timber rather than chipboard, it is attractive in itself.

Floor screed or not?

The traditional method of putting in a concrete floor was to lay a rough floor slab, and then, after the shell had been built, to put down a 5 cm floor screed. However, the screed is often dispensed with nowadays, simply by giving a good finish to the slab when it is laid. This makes a lot of sense, saving both materials and time; and for the ownhander, it also saves the need to learn yet another skill, screeding. It's easier to make a floor flat with a straight tamping board when laying the concrete, than it is by screeding it. (If you try screeding yourself, you may end up using expensive levelling compound to get it flat.)

However, it is easier to incorporate ducts for plumbing pipes into a screed than a slab.

Wall construction

Until very recently, the orthodox construction of a wall was an inner leaf of blockwork, a cavity, and an outer leaf of brickwork. But nowadays, the cavity often contains insulation. It may be partially filled, which preserves a cavity to deter damp. Or it may be totally filled. In this case, the insulation should have an Agrément Certificate to show that it resists damp penetration. Furthermore, in the modern, rather air-tight house, the material should preferably be permeable in order that unwanted gases and odours can diffuse out through the walls.

Some variations for part or all of the outer leaf:

Stonework, usually reconstituted

Blockwork, faced with render, tiles or boarding

Bare blockwork. This can be made to look attractive, but has it ever been tried on a British house?

Window frames

The window frames have a lot of influence on the overall appearance of a house. Collect the glossy brochures put out by the joinery manufacturers. The choice of style is more limited than would be expected, since by and large they carry the same range of styles. Make sure that the rebates are wide enough for your sealed units. (Most units are 14 mm thick: better units are 20 mm.)

Select metric frames; heightwise, these fit the $7\frac{1}{2}$ cm gauge of metric brickwork.

The depths of windows usually varies. Living rooms have deep windows to allow a view of gardens; kitchens and bathrooms have higher window sills which will be above any appliances and which will preserve privacy. Note that window and door heads are invariably in line.

Gable or hipped roof?

The carpentry and tiling are much more difficult for a hipped roof than for a gable roof. On the other hand, the brickwork is easier – it is finished level all the way round, without any gable. Overall, it is easier and, doubtless, cheaper to do as most builders do, and to put on a gable roof.

Trussed rafters or traditional roof timbers?

The modern construction uses prefabricated trussed rafters. These can be erected quickly, with little skill. They can span a wide distance – up to 10 metres – without the need for support. The disadvantage is that the loft is a forest of spars, incapable of being converted into usable space.

The traditional method, using heftier timbers cut on site, does result in a more useful loft space. About 30% more timber is used than with trusses, but the actual material cost is less because there is no prefabrication. The purlins need support from struts off a load-bearing wall, and this reduces the flexibility in the layout of rooms. More skill and time are required to build the roof. Nonetheless, the construction of a simple gable roof should be within the capabilities of an ownhander. Be warned: A hipped roof is a good deal more difficult!

Overhanging or flush verge?

Assuming a gable roof, there are two popular choices for the detail at the verge. One is to use a pair of 'gable ladders' to take the roof out over the gable. A ladder is finished with a barge board and soffit. In the past, these were invariably painted white, standing out as markers of private, as opposed to Council, housing.

The Local Authority housing usually used a cheaper and maintenance-free verge. Dubbed by some a 'Council verge', this used a strip of asbestos board to carry the tiles over the gable with a narrow overhang. This style is now very much in vogue, albeit with decorative brickwork at the verges. (Non-toxic cement/fibre boards are available instead of the asbestos board.) But a side-effect of this method is that the gable wall needs corbelling out (to block off the gap beneath the eaves). This corbelling, usually built nowadays in brick, looks attractive, but it is a complication. The cut line of brickwork up the verge needs to look neat, as there is no barge board to hide it.

Eaves

The most popular treatment for the underside of the eaves is to box them in with a fascia and soffit. A more rustic effect is obtained by leaving the rafter feet exposed – block off between the trusses with metal mesh to prevent birds nesting on top of the wall.

Roof pitch

A roof pitch that imitates neighbouring roofs helps to harmonise the buildings. But that is not the only criterion:

A steep pitch makes a house look more impressive (is status what you seek?), but it require more materials and so is a little more costly. If built with traditional timbers, a steep roof yields a usable loft space.

Shallow pitches can influence the tiles used. Plain tiles need a steep slope: 35°, or more. Single-lap tiles are weather-tight on shallower roofs – generally down to a pitch of 30°, though some designs can be used even at 22°.

That sort of slope feels quite comfortable; it's easy to walk directly on the tiles. Most ownhanders will feel more relaxed working on a shallow pitch.

Flat roof

Flat roofs are even easier to walk on! And they are easier and cheaper to build. However, they do have a reputation for leaking, due to bad maintenance or bad design. New materials, with 20-year guarantees, should make this less of a problem.

Flat roofs don't have to look ugly. There are fine looking houses and bungalows with flat roofs. They merge with their natural surroundings, rather than trying to dominate them.

The architect, Walter Segal, used a novel design of flat roof in his system for selfbuilders. If you want to use a flat roof, look at his method.

But can you get Planning permission with a flat roof?

Chimney

A chimney is embedded in the national psyche as being an integral part of 'home'. (Would Freud have had something to say about that?) As an occupier, you may well wish your house to have a chimney. What is more delicious than the aroma of a woodstove in winter? But as a builder, you may come to see the chimney in a different light – as a ponderous relic of bygone times. It needs deep foundations, a lot of brickwork, and complicated timber, tile and lead work where it emerges from the roof. Simplicity says to do without the chimney if you can. (If you can't, or won't, it's possible to get prefabricated, lightweight sections for quicker and easier chimney building. But above the roof, use brickwork for show.)

Stairs

The simplest and cheapest stair is a straight flight, but if it is broken up by a landing, the ascent seems easier. A landing also allows a turn, either right-angled or dog-legged (180°). If space is limited, winders can be used for the turn. But they make the construction, and perhaps the fitting, much more complicated.

If you are intending to use a ready-made stair, design the height of the upper floor to suit it. The most usual rise is 20 cm, with a 'go' of 22·3 cm. This gives a total rise (finished floor level to finished floor level above) of 260 cm (13 × 20 cm). The total go is 267·6 cm (12 × 22·3 cm).

There are a couple of points to note in that last sentence. Is the number of steps 12, or is it 13? Do you realise why there is this apparent oddity in the arithmetic? The other point is to allow for the floorboarding (and possibly a floor screed) to make up the finished levels – remember this when ordering stairs.

Plumbing

There's a very good plumbing book which states "For really successful single stack installation, the building should virtually be designed round the plumbing system"! Perhaps this is an exaggeration, yet there is some truth in it. Ideally, kitchen and utility room are adjacent, and the bathroom and WC above them. The runs for the water supplies can be kept short, saving the pipework and the wasted hot water of long runs. More crucially, the waste runs can also to be kept compact. Long runs to the stack, across the lie of the floor joists, can be difficult or impossible.

For two decades the Building Regulations required the waste and soil pipes to be within the fabric of the building. This gave a clean, uncluttered appearance to the outside of a house. But it is no longer a requirement of the Regulations. Placed inside, a stack pipe needs sound proofing and boxing in; yet still the sound of waste running down it can be obtrusive. So you may prefer to fix the stack and its associated waste pipes to an inconspicuous outside wall. Placed outside, the pipework can spoil the appearance of the house; there's also a small chance that a dripping tap in frosty weather could cause a waste pipe to freeze up. Neither option is a good one!

The position of the stack is important; so also is the position of the hot water cylinder and its associated airing cupboard. This should be given consideration at the design stage, especially if there is to be solid fuel boiler with gravity hot water circulation.

Insulation

The standard of insulation required by the Building Regulations has for long been a minimum standard, rather than an economic one. But the standard has been steadily rising over the years and, at last, is reaching a sensible value. Even so, you may still wish to treat the present requirements as the minimum, not the optimum. Design in for full insulation. It's cheaper and easier than upgrading later. Part of the cost is immediately offset by the savings on a smaller central heating system. The rest is soon repaid by the smaller fuel bills and increased comfort in the future.

Alternatives

You don't have to design a brick-and-block house. You could design your own timber-frame house using TRADA's book, *Timber Frame Construction*. (See 'Books', Appendix 4.) Then send your design out to the timber-frame manufacturers for quotes for making it. (And you could ask them to check the design over!)

Walter Segal had ideas about people doing their own designs as well as their own building. Find out more from the Walter Segal Trust. (See Appendix 4 again.)

Design life

The design life for most contemporary housing is 60 years. The intended life of a building can affect how it is built. A small example: Using galvanized nails for roofing may be good enough for a life of 60 years, but if you're aiming for 100 years, use alloy nails.

Don't presume, though, that to build to last so long is necessarily a good thing. There may be physical obsolescence of the building. And who can say how people will want to live in 100 years' time? As social patterns change, our housing – even the street – may become socially obsolete.

Fine details:

Size and shape of rooms

You might like to consider some possible layouts for the furniture and fixtures in your proposed rooms. Will it all fit together? To this end, make scaled cut-outs to represent the furniture and fixtures (cupboards, sanitaryware, kitchen appliances, and the like) and see how they fit onto the plans. It's better to find that room dimensions are unsuitable before building, rather than later.

Kitchen

There's plenty of awareness of the need to plan an efficient layout for the kitchen; using the above method is particularly helpful here. The kitchen is usually so full of appliances and cupboards that it's difficult to find space for everything, particularly a radiator.

The appliances of today and tomorrow are: sink (single or double), oven and hob (together or separate), fridge, freezer, clothes washer, clothes drier, and dish washer. Some of these can be kept in a utility room, of course. You may well not want all of them, but for future convenience it is as well to allocate space.

Doors

Rooms are generally more usable if the doorway is near a corner rather than in the middle of a wall. But don't place a doorway tight into a corner: Allow space for a comfortable passageway, or at the very least, for the architrave. In confined spaces, a narrower door can be used. For internal doors, there's a choice between the metric size and the much more widely available imperial size.

Doors usually open into a room. Which side for the hinges? A general convention is to preserve the privacy of the room by hanging the door so that it opens towards the side, not the centre, of the room. But this is not a rigid rule and may be over-ridden (eg, for a kitchen door, easy access is more important).

Special features

It is much easier to put in special features at the design stage rather than to add them to a finished house. Such things as:

A wide hatch from kitchen to diner
Plentiful telecom, TV, and hi-fi sockets
Feature arches
Built-in cupboards, etc

– these can all be built in easily during construction. Take the opportunity, as a selfbuilder, to build a home to suit yourself.

It need not be like the anonymous product of a speculative builder.

Construction drawings

There is some confusion of terminology with respect to drawings. Lay people tend to think of 'drawings' in an artistic context; the diagrams that an architect produces they call 'plans'. But architects themselves call their diagrams 'drawings', and 'plans' are one special type of them – horizontal projections. Interestingly enough, the Building Regulations refer to 'plans', not 'drawings'. However, this book follows the architects' terminology.

Some people may be familiar enough with house-building to be confident about producing their own architectural drawings. The following drawings will be needed (with convenient scales indicated):

Combined location and site plan, 1:500. This identifies the site; shows its boundaries and trees; gives the outline of the house and the driveway; and shows the drains and rodding access.

To produce this, you need a plan of the plot. When you purchased the plot, you were probably given one. If not, try the Local Authority – they may have a plan showing its boundaries.

Ground floor and first floor plans, 1:50. These are horizontal sections taken halfway up the window frames for each floor. The ground floor plan may also show the foundation trenches by dotted lines. (Selected details not in the actual plane of the section are shown dotted.) The upper floor plan may indicate the floor joists. Stairs need to be shown. It's sensible also to show the fitments in the kitchen, the sanitaryware in the bathroom, the hot water cylinder, and the boiler.

Four elevations, 1:50. These are views of the front, back and two sides.

The above are needed for an application for Full Planning permission. (For Outline permission, only a location plan is required.) Additionally, for the building inspector:

Vertical section, 1:50. This is generally taken in the direction of the roof trusses. It extends below ground to show the foundations and floor slab.

And lastly, for yourself or subcontractors:

Details, 1:5, 1:10, 1:20, etc. These may be included to show some involved construction. (For example, Fig. 5, Chapter 7 shows a typical eaves detail.)

A few selfbuilders do produce their own drawings. There need be no mystique about this. The drawings don't all have to be aligned on large sheets of paper, although nowadays, with a print shop on every high street, this is not difficult to achieve. An easy way to produce constructional drawings is to use graph paper with light green squares. On a copier set for high contrast, these can be blanked out – check beforehand. (An architect uses a special drawing board which makes the production of vertical and horizontal lines easy.)

Remember to put a scale with the drawings. Also, it's common practice to mark off, around the outside of plans, the measurements for the main features – walls, frames and the like. (By the way, if the written and drawn dimensions don't agree, the written figure is taken to be the correct one.)

And lastly, how many copies do you need? – Many more than you think! To start with, four for Planning applications and two for Building Regulations. If you are subcontracting everything and getting three quotes for each trade, that's another 21 copies. (You can ask for your drawings back, but they rarely do come back.) If you are doing the work yourself, let's say that you'll use just one for each trade (eg, to mark on the electrical circuits). Do you want three quotes for your roof trusses? – that's another three copies. Then there's one you need on site, one in the office, one that blows away, one that gets sodding wet, one for a future purchaser of your home, one for a souvenir... A lot!

Model

Drawings are the usual way to represent a design, but a model is more effective. A high quality model can be made from balsa wood, obtainable from model shops. But for exploring the design, a simple and quickly made cardboard model is all that is needed. It can give you a much better picture than construction drawings. Don't think that it marks you out as an amateur. Some architects too work with models.

Building Regulations

If a builder erect a house for a man and do not make its construction firm, and the house which he built collapse and cause the death of the owner of the house, that builder shall be put to death – The Code of Hammurabi. (Hammurabi was King of Babylon from 1792 – 1750 BC.)

Regulations for building have been around for a long time! Our present ones, less harsh but more comprehensive than the code above, originated as model byelaws in the last century. Local Authorities were made responsible for drawing up the actual byelaws and enforcing them. The concern was the safety and sanitation of the populace. Periodically since then, new versions of the Regulations have been introduced.

The last such major reform was in 1985, when the Building Regulations were completely recast. Prior to 1985, the Regulations described the methods of construction required. They now state, instead, the objectives to be achieved. This should allow more flexibility in constructional methods in the future.

And they are now expressed in proper English, instead of Legalese. For example, Requirement C4 of Schedule 1 is: *The walls, floors, and roof of a building shall adequately resist the passage of moisture to the inside of the building.*

That's easy enough to understand. But perhaps it is rather vague in the context of an actual, practical application. So the Regulations are backed up by 'Approved Documents' which show practical ways of complying with the Regulations. For example, Approved Document C for Regulation C4 has four pages showing various ways of constructing walls to resist the passage of moisture.

There is much more flexibility in the new Regulations. Not only do the Approved Documents embrace a much wider spectrum of possibilities than the earlier Regulations, there is no assumption that these are the only possibilities. You can use other methods as long as you can convince the building inspector that they satisfy the requirements of the Regulations.

If you are designing your house yourself, one of the guides to the Regulations might be useful (though expensive).

Applying for Building Regulations approval is simple. Obtain a form from the building inspectors and return it with a couple of copies of 'Full Plans'. The fees (in 1990) are £60-95 to deposit plans (ie, to have them checked), and £162-15 for inspections. These prices include VAT – remember, the selfbuilder can't reclaim VAT on fees. You should hear the result within a month. If the plans are approved, you will receive a set of postcards to send to the inspector at each inspection stage. (In fact, it is generally easier to phone.) Most of the inspections concern the foundations and drains – work which will be covered over and inaccessible later.

A theoretical alternative to the 'Full Plans' procedure is the 'Building Notice', in which it is not necessary to submit plans at all. That sounds good but isn't. The inspector checks that what you are building complies with the Regulations as you build it. But what if it doesn't? It is better by far to make changes on the drawing board than on the ground.

(It may possibly be worth pointing out that, if you don't want to be bound by some particular Building Regulation, you can apply for a 'relaxation' of the regulation.)

Agrément Certificates

The British Board of Agrément is a limited company controlled by the Government; they test new building products. If a test product is found to be satisfactory, an Agrément Certificate is issued for it. Submission for testing is voluntary, but if a product receives a certificate, its manufacturer invariably advertises this as a selling point. It's a very good system for allowing innovation into an industry rather constricted by tradition. A certificate allows a product to be used with some confidence. (The certificate often gives useful, practical information about the product, eg, its installation.)

Under the earlier Building Regulations, the certificates had no status. For example, some Local Authorities would not allow air admittance valves on the top of a soil stack, even though the valves had an Agrément Certificate. That can no longer be the case. Regulation 7 states:

"Any building work shall be carried out with proper materials and in a workmanlike manner."

The Approved Document that backs this up lists criteria for establishing the fitness of materials. These include:

Past experience (can Devon cob make a comeback?)
Agrément certificate
Conforming to a British Standard
Tests or calculations that show the materials to be adequate.

British Standards

While Agrément certificates establish the fitness of an innovatory product, British Standards deal with established ones. They cover a vast number of products, from humble stuff like sand to complex items like trussed rafters. As noted above, compliance with a British Standard infers compliance with Building Regulation 7.

Pan-European standards are slowly being established. During the Nineties, British Standards will gradually be changed to conform with these Eurocodes. In the present Standards 'covert imperialism' is rife. Lip service is paid to the metric system by quoting quantities in metric although their underlying logic is imperial – a case of falling between two stools. Hopefully, Eurocodes will put an end to this nonsense.

20

MORTAR AND CONCRETE

☆

☆

☆

☆

☆

☆

☆

SAND, STONE AND CEMENT are the humble materials which support houses and stick them together. They seem so simple, yet they do have their subtleties. Most builders get to know their properties intuitively over the years, but some simple theory can help the selfbuilder. They are versatile and robust materials that can withstand a lot of abuse; but an understanding of their properties enables better results to be obtained from them.

Aggregate

Sand is merely small stones, and sand and stone are both technically called 'aggregates'. 'Coarse aggregate' is the rather awkward term for stone – it will not pass through a $\frac{1}{2}$ cm square sieve. 'Fine aggregate' (sand) will do so. The aggregates give bulk to mortar and concrete. They are inert, and do not react chemically with the cement – the aggregate is just bound together by the cement paste.

The size and shape of the aggregate have a marked effect on the properties of a mix. Angular particles interlock and help to yield a strong concrete. In a mortar, on the other hand, round particles are better: They flow over each other more easily and so enhance the workability of the mortar.

The size of particles influences the effects of surface tension in the water of the mix. Water is attracted to many solids, as children learn at school by seeing water rise up a glass capillary tube. The narrower the tube, the higher the water is drawn. The same effect is at work in a mix. The smaller the particles in it, the smaller the voids between particles and the more strongly water is drawn into the voids. The water is attracted to the particles and helps to stick them together, resulting in a more cohesive mix. This is highly desirable in a mortar (or plaster). Another desirable result due to the presence of small particles is that water retention is improved. (See 'Mortar', later in this chapter.)

But in the 'bulking' of sand, the effects of surface tension are a bit of a nuisance. If dry sand is dampened, it expands. Tiny drops of water are attracted between touching grains of sand. The pressure due to surface tension forces the grains apart, and the sand swells up. As more water is added, the drops coalesce, and eventually all the separate surfaces of the water disappear. There is then no longer any surface tension effect, and the sand returns to its former volume. (An observant reader may be puzzled that it was previously stated that water helped to stick the grains together, while now it is being said that water forces them apart. In fact, there is no contradiction. A droplet of water may be attracted between two grains of sand, thereby forcing them apart, but it then helps to hold them in this separated position.)

A fine sand can increase its volume by 40% when dampened by 10% of water. A coarse sand only bulks by half of this, with half the water. (You can verify these effects for yourself by drying some sand in an oven and then gradually wetting it.) Typically, washed sand from a quarry can be taken to be bulked by 20%. This is a factor to bear in mind when measuring out for a mix. (Recipes for mixes assume this slightly damp sand.)

'Grading' is the mixing together of aggregates of different sizes. This mixing may be natural: 'As-dug' or 'ballast' is a natural mixture of stone and sand in proportions roughly suitable for concreting. More often, though, aggregates are separated out into different sizes and then remixed in desired proportions. There are even British Standards for grading aggregates. A sand for mortar has a specification with predominantly fine particles, whereas a concreting sand contains substantially coarser particles; a sand for plastering/rendering/screeding is intermediate between these two. There are also grading specifications for 'all-in' aggregate for concreting. Fortunately, all this can be left to your supplier. (As-dug is unlikely to fit in with the grading specification, and should be used only for non-critical concrete work.)

Gravel is a natural stone derived from quartz (silica rock) and naturally rounded by the action of water aeons ago. Other stone is obtained artificially by crushing limestone, granite or sandstone. Sand is a smaller version of gravel. It may contains impurities such as clay – tiny amounts of this can aid workability. But there is too much of it if a handful of sand, after being squeezed together, leaves the palm stained.

It's usually cheaper to purchase sizable amounts of aggregate direct from a quarry rather than from a builders' merchant. (See 'Sand & Gravel Suppliers' and 'Quarries' in the *Yellow Pages*.)

Lime

Lime was one of the earliest materials to be used for binding aggregate together. It is made by heating limestone or chalk, which are both forms of calcium carbonate. Calcium dioxide gas is driven off to leave quicklime:

$$CaCO_3 = CaO + CO_2$$

Before it can be used, the quicklime has to be slaked with water to give hydrated lime (calcium hydroxide):

$$CaO + H_2O = Ca(OH)_2$$

A few decades ago, the first job to be done on a building site was to dig a pit in which quicklime was left to slake. These days, the lime is delivered as a convenient powder, already slaked. This form of lime depends on cement to give strength to a mix, although the lime does very slowly harden by reacting with carbon dioxide from the air. The lime reverts back to calcium carbonate, giving off water:

$$Ca(OH)_2 + CO_2 = CaCO_3 + H_2O$$

This is a good reason for leaving plasters which contain lime for several months before papering.

There are, however, other, less common forms of lime. Some limestone contains clay impurities, and when it is heated more complex compounds are formed. These can be slaked with a limited amount of water to yield 'hydraulic' lime. This is so called because it reacts with (further) water to set (not combining with carbon dioxide like the non-hydraulic lime described above).

Cement

If, instead of relying on clay impurities in the limestone to make hydraulic lime, extra clay is added (about a quarter clay), then the result after heat treatment is cement. Portland cement was patented in 1824 and since then has replaced hydraulic lime as a binder. It is composed of compounds (calcium silicates and calcium aluminates) not unlike the ones in hydraulic lime. It could be called hydraulic cement because it too sets by hydration. Interlocking needles of the hydrated crystals are formed. The result is much stronger than that of hydraulic lime. And a paste of cement and water not only sets very hard, it also adheres to aggregate, steel, etc.

Most cement used is ordinary portland cement, but there are variations. Rapid hardening cement has been ground extra fine, allowing hydration to occur more rapidly. White cement, useful sometimes for visual reasons, is made by using china clay. (It is expensive, about double the price of ordinary cement.) Other special cements are made by varying the proportions of the different compounds.

Mortar

The novice may think of mortar as simply a mix of sand, cement and water that sets to hold bricks together. In fact, if it is to do its job, a mortar requires several properties that are not immediately obvious.

In the plastic state, a mortar should:

Be cohesive, ie, it should stick together. With a well graded sand, the voids between large grains of sand are filled by smaller grains, so there are only small voids between the grains. This gives a strong surface tension effect, holding the grains of sand together.

Be pliable, ie, it should flow easily into any shape that it is forced into. The sand grains should be rounded, rather than angular, and, again, well graded.

Retain water, ie, some, but only some, of the water should be sucked out of the mortar into the surrounding porous bricks or blocks. This quickly stiffens the mortar enough to support subsequent courses until the chemical setting takes effect. The mix must retain some water both to set and to minimise drying shrinkage. If too much water is sucked out, then the mortar (or render) can only shrink. With a well graded sand, the voids between the grains are tiny, so they strongly attract water, ie, water retention is good.

In the set state, the properties required are more obvious. The mortar should be:

Strong; ideally, it should be as strong as the bricks, though not stronger. The proportion of cement in the mix affects this.

Durable; in particular, it should be able to withstand weathering.

Adhesive; it should adhere well to bricks and blocks.

The sand to use is called 'soft' or 'building' sand, and is composed of well graded, rounded grains that give a workable mortar. A common mix is 1:6 of cement and sand, with a liquid plasticiser to improve the workability.

Adding lime instead of plasticiser has numerous small advantages which are becoming recognised. Not least of these is that the mortar is more durable. The fine grains of lime fill the voids between the sand to give a more impervious mortar. It probably won't affect you, but the brickwork will last longer without repointing! Another desirable effect is that mortars containing lime accommodate any settlement by developing numerous tiny and harmless cracks. Mortars without lime are more brittle, and they give way with a single and undesirable, wide crack. Furthermore, in the wet mix, fine lime particles aid cohesion, pliability, and water retention: ie, the lime improves workability.

A common mix for 'compo' (ie, 'composition' mortar, also called 'gauged' mortar) is 1:1:6 of cement, lime and sand.

The desirable effects of lime on workability can be improved even further by soaking the lime overnight before use. Add the lime to water and stir it to a slurry. Leave it to settle; surplus water can be skimmed off before use. This lime putty can be kept a long time. Few people bother with this soaking, but it is reckoned to be desirable. (In some countries, lime is always sold as a putty in a tub, never as a powder in a bag.)

Taking this a stage further for even better effects, lime and sand in the appropriate ratio can be mixed with water to give 'coarse stuff'. This too is left overnight, or longer. The stuff is used, as it is required, by adding cement (and further water). In fact, premixed coarse stuff can now be purchased. (See 'Mortar suppliers' in the *Yellow Pages*.) If you are intending to use a pigmented mortar, note that the colour lasts better with lime in the mix. So some pigmented coarse stuff from a mortar supplier would be very sensible. Protected with polythene above and below, it keeps for many weeks.

Mortar mixes

A plain mix of sand, cement and water gives a mortar that will set satisfactorily. But generally its workability is improved by using one of the following methods:

Add a proprietary plasticiser (eg, 'Febmix')

The plasticiser is added to the water. Don't add extra plasticiser – it doesn't improve the mortar.

Minute bubbles are produced in the mix and they both 'lubricate' the mix and bind it together. (In emergency, washing up liquid has been used.) This is a good method to use if frost is imminent: Small ice crystals are harmlessly formed inside the bubbles.

1:6 of cement and sand.

Below the dpc use a stronger mix – 1:4.

Use masonry cement

Powder plasticisers are premixed with the cement. This is a more expensive method.

1:4½ of masonry cement and sand.

Add lime

The beneficial effects of lime have been described above. 1:1:6 of cement, lime and sand.

For internal blockwork a weaker mix can be used – 1:2:9.

To make up a mortar, the dry ingredients are mixed together first, and then the water is added. (Though some say: Add half the water at the start.) The wetness required takes some experience to judge. If the mortar is too dry, it won't flow; and the bricks need more than light pressure to position them. If the mortar is too wet, it will be too sloppy to control properly, and it will not support the weight of further brickwork on top. Use mortar within a couple of hours of mixing – or less in hot weather, when the chemical process proceeds faster. 'Knocking up' – the addition of more water to stiffened mortar – is disapproved of.

The colour of mortar depends upon the sand used. Different quarries may produce differently coloured sands. As would be expected, cement makes mortar greyer, and lime tends to whiten it. For special effects, white cement or coloured pigments (cement colours) can be used. These are expensive.

Don't lay bricks in frosty weather – freshly laid mortar is spoilt if it freezes. Air-entraining plasticisers do help in cold weather, but they should not be relied upon.

It's a common practice to measure out the ratios of mixes by shovelfuls, but this is not accurate. A 'shovelful' of cement may have only half the volume of a 'shovelful' of sand. For more precision, measure volumes by bucketfuls.

Quantities

Let's look at a 1:1:6 mix. How much cement, lime and sand is needed to make up 1 cu m of mortar?

We can take the volume of sand as the final volume of mortar, and the density of sand as 1·6 tonnes per cu m. So the weight of sand required is 1·6 tonnes.

The volume of cement required is 1/6 cu m. A bag of cement (50 kg) occupies ·035 cu m. So 4·8 bags of cement are required $\left(\frac{1}{6 \times \cdot 035}\right)$.

A bag of lime (25 kg) occupies ·042 cu m. And so 4·0 bags of lime are required $\left(\frac{1}{6 \times \cdot 042}\right)$.

How much mortar is needed for a square metre of stretcher bonded brickwork?

Mortar joints are 1 cm thick and 10 cm wide; each brick requires 290 cu cm of mortar ($[21\frac{1}{2} + 6\frac{1}{2} + 1] \times 10$). There are 60 bricks in a square metre of the brickwork. So ·017 cu m of mortar are required ($60 \times 290 \div 1{,}000{,}000$).

(Some books erroneously quote a figure twice as large. The mistake doubtless arises from considering an isolated brick enclosed by two bed joints and two cross joints. But as part of an area of brickwork, only one bed joint and one cross joint can be assigned to an individual brick.)

In a similar way, we can work out how much mortar is required for a square metre of blockwork. Each block requires 665 cu cm of mortar ($[44 + 21\frac{1}{2} + 1] \times 10$). There are 10 blocks per square metre; so ·0066 cu m of mortar are required.

Using these figures, estimates for the quantities of cement, lime and sand can be made. Cement and lime can be purchased as work progresses, but it's best to order the sand in one batch – it's considerably cheaper in bulk and the colour won't vary. (Allow 15% for wastage and over-order – sand is always useful.)

Concrete

Concrete is mortar with stone in it. Or put another way, it is stone and sand, stuck together with a cement paste. The ratio of stone to sand is usually 1:2, which gives a well graded aggregate with only a small volume of voids. The cement paste that fills the voids is the costly item, so minimising the voids keeps the costs down.

(As a matter of passing interest, there is another, completely different, approach. 'No fines' concrete is made without sand. Lots of air voids are left in the concrete; only the surface of the stones is covered with the cement paste. This concrete has some desirable properties: It is lighter, a better heat insulator, and it has a well keyed surface for plastering or rendering. But the selfbuilder is unlikely to come across it.)

Ready-mixed concrete by the truckful is nearly as cheap as the materials for mixing your own. It saves a lot of effort and is better mixed. A full-sized truck of six cubic metres carries about 15 tonnes of concrete. Imagine mixing that yourself, a shovelful at a time! For smaller amounts, smaller trucks are available; but the unit price goes up and it may be worthwhile to mix your own.

The usual maximum stone size is 2 cm. (It shouldn't be more than a quarter of the thickness of the concrete.) The usual mix is 1:3:6 of cement, sand and stone; a common stronger mix is 1:2:4. These proportions are by volume – good enough for house-building, though for more critical work, like bridges, the ingredients would be weighed for more accuracy.

The strength of concrete is determined by the ratio of cement to water. There is a necessary amount of water required for the hydration of cement (12 kg of water for a 50 kg bag of cement). Any water in excess of this evaporates, thereby leaving tiny voids which weaken the material. But this theoretical ratio results in a mix which is much too dry to be worked. It can't be shaped, and air voids are left which weaken the concrete. So in practice, 20 kg to 40 kg of water per bag of cement are contained in a mix. (The water is not measured on site – there is an unknown amount of water in the damp aggregate.) Even over this range, there is a big variation in strength. The wetter mix results in a concrete only a third as strong as the rather dry mix. Avoid the soup-like concoctions of many amateurs! The concrete should be just wet enough to compact. (A wet mix may also suffer other faults. It may 'bleed' – water rises to the surface and dries off to leave a cement dust. And as the mix dries, it may shrink and so crack.)

When you order ready-mixed, the company may well ask you what slump you want. If this question bamboozles you, just say what the concrete is for and they will answer the question for themselves. The slump is a measure of the workability of the mix. It is measured in a simple way. A metal cone, 30 cm long and looking something like a megaphone, is filled with the wet concrete and stood on a flat surface. The metal cone is then lifted up to leave behind a 30 cm high cone of wet concrete. But its weight causes the top of the concrete to drop and the sides to bulge. The drop is measured and gives the slump; 5 cm is a common slump. The workability can be increased by adding water. The slump will increase and the strength decrease. (If the weather is hot or you are short-handed, rather than add extra water ask to have retarder added when you order the concrete. This will slow down the setting time.)

Something else to be aware of, when ordering, is that most ready-mixed suppliers specify a mix by its design strength, not its nominal composition. But if you ask for a composition, they will do the conversion for you. For example, a 1:3:6 mix with a maximum stone size of 2 cm and a slump of 5 cm is pretty well equivalent to a mix specified to have a strength of 14 N/mm^2 after 28 days from laying. The stronger 1:2:4 mix is more or less equivalent to a 21 N/mm^2 mix.

All these strengths refer to the crushing strength of concrete. A disadvantage of the material is that it is much weaker in tension, only about a tenth as strong. To overcome this, the great tensile strength of steel can be used. The concrete is cast with steel bars within it for reinforcement. For a beam, the tension occurs on the underside, so the steel bars should be placed there – say a couple of centimetres in from the surface for weather protection. Lintels are sometimes cast *in situ* like this. Use twisted bar, or plain bar with the ends hooked up. (6 mm is about the right diameter.) Reinforce posts with a bar at each corner.

Many ready-mixed suppliers have technical representatives who will be pleased to visit you on site and discuss your requirements. This is a good chance for you to pick their brains.

Practicalities:

Preparation

To contain wet concrete, stout formwork, or shuttering, is required. It must be firm enough to withstand the tamping. $2\frac{1}{2}$ cm sawn timber is suitable, held by 5 cm square pegs. For finer work, planed timber is better, brushed with mould oil to release it from the concrete. Formwork must be designed so that it can be stripped without disturbing the concrete. For simple shapes this is no problem. (If they are to hand, double-headed nails are useful. They can be readily removed to release the formwork.)

If concrete is being laid onto the ground, hardcore is generally put down. This acts as a cheap filling to give the depth required.

Estimating quantities

The length and width of a slab are obvious enough. The depth is tricky if it is variable. In this case, measure the depth at regular spacings over the slab and calculate an average. Remember to express all three factors in metres to obtain the volume in cubic metres: obvious enough, but easily overlooked.

It is sensible to slightly over-order, eg by 10%. If you have somewhere ready to use up any surplus – fine. If not, the truck will take back any that it hasn't discharged. But you still have to pay for it.

If you are mixing concrete yourself, you will need to estimate quantities for the different ingredients. DIY manuals contain charts to help with this. Otherwise, it is easy enough to work our directly. Find out from your suppliers the density of their aggregate, eg, for a typical ballast, 1·9 tonnes per cubic metre. The volume of ballast will equal the volume of concrete, as the cement fills voids in the ballast. For a 1:4 general purpose mix, divide the ballast volume by 4 to give the volume of cement. Since a 50 kg bag of cement occupies ·035 cubic metres, the answer can be converted into the number of bags required – eg, 7 bags per cubic metre for 1:4 concrete $\left(\frac{1}{4 \times \cdot 035}\right)$.

If you are using separate stone and sand, their combined volume is less than you might expect – some of the sand fills voids in the stone. Thus a 1:2:3 mix of cement, sand, and stone is equivalent to a 1:4 mix of cement and ballast. A cubic metre of typical stone weighs 1·4 tonnes, and sand 1·6 tonnes.

Mixing concrete

If you are mixing your own concrete, there are several different sequences recommended. The following is advised by the British Cement Association:

1) Add half the stone and half the water to the mixer. Let the mixer run to help scour itself clean.

2) Add most of the cement and sand.

3) Add the remaining ingredients gradually, keeping the mix wet until the end to prevent build-up on the drum.

4) Mix for a further two minutes.

The consistency is somewhat difficult to judge in the mixer, but the material should fall from the blades without looking crumbly.

In general, keep the materials on one side of the mixer, and barrow the concrete off from the other.

Laying concrete

If you are using ready-mixed, get the truck driver to discharge the concrete where it is to be laid. Otherwise, you will have a lot of extra work on your hands – a cubic metre of concrete is equivalent to about 20 barrow-loads. The chute on the truck can be swivelled to direct the ready-mixed towards its destination. Ask the driver to change the truck's position if that will save you work.

Spread the wet concrete quickly by shovel, working it well into the sides and corners to avoid air pockets. Level it off with a rake. The faster the work is done, the easier it is. This really is a case of 'Many hands make light work'. At this stage, the concrete level should be a centimetre or two above the formwork.

Next, the concrete is compacted to drive out air voids. A tamping board is passed across the surface with a chopping action. (A straight scaffold board is suitable. Handles on it will let you and your helper work standing up.) Advance the board half its thickness for each chop, and do a couple of passes over the surface. Don't overdo the tamping as this will bring the cement paste to the surface.

Level off the surface by 'sawing' the tamping board across it, supporting each end of the board on the formwork. When an excess of concrete builds up in front of the board, shovel it away. (This is a three-person job.) Fill in any hollows. Repeat until the surface is level. It's a good idea to go along the formwork, hitting it with a lump hammer to settle the concrete.

Finishing

Concreting requires little skill – people rarely claim with pride to be concretors. But some finesse is possible with the finishing. Here are a few options:

As tamped: A rough and ready finish – OK for farm drives.

Struck off: Saw gently across the surface with the front edge of the tamping board raised. (Or use a round scaffold pole.) This gives a lightly rippled surface.

Brushed finish: A soft broom on fresh concrete gives a fairly smooth finish. For a corrugated texture – good for paths – trail a stiff nylon broom across the surface.

Exposed stones: Carefully brush the concrete with a soft broom about an hour after laying it, just to remove the laitance. When the concrete is fairly firm, water it from a watering can with a rose, and brush it with a stiff broom to expose the stones. Timing is critical. Too soon, and the stones will be dislodged; too late, and they won't be exposed.

For the best results with this method, small stones should be left out of the mix: Use a 3:4:9 mix of cement, sand, and stone (1 cm to 2 cm only).

Lightly textured: Soon after tamping down, rub a wood or polythene float over the surface in a loose circular motion.

Smooth: First, go over the surface with a wood or polythene float, as above. Wait until the concrete is going off, and then polish out the texture with a steel trowel.

Be sparing with a steel trowel on fresh concrete. Over-trowelling brings excess water to the surface, resulting in a weak, dusty finish. But using a steel trowel later, when 'bleeding' has stopped, produces a hard finish. In fact, for a really smooth, dense surface, go over the work with a steel trowel a few times as the concrete progresively stiffens. Firm pressure is needed towards the end, with the blade at an angle to the surface. For the last session, the trowel is almost scraped across the surface at an angle of 40°.

Follow-up

In hot weather, the concrete should not be allowed to dry out too fast – it may shrink excessively and crack. Cover the surface over or keep it watered, especially for the first couple of days.

Cold weather brings other problems. Below 5°C, setting is extremely slow, so in cold weather add an accelerator to the concrete. Below zero, frost may damage the concrete. If frost is imminent, avoid concreting. But if you are caught out, cover the surface with straw, etc. Heat generated as the concrete cures tends to raise its temperature.

After a week of normal temperatures, concrete will have developed about two-thirds of its final strength.

Formwork can be stripped from the sides after a day or two. But if there is any soffit supporting concrete above (eg, for a lintel cast *in situ*), then leave the soffit in place for a week.

21
BRICKLAYING

Tools
Building up corners
Bricklayers' profiles
Laying to the line
Jointing
Blockwork
Cavity walls
Practice

THE PROSPECT of bricklaying is daunting to the uninitiated, but in fact, it is not such a difficult skill to acquire. Unlike plastering, the novice has time enough to get it right. And the modern house uses only stretcher bond, the simplest of all brickwork bonding. The main difference between amateur and professional is speed. The professional brickie can lay bricks almost as fast as he can pick them up and put them down. After all, he gets enough practice; in his career he may lay millions.

First, some terminology: a 'stretcher' is a brick showing its long face laid horizontally. Almost all the bricks in the cavity walls of a modern house are stretchers. Sometimes a few may be vertical (eg, above window openings), and they are then called 'soldiers'. (In solid walls, on the other hand, many 'headers' are used. These are bricks laid across the wall, with their ends showing in the face of the brickwork.) Another term used is 'bonding'. This is the overlapping of bricks so that vertical joints are not directly above each other. Lines of weakness along the joints are minimised, and the brickwork holds together as a unified whole. The 'cross joints' (also called 'perpends' in textbooks) are the vertical joints in the face of the brickwork; the 'bed' is the horizontal joint. A 'return' is the other arm of a corner.

The dimensions of a brick facilitate bonding. A stretcher occupies the same space as two headers. And if the stretcher is vertical, ie a soldier, its height is that of three courses. In fact, the brick format, which consists of a brick plus mortar joints, is $22\frac{1}{2} \times 11\frac{1}{4} \times 7\frac{1}{2}$ cm. The mortar joints are taken to be 1 cm thick, so the actual brick size is $21\frac{1}{2} \times 10\frac{1}{4} \times 6\frac{1}{2}$ cm. (See Fig. 1.)

Figure 1: Brick and block formats

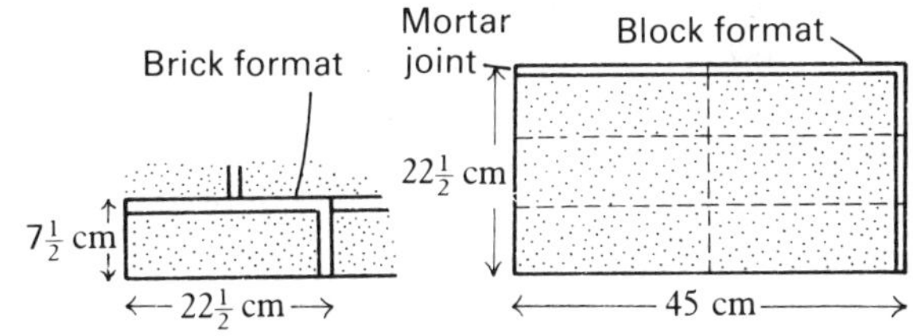

* Block format is equivalent to six brick formats.
* Actual sizes are 1 cm less – the thickness of the joint.

The usual block size is equivalent to six bricks. The face format is $45 \times 22\frac{1}{2}$ cm (two stretchers along, three courses up). The actual size is $44 \times 21\frac{1}{2} \times 10$ cm. Numerous other sizes are available for blocks, including a brick size.

Tools

Brick trowel – get a good-sized one (30 cm) to carry plenty of mortar. One edge is slightly curved for cutting bricks, the other is straight for scraping up mortar off the spot board. (Left-handed versions are sometimes available.) Cutting bricks with a trowel requires a knack, and most amateurs use the more reliable bolster instead. Keep the blade of the trowel clean and smooth – don't let mortar harden onto it between work sessions.

Pointing trowel – much smaller, about 15 cm long.

Small hawk – about 15 cm square. A home-made item. (See Fig. 1, Chapter 25.) It carries a small amount of mortar for pointing.

Club or lump hammer – different weights are available: 1 kg is about right. It is mainly used for hitting a bolster or cold chisel.

Bolster – an all-steel chisel with a wide blade. Get one as wide as a brick, ie, 10 cm. It is used for cutting bricks: Lay a brick on a flat bed (eg, sand or a board). Place the bolster across the face of the brick, and strike it sharply with a club hammer. For more precision, score a line across the back face of the brick first.

Blocks are also cut with a bolster (though aircrete blocks can be cut more precisely with a masonry saw).

Stone-cutting disc – use in an electric drill or angle grinder. To cut a difficult shape from a brick, use the disc to score it deeply. Even the pros use the technique!

It's prudent to wear goggles.

Cold chisel – occasionally useful for chasing, etc. ('Chasing' means cutting a channel in the surface of a wall, eg, for cable.)

(*Brick hammer* – used for trimming bricks. Optional.)

Line blocks – not items that are sold in shops; brickies make their own. They are clever and simple devices for holding a line stretched between two external corners. (See Fig. 7.)

To make one, take some timber, say 8 × 8 × 3 cm, and saw a square off a corner to leave an 'L' shape. Make a saw cut down one arm – the line passes through this. And knock in a couple of nails round which to wind surplus line. They are used in pairs; the tension of the line holds the blocks onto the corners.

A line block at the very top of a corner needs extra support – rest an extra brick or two on top of the corner.

Pins – used for stretching a line where line blocks can't be used, eg, at internal corners. (If you wish to put them into hardened mortar, make a hole with a nail first.)

Tingle – on a very long stretch (over 10 m), the line may sag, but it can be supported midway with a tingle. This may be simply a piece of card folded over the line and held in place with a brick. (See Fig. 2.)

Figure 2: Tingle with gauge rod

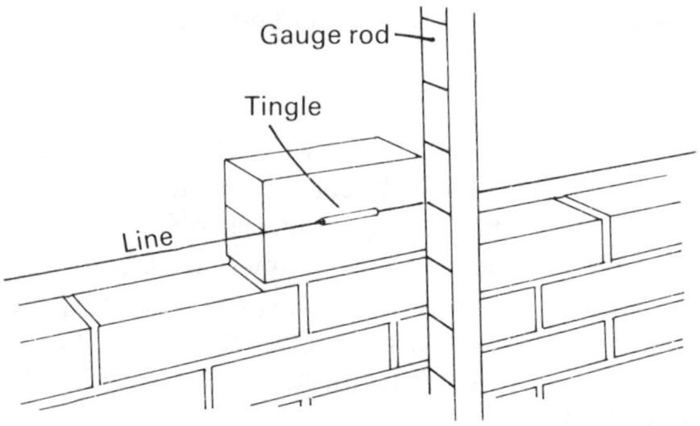

* Tingle prevents a long line from sagging. It can be folded card, as shown, or a purpose-made metal plate.
* Gauge rod checks the course levels.

Sight along the line from a corner to check that it is straight; or use a gauge rod from the dpc.

A tingle is also useful if the line is being blown about by a strong wind.

Spirit level – at least a metre long, and preferably with a plumb bubble at both ends.

Small spirit level – say 20 cm long; occasionally useful.

Level-board – a board about three metres long with straight and parallel edges. With a spirit level resting on its top edge, it effectively forms a very long spirit level. For accurate work over a long distance, reverse the direction of the board at each step to cancel out any bias. (See Fig. 5, Chapter 5.)

Spot boards – pieces of ply, or whatever, about half a metre square, onto which a bucketful of mortar can be turned out. For convenience, raise them with a brick at each corner. Several are required, spaced every couple of metres near to the wall being laid. Between the boards, put little stacks of bricks. (Take bricks from different pallets to even out any colour differences.) The intention is that wherever you are working on the wall, bricks and mortar are to hand.

Builders' square – is it a square, or a triangle, or maybe a square triangle? For a useful building size, take three pieces of timber and fix them together to form a 60–80–100 cm triangle. (See 'Squareness', Chapter 27.)

Gauge rod – made from a straight piece of timber, say 5 × 3 cm and three metres long. Score it every $7\frac{1}{2}$ cm with a saw. Held vertically, the rod gives the levels of the brickwork courses. (See Fig. 2.)

Mixer – a portable cement mixer is more than sufficient for keeping up with a two-and-one bricklaying gang. But don't get a very small one – they don't mix well. A 'half bag' size is right. They can be hired, but it is probably more economical to buy one second-hand and re-sell it later.

At the end of a day's work, clean the mixer by churning round a few half bricks with some water. What a happy sound that comes to be!

Sundries – water tub, hose, buckets, shovels, barrow, polythene to cover cement, etc.

Technique of laying

Make up a mortar according to one of the recipes in the previous chapter. Judging the wetness required needs a little experience. Too stiff – the bricks will need too much tapping with the trowel to position them. Too sloppy – the mortar will be difficult to control with the trowel and the fresh brickwork will not be held firmly. Ideally it should be possible to just place a brick into position.

Let us look at the laying of a single brick.

The first step is to take up a trowelful of mortar, but there is technique even in this. From a mound of mortar on the spot board, 'saw' away a portion, enough for a good trowelful. Scoop it up, and flip it back over onto the board. Scoop it up again, and the lump of mortar will have become a cohesive, fat 'sausage'.

Now to turn it into a 'bed' on top of the wall:

With the point of the trowel towards the brick last laid, pull the trowel along and above the top of the wall. At the same time, roll the trowel blade over, and the result should be a line of mortar deposited along the wall. Put the point of the trowel in the mortar, and 'snake' it down the line at a flat angle to make a furrow. (See Fig. 3.)

Figure 3: Laying a bed of mortar

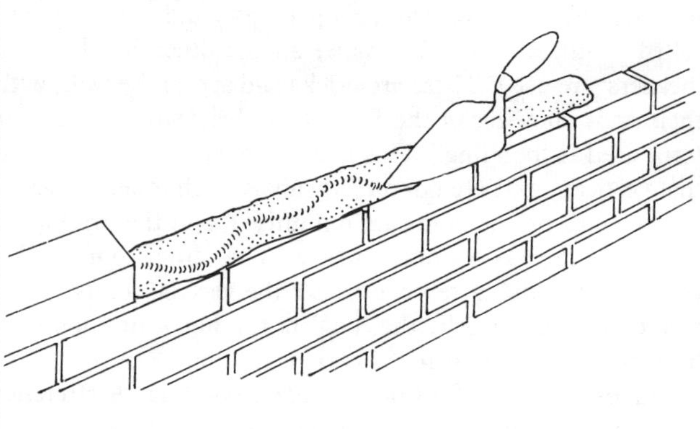

* Spread the mortar to each side and to an even depth.

This pushes the mortar out to each edge, giving a fairly even bed to lay on. Trim the edges. The amount of mortar originally taken up should be enough to give a bed for three bricks – when you are competent. (The process is simpler than the description; watching a brickie at work will make it clear.)

Take up a brick and 'butter' one end of it. This is done by taking a small amount of mortar on the trowel, and scraping the face of the trowel on each of the four edges at the end of the brick. This should produce a flat pyramid of mortar (and clean the trowel). When this is butted up to the previous brick, a solid cross joint is obtained. The amount of mortar used influences the thickness of the joint.

That's the 'proper' way of doing the cross joint. An easier way is just to put two lines of mortar on the end of the brick, by scraping the trowel over the face edge and the back edge. With this method, it is easier to adjust the thickness of the joint to what is required. Rather surprisingly, this does not appreciably reduce the strength of the finished brickwork. Whichever method is used, the face of the cross joint should be full of mortar – it is tedious, when jointing, to have to fill in hollows. The same applies to the bed joint.

So with one end buttered, the brick can be laid. But which way up? The question arises with those bricks which have 'frogs', the rather odd name for an indentation in the brick. (See Fig. 4.)

Figure 4: Facing bricks

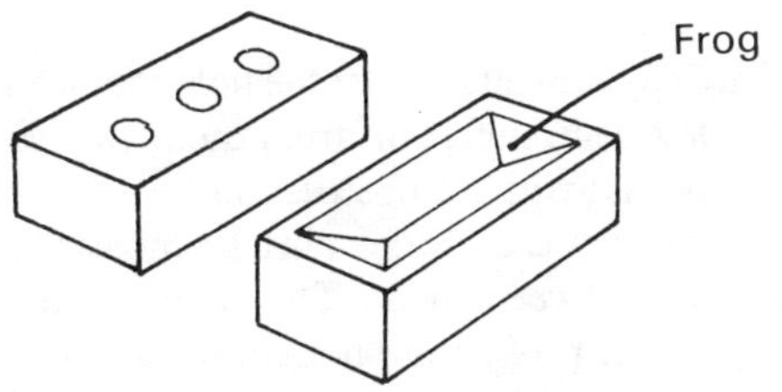

Properly, the frogs should face upwards, which makes for stronger brickwork. But you're building a house, not high-rise flats. Laying the bricks with frogs downwards is quite strong enough. It uses less mortar, and the bricks are more easily positioned when they are being laid.

So, one way up or the other, the brick is ready to lay. Position it, as explained below, either at a corner or along a line. Keep to the required thickness for the cross joint (nominally 1 cm), and keep the cross joint plumb above those below. If the mortar is the right consistency, a brick can often be placed directly into position. But sometimes it needs a light tap with the edge of the trowel. If a heavier tap should be necessary, use the base of the trowel handle. (A heavy tap may be necessary for blockwork, but for brickwork it indicates a mortar that is too stiff.) Keep the brick level – this is affected by whereabouts the brick is tapped. (For a strong bond, lay the brick right first time – don't fiddle about repositioning it.)

You should find that a little mortar has been squeezed out from the bed joint. Cut this away upwards with the trowel – scraping the trowel along the joint smears the bricks. Use this surplus to butter the end of the next brick.

When brickwork is being laid, water is sucked out of the mortar by the bricks. This stiffens the mortar so that it is strong enough to support the brickwork until the mortar hardens chemically. If the bricks are already saturated by rain, not only are they much heavier, but also they won't suck the water out from the mortar: the brickwork flops. Moreover, wet bricks are liable to effloresce as they dry out, leaving white salts on their face. (This can be removed with 'Disclean', but prevention is better than cure.) So keep bricks covered in heavy rain.

On the other hand, in a heat-wave, the bricks can become too dry, and suck too much water out from the mortar. This makes laying more difficult and interferes with the chemical process, resulting in a crumbly mortar. So in a hot spell, hose the bricks down before use.

The above is a general description of how to lay a brick. But where precisely is it to be placed?

In the building of a wall, firstly the two corners are built up, with the position of each brick being found by reference to those already laid. It is critical that the corners are built accurately, and this is slow work.

Once the two corners have been built, a line can be stretched from one to the other, and this is used as a guide to lay the bricks in between. 'Laying to the line' is fairly quick and easy.

That's the outline of the method. The sections below give the details.

Building up corners

To start building up the walls of a house, first of all the corners have to be built up off the concrete foundations. To find the positions of the corners, the profiles are used, and ranging lines stretched between them. How to transfer these lines onto the concrete and lay each corner brick is explained in Chapter 5: *Foundations*. Start laying the bricks for the first course along one arm of a corner. Use the line marked on the concrete, and keep the cross joints to the required thickness. Check with the spirit level that each brick is level with the corner brick. Repeat along the other arm.

Now for the second course. Lay the corner brick (reversing the bond, of course) with care. The bed joint must be the required thickness so the brick is at the right level. Normally the bed joint is 1 cm thick, but for the first few courses this may be adjusted to compensate for variations in the level of the concrete. The two outside faces of the corner brick must be plumb above the brickwork below. Check this with the spirit level. Next, run the course out along an arm. To get the direction to lay to, use the spirit level as a straight-edge: slant it from the corner brick just laid, out along the arm of brickwork below. Keep the cross joints so that they are central above the brick below. Lay the spirit level along the top to keep the coursing horizontal. Because of the bonding effect, each course will be shorter by half a brick than the course below. This is called 'raking back'.

In this manner, a corner can be built up. Because the arms are short, the corner can only rise a few courses. After the brickwork has been run in between these initial corners, longer arms can be laid for subsequent corners so that they can be raised higher (six or twelve courses). Use the gauge rod to check the coursing. Check the raking back with the straight-edge of the level: If the joints are even, the bricks should touch the (slanted) straight-edge. (See Fig. 5.)

Figure 5: Brickwork corner

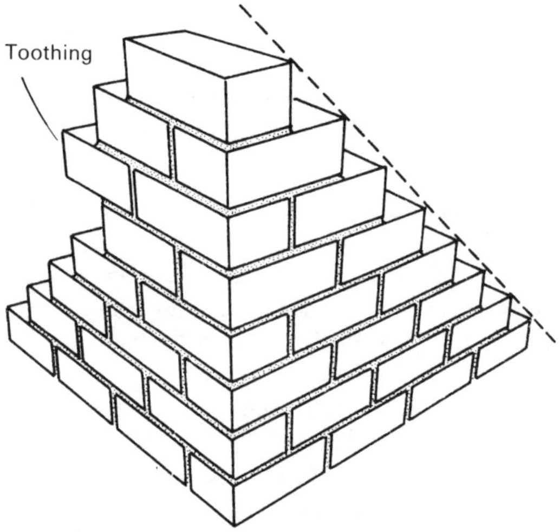

* Check the raking back with a straight-edge (dashed line).
* Toothing is occasionally useful.
* Technical term for the corner is 'quoin'.

As you are building a corner, periodically check that the two faces are plumb and in line (use the straight-edge on a slant). If a brick has become displaced, tap it back.

(The description above is based on strip foundations, but it can easily be adapted for the lesser amount of brickwork involved with trenchfill.)

Once bricklaying has been tried, it will be readily appreciated that laying bricks at corners is much slower than laying to the line between them. It is a not uncommon practice to decrease the number of bricks involved in a corner by projecting a course instead of raking it back. This 'toothing' is frowned upon because it is difficult to get a good bed joint underneath. Use it sparingly. It does save time (and space). (See again Fig. 5.)

Bricklayers' profiles.

From the above description it can be seen that building up corners is a tricky task. But there is another way, rarely seen in Britain, which is easier, and which could well appeal to the ownhander – the use of bricklayers' profiles. The first few courses are built up off the footings as before. Then the profile can be erected. This is basically an upright metal pole that can be fixed at its lower end to a brick corner already built. (See Fig. 6.)

Figure 6: Bricklayers' profile

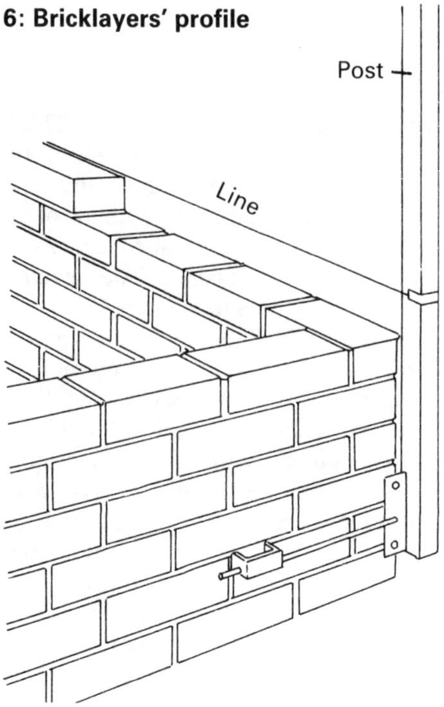

* Eliminates the need to build up corners (except for the first small corner).
* Post can be adjusted plumb.

There are adjustments so that the pole can be made plumb. It stands a few centimetres off from the corner so that corner bricks can be laid without obstruction.

With a profile at each corner, bricks can easily be laid to a line stretched between them. The gauge is marked on the profile pole. The profiles are not cheap, and the ownhander would have to think hard before buying some. They should be available from hire shops, but they aren't (yet?).

Laying to the line

After you have built up the corners, laying to the line is easy. Using line blocks (or perhaps pins), stretch a line taut from corner to corner to guide the top edge of the bricks to be laid. (See Fig. 7.)

The line should be about 2 mm off from the brickwork to allow for irregularities. (To this end, score a line down the inside face of the line blocks.) Lay each brick so that its face is flush with the bricks below, while the top edge is along the line (keeping the 2 mm gap). Keep an eye on the cross joints so that they stay in line with the ones below – else, the last brick in the course won't fit! (Butter both ends of this brick.)

Having run in one course between the corners, repeat on upwards, course by course. (While changing the position of the line, you'll appreciate why brickies usually work in pairs – one for each end of the line!)

Jointing

Every so often while laying bricks, before the mortar gets at all hard, have a session of 'jointing' – smoothing off the mortar joints. The joints need to be 'tooled' not only to look better, but also for weathertightness. (See Figs. 8 and 11.)

Figure 7: Laying to the line

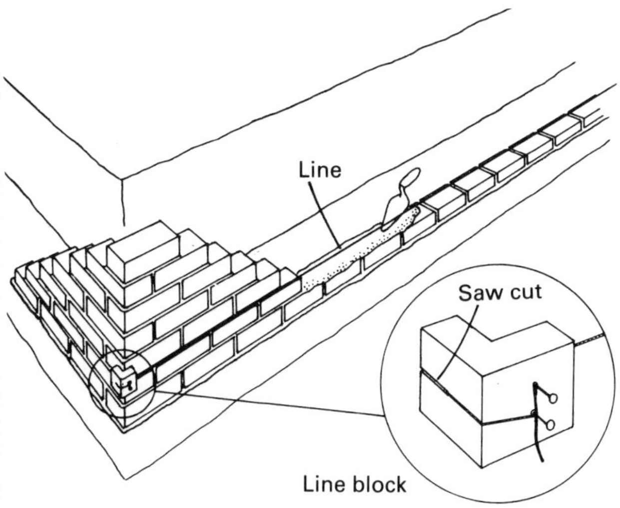

* With the line as a guide, brickwork can be kept straight, plumb, and to the correct coursing.
* Tension in the line keeps the line blocks in position.

Figure 8: Tooling the joints

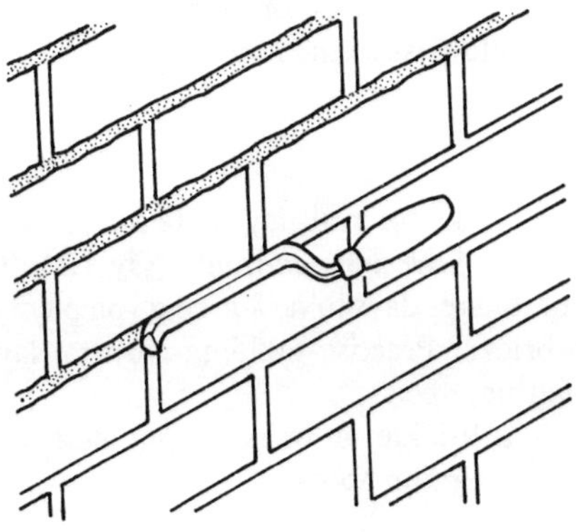

* Tool the cross joints before the bed joints.

A common, simple, and effective jointing is called 'bucket handle'. In the days before plastic buckets, a piece of handle from an old galvanized bucket was the tool used. Nowadays a brick jointer can either be cheaply purchased or improvised from a short piece of copper pipe. By rubbing the rounded blade of the tool along the joint, the mortar is compressed to give a smooth, hard surface. Tool the cross joints first, then the beds. It's a simple job.

Where there is insufficient mortar in the joint, more must be added. Using a somewhat stiff mix, press it down onto a small hawk to form a layer a centimetre thick (to match the thickness of the joint). Cut a portion off onto the back of a pointing trowel, and press it into the joint. There should be no smudge on the face. (It's better to avoid the job in the first place by applying enough mortar whilst laying the bricks.)

Blockwork

Fairly similar methods are used for laying blocks. An individual block is equivalent to six bricks but it takes longer to lay. Overall, blockwork can be laid about twice as fast as brickwork.

The blocks are usually laid in a stretcher bond. On alternate courses at the corners, quarter blocks are needed to maintain the bond. (See Fig. 9.)

Figure 9: Blockwork corner

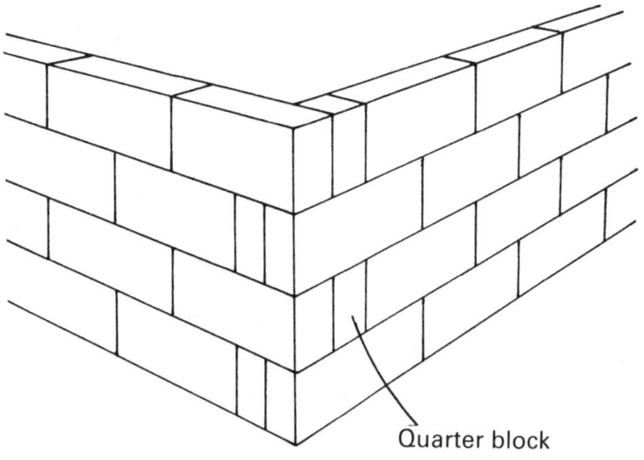

* Quarter block enables stretcher bond to be maintained.
* Cut blocks with a masonry saw, or chop with a bolster.

Figure 10: Alternative blockwork corner

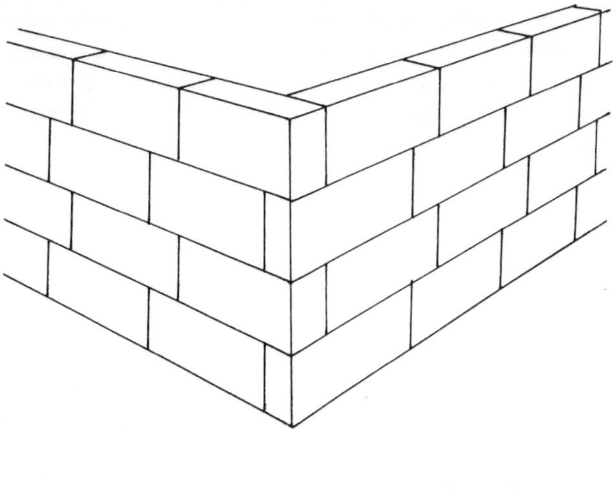

* No cut blocks are necessary but the bond is weaker.

Alternatively, blocks can be laid in an off-centre running bond with cross joints over a quarter point of the block below. The blockwork will be slightly weaker, but the method saves on the cutting of blocks. (See Fig. 10.)

With a heavy concrete block, a stiffer mix is required, and two hands are needed to lift and place the block. Sometimes a lump hammer is more appropriate than the trowel for tapping a block into position.

Cavity walls

The original purpose of separating inner and outer leaf of a wall was to prevent damp from passing across the wall. Nowadays, it has the additional purpose of containing insulation. The outer leaf is usually in stretcher bonded brickwork, and the inner leaf in blockwork. To give some structural stability, the two are connected together by ties. These are placed at intervals of six brick courses upwards, and four stretchers along. (Or, in terms of blocks, this is two up and two along.) This spacing fits in with the size of insulation slabs. (At the sides of openings use more ties – every block up.) In very wet and windy weather, the outer leaf can become so saturated that water runs down the inside of the brickwork. The ties are designed so that this water cannot run across them to the inner leaf.

As originally conceived, the cavity was empty, but nowadays, it is often filled with insulation. (Obviously the insulation should not transmit water.) Sometimes only half the width of the cavity is filled, leaving the other half clear as a damp barrier. Cavities can be kept to the original 5 cm width, or increased to $7\frac{1}{2}$ cm. (See Fig. 11.)

The construction method varies a little with the type of cavity insulation used. The following applies to full cavity insulation:

It is usual to lead with the brickwork, though the blockwork can lead, eg, at gables. (If partial cavity fill is being used, it's preferable for this to be attached to the inner leaf. In this case, lead with the blockwork.) It's best to build up the cavity wall one row of insulation batts at a time, ie, lay six courses of brickwork, with a row of ties under the top course. (Though in fact, it's not uncommon to lead with 12 courses of brickwork.) Put the batts into place, and catch up with the blockwork. (It may help to bend the ties upwards in order to place the blocks in position.)

Figure 11: Section through cavity wall

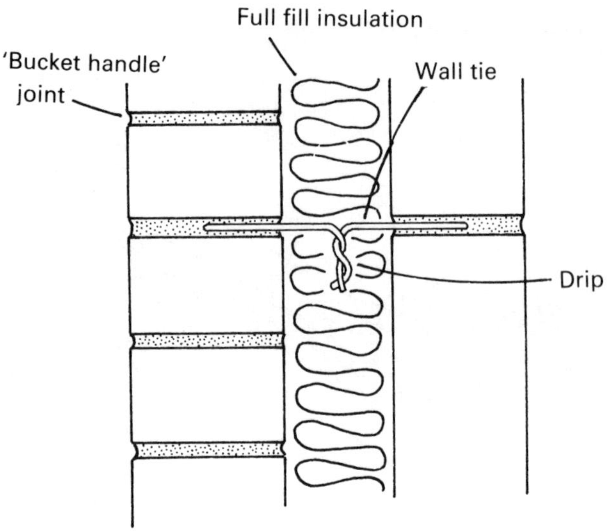

* If a clear cavity is required, use partial fill insulation secured by special wall ties.

Don't let mortar droppings lodge in the cavity, where they can form a bridge that transmits dampness. (Some people rest a board along the top of the blockwork to catch falling mortar.) By the way, the insulation should be carried up to the top of the gable – not to keep the loft warm, but to prevent the top of the insulation from forming a bridge over which water could pass to the inner leaf.

Practice

Before laying bricks for real, lay some for practice. Make a special mortar of lime and sand only (say 1:5). This mix is workable but it takes days to set – giving you plenty of time to recycle the bricks. Practise building corners, laying to the line, and jointing.

And watch a brickie at work to put flesh on the bare skeletons of description above.

22

PLUMBING AND HEATING

☆

☆

☆

☆

☆

☆

☆

Vented and unvented systems
Combination boiler
Condensing boiler
Other options
Cold supply
Heating circuit
Hot supply
Radiator circuits
Boiler
Pump
Circuit details
Thermal store
Pipework
Cutting
Bending
Fittings
Discharge system

PLUMBERS and electricians are traditionally the best paid of the building trades. When the plumbing includes the heating system, it can become a very complex subject, and you may think that plumbers well deserve their premium. Now that unvented systems, the norm on the Continent, have been allowed into Britain, there is even more to know about. The plumbing trade is changing fast. Combination boilers, condensing boilers, electric boilers, unvented boilers, unvented cylinders, thermal stores – they are all recent innovations that many people will be unfamiliar with. It can all be quite confusing.

First of all, let us look at the differences between the traditional, vented systems and the new, unvented systems.

Vented and unvented systems

When water is heated, it expands, and if the pipes are not to burst, this expansion has to be accommodated in some way. In a vented system, the water can expand up an open pipe. If the water in the system were under mains pressure, then this vent pipe would have to be many storeys above the top of the roof – impossible. So the pressure in the system is reduced by feeding it not from the mains, but from a cold water tank in the loft. When water in the system is heated, it is free to expand by pushing up the water level in the open pipe.

An unvented system works completely differently. The expansion of the heated water is taken up by an expansion vessel. This is a sealed container divided into two compartments by a diaphragm. On one side is a compressed gas; on the other is the water system connected to the mains via a one-way valve. When the water expands as it is heated, it pushes out the diaphragm against the pressure of the gas.

An unvented system does not require tanks in the loft, nor the associated pipework. There's an obvious cost saving here, but this is lost because of the higher cost of the complex equipment required: expansion vessel, extra controls, etc.

Advantages of unvented systems are:

There are no pipes or tanks in the loft to freeze up.

The pressure is high throughout the system, which is especially beneficial for showers.

Water from hot taps is drinkable.

Advantages for a vented system are:

There's a reserve of water should the water supply be interrupted.

It is widely understood.

There are less potential dangers with it, and it can be installed by an unqualified person.

This last advantage is decisive for the ownhander. The Building Regulations expect an unvented system to be put in by a British Board of Agrément 'Approved installer'. If you wished to put such a system in yourself, you'd have difficulty in convincing the building inspector of your competence.

Commonly there are two separate circuits involving hot water:

1) Boiler, radiators and cylinder heat exchanger.
2) Cylinder hot water store and pipework to taps.

In traditional systems, each needs a tank and vent pipe. In either circuit, a tank and vent pipe can be replaced by an expansion vessel. Thus there are both unvented boilers and unvented cylinders, and both have an expansion vessel. They can be used independently of each other (ie, with one circuit vented and the other unvented). Unvented cylinders have to be stronger than vented ones because of the higher pressures inside them (the pressure of the mains). They are sometimes called unvented hot water storage units, but this should not be confused with thermal stores. (See 'Thermal Store', later in the chapter.)

Combination boiler

With a combination boiler, the hot water cylinder is abolished. The hot supply is heated directly from the mains as it is required (like in the 'Ascot' heaters of days gone by). This takes precedence over heating the water in the unvented central heating system. Commercially, combination boilers are heavily promoted, but both their theory and practice are poor:

They are inefficient. They are big boilers which start and stop frequently. (Small boilers running flat out are more efficient.)

When a hot tap is turned on, the water takes a fair time to become hot, and its temperature varies with the flow rate.

Maximum flow rates are insufficient. With a traditional vented system, a bath tap delivers hot water at about 20 litre/min. Combination boilers manage an output of only about half of that. Too bad if two hot taps are on at the same time!

In short, don't fit a combination boiler.

Condensing boiler

A condensing boiler, on the other hand, is very efficient. In use, it is about 88% efficient, significantly better than the 80% efficiency of a modern conventional boiler. And when it is working at low outputs (eg, in spring or autumn), efficiency remains high, unlike a conventional boiler.

How does it do it? Conventional boilers give off hot gases into the atmosphere. A condensing boiler extracts the heat from these gases, cooling them down to about 50°C. Some of the gases, in particular steam, condense and give up their considerable 'latent heat'. The cooled waste gases are dispersed by a fan through a small flue outlet. The acidic condensate needs a waste pipe to lead it away to a drain, either internally, via the waste system, or externally, via a gully. (The condensate is no more acidic than the world's most popular soft drink. Since other effluent is mainly alkaline, some acidity is not unwelcome.)

Condensing boilers are something of an innovation in Britain, though they are popular in Holland where their use has been pioneered. They are available for both vented and unvented systems. They are more complex and costly than conventional boilers. (About twice the price at the time of writing, though the differential is likely to come down.) They make more economic sense in a large house, where the extra cost will be more quickly recouped by fuel savings. You will have to work out for yourself whether they are cost effective in your particular circumstances. (In general, put your money into insulation, not into heating systems.)

Other options

So far, we have presumed one sort of heating system – a gas-fuelled wet system with radiators. This is versatile, cheap to run, and popular. But there are many options. Instead of radiators, you may prefer under-floor heating, which is very popular in Germany and said to be healthier. (But it is somewhat unresponsive for our very changeable climate.) Or gas can be used to fuel a warm air system. (But sound insulation can be a problem with this sort of system). If mains gas is not available, there is a wide choice of more expensive fuels:

Cheap to install and reasonably cheap to run are electric storage heaters, which use cheap night electricity. But they are not very responsive. If you want that, you can have a conventional radiator system fuelled by a night electric boiler (the boiler stores heat for daytime use). Yet a third electrical option is to use a solid floor to store cheap heat overnight, and to top up the heating requirements during the day with electrical ceiling heating.

Solid fuel systems are cheap to run, and if you choose a multi-fuel room heater, you can have the gorgeous smell of burning logs. For more convenience, there is oil or stored gas; the unsightly tanks can be buried.

Altogether, there's a bewildering choice. In this book, there is space only to describe in detail the single most popular system: a vented, fully pumped, two-pipe radiator system, using a conventional gas boiler.

Cold supply

Before we immerse ourselves in the hot water system, we had better deal first with the cold supply. Even here, there is a choice between two systems, direct and indirect. In the direct system, the rising main feeds all the cold supplies. In the indirect system, widely used in Southern England, the rising main feeds the kitchen tap (to give drinking water as pure as the supply from the Water Company), the storage tank and header tank in the loft, and perhaps an outside tap. (By the way, you might like to plumb in a water purifier in the kitchen for improved drinking water.) Other cold supplies, to basins, WC's, etc, are fed from the storage tank. (See Fig. 1, Chapter 9.)

The direct system uses less pipework, and gives drinking water from all the cold taps; the storage tank can be smaller. But special shower mixer taps have to be used to cope with the different pressures of the hot and cold supplies. The indirect system gives a reserve water supply and is said to refill WC's more quietly.

Heating circuit

The flow of hot water from the boiler divides into two separate circuits: one pipe goes to the radiators, and the other to the heat exchanger in the hot water cylinder. (See Fig. 3, Chapter 9.)

The modern cylinder is described as 'indirect'. In this context, the word means that the cylinder has a heat exchanger. Water for the hot supply is heated by the heat exchanger and stored; it is quite separate from water in the primary circuit (boiler, radiators, and heat exchanger). The advantage of using an indirect cylinder is that the water in the primary circuit remains unchanged and so very little scale is deposited.

The flow of water around the circuits can be controlled by motorised valves. These are switched electrically, and are usually controlled by a cylinder or room thermostat. The simplest type is a two-port valve, which just opens or closes to the flow in a pipe. (They are sometimes called 'zone' valves, because they can control the flow to a zone of radiators, eg, the radiators on one floor.) A fairly simple system would use one of these valves, controlled by a cylinder thermostat, to regulate the flow to the cylinder, and another, controlled by a room thermostat, to regulate the flow to the radiators.

But the simplest system uses a three-port motorised valve (forming a T-junction) to switch the flow between heating and cylinder circuits. The valve is available in two variations. A 'diverter' allows either hot water heating or radiator heating, but not both. The more sophisticated 'mid-position' valve can allow both at the same time. But the logic of this is that either a larger boiler is required, or hot water recovery is slower. With a well insulated house, the diverter is quite satisfactory, and it is assumed in the following account.

The diverter is controlled by a thermostat strapped to the side of the cylinder. When the cylinder water is below the required temperature, say 60°C, then all the hot output from the boiler goes to the cylinder heat exchanger. While the cylinder water is being heated up (usually half an hour from cold), the supply to the radiators is cut off. When the cylinder water has reached the set temperature, the diverter switches all the boiler output to the radiators. The system is described as 'fully pumped' because the water is pumped to both the cylinder and the radiators.

(The gravity method is not much used nowadays, except for solid fuel boilers – in which case, for safety reasons, the method must be used. Only the central heating has a pumped circuit – a separate 'gravity' circuit heats the cylinder by natural convection. For a good gravity flow, the pipework should rise continuously, and the cylinder should preferably be near the boiler. The fully pumped system allows much more flexibility in the placing of the cylinder relative to the boiler.)

Hot supply

As described above, hot water is circulated through the heat exchanger in the cylinder, either by a pump or by convection. A cold feed, from the storage tank in the loft, enters the bottom of the cylinder. The cold water is heated by the heat exchanger and rises up to the top of the cylinder; from there, it is drawn off to the taps. (See Fig. 2, Chapter 9.) The vent pipe, which allows for the expansion of the hot water, is tee'd off from this hot supply, and reaches up above the cold tank. Lest the water in the system should ever boil and be expelled out from the vent, the pipe is bent back over into the top of the header tank.

Radiator circuits

The 'two-pipe' system is the better, modern method. Each radiator receives hot water from the hot flow, and returns cooled water via a separate return pipe. (See Fig. 3, Chapter 9.) The flow from the boiler is switched to the radiators by the motorised valve mentioned previously.

Radiators

Despite their name, radiators give off most of their heat by convection. Many have fins to increase this heat output; the output from double panel radiators is even greater. (Incidentally, radiated heat is reckoned to be more pleasant than convected heat.) The radiators are usually made of steel, and come in a multitude of sizes; the corresponding nominal heat outputs are given in the manufacturers' brochures. (These assume a 60°C temperature difference: average temperature of the radiator at 80°C, room temperature at 20°C.) The pipework to a radiator, or a group of them, must obviously have a sufficient capacity (ie, diameter) to carry the heat required for the radiator(s). (See 'Circuit details', later in the chapter.) The outlet from each radiator is fitted with a lockshield valve. When the system is being commissioned, these valves can be adjusted so that the flows through the individual radiators are balanced.

At the inlet (ie, the flow), it is sensible to fit a TRV (Thermostatic Radiator Valve). The householder can set the valve to some particular cut-off temperature. When the air temperature is higher than this, the valve shuts off the flow through the radiator. These valves really are a most useful innovation from Scandinavia. They make temperature control of the system easy for the ownhander to install, and simple for the householder to use.

Boiler

The conventional balanced-flue boiler is a neat piece of equipment that can be wall-hung out the way, or fitted beneath a worktop. (In a bungalow, it may be preferable to use a floor-mounted boiler so that the header tank is sufficiently high above it.) If no external wall is available, a fan-assisted boiler can be used, the gases being blown out through a duct. (But consider: A fan is not silent.)

In the past, rather oversized boilers have often been fitted. The modern theory is to use a smaller boiler and to work it hard. This is more efficient, as heat is wasted when a large boiler cycles off and on. With a very well insulated house, you can install a very small boiler; if you are subcontracting to a plumber, it's a good idea to take the size smaller than his recommendation!

Most boilers nowadays have a 'low water content' and can only be used with a fully pumped system. The pump has to continue working for a short time after the boiler has been switched off to dissipate heat; otherwise the water would boil. (Anyway, it is more efficient to use up the residual heat in the boiler.)

Pump

In days gone by, the size of the pump had to be matched with the frictional resistance of the circuit; this involved lots of sums. Once again, technical advances have made life easier for the ownhander. Pumps now come with a speed switch so that you can just set the flow to the lowest speed that gives the required temperature drop at the radiators.

It is reckoned nowadays that it is generally preferable to put the pump in the flow rather than the return.

Circuit details

The boiler circuit, like the hot water supply, needs to be vented and to have a low pressure cold feed. This can't be taken from the main storage tank, not least because this would preclude the use of a corrosion inhibitor. Rather, the circuit needs its own small header tank (20 litres) in the loft. When the whole system is cold, this tank should be only a third full.

The feed from the header tank goes into the return to the boiler. (See Fig. 3, Chapter 13.) When the water is heated up, this pipe allows the hot water to expand upwards into the tank's spare capacity. (Hence the pipe is called the feed-and-expansion pipe.) There is another pipe, the vent, which is usually connected into the flow from the boiler and which rises to curve over the top of the header tank. Its primary purpose is to allow air to escape when the system is initially filled with water. It also acts as a safety outlet should gross overheating occur.

Where the feed connects to the return, the water is at a fixed pressure, that due to the head of water. This is called the neutral point. In front of the pump as far as this point, the water is under extra pressure; behind the pump, for the rest of the circuit back to the neutral point, the water is under reduced pressure.

There is an inter-relation between the positions of the pump, and the feed and vent connections. These are not arbitrary, and you should follow some recommended system. Placing them wrongly can lead to troubles such as 'pumping over': A circulation is set up with the pump forcing water up the vent pipe into the header tank, from where it is sucked back through the feed pipe. (There are other traps lying in wait for the unwary.) So, the ownhander may well want to use a boiler or cylinder that is pre-fitted with integrated controls (programmer, motorised valves, pump, etc). This greatly simplifies the plumbing, as well as the electrics.

As mentioned previously, each radiator receives hot water from the boiler via a flow pipe, and returns the cooled water via a return. Sometimes the pipework is all done in 15 mm copper pipe, but microbore (ie, 6, 8, or 10 mm pipe) is also widely used. 'Manifolds' are often associated with microbore, whereby each radiator has its own microbore circuit from a central manifold. But this system is wasteful of pipe, and creates high friction for the pump to overcome. A better system is an 'arterial' distribution, in which the size of the pipe matches the flow of hot water (ie, heat) required.

What diameter pipe is needed for any particular stage? Guidelines for this have been be worked out, based on a 11°C drop in temperature at the radiator(s), and a reasonable flow rate – high flow rates are noisy and shorten pump life. So we have:

Pipe diameter, mm	6	8	10	15	22	28
Max flow of heat, kwatts	1	2	3	6	13	23

To decide what size pipe to use, compare its capacity to transfer heat, given in the table, with the outputs required from the radiators. (The return pipework will be the same size as the flows.)

Thermal store

The system described above is common practice in Britain. However, a thermal store is an ingenious and simple innovation which has much to commend it, especially to the ownhander. It is vented – but there are no tanks in the loft! The prime purpose of the store is to act as a buffer between the boiler and the intermittent demand for heat by taps and radiators. Intermittent cycling of the boiler is eliminated, and hence its efficiency is increased.

The boiler heats water in the store to 80°C, and this is pumped round to the radiators. (See Fig. 1.)

Figure 1: Thermal storage system

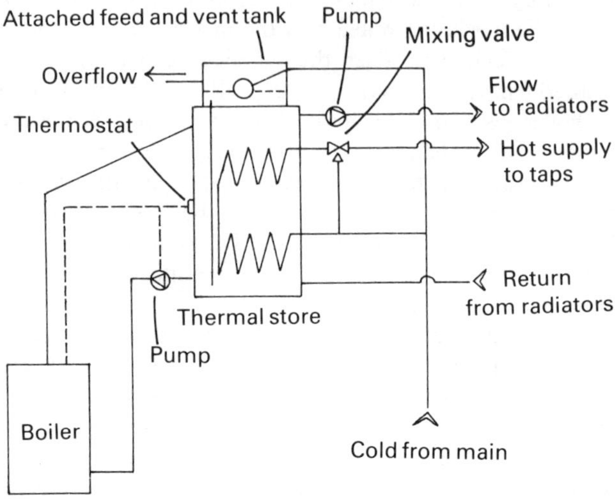

* The thermal store contains water at 80°. It acts as a buffer between the boiler and the demand for heat – from the radiators or from the hot taps.
* For the hot supply to the taps, water is heated instantaneously in the heat exchanger of the thermal store. Cold water is mixed with it to bring its temperature to 60°.
* No tanks are required in the loft – but the system is vented.

If the temperature of the store drops, a time delay postpones the start up of the boiler to prevent intermittent operation. The thermal store has sufficient heat capacity to meet the demands of the heating and hot water systems during this interval. The store is vented, with a feed tank on top as an integral part of the unit.

Hot water for the taps is obtained instantaneously by passing water from the mains through a heat exchanger in the store. The very hot water then passes through a mixer valve, where cold water is added to reduce its temperature to 60°C. Good flow rates are possible – up to 40 litre/min.

Besides the extra efficiency, other advantages are:

There are no tanks or pipes in the loft

Hot supplies are at mains pressure, which is especially good for showers

The hot water from the taps is drinkable.

The equipment is a little more complex than that for a conventional system. An extra pump and a mixer valve are needed. But these extras are supplied as an integral part of the unit, so installation for the ownhander is simple enough.

(A disadvantage of a thermal store is that it cannot take full advantage of a condensing boiler. The return temperature from the store is about 70°C, whereas a condensing boiler needs the return temperature to be below 55°C for fully efficient operation.)

Pipework

Copper pipe is ubiquitous, but the ownhander could consider plastic. Might it be only craft inertia that keeps copper supreme? Some plastic systems have Agrément Board approval for both hot and cold use. According to the system, fittings are joined to the pipe either by push-fit – it can't be simpler than that! – or by solvent welding, which again is pretty simple. Some systems use flexible pipe, which can be easily bent or threaded through joists.

So plastic pipe is worth investigating; but since this book is dealing with orthodox techniques, the methods described are for copper pipe.

Copper tube comes in three and six metre lengths, in 15 mm and 22 mm outside diameters. (For a gravity circuit, 28 mm is also available.) Microbore is usually available in 8 mm or 10 mm diameter, in coils of ten to fifty metres. It is easily bent to shape, and it can be laid rather like electric cable.

Pipework needs supporting. It is light enough when installed, but heavier when filled with water! 22 mm copper pipe needs clips every 2 metres, 15 mm pipe every 1·2 m. (For vertical pipes, these intervals can be increased a little.) Too few clips may result in a noisy system.

Cutting

For only a few cuts, a hacksaw can be used. (Remove the burr afterwards with a file.) But generally, it's worth buying a pipe cutter (with a reamer on the end). It's a simple tool to use: Tighten the cutter onto the pipe and rotate it around, tightening again as necessary. De-burr the inside of the cut pipe by twisting the reamer around inside it.

Bending

Microbore can be simply bent by hand, though external bending springs can also be used. For a few bends in 15 mm or 22 mm pipe, internal bending springs can be used. (Slightly overbend the pipe and then bend it back to make it easier to release the spring.) But for a houseful of plumbing, it is worth hiring a pipe bender. The basic operation of the tool is simple enough: Open out the handles and hook the pipe in place so that it is sandwiched between the straight and curved formers, and then bring the handles together.

At a bend, the walls of the pipe remain parallel. The wall on the outside of the curve is stretched, and the wall on the inside is compressed. The original length is unaltered along the centre line of the pipe. Gauging the exact position on the pipe and the angle of a bend is not easy. Consult a textbook for the method. But if several bends are required in a pipe, it is simplest to produce the pipework in sections, with one bend per section. Make the bend before cutting the section to length. (A tip for checking right-angled bends: place the bend in the right angle at a door lining or window reveal.)

In general, bends are better than elbows because they give a smoother flow and are cheaper.

Fittings

Only a couple of spanners are needed to fit compression fittings. In these, a nut is tightened up against a soft copper ring (called an 'olive'), forcing the ring to grip the pipe. To ensure a watertight joint, lightly smear the olive with Boss White (or Boss Blue) before fitting it. Don't overtighten the nut as this may produce a leak. (There is another type of compression joint, the 'manipulative' type: Instead of an olive, the end of the pipe is flared out. But the selfbuilder is unlikely to need this joint.)

Compression fittings are used for connections to appliances, and are useful for an occasional joint. But they are bulky and costly. A houseful of plumbing requires a lot of fittings, so it's worthwhile for the ownhander to become accustomed to capillary fittings. With these, molten solder is sucked around the narrow gap between the fitting and pipe, and this produces a seal when it sets. The cheapest are end-feed fittings, to which the plumber adds the solder. (A tin-based, lead-free solder should be used for drinking water pipework.) But easier to use are ring capillary fittings (eg, 'Yorkshire' fittings); they have a ring of solder already set in them. Lead-free versions are obtainable.

To fit a Yorkshire fitting, clean the end of the pipe and the inside of the fitting with wire wool, to make them shiny. Brush flux onto the end of the pipe; push it home into the fitting and rotate it to spread the flux. With a blow torch (or powerful hot-air blower), warm the pipe; then heat the fitting until a complete ring of solder appears at its mouth. (Don't overheat or the solder might flow away.) Leave the joint quite still for half a minute, to let the solder set. This is important to bear in mind when working on (springy) floor joists – it's best to stay still by the joint for half a minute. There are many, many joints to be made, and you want every one to be good.

It's best to solder all the joints on a fitting at the same time. But if one pipe is not ready for connection, put a wet rag round the empty solder ring. Later on, when fitting the pipe into this ring, put wet rags round the other joints to prevent their solder remelting. (Alternatively, this may be a time to use a compression fitting.)

Wipe the joints over with a rag to clean away burnt flux.

A recent technical innovation might interest some ownhanders: push-fit plastic fittings for copper pipe. Just push them on – no need for soldering.

The discharge system

It is the plumber's work not only to supply water, but also to get it away to the drains after use. This is done via plastic pipework arranged in a single stack system. (See Fig. 4, Chapter 9.) Formerly, a two-pipe system was used, keeping WC waste separate. The single stack system was introduced from the USA in the Fifties.

The pipework is usually inside the building, leaving external walls uncluttered. An exception to this can be made on the ground floor, where wastes may run into a trapped gully outside. This might save an inconvenient, or even an impossible, waste run inside. But in general, wastes run to the stack. This is an 11 cm soil pipe which runs up inside the house, from the drain at ground floor level to an air valve in the loft. Note that a ground floor WC may discharge into its own drain, without any stack. The handbasin can also discharge into this drain.

To prevent obnoxious smells, all wastes have a water seal. These are built into lavatory pans, of course; but for the rest, the plumber must incorporate a U-trap or the neater looking bottle trap. In a single stack system, all the traps are supposed to be 'deep-seal', $7\frac{1}{2}$ cm deep. This is reckoned to be deep enough to prevent siphonage sucking out the seal:

When waste water flows away, it can suck through the trap the water which ought to be left to form a seal. This is most likely to happen with narrow waste pipes in long runs with strong falls. It can also happen if one waste pipe runs into another – water running down one pipe can suck out the seal in the other. So it's prudent if each waste pipe individually runs into the stack.

The top of the stack is often taken out through the roof and left open, but this is ugly. Better and simpler is to terminate it in the loft with an air admittance valve. This is another innovation, from Scandinavia, which makes the job easier. The valve allows air to be sucked into the stack as waste runs away, but it prevents foul drain air getting out. If you feel a bit squeamish about their efficiency be assured that they have Agrément Board approval. (Actually, the Building Regulations once again allow the stack to be fixed on an outside wall. In this case it can be terminated at eaves height and left open.)

There are two systems for jointing waste pipework:

The 'push-fit' type relies on a rubber ring for a seal:
Cut the pipe square with a tenon or hacksaw; chamfer the end, if need be, with a rasp; lubricate it with water or washing-up liquid; push the pipe home, mark it, and then withdraw it 1 cm to allow for expansion.

The other system uses solvent welding:
Clean the end of the pipe and the inside of the fitting with the proprietary solvent cleaner. Brush solvent cement onto these surfaces. Quickly push the pipe home, and rotate it to spread the cement. Hold the joint firmly together for half a minute, and then wipe away the surplus cement. Leave it undisturbed for several minutes. (On a straight run longer than two metres, an expansion coupling should be incorporated.)

To prevent pipework sagging, support it by clips – every half metre horizontally, and two metres vertically.

The wastes run into the stack via bosses. For a sink waste, which may be carrying nearly boiling water, a bossed pipe should be incorporated into the stack. For other wastes, the versatile 'patch' boss is useful. To fit this to the stack, drill a hole into the soil pipe with a hole saw, and attach the boss with solvent cement. Don't run a waste into the stack opposite, or just below, a WC discharge, in case of blockage. The better position is above the WC discharge; otherwise, at least 15 cm below it. Or else use a manifold; this is fitted at floor level to accept a WC discharge and one or more waste pipes.

23
ELECTRICS

☆

☆

☆

☆

☆

☆

☆

Simple theory
Meter box
Consumer unit
Power circuits
Cooker circuit
Light circuits
Control and power for the central heating
Bonding
Cable size

SOME PEOPLE will turn their hand to any of the building trades except electrics. Indeed, in some countries, amateurs are even forbidden by law to carry out their own electrical work. Because it can't be seen, there seems to be something of a mystique about electricity; and mistakes, of course, can be lethal. Yet in one way, it is the skill most amenable to the ownhander. The knowledge required for it is nearly all intellectual, and so can be learnt from books – there is hardly any 'knack'. Provided that you do understand what you are doing, there is no reason why your work should be inferior to that of a professional. That can hardly be said about plastering, for example!

To aid this understanding, here's a brief account of some of the basics of electricity. Many readers will be confident enough to skip it.

Simple theory

The flow of electricity is often likened to the flow of water in a pipe:

Imagine water being forced by a pump to flow round a circular loop of pipework. The pressure head developed by the pump forces the molecules of water to flow round the loop back to the pump.

Now consider a battery with a wire connecting its two terminals. An electric current flows round the wire. The voltage developed by the battery forces electrically charged particles, called electrons, to flow round the wire back to the battery. The electric current can be compared to the flow of water, and the voltage developed by the battery to the pressure head developed by the pump.

The resistance to the water flow in the pipework decreases for a bigger pipe and more water flows along it. And so it is electrically – a thicker wire has lower resistance and more current flows along it. In fact, this can be expressed more precisely in the most fundamental law of electricity, discovered less than two-hundred years ago by a certain Herr Ohm in Germany:

$$I = \frac{V}{R}$$ where I – current (amps)
V – voltage (volts)
R – resistance (ohms!)

How marvellous that Nature should be so simple!

There's another fundamental law of frequent use, and that relates to power, the rate at which work is performed. Going back to our water analogy, let us imagine that we put a water turbine in the circuit. The water turns the turbine which can perform work. The greater the flow of water in the pipe and the more the pressure behind it, the more powerful the turbine. And so it is with electricity. If we put an electric motor in the circuit, the greater the current round the circuit and the greater the voltage behind it, the more the power of the motor. In fact, it is found again, that a simple relationship holds:

$W = V \times I$ where W – power (watts)

Here, for example, is a practical use of this equation:

Light circuits are usually protected by a 5 amp fuse. So how many lights can we put into one circuit? –

As is well known, the mains voltage is 240 volts. Hence, if the maximum current is 5 amps, the maximum power the circuit can deliver is 1,200 watts (240 × 5). If the power of each bulb is 100 watts, the maximum number of bulbs in the circuit is 12. (In practice, a lesser number, 8, is taken as the design maximum. This allows for the possible use of 150 watt bulbs, and the possible expansion of the circuit later.)

After that practical aside, let's return to theory. The water analogy had water flowing steadily in one direction, corresponding to a direct electric current. But the mains voltage is alternating. The analogy would have the pump pulsing the water one way and then the other – an unlikely analogy. Alternating current is used in the mains supply because it is both easier to produce and easier to use than direct current.

In the mains, the neutral wire is kept at about zero voltage, or earth potential. (In modern installations with PME, 'Protective Multiple Earth', the neutral is kept strictly at the earth potential.) But the live oscillates between a positive and negative potential at 50 cycles per second (or hertz, as the unit for the rate of cycling is known, after a certain Herr Hertz). However, you don't really need to understand about alternating current. If you wired up the circuits to have a positive potential in the live and a zero potential in the neutral, the circuits would come out right.

Domestic appliances are all made to work at the same mains voltage. So that they can all be fed with this voltage, they must be connected 'in parallel'.

Imagine connecting up a couple of 100 watt bulbs. In parallel, they are both fed with the full voltage and both shine brightly. (See Fig. 1.)

Figure 1: Parallel and series circuits

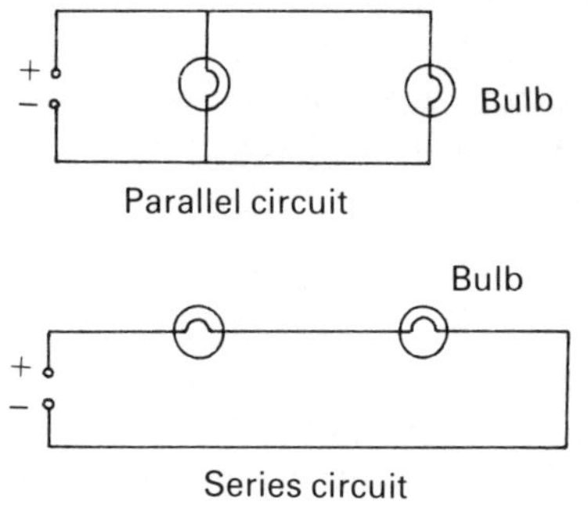

* Only parallel circuits are used in household wiring.

The other possibility, though, is 'in series' – the voltage is applied across the two bulbs arranged one after the other. In this case, each bulb only receives half the full voltage, and each shines dimly. This is not very useful, and so all domestic circuits are wired in parallel. In practice, this is simple enough. All the live terminals (L) are connected together (by the red wire of a cable), and all the neutrals (N) are connected together (by the black wire). And for a continuous earth protection, all the earth terminals (E) are connected together (by the bare copper wire).

Now, with some basic knowledge of electricity, let's look at the wiring of a house.

Meter box

The box, and a conduit shaped like a hockey stick are supplied by the Electricity Company for installing by the builder. The main service cable enters the box to a 100 amp fuse (which is to protect the mains, not the household). An earth terminal is also supplied.

The main item in the box, of course, is the meter – or meters. In many households, it is economic to heat hot water in summertime by Economy 7 electricity. The extra meter for this measures the electrical consumption in a 7-hour period during the night. (During this period, electricity costs about a third of its usual price.)

Consumer unit

From the meter box, the supply is taken via a pair of 16 mm^2 cables to the consumer unit. This has a switch to disconnect the supply. But the main purpose of the unit is to split the supply into several circuits, each protected against overload by a cartridge fuse or a miniature circuit breaker (initialised to MCB). An MCB is a switch which trips out when the current through it becomes excessive. When the fault has been rectified, the MCB can simply be switched back in. And like a fuse, it can also be used to purposely disconnect its circuit. In other words, fuses and MCB's do the same job, but fuses are cheaper and MCB's more convenient.

In a typical house the circuits might be:

Separate power circuits for upper and lower floors
Separate lighting circuits for upper and lower floors
Cooker
Immersion heater
Garage and outside.

So an 8-way consumer unit would be used, leaving one fuseway spare for a future use. (For a small bungalow, a cheaper 6-way unit would be sufficient.)

Some consumer units have another form of circuit breaker besides the MCB's. Why is this needed?

Consider for a moment what would happen if you should carelessly touch a live wire. A big surge of current could pass through you, big enough to trip the MCB – but not quickly enough. By the time the circuit was broken, you might no longer be a live wire yourself but a very dead one!

What happens, if you touch a live wire, is that current can flow through your body and back through the earth to the sub-station, so completing a circuit. Normally, the currents in live and neutral wires are equal, but in this case, with some current flowing to earth, the current in the neutral is less than the live. This difference can be detected; it is the basis of a sensitive safety device called a (current operated) Earth Leakage Circuit Breaker. This mouthful is shortened to ELCB. It also used to be called a Residual Current Circuit Breakers – shortened to RCCB. Nowadays, the preferred name is Residual Current Device (RCD).

Every year in Britain, several people are electrocuted by their lawn mowers. Many more though are killed indirectly – about 200 people a year die from fires started electrically. Many of these deaths could be prevented by consumer units fitted with RCD's. These can detect tiny differences (eg, 30 milliamps) between the currents in the live and neutral wires, and break the circuit in 1/50 second – quickly enough to prevent electrocution and quickly enough, without doubt, to prevent a fire.

It would be foolish to put in a new consumer unit without an RCD. But they do have a disadvantage. They are so sensitive that they are subject to 'nuisance tripping', ie, breaking the circuit without good cause. If this should happen while you were away on holiday and the deep freeze was full of food – misfortune. So it's a good idea to buy a split consumer unit, with most of the fuseways protected by the RCD – but some not, so that separate, unprotected circuits can be taken to the freezer, some lights, and possibly a computer terminal.

Now lets look at the different circuits that can be run from each fuseway.

Power circuits

These are simple. Usually they are a ring circuit. The conductors run from a fuseway, round to each of the sockets, and then back to the same fuseway. (See Fig. 2.)

Current flows along both branches to reach the socket. As is required, all the sockets are in parallel, with a full voltage across them. The basic thinking behind a ring main is that it is economical on cable, which it uses it to full advantage.

We've worked out previously the number of lights that can be put into a light circuit. So, how many sockets can you put in a ring circuit? The answer is surprising – as many as you like, as long as the floor area served by the circuit is less than 100 square metres. Why no limit, and what does floor area have to do with the question? The answer lies in a concept called 'diversity'. In a given area there may be many sockets; but the use made of them and the current consumed is likely to be within reasonable limits. In fact, ring circuits are protected by 30 amp fuses. Appliances can take up to 13 amps from a socket. 3 × 13 is greater than 30, so just three sockets delivering full power would be enough to blow the fuse! But the only household appliances that take these large currents are electric fires: A 3 kw fire uses 12·5 amps (3,000 ÷ 240). So three such fires in the circuit would blow the fuse. In practice, the need for three fires is unlikely, and since other appliances use far less power, the principle seems justified in practice.

Figure 2: Ring main with spurs

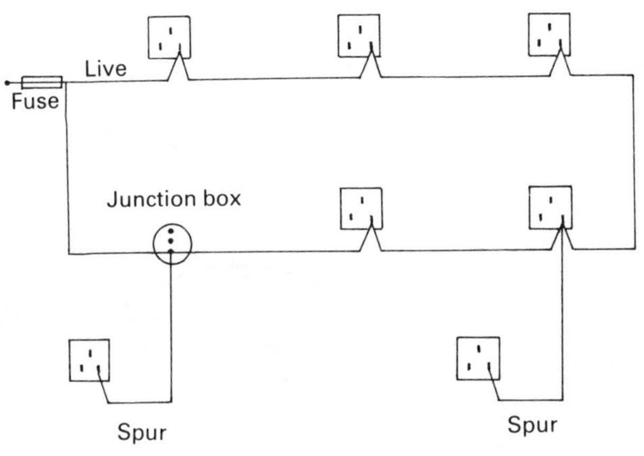

* Neutral and earth not shown for clarity.
* Current can flow in both directions around the ring to the socket.

Sometimes, there's a distant socket required, separate from the general run of the ring. To extend the ring by looping the cable out to it (ie, using two runs of cable) would be wasteful, so a spur of single cable may be used. The spur can be connected into the ring either at a socket or at a junction box inserted into the ring at a convenient position. Note that only one double socket or two single ones may be connected on one spur. And also note that you may not have more sockets on spurs than there are sockets on the ring itself.

In general, 'point to point' wiring is preferred, ie, take a spur from a socket, not a junction box. This way, the circuits are more obvious for any future alterations.

Any fixed appliance, up to 3 kW, is connected as a fused spur. (Except, that is, for an immersion heater, which should not be connected – it is considered to require a continuous load, which would substantially decreases the capacity of the ring.)

Circuits don't have to be based on rings. Simplest of all is the radial circuit. (See Fig. 3.)

Figure 3: Radial circuit

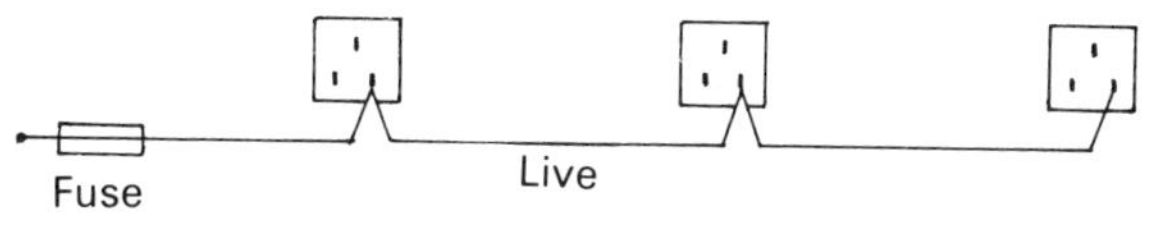

This would be preferred, for example, if you were running a supply to a detached garage – you would only want to run one cable out to the garage.

Immersion heater circuit

Because of its fairly high and fairly continuous load, an immersion heater is connected directly to its own fuseway with a 15 amp or 20 amp fuse. (A 3 kW heater takes 12·5 amps.) For extra safety, it is connected via a double pole switch. (Socket switches disconnect only the live circuit, but a double pole, or 'dipole', switch disconnects both live and neutral.)

Usually, a timer is also incorporated into the circuit.

Cooker circuit

A electric cooker takes by far the biggest load of any appliance. It needs its own circuit, which is protected by a 30 amp fuse and which incorporates a cooker control unit (essentially, a double pole switch).

Figure 4: Loop-in lighting circuit

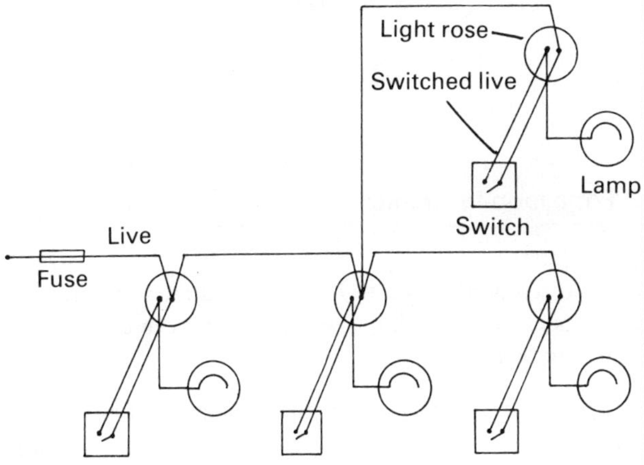

* Neutral and earth not shown for clarity.

A cooker with all its heating elements working may use 12 kW, taking 50 amps. So why a lesser fuse? The answer again lies in diversity. Very seldom will the cooker be used to its full capacity; and even then, the individual thermostats which control each heating element will be switched off much of the time. So in practice, 30 amps is sufficient.

For a separate oven and hob, a single cooker control can be used, provided that both oven and hob are within two metres of the control. A single, shared cooker outlet or two separate ones may be connected to the control.

Light circuits

These are more complex than power circuits because associated with each outlet is a separate switch.

The 'loop-in' system is the modern method. (See Fig. 4.)

The cable runs round from light rose to light rose, with a separate cable running from each rose to its switch. So there are generally three cables at a rose. One feeds in the live, neutral and earth, and another takes them onto the next rose. The third takes the live (and earth) down to the switch, and returns a live if the switch is 'on'. (See Fig. 5.)

Figure 5: Connections in a light rose

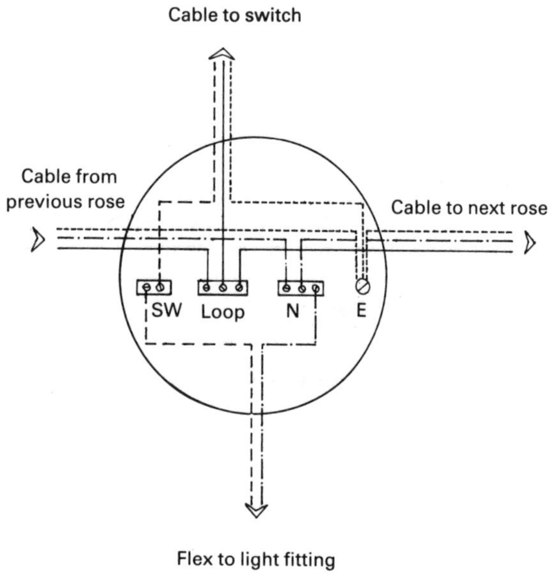

* For a loop-in circuit.

The roses don't have to be connected all in a line. The circuit can branch, with the spur cable connected at a rose or a junction box.

So much for the basics; now for the complexities:

Two lights and one switch

This is the easiest variation. If a pair of lights are to be controlled from one switch, run a cable from the 'switched' rose to the other one. (Connect the corresponding switch, neutral and earth terminals.)

Two switches and one light

This often occurs at a staircase, and sometimes in a bedroom, with the extra switch by the bed. The essence of the method is to run a three-core-and-earth 'strap' between two two-way switches. (See Fig. 6.)

Figure 6: Two-way switching

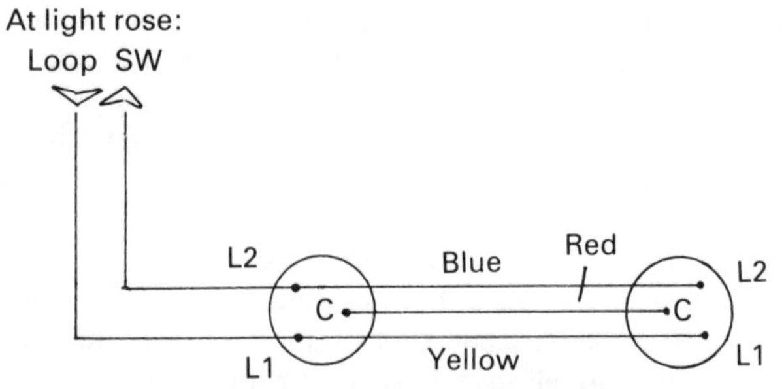

* Light can be switched from either position: To complete the circuit, one switch must connect L1 and the other L2. Whichever terminal is connected at one switch, the other switch can be connected to the same terminal (light off) or the opposite terminal (light on).
* Three-core-and-earth strap between switches.

Figure 7: Lighting with junction box

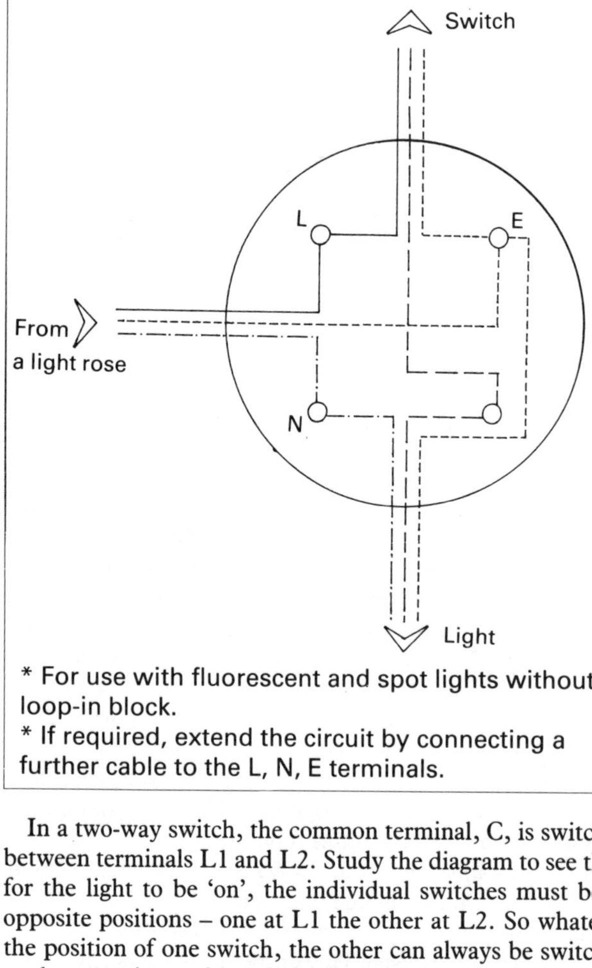

* For use with fluorescent and spot lights without a loop-in block.
* If required, extend the circuit by connecting a further cable to the L, N, E terminals.

In a two-way switch, the common terminal, C, is switched between terminals L1 and L2. Study the diagram to see that, for the light to be 'on', the individual switches must be in opposite positions – one at L1 the other at L2. So whatever the position of one switch, the other can always be switched to the opposite position (light 'on') or the same (light 'off').

Three switches and one light

This is not common in a house, but if there is to be yet

another switch, a special 'intermediate' switch is inserted in the strap to interchange the connections of the blue and yellow wires.

Fluorescent and spot lights

The cheaper versions of these do not have a 'loop-in' block; the 'point to point' method of wiring cannot be used. Instead, use the older, junction box method. (See Fig. 7.)

Control and power for the central heating

The circuit for controlling the boiler, pump and zone valves can be complex! (See Figs. 8 and 9.)

Figure 8: Circuit for a simple central heating system

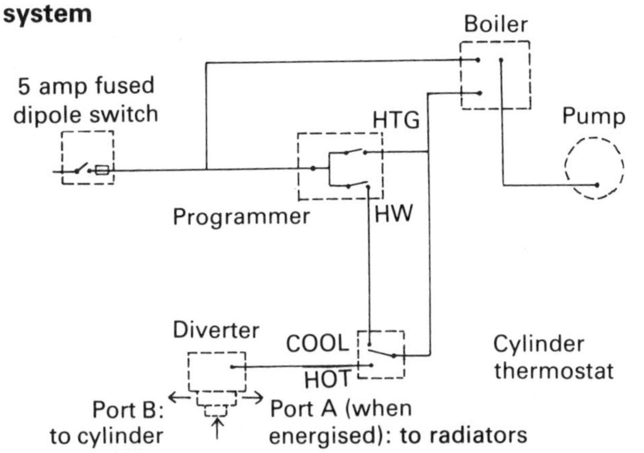

* The diverter is only energised when heating is required and the cylinder is hot. It then switches the flow to the radiators via port A.
* For clarity, the neutral and earth conductors have been omitted.

The diagrams show a circuit for a basic heating system – there are many variations, mostly more complex.

Spur the circuit off a ring main, taking 1·5 mm² cable to a 3 amp fused dipole switch.

In the example given, the boiler requires 'pump over-run'. So the pump is powered from the boiler, which has a terminal controlled by a time delay. The boiler needs a permanent power supply.

The diverter switches the flow to one port (A) when energised, and returns by spring action to the other port (B) when not energised. Even for this relatively simple system, working out all the possible combinations of switching is not easy unless done methodically:

	STATE OF SYSTEM (SWITCHES)							
Heating	on	on	on	on	off	off	off	off
Domestic hot water	on	on	off	off	on	on	off	off
Cylinder water	hot	cool	hot	cool	hot	cool	hot	cool
	RESULT							
Boiler	on	on	on	on	off	on	off	off
Diverter	htg	dhw	htg	dhw!	–	dhw	–	–

In this example, the cylinder thermostat energises the diverter when the cylinder water is 'hot'. So the diverter switches the flow to heating, 'htg', via port A. When the diverter is not energised, the flow is switched to the cylinder, or domestic hot water, 'dhw', via port B.

Note that this system has 'hot water priority'. When both heating and hot water are called for, only the demand for hot water is met – until the water in the cylinder becomes hot.

Figure 9: Central heating circuit with junction box

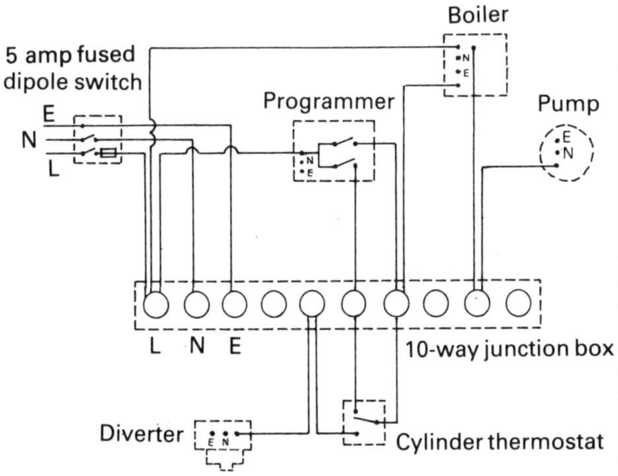

* This corresponds to the circuit in the previous figure (and Figure 1, Chapter 10).
* For clarity the neutral and earth wires are not shown. All the neutrals are connected from terminal 2 to the devices, and the earths from terminal 3.
* Use a 10-way junction box designed for central heating circuits and wire according to the instructions.
* A 'wiring centre' makes connecting the circuit together even simpler.

Note also that, when the Heating is switched 'on' and the Domestic Hot Water is switched 'off', hot water is nevertheless delivered if the cylinder is cool. This aberration of the system is generally acceptable – it is, in fact, a popular control system (Honeywell's Sundial Plan W).

The ownhander can avoid working out all this by following the instructions that come with a special junction box or wiring centre. The complexities can be avoided altogether by using a boiler or cylinder pre-fitted with all the controls. (See 'Circuit details', Chapter 22.)

Bonding

Bonding is the electrical connection of the metalwork in a house (mostly copper pipework) so that it is all at the same (earth) potential. If a copper pipe, for example, is inadvertently in contact with a live wire, then the whole pipe becomes live and potentially dangerous. But if the pipework is earthed, a large current flows to earth, blowing the fuse and breaking the circuit. So all metalwork is connected together and maintained at a safe, earth potential.

'Main bonding' is the earthing of incoming water, gas and oil pipes, just after their entry into the house. An earth conductor connects them to the main earthing terminal, which is usually taken to be the earthing terminal in the meter box. Use 10 mm^2 earth cable, connected to the pipes by earth clamps.

In a bathroom or shower-room, 'supplementary bonding' is required. All the pipework, and metal bath, etc should be cross-bonded together and earthed. Supplementary bonding in the kitchen and utility room is also desirable. Cross-bond the hot pipework and metal sink to the cold (ie, to the rising main, which has been earthed by main bonding). For supplementary bonding, use 4 mm^2 or 6 mm^2 earth cable.

Cable size

Conductors are not perfect. They have some resistance, which results in some power being lost in the cable.

As a matter of academic interest, we can combine the two equations given previously:

$$V = I \times R$$
$$W = I \times V$$

to give

$$W = I^2 \times R$$

(and you can hardly have easier algebra than that!)

So we see that the power (W) lost in the cable depends greatly upon the current (I) – as its square, in fact. This power loss appears as heat, and with extreme overload the insulation of a cable could melt. The other adverse effect is a voltage drop along the cable, given by the first equation. If the current is large, the resistance must be small to keep the voltage drop within limits. In other words, larger currents need larger cables.

The Regulations of the Institution of Electrical Engineers (IEE) state that the voltage drop from meter box to any part of the circuit must be within 2·5% of the mains voltage. And as this is, itself, allowed to vary within 6%, in the worst case the drop in voltage from the nominal 240 volts could be 8·5%, a quite significant amount.

The ratings for cables of different sizes are as follows:

Cable size, mm^2	1	1·5	2·5	4	6	10
Max current, amp	15	19	27	36	46	63

These figures are extracted from the Fifteenth edition of the 'Regulations for Electrical Installations', published by the IEE. The ratings are lower if the cable is likely to be extra warm. For example, if the cable is insulated on one side (eg, it lays on ceiling board and is covered with loft insulation), the ratings should be reduced by a third.

Anyway, the following are the usual practical arrangements:

	Fuse – ie, max current (amps)	Fuse Colour	Cable size in mm^2
Lighting	5	White	1, 1·5
Immersion heater (up to 3 kW)	15	Blue	1·5
Immersion heater (over 3 kW)	20	Yellow	2·5
Radial circuit (up to 20 m^2 floor area)	,,	,,	,,
5 kW instant water heater	,,	,,	,,
Ring circuit	30	Red	,,
Radial circuit (up to 50 m^2 floor area)	,,	,,	4
7 kW instant water heater	,,	,,	,,
Cooker, up to 12 kW	,,	,,	6
Large cooker	45	Green	10

24
CARPENTRY

☆

☆

☆

☆

☆

☆

☆

THE TWO TERMS, 'carpentry' and 'joinery', are widely used, but their meanings vary somewhat in different parts of Britain. In most of England, carpentry is the rougher timber work done on site, usually with timber of a substantial size. Joinery is finer work with planed or moulded timber.

In days gone by, some of the joinery – windows, stairs, cupboards, etc – may well have been made on site, but nowadays these things invariably come from a factory. So in this book, the single term 'carpentry' is used for all the timber work done on site.

Most practical people tend to have a preference for one particular medium, be it timber, metal or stone. Timber seems to be the favourite. Working with wood always remains interesting – there is an inexhaustible fund of technique and know-how to acquire. Yet useful things can be made of wood by only simple methods, and it is a forgiving medium – if you don't get it right first time, there's usually a second chance.

Carpentry is the most comprehensive discipline of the building trades; many builders started out as chippies, but few, for example, as plasterers.

Materials:

Timber

As most people know, timber can be classified into two groups: hardwoods from broad-leaved trees, and softwoods from conifers. In times gone by, there was plenty of hardwood available as forest was cleared for farmland. So people could build in oak to last for centuries. But Britain is now the least forested country in Europe, and most of our timber is imported. In fact, we are Europe's biggest importers of tropical hardwoods. These come from countries which are now doing what the Europeans have done already – clearing their lands. Scientists say that this is gravely damaging the biosphere.

Softwoods are more bio-friendly in that they come from renewed forests. The timber tends to be weaker and less durable than hardwoods, but easier to work. However, this is only a generalisation – balsa is a hardwood!

Redwood is a commonly used softwood, derived from Scots Pine – it is strong, durable and easily worked. It is used, for example, for floor joists.

Whitewood is a little inferior in its properties, but it is quite satisfactory for a lot of internal work. It is converted from the largest European tree, the spruce.

Lesser used softwoods come from North America. British Columbian Pine (from Douglas Fir) is the best of all, somewhat stronger than Redwood, and available in very long lengths. Hemlock is a pale timber with little resin, and therefore not very durable. But it is strong, and used for internal joinery, eg, balusters.

From South America comes Parana Pine. This is fairly free of knots, and the yellow timber can have exotic streaks of red, grey and bluey-green. It is used in good class work for stairs and window boards.

Softwoods come in standard lengths, at 30 cm intervals from 1·8 to 4·8 metres. (Why not simply quarter-metre intervals?) Longer lengths can be obtained. Standard thicknesses for sawn softwood are 1·6, 1·9, 2·2, 2·5, 3·2, 3·6, 3·8, 4·4, 4·7, 5, 6·3, 7·5, 10 cm. (If you want to make sense of these sizes – think imperial!)

Planed timber comes as PAR (Planed All Round) or, more precisely square, as PSE (Planed Square Edge). Its size is quoted, rather misleadingly, as the size of the sawn timber from which it is planed. In reality, this needs to be reduced a few millimetres. For example, 'ex 25 × 50 mm' might measure 21 × 46 mm.

Trees grow high but not wide. So timber is long and narrow. Even if boards were wider, they would not be satisfactory. Timber is very stable in its length, but across the grain it shrinks as it dries, and swells again if it becomes damper. A lot of joinery technique was developed to accommodate this, but nowadays, stable artificial boards are used and techniques are simpler.

Plywood is the most attractive of these boards. The more plies for a given thickness the better. For exterior work, use WBP grade – Weather and Boil Proof. (Actually, this applies to the glue used, not the timber.) Another common grade is INT (Interior use). Note that the timber description, eg Birch, refers only to the two face plies – the inner ones may be different. Letters refer to the quality of the face plies, with 'A' being the best. A common description is B / BB: one good face, with the other one having some knots (which have actually been removed and replaced with sound timber). And lastly, note that the first dimension to be quoted in the size gives the direction of the grain of the face veneers. For example, 122 × 244 cm ply has the grain across its width.

Chipboard is a lot of woodchips stuck together under pressure; it is often denser at the surface than the middle. Tongued-and-grooved chipboard is very suitable for flooring, and a water-resistant grade is available for bathrooms, etc. Plastic-coated chipboard is very popular for cupboards. Medium Density Fibreboard (MDF) is a board that can be worked like wood; it is useful for cupboards and general construction.

Hardboard is becoming less popular. To fix it taut, wet the back of it the day before pinning it into place. Nor is blockboard so widely used.

A new type of board, OSB (for 'Orientated Strand Board') is available. The technology has been brought over from Canada to use Scottish trees. In its properties and price, it lies between plywood and chipboard. It is suitable for external use.

Completely different types of board use cellulose fibres bound together with cement (eg, 'Tacboard') or calcium silicate (eg, 'Masterclad'). These are very stable, can be used externally, and are fire resisting.

Nails

For rough carpentry (eg, studwork), round wire nails are generally used. In more visible work, ovals are used; their heads can be punched below the surface and the holes filled (eg, for architrave). If the oval is lined up with the grain, the nail is less likely to split the wood. Lost head nails can also be punched below the surface. They are even less obtrusive than ovals, and do not bend so easily. Smaller versions are called panel pins (used for fixing matching, beading, etc). Ring-shank nails (with a jagged shank) give a very strong grip. Clasp nails also have a strong grip and are useful for fixing directly into blockwork (eg, for skirting). They are relatively expensive – like the other cut nail, the floor brad (used for timber floorboards).

Clout nails have large heads. (Galvanized types are used for plasterboarding and roofing.) On roofing, galvanized nails are said to be good for a 60-year life, alloy nails for 100 years.

In general, use nails about $2\frac{1}{2}$ times as long as the thickness of the timber to be secured.

Splitting is a common problem when timber is being nailed near its end. There are several ways of avoiding this. Strangely enough, it helps to blunt the nail: Nip off the point with pincers, or knock it back with a hammer. The nail then tends to cut the fibres, rather than riving through them. Avoid knocking in a pair of nails along the same line of grain. And when there is a choice, nail first and saw the end off afterwards (eg, with the horns of a door lining). If you are really having trouble with splitting, drill a pilot hole.

Nails are not always driven in square. Sometimes there is no choice but to skew nail them (eg, when nailing a roof truss to the wall plate). But sometimes it is by choice, and 'dovetail' nailing – putting several nails in at different angles – makes for a very strong union. This can be used, for example, in joisting – nail a pair of joists together to make a strong trimmer.

As a guide to numbers, here are some quantities for a kilo of nails in common sizes:

	2 cm	5 cm	$7\frac{1}{2}$ cm
Round wire	4,000	420	150
Ovals	4,400	450	130
Clasp		300	120
Lost heads		450	130
Clout	1,100	250	

Screws

Screws give a stronger fixing than nails, and one that can be unfixed. Screws of the same gauge have the same size shank and head.

The common wood screw has a countersunk head for fixing timber. To fix a metal fitting, use a round head screw – but if the hole in the fitting is countersunk, use a raised head screw. (The exception to this is on door hinges; countersunk screws have to be used to let the hinges close.) Use brass screws with brass or brassy fittings. Large screws need a pilot hole for the thread, and a wider clearance hole for the shank. These are especially required for brass screws, which are weak and tend to shear off. For small screws, starting a hole with a bradawl is sufficient.

Cross-head screws have some advantages over the traditional slotted head. The cross-head allows the screw to be held on the end of a screwdriver – which is useful for reaching into difficult positions. And the screw can be turned from an angle. Twin-threaded screws can be driven home with fewer turns.

Coach screws are used for heavy constructional work; they are turned with a spanner rather than a screwdriver.

Other fixings

'Woodhog' nail plates are useful for butt joints in difficult circumstances (eg, a row of noggings in line).

Polyurethane foam from an aerosol fixes and seals across gaps (eg, in the USA, it is used around door linings).

Tools

Chippies need considerably more tools than other tradespeople, a fact which reflects the greater number of techniques they need to master. Here's a list of the most useful tools:

Claw hammer: When hammering, try to hit the nail! A miss can cause an indentation – a 'half-crown' as it used to be known. This spoils the appearance of planed timber. (To remove the half-crown, wet it with hot water, so that the fibres swell. Allow it to dry, and then sand flat.)

The claw may have only enough leverage to partly extract a long nail. In this case, pack underneath the hammer head with a thick off-cut and try again. (If that fails, use a 'wrecking bar'.) Some thin packing underneath the claw will protect a delicate surface.

Punches: Keep two different sizes for knocking large and small nail heads below the surface.

Pin push: This deserves to be more commonly used than it it. It inserts panel pins quickly and easily (especially if you hit the handle with a mallet). The barrel bore should suit the size of the pins; a medium bore is most useful.

Pincers: For extracting nails.

Screwdrivers: A range of screwdrivers is needed for both slotted and cross-head screws. The longer the screwdriver, the more the torque that can be exerted; and a fat handle helps too.

Panel saw: This is a general-purpose saw both for ripping along the grain and for cross cutting. Having it set and sharpened occasionally can make an amazing difference to its performance. A long blade helps the eye to keep the saw in line.

Tenon saw: Use this for smaller work, on joints and the like.

Coping saw: For cutting curves, eg, for scribing skirting. It can be used to cut on the pull (like Japanese saws) or on the push, depending on which way round you insert the blade. This is influenced by which side of the work needs a clean cut finish.

Chisels: For cutting mortises, housings, etc. The bevelled-edge chisel is the most generally useful type, and about three widths should suffice, eg, 6, 12 and 25 mm.

Mallet: This punches a chisel through wood more effectively than a hammer.

Brace: This is the traditional tool for drilling holes. To prevent a ragged edge at the back of a hole:

1) When the centre of the bit has just started to break through the back surface, withdraw the bit, and finish the hole from the other side.

or 2) Hold some waste timber against the back surface, and drill through into that.

Four bits are plenty, say 10, 15, 25 and 32 mm, preferably 'Jennings' pattern. (You could, perhaps, manage with only a power drill.)

Wheelbrace: For drilling smaller holes. Optional. A cordless drill may replace it.

Bradawl: Makes pilot holes for screws. Keep it sharp so that it cuts across the fibres.

Countersink: In neat work, this is used to make a recess for a screw head. A countersink with a handle for hand operation is more convenient than one that requires a drill.

Plane: This is the most complicated of these hand tools. Most amateurs buy a small smoothing plane, but the longer jack plane (about 35 cm in length) is preferable. A longer sole plate results in a straighter surface.

After sharpening the blade (as described below), the plane needs to be re-assembled. The cap iron should be set about 3 mm above the edge of the blade (less for hardwood). When assembled, to ascertain the position of the blade, hold the plane upside down and look along the sole plate. Adjust the squareness of the blade with the lever. Rotate the knob so that the blade just protrudes from the sole plate – trial and error will show by how much, so that shavings are neither too fine nor too coarse. Rubbing a candle over the sole plate helps the plane to slide over the wood. (Saws also benefit from this treatment.)

After perhaps an hour's use, the blade will need resharpening.

Oilstone: Spread a little machine oil over the stone before use. It is used for re-sharpening chisels and plane blades – both to 30°. Keep this angle constant as you push the blade back and forth. (See Fig. 1.)

Figure 1: Sharpening a chisel

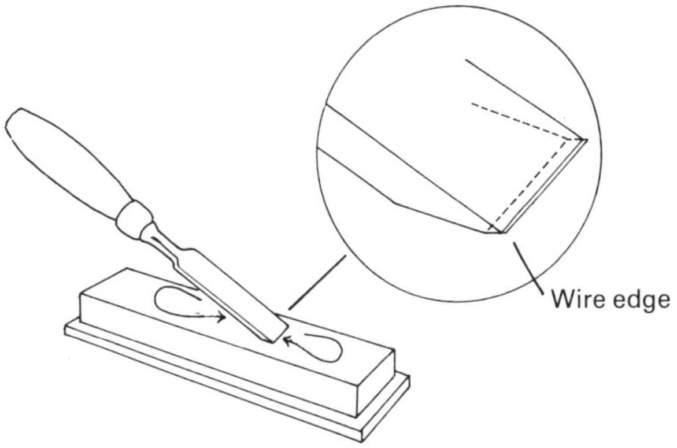

* Hold the blade at a steady angle when moving it – approximately 30°.
* A 'wire edge' is formed – remove this by stroking the face of the blade flat across the stone.
* A plane blade is sharpened in a similar fashion – but move it back and forth, not in a figure-of-eight.

Continue this until a 'wire edge', or burr, can be seen all along the edge. (Or feel it, by sliding a finger off the back of the cutting edge.) It is pointless to try and sharpen the blade further. Remove the burr by pulling the blade flat over the stone a couple of times. (Note that the cutting edge of a jack plane is not straight, but has a slight convex curve.)

After a lot of use, or a little misuse, chisels and plane blades need regrinding to an angle of 25°. A small electric grinding wheel can be used for this. Keep the blade wetted and keep it moving across the wheel; otherwise it becomes red hot, and the steel softens. (In that case, the blade should be ground down further to remove the suspect steel.)

Combination square: This has a multitude of uses. It can be used as a try square to check that timber is flat and square. It can be used to mark across timber, either square or at 45°. And it can be used to mark a margin. (See Fig. 7.)

Bevel: This is used for marking non-square angles, eg, a plumb cut at the end of rafters.

Workmate: Invaluable.

Power tools: Power tools can be most useful on site, if mains electricity is available. If not, battery-operated tools are a possibility, but with the exception of cordless drills, they are rather ineffective for building work.

Circular saws cut faster, straighter and squarer than jigsaws. They are very useful for floorboarding and a lot else besides. For cutting any glued material (eg, plywood or chipboard), a TCT blade should be used. A 'Tungsten Carbide Tipped' blade needs only occasional resharpening. (Try 'Saw Sharpening' in the *Yellow Pages*.) The more teeth, the neater the cut. Jigsaws are invaluable for cutting curves, but they can cut straight too. They are versatile; with a change of blade, they can cut metal.

A drill is the other frequently used power tool. In fact, it may be worth having two or three: a general-purpose, DIY drill, a cordless drill, and a pneumatic hammer drill for masonry work.

For safety, it's considered best to use a power tool with the cable over your shoulder, out of the way.

Techniques:

Preparing timber

Timber is converted from the indeterminate shapes of tree trunks into boards, which should be straight and square. For building work, the timber will usually have been prepared true enough. Here is how to check it:

Figure 2: Checking timber for straightness

* View the timber from an end – any bowing is optically exaggerated.

Figure 3: Checking timber for flatness

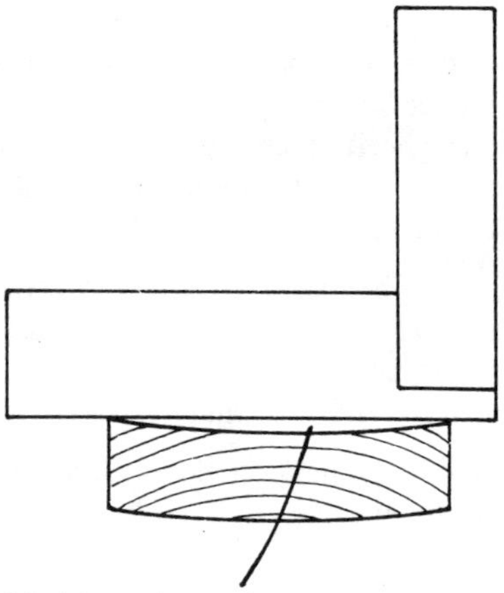

* View the timber towards a light source to see if there is a gap through which light can shine.

Straightness: A quick test is to look down the length of the timber. (See Fig. 2.)

Deviations from straightness appear exaggerated. Alternatively, hold the timber against a known straight edge.

Flatness: Hold a straight-edge, eg, the blade of a try square, across the 'flat' surface. (See Fig. 3.)

Look along the timber to check that there is no gap between the surface and the straight-edge. Hold it up to the light to see if light shines through.

Squareness: Hold a try square against the 'square' angle. (See Fig. 4.)

Figure 4: Checking timber for square

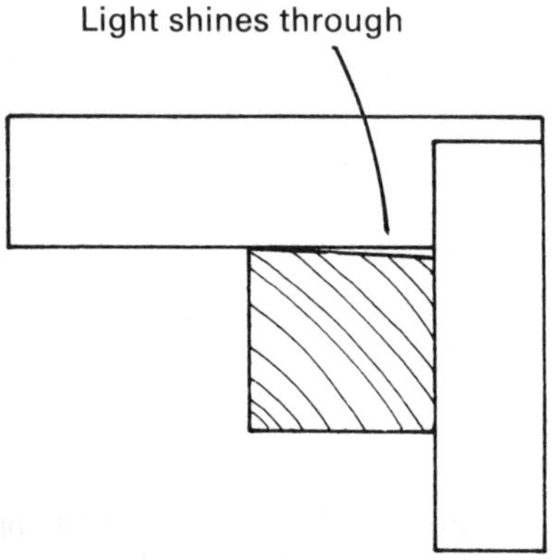

Again, check that no light shines through. Repeat the test at other positions along the timber.

Twist: A piece of timber can satisfy all the above tests, yet still not be true. It can be slightly twisted, or 'out of wind'. This has nothing to do with being puffed out as the word is pronounced as in 'a winding road'. To test for this twist, two winding sticks are used. These are pieces of timber, say 1 × 3 cm in cross section and 40 cm long. Place them on the surface to be tested, one across each end. (See Fig. 5.)

Figure 5: Checking timber for twist

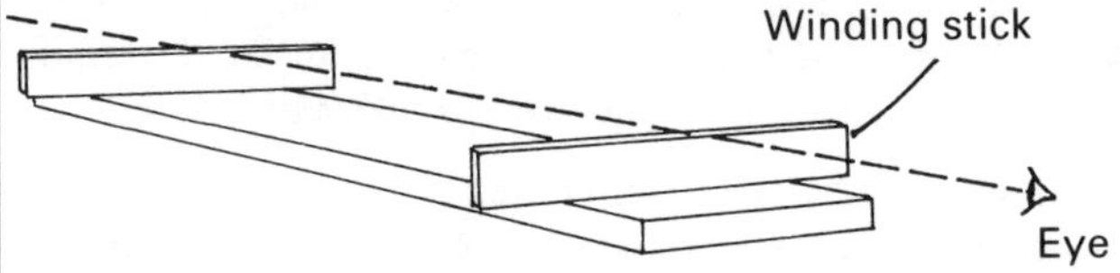

* View as shown to see if the tops of the winding sticks are parallel.
* On long boards, use a third winding stick in the middle.

Look down the length of the timber to check that the top edges of the sticks are parallel. If not, the timber has warped. (Doors are liable to go out of wind.)

Marking out

For cutting an end square, mark square across a face and an edge with a try square.

Given several pieces of timber which are all to be cut to the same length, a novice will measure off each length individually. To do it professionally, place them side by side and all lined up at one end. Measure the length, and then mark square across them all. (See Fig. 6.)

Figure 6: Multiple marking

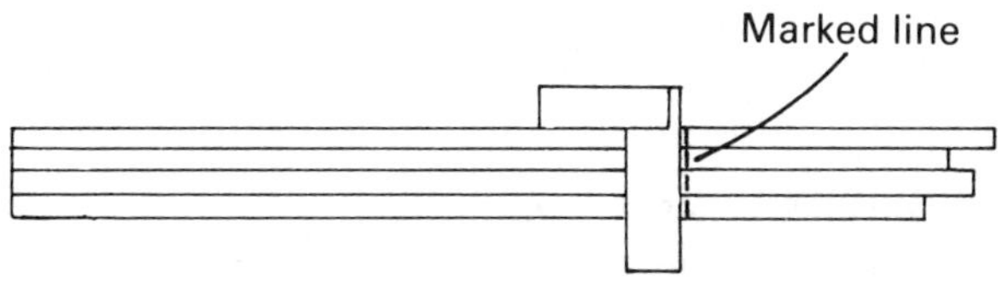

* Quicker and more reliable than marking each piece separately.

This is quicker than doing the job piecemeal, and it leaves less chance for a wrong measurement. (With one measurement, you take care; with half a dozen, you may become careless.)

In another type of repetitive marking out, the marks are transferred from a 'rod'. This is a straight piece of timber inscribed with the required marks.

Figure 7: Marking a margin

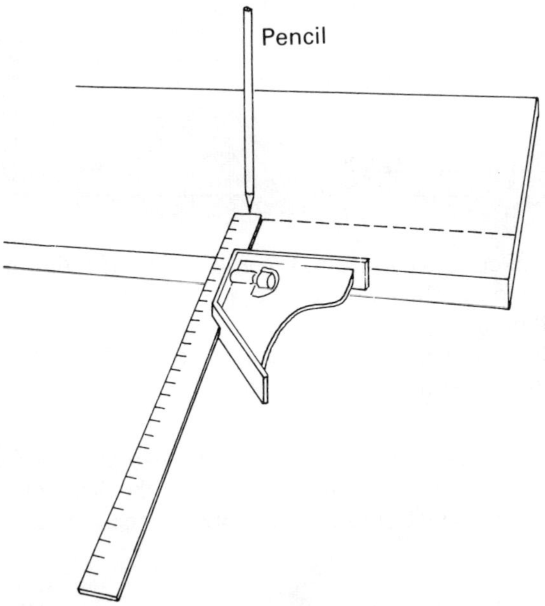

* Set combination square to required margin.

It is mostly used in a joiners' shop, but an example of its use on site occurs in the making of studwork. The head is marked out and then used as a rod to transfer the marks to the sill and noggings. (And bricklayers use a gauge rod for the coursing of brickwork.)

To mark a margin down a board, a combination square is used. Extend its rule to the margin required, and run the square down the board, holding a pencil against the end of the rule. (See Fig. 7.)

An approximate margin can be marked well enough by hand: Run the pencil down the board while steadying the hand with the little finger held against the edge of the board.

Another method of marking a margin is with a marking gauge. Sometimes the cut line produced by this helps to give a neater finish. Push the tool down the timber, dragging the pin through the wood to cut a line.

Sawing

'Measure twice and cut once' is a well-known saw (please accept the pun!). Follow this and you will waste less material and time. (A Russian proverb is even more cautious: 'Measure your cloth seven times, because you can only cut it once'.)

In accurate work, saw on the waste side of the line, leaving the line just visible on the very edge of the timber. A saw kerf has an appreciable width, and just to saw down a line and obliterate it is too inaccurate for fine work.

Often a straight line needs to be cut across a wide board with a circular or jig saw. To guide the saw, keep its sole plate against a straight batten clamped to the board. (To find the position for the batten relative to the required cut, measure the distance from the edge of the sole plate to the face of the blade – the nearer or further face, according to which side the waste will lie. This is a subtle point that you will probably forget until you learn it through your mistakes!)

Another point that should be born in mind about sawing is to anticipate the neatness of cut required. A saw blade leaves a ragged edge on the side from which it leaves the timber – particularly so with circular saws. In fine work, this factor determines which side of the timber you saw from.

To saw an aperture with a jigsaw, drill a small hole to take the jigsaw blade at the start. Alternatively, the cut can be started just with the saw itself:

Begin with the sole plate tilted on its front edge so that the blade is only just cutting through the surface. Gradually pivot the saw into its normal position as the blade cuts into the surface. The method is tricky but convenient.

Planing

Knowing how to plane timber straight, square and flat is a basic requirement in joinery work. Fortunately, the techniques are seldom required on site, where window frames, etc. are ready-made and timber pre-planed if necessary. However, some planing is necessary, in particular, when fitting doors.

Keeping the blade sharp and properly adjusted is important for easy working. If you are working hard to very little effect – probably the plane needs sharpening! (See 'Oilstone', earlier.)

Planing across end grain is not so easy as planing with the grain. Beware at an edge – some fibres may split away (eg, from the lipping when you plane the top of an internal door). Avoid this by planing into the edge, not off it.

An electric plane is very productive – though not for delicate work.

Chiselling

The main use of a chisel is to cut a mortise (ie, a rectangular hole):

Mark out the rectangle for the mortise with a marking gauge. (Preferably, the width of the mortise will be the same as your chisel.) Chop a series of cuts into the wood across the grain, aligning a side of the chisel to an edge of the mortise. Hold the chisel upright and hit it firmly with a mallet. Try to gauge the depth of cut required. (See woodworking books for more details.)

For the very shallow housings for hinges, it is more effective to chop slanting cuts at 30°. (See Fig. 3, Chapter 15.)

At the other extreme, for a very deep mortise, drill a series of holes first, and then cut out the rest of the waste with a chisel.

Mitring

The angle of a mitre is half the angle of the corner it is fitting into; so it is nearly always 45°.

For mitring the width (eg, for architrave), a mitre box is used to hold the saw at the required 45° angle. A mitre box can be purchased for a few pounds, or simply made. (See Fig. 8.)

Figure 8: Mitre box (unfinished)

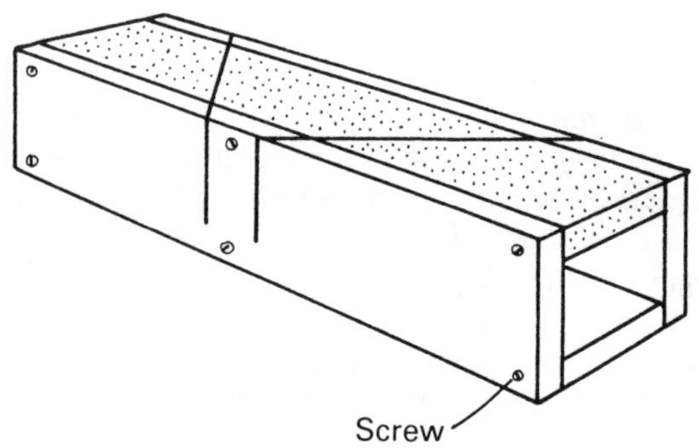

* To finish the box, remove the shaded piece.

The construction of the box is simple, but the cuts in it need to be made carefully.

If a length of batten is fixed to it underneath, the box can be held securely in a Workmate.

For mitring the thickness (eg, for skirting), a mitre box is usually too shallow. A professional uses a mitre block, which is even more simple to make than a box. But an amateur can get a better result using a circular saw: Bevel the sole plate to 45° and guide the saw with a batten clamped across the board.

Scribing

This term means the cutting a workpiece so that it can fit against a non-flat surface. There are two main applications, rather different in nature:

Scribing to a wavy wall

A typical example of this occurs in the fitting of kitchen worktops, when a wall may turn out to be less flat than it looks.

Place the worktop in position against the wall and mark on it a margin at an even distance from the wall. To do this, use a pair of compasses set to slightly more than the biggest gap between the worktop and the wall. (Or use a small wood block cut to this size.)

Cutting along the line should result in a good match with the wall.

Scribing skirting board at internal corners

Amateurs often mitre skirting boards at corners. But the result, at an internal corner, is not as neat as scribing one piece over the other. With this method, the first board just butts up to the wall. The second board butts up to the first. But skirting boards are usually moulded, not flat, and the problem is to cut the end of the second board to match the profile of the first. The solution is ingenious:

First, mitre the end of the second board. If you look at the shape of the cut edge, you will then see that it traces out the profile required to fit over the skirting. (See Fig. 9.)

Figure 9: Scribing skirting board

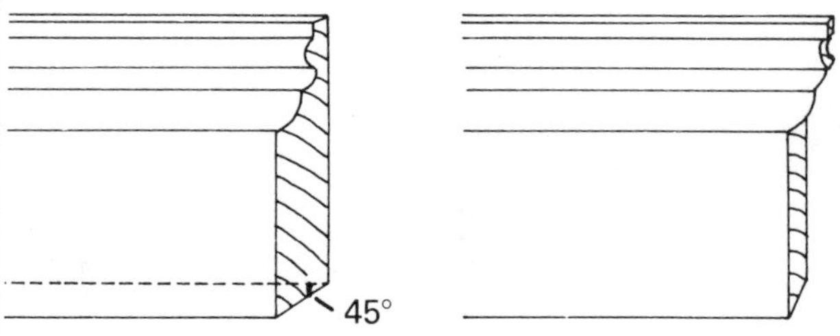

* First cut a 45° mitre at the end of a board. Along the edge of the cut, a profile of the board is outlined.
* Cut to this profile with a coping saw. The end will now fit over the adjoining board.

Cut this shape out with a coping saw. (In practice, a better result is obtained if you aim to 'undercut' the shape a little.) To understand why this method works, it's best to do it!

Joints:

Butt joint

This, the very simplest and easiest of joints, is held together by nails. It is used, for example, in studwork and herring-bone strutting. (See Fig. 10.)

Skew nailing may be required; this tends to split the wood. If this is a problem, pre-drill a tight hole – or else use the ingenious 'woodhog' metal plate.

Splay joint

Instead of just butt jointing lengths of fascia or skirting, in good quality work they are splayed: The two ends are mitred in their thickness so that one overlaps the other. (See Fig. 11.)

Figure 10: Butt joint

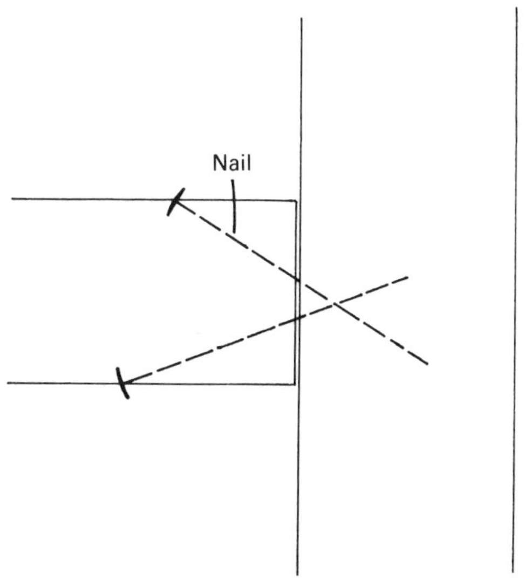

* If it is not possible to nail through directly from the back, skew nailing is necessary, as shown.

Figure 11: Splay joint

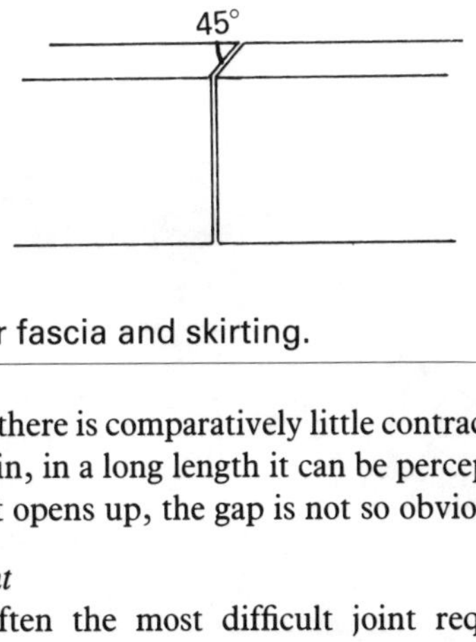

* Used for fascia and skirting.

Although there is comparatively little contraction in timber along its grain, in a long length it can be perceptible. But if a splayed joint opens up, the gap is not so obvious.

Half-lap joint

This is often the most difficult joint required on site nowadays – and it's very simple!

It is used to join lengths of wall plate, usually in line but sometimes at a corner (eg, for a hipped roof). (See Fig. 12; and Fig. 17, Chapter 6.)

Tongued-and-grooved joint

This machined joint is used for chipboard flooring and for 'matching' – timber cladding with a chamfer to disguise the joint.

To make a tight joint, place a grooved off-cut over the free tongue and hit the off-cut with a mallet.

For secret fixing, nail through the tongue. (Use panel pins for matching.) Skew the nail so that it goes through the lower shoulder – this tends to tighten the joint.

Figure 12: Half-lap joint

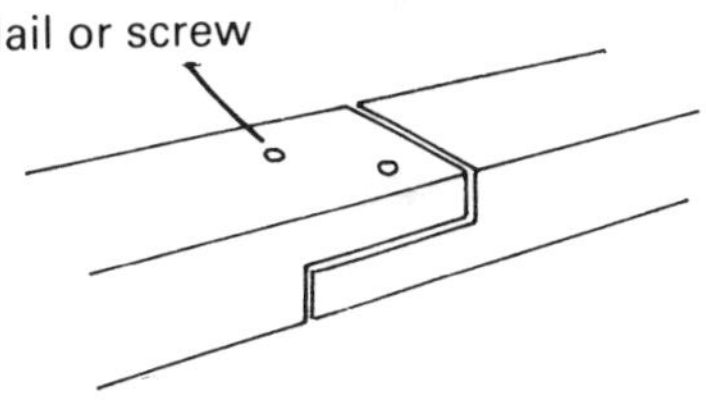

* Used for wall plate.

Draw-pinning

This is a method of holding mortise-and-tenon joints very tightly together. It is used for stairs, for example.

Some dowel is needed. Remove the tenon from the joint and drill a hole, of the same diameter as the dowel, to pass through the mortise. (For neatness, there is no need to break out through the far cheek of the stock.) (See Fig. 13.)

Figure 13: Draw pinning a mortise-and-tenon joint

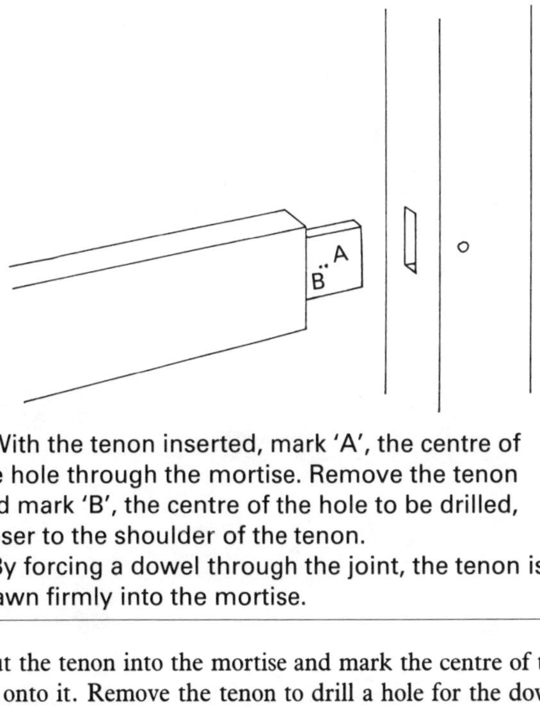

* With the tenon inserted, mark 'A', the centre of the hole through the mortise. Remove the tenon and mark 'B', the centre of the hole to be drilled, closer to the shoulder of the tenon.

* By forcing a dowel through the joint, the tenon is drawn firmly into the mortise.

Put the tenon into the mortise and mark the centre of the hole onto it. Remove the tenon to drill a hole for the dowel through it. But the essence of draw-pinning is to displace this hole towards the shoulder – by about half the radius of the hole. When the dowel is forced through the joint with a mallet, it will then draw the tenon's shoulder hard up against the stock.

(To make it easier to insert the dowel, chamfer its end first. And coat it with a little glue before inserting it.)

Fixing to walls

A common task is to fix a length of timber to a masonry wall.

The problem is to drill holes in the wall so that their positions exactly match holes already drilled in the timber.

The first two holes are easy. Drill the first hole, plug it, and screw on the timber. Mark the position on the wall for the second hole, and swivel the timber out the way. Drill and plug this hole, and fix the timber in position with another screw.

The laborious way, now, would be to mark the remaining holes on the wall and then take down the timber to drill the holes and plug the wall. Instead, leave the timber in place, and drill the remaining holes in the wall. With the timber in place, how can the plugs be inserted? –

Plugs with small shoulders are required. Start a screw in one, and push the plug into a hole. Tap the screw with a hammer to force the plug past the timber and home into the wall.

Folding wedges

'Folding wedges' are used to exert pressure. Jam a pair of wedges into a given gap, in opposition to each other; hammer them in to increase the pressure. They are used, for example, at the end of floor strutting to make it tight. (See Fig. 13, Chapter 6.)

To make a pair of folding wedges, take a rectangular block of wood of suitable size, and cut across it slant-wise.

25
BASICS OF PLASTERING

☆

☆

☆

☆

☆

☆

☆

Plasterboarding
Plastering
Tools
Floating coat
Skim coat

Plasterboarding

Though plastering may require a knack, the simple techniques of boarding are quickly learnt.

Plasterboard is usually available in two thicknesses, 9·5 mm and 12·7 mm (ie, $\frac{3}{8}''$ and $\frac{1}{2}''$). There are a variety of sizes, some all metric, and some imperial lengths with metric widths. There are three different profiles for the long edges. Square-edged is the usual, but the rounded edge of plaster lath needs no scrimming, and tapered-edge board needs no skimming. The grey surface of the boards is for skimming; a white surface is for painting, papering or texturing. Boards should be stored dry and flat.

The ease with which plasterboard can be cut is one of its virtues. The technique is simple. For a straight cut across, score the line with a Stanley knife and a metal straight-edge. A sharp blow against the line from the other side (eg, with a knee) will crack the plaster core. With the board creased back, slice down the other paper surface. (Sometimes it may be necessary to smooth this edge: Scrape the knife blade or a Surform over it several times.) Curves are a little more difficult: Cut right through the board with the knife. Or a jigsaw will cut the curve like the proverbial knife through butter.

Plenty of galvanized plasterboard nails are needed – every 15 cm along each joist (or stud, or nogging). Use 3 cm nails for the thin boards and 4 cm for the thicker ones. Make sure that the nails are hammered in tight. (Loose nails may snag the trowel when the board is skimmed, and they also allow the board to move.) But don't knock the nails in too far and so puncture the paper. A professional can hammer a nail home with just two blows. Keep 1 cm from a bound edge, somewhat more from a cut edge. In general, fix the middle of a board first, and work outwards.

An alternative is to use plasterboard screws with a cordless screwdriver. (Use screws of the same length as given above for the nails.)

(For special requirements, there are plasterboards reinforced with cellulose or glass fibres. Such boards are much stronger and better able to resist damp. Some of them can also bend – curved walls?)

Plastering

Plastering is something of a knack that takes some practice to acquire. Nonetheless, it does help to understand what is supposed to be happening at each stage, rather than seeing it all as sleight of hand.

Even knowing some chemistry may help! The gypsum plasters are obtained by heating an ore, gypsum ($CaSO_4.2H_2O$), to drive off some of the water of crystallisation. This gives Calcium Sulphate Hemi-hydrate ($2CaSO_4.H_2O$), which is otherwise known as Plaster of Paris. When this is mixed with water, the material reverts to its earlier form, and it sets as a mass of interlocking, minute crystals. However, this happens too rapidly for building work, so retarders are added to slow the set down. This is the basis of the 'Browning' and 'Finish' plasters. They should not be retempered once they have started to set because this breaks up the crystalline bonds and results in a weaker plaster.

Physics too plays a part in the process. When plaster is applied, be it floating coat or skim coat, water is sucked out of it into the backing material. This suction is beneficial as it rapidly stiffens the material and helps it to be worked. The chemical setting takes place later, after an hour or so.

Plaster very definitely needs to be stored in dry conditions. Even so, it deteriorates, and after a couple of months, or so, its setting time will have become too short and the plaster will be unusable.

Tools

The plasterer's tools are simple. They should be kept particularly clean. Don't let plaster harden on them.

Hawk: Make your own from a square piece of ply (30 × 30 cm), screwing a short handle to its centre. (See Fig. 1.)

Or buy an aluminium one.

Figure 1: Home-made hawk

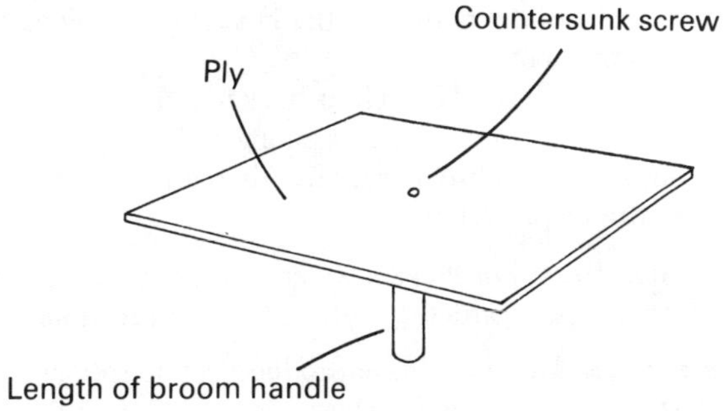

Trowels: A floating, or laying-on trowels, has five to seven rivets. A skimming trowel has a thinner blade and needs eight to ten rivets. An internal angle trowel is optional. (This has two small blades at right angles.)

Floats: Polythene is tending to replace wood as it keeps its shape better. A skimming float gives a flatter surface than the somewhat flexible blade of a steel trowel.

A scratch, or devil, float, is used to both flatten and scratch the floating coat. Stick some nails into the toe of a float so that the nails just protrude. (See Fig. 2.)

This float is somewhat larger than the skimming float.

Figure 2: Scratch float

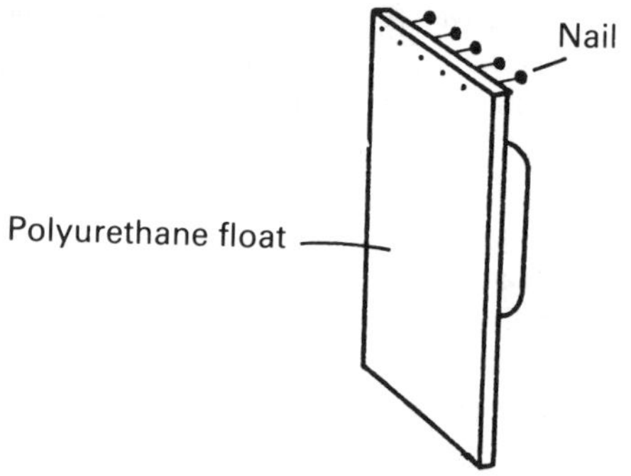

* To give a key to the floating coat, rub a scratch float over it. The nails score the surface.

Feather-edge rule: This rule is about two metres long, and has a chamfered edge to get into corners. Some wide skirting board may be satisfactory – it must be straight!

Darby: This is a broad straight blade, a metre or two long, with a couple of handles at the back. Aluminium versions are available. Use it to press the floating coat in, as well as flattening it. Optional.

Spot board: A board about a metre square, supported at table height.

Mixers: A cement mixer for cement/lime/sand. For mixing gypsum browning, some people use an old bath. An alternative is to make a simple box with some ply (say 1·2 × 2·4 m) and four short lengths of scaffold board. Lay the ply on the floor and fix the boards on edge around it. To prevent plaster seeping out from the bottom of the box, lay sand along the joints with the floor.

For finish plaster, a large clean bucket and a plunger are needed. You can make your own plunger: Fix a push-chair wheel onto a piece of broom handle. Alternatively, a plunger or whisk can be purchased.

Broad paint brush: For flicking water onto a dry background (some people use a garden spray), and for cleaning tools.

Platform: The Americans have produced some special stilts which strap to the legs and enable a plasterer to walk tall and reach up to any part of the ceiling. The more mundane and, perhaps, safer way is to build an extensive platform of scaffold boards. 'Split heads' can be made to support scaffold boards on edge. (See Fig. 3.)

Figure 3: Support for a platform of scaffold boards

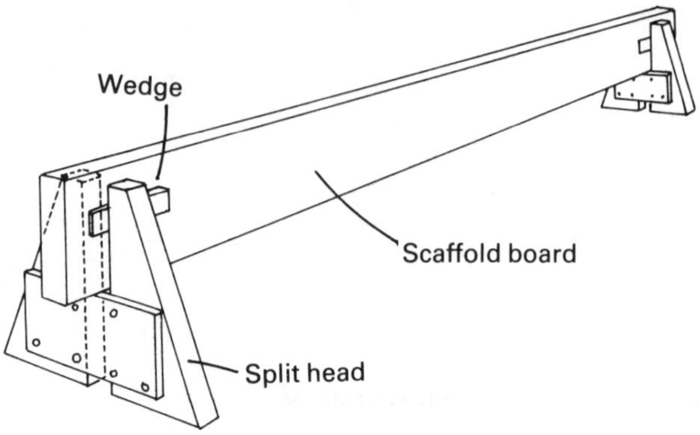

* Two 'split heads' hold a scaffold board on edge. Two or more such bearers can be used to support a platform of scaffold boards.

Then lay more boards across these to make a platform. (Or use bottle crates to support the boards.) Leave a gap at the walls so that you can step down and view the whole ceiling comfortably.

Floating coat

The purpose of the floating coat is primarily to produce a flat surface and also to help even out differences in the suction of different backing materials. Pronounced differences would affect the skim coat – where the backing is more absorbent, the skimming coat would tend to be thicker. Such slight variations cause the background to 'grin through'.

In the past, a mixture of sand and plaster, called browning, has been used for the floating coat. Nowadays, the sand is replaced by a lightweight aggregate to make the job easier. One aggregate is perlite, which consists of tiny glass bubbles obtained from a volcanic glass ore found in the USA. Another is vermiculite, which is expanded mica. The mix of aggregate and gypsum is sold in bags as 'Carlite Browning'. An old bath is a favoured vessel for mixing; or else make up a box as described earlier. Mix the browning with water, stirring it around with a shovel.

To get the right consistency, think of whipped cream. A 35 kg bag of Carlite Browning will cover about 5 square metres, at a thickness of 1 cm. Alternatively, a 1:1:6 mix of cement, lime and plastering sand may be mixed in a cement mixer. This makes a harder plaster, but it also makes for harder work! At a thickness of 1 cm, 100 square metres of plaster have a volume of 1 cu m. For the quantities of cement, lime and sand required for this, see 'Quantities', Chapter 20.

Whether you have made up a cement or gypsum plaster, place a couple of bucketfuls of the mix on the spot board. With a trowel, cut away a dollop of plaster and push it off the spot board onto your hawk. Apply the plaster to the wall with a laying-on trowel:

Start at the top right-hand side of the wall (for a right-handed person) and lay on a band of plaster about a metre and a half wide. Start at the top and work from right to left. (See Fig. 4.)

Figure 4: Applying floating coat

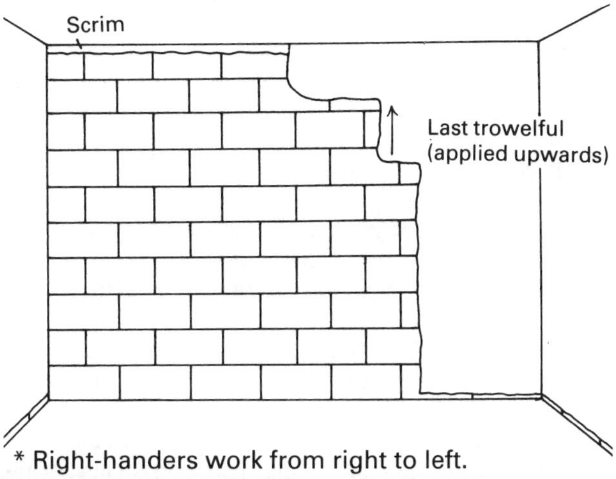

* Right-handers work from right to left.
* For a flatter result, use horizontal screeds near the top and bottom of the wall, or a series of vertical screeds.

The material can be swept off the hawk with an upward push and transferred straight onto the wall with a broad, vertical stroke. At the start of the sweep, the trowel is quite oblique to the wall, but as you push it upwards with less and less material, roll it over to make the blade flatter to the wall. In this way, push the material onto the wall with an even thickness. (See Fig. 5.)

The thickness is controlled by the distance between the bottom edge of the trowel and the wall. A regular stroke helps to obtain a regular thickness. (It's better, in fact, to apply the floating coat in two thicknesses, pressing the first coat well into the wall, and applying the second straight after the first.)

There's a technique for getting the plaster up into the angle with the ceiling. ('Angle' is the plasterer's term for a corner.) At the top of the sweep, roll the trowel over, squeezing the material up to the top edge; then sweep downwards to distribute it evenly. After each trowelful, rotate the hawk in your hand through 90° – that way, the material left on the hawk stays approximately balanced in the centre.

Suction is an important factor. Some water should be sucked out to make the plaster stiff so that it stays in place. But if too much is sucked out, the plaster won't set properly. So if the blockwork is very dry and porous, flick some water onto it beforehand (or use 'Carlite Browning HSB' plaster). On the other hand, if the suction is insufficient, eg, on unporous brickwork, then the suction may not be enough to hold the plaster in place. In this case, use 'Carlite Bonding' plaster. Or paint the surface with diluted PVA (1:4); when it's tacky or dry, apply the plaster.

Test the suction by flicking water onto the wall. If it is absorbed immediately, the suction is high; if it runs down the wall, the suction is low.

Figure 5: Applying plaster

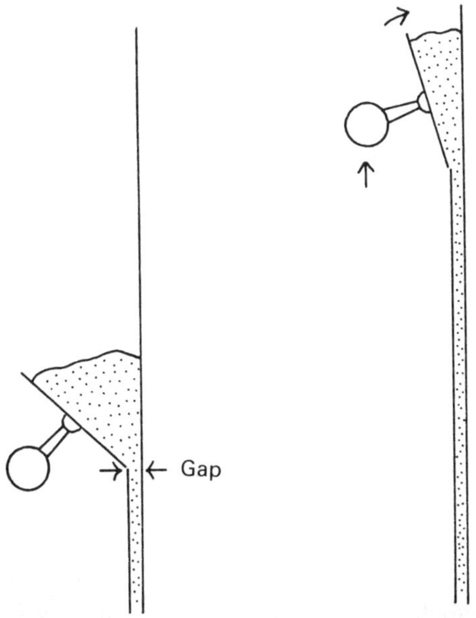

* Rotate the trowel as it empties.
* Gap between edge of trowel and wall controls thickness of plaster.

If the ceiling has been plastered, dampen it around the edge in order to prevent it absorbing water from the floating coat.

In increasing order of trueness, here are several methods of getting a flat floating coat:

Using a darby:

The darby presses the floating coat onto the wall and flattens it.

Apply the plaster to the wall, as described above. Then use a feather-edge rule at an internal corner to get a straight surface. Start off from this, using it as a guide for the darby. Push the darby up the wall, scraping off the high spots and filling the low ones. Hollows that remain can be filled with extra material. Work across the wall, and then repeat again over the whole wall until the surface is reasonably flat.

Using a feather-edge rule:

With the rule upright, pass it over the surface with a sawing motion to remove high spots. The low spots will show up and can be filled with extra material. Pay particular attention to the corners.

Horizontal screeds:

Screeds are used to give a guide for flatness. A professional may well make the screeds out of plaster, but the ownhander will find timber easier. The battens run along fairly near the top and bottom of the wall. (The rule must be long enough to span them with a little to spare.) Nail the 1 cm thick battens to the wall – pack them out at hollows, and check that the lower row is plumb beneath the upper one.

The feather-edge rule is sawed along the surface using the battens as a guide. Fill in hollows, and repeat the process until the surface is flat.

When the plaster has become firm, the battens can be removed and the bands along top and bottom filled in.

Vertical battens as screeds:

This method gives a high class (ie, flat) result; it is easy for the novice, but slower.

A series of vertical battens are fixed to the walls, at intervals of about two metres. Check them for plumbness – pack out where necessary. For a perfect job, check also that they are in line, by stretching a cord between the two end battens and checking the alignment of the ones in between. (This can be done more easily by cutting off three blocks of equal thickness from some batten. Use two to push the cord out at each end batten, and the third to check the gap between cord and test batten.)

Plaster alternate bays, ruling off across the battens to obtain a flat surface. When the plaster is firm, remove the battens and fill in the remaining bays.

Whichever method is used, scrape the rule or darby clean after each application. Pick up droppings from the floor and return them to the spot board. (It may be worth putting a clean board along the base of the wall to catch the droppings.)

The floating coat should finish flush with door linings (or slightly below). If need be, adjust the thickness of the plaster, graduating it away from the linings. At a junction with the ceiling or another walls, clear out the angle by pressing the trowel along the angle. (See Fig. 6.).

Figure 6: Cleaning out an angle

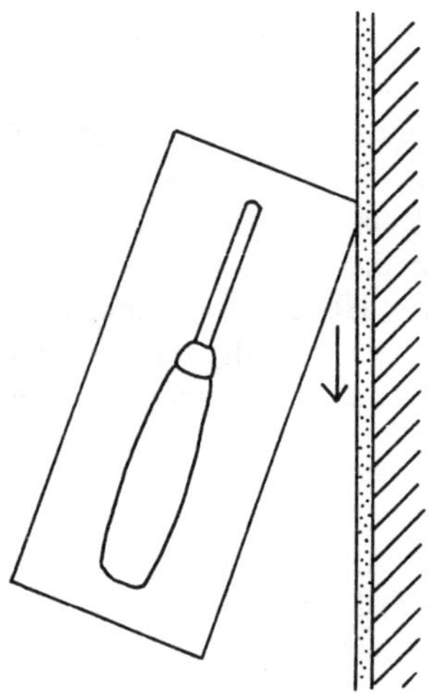

* Place the trowel flat on the floating coat and score down the adjoining plaster.

If necessary, wash stains off the ceiling with a brush and water. Finally, before the plaster sets, it needs to be keyed to take the finish coat. Rub the scratch float over it in a loose scrolling motion. The result should be a lightly scratched, but otherwise flat, surface.

Clean up well.

Skim coat

The plaster to use depends on the backing. Over Carlite Browning, use Carlite Finish – a 40 kg bag will cover about 20 square metres, at 2 mm thickness. Over a cement/lime/sand render, use Thistle Multi-Finish. A bag of this will cover about 16 square metres at the same thickness. On plasterboard, use Thistle Board Finish. A 40 kg bag of this will only cover about $6\frac{1}{2}$ square metres, as it is usually put on to a thickness of 5 mm. (Thistle Multi-Finish can be also be used on plasterboard; as it sets more slowly than Board Finish, it could be better for the amateur.) (British Gypsum seem to have a near monopoly of plaster, and their trade names are ubiquitous.)

Care is needed with the mixing. Start with a clean bucket, fill it a quarter full with clean water, and then add the plaster, stirring it in with a stick. Vigorously plunge a mixer up and down to make the mix homogeneous, gradually adding a little more plaster until the mix has the right consistency. If the mixer is taken out of the plaster, it should leave a crisp impression on the surface. If the mix is too sloppy, controlling it on the trowel will be difficult. When satisfied – and you may need to gain some experience the hard way first – turn all of the mix out onto a damp spot board, and straightaway wash clean the bucket and mixer. If residues are left to get into the next mix, they will catalyse an earlier set.

The plaster is applied to the wall in a rather similar manner to the floating coat, but the quantities are smaller and applied from left to right. Apply a first coat with adjacent vertical sweeps of the laying-on trowel. Keep the toe of the trowel tight to the adjacent layer, in order to prevent a double thickness at the overlap. The thickness of this coat depends on the final thickness required, which is 2 mm for skimming over a floating coat, and 5 mm over plasterboard. In this latter case, only apply the first coat between the scrim, bringing the surface level with the scrim.

When the surface appears drier, test that it is firming up – if touched lightly, the plaster shouldn't stick to the fingers. Apply a second, thinner coat with the skimming float. Apply it on the upstroke, and at the top of the stroke rock the float over to sweep down with the surplus. So obtain a flat surface. Check internal angles with a vertical feather-edge rule, filling or removing irregularities. Rub in internal angles with the float, and then clean them out with the finishing trowel.

When this plaster is firm to light finger pressure, apply a thin third coat (just enough to lubricate the trowel). Use long sweeps with the skimming trowel held at 20° to the surface. Let the toe of the trowel remove the heel line of the previous stroke.

Altogether, work quickly and methodically. (Often these operations are combined into two coats only.)

Lastly, when the plaster is losing its wet appearance and starting to set, it can be trowelled up. (To test that the plaster is ready, lightly touch it – again, the plaster should not stick to the fingers.) Have a wet brush in one hand to flick water onto the plaster a little in front of the trowel. Hold the clean trowel at 35°, and pass it firmly over the surface a couple of times. The object at this stage is primarily to remove any ridges. But look out for blemishes and apply a tiny dab of plaster to any remaining hollows. When the plaster is really hardening it can be trowelled for a second time. A highly polished surface looks nice, but it is considered to be undesirable.

In between the trowellings, give the corners care and attention. It's easier if plaster on the side walls has been allowed to set beforehand. Pass a float, lightly wetted, up and down the angles. Clean out any superfluous 'fat' with a damp flat brush. But if both sides of an angle do have to be finished together, an internal angle trowel may be useful. Pass the clean trowel down the angle; or, to fill hollows, put a little plaster onto the end of the trowel to apply it to the angle.

All these operations have to be done before the plaster sets in an hour or two. There is not much time to dally on any stage. It requires concentration – even from professionals who have been doing the work for years. Be modest in your ambitions at first, and only attempt small areas.

26

INSULATION AND VENTILATION

☆

☆

☆

☆

☆

☆

☆

Building Regulations
Wall insulation
Loft insulation
Window insulation
Door insulation
Draught stripping
Chimneys
Floor insulation
Thermal capacity
Ventilation

Building Regulations for insulation

In 1990, the standards of insulation required by the Building Regulations were upgraded. Nearly 20 years after the energy crisis of the early Seventies, they have at last become something like a sensible standard. However, they should still be regarded as a minimum. Unlike a commercial builder, who will build down to this standard, a selfbuilder will doubtless be building to a higher, optimum standard. (The introduction of the upgraded Regulations was resisted by the House Builders' Federation, who dismissed them as 'a cosmetic exercise'. They result in a 20% cut in heat losses.) Good insulation not only makes economic sense, it is also eco-friendly.

Under the upgraded Regulations, the target U-values (in watts / metre °C) are:

Walls ·45
Roof ·25
Floor ·45 . . . only expected if there is single glazing.

(The U-value is the 'thermal transmittance coefficient'. It is a measure of how easily heat passes through some particular form of construction. The lower the value, the better. See Appendix 2: *Thermal Sums*.) If the target U-values above are met, and the area of the windows is less than 15% of the total floor area, then single glazing is permitted – but any selfbuilder tempted by such an option must be very short of capital.

(For the record, it is possible to meet the requirements even though not all the target U-values are met. But you must be able to show by calculation that the overall heat losses from your proposed building are no greater than the losses from a hypothetical building of the same size and shape whose U-values are the target values above. This calculation method gives flexibility to the Regulations, but a selfbuilder is unlikely to need it.)

Wall insulation

See the tables below for some forms of wall construction that give a U-value within the target value of ·45.

Cavity walls

Outer leaf	Cavity	Inner leaf	U-value
Brick	5 cm mineral wool	Aircrete 650	·42
Brick	$7\frac{1}{2}$ cm mineral wool	Aircrete 650	·34
Brick	4 cm mineral wool / 4 cm clear	Aircrete 650	·45
Aircrete 650:			
Rendered	5 cm clear	Aircrete 480	·45
Tile hung	5 cm clear	Aircrete 480	·43

In the above, Aircrete 650 is the standard aircrete block of density 650 kg / cu m (eg, 'Celcon Standard', 'Thermalite Shield'). For the better insulating Aircrete 480 block (eg, 'Celcon Solar', 'Thermalite Turbo'), a thickness of 13 cm has been used, although many other thicknesses are available. It has been assumed that the inner leaf is plastered.

Solid walls

Aircrete 480 blocks, $21\frac{1}{2}$ cm thick:	U-value
Hung tiles outside, plaster inside	·43
Rendered outside, plasterboard on dabs inside	·45

Popular insulation materials are mineral wool (rock wool or glass wool) and polystyrene. The later is impermeable, not allowing water vapour and other gaseous wastes to diffuse away through the wall.

Loft insulation

The usual materials for loft insulation is mineral wool. Note that rock wool melts at 1,000°C, whereas glass wool melts at half that. In a fire, the difference could be significant. They are both available in rolls of 60 cm (or 45 cm) width to fit between the trusses. Alternatively, rolls of 1·2 m width can be purchased. These are easily cut with a panel saw (before being unwrapped) to any required width.

To meet the Building Regulations target U-value of ·25, just under 15 cm of rock wool loft insulation is required, but 20 cm is more of an economic optimum. Avoid burying electric cables – they become difficult to trace and might overheat. (It's best to foresee this when putting in the cables – raise them above the insulation level.) Don't forget to insulate the hatch door.

At the eaves, don't let the insulation block the passage of air up into the loft. (It would have been prudent to take precautions against this before the roof was covered in. See 'Carpentry along the eaves', Chapter 7.)

Window insulation

Single glazed windows are the weakest component of a house – thermally as well as structurally. The standard U-value of single glazing is an enormous 5·7. Even with sealed units it is a high 2·8.

However, a technical innovation, low-emissive glass, can reduce this substantially. One surface of the glass is coated with a metallic film, which is transparent both to light and to radiant heat of short wavelength – such as the radiation from the sun. But the film is opaque to heat radiation with a long wavelength – such as from the walls of a room. So heat radiation can enter the room, but not escape out. (The same effect happens with ordinary glass to a lesser degree – the 'greenhouse effect'.)

The transparent coating is delicate, so it is placed inside a sealed unit for protection. The effect is that the U-value of a sealed unit is reduced to 2·0. This is the same value that is obtained with triple glazing, ie, sealed units with low-emissive glass are as effective as triple glazing in cutting heat losses. (Actually, the U-value can be improved even further, to 1·6, if Argon gas is used instead of dehydrated air within the sealed unit. Such units are more costly.)

Good though these figures are, they are still considerably more than the U-value of a wall. It might be deduced from this that the less the glazing the better, as far as insulation is concerned. Fortunately for people who like a view, this is not so. Glass lets the sunshine in! Solar gain effectively decreases the U-value of windows.

The strength of this effect obviously depends on the orientation of the window. The gain in heat, disregarding unwanted heat in summertime, can be converted into an equivalent reduction in U-value.

For a south-facing wall, effective U-values are:

Single glazing	3·0
Sealed unit	·8
Low-emissive sealed unit	·1

The last is a surprisingly beneficial figure. (Admittedly, the figures are those claimed by a glazing manufacturer!) There is a net radiation loss through the worst three months of the winter, but the greater gains in spring and autumn give an overall solar gain.

Even for a north-facing window there is solar gain from the sky, and the effective U-value for a low-emissive sealed unit facing north is 1·0. (The radiation from the sky when the sun isn't shining is more than one imagines.)

So sealed units with low-emissive glass seem to be highly beneficial. But be wary! The seals around the edges of sealed units are liable to break down; this allows water vapour in, and condensation occurs. So the units may need replacing in the future. Moreover, the low-emissive coating is not perfectly transparent to light, and only two-thirds of the light falling on such a sealed unit is transmitted through. In practice, however, this loss is hardly noticeable.

Though sealed units are so convenient, it may be worth considering secondary glazing instead. This will be especially so if you want sound insulation also. The wider gap between the panes of glass is much more effective acoustically. (But the optimum is over 15 cm.)

Door insulation

The thermal conductivity of timber is ·13 watts / m °C approximately. So the U-value of a solid timber door, 4·4 cm thick, is 3·0 (·13 ÷ ·044) – doors, not windows, are the weakest component of a well insulated house. Although joinery manufacturers indulge the public's taste for nostalgia by producing front doors in wide ranges of traditional styles, their catalogues show not one well insulated door. Some back doors are particularly bad, sometimes having panels of ply. (You can improve such a door by sandwiching some polystyrene between the ply and an extra panel of ply.)

Draught stripping

Draughts used to be a major source of heat loss, but modern door and window frames have very effective draught stripping. To continue to be effective, the stripping must retain its original profile. EPDM rubber has a good 'memory', and silicon rubber even better.

Chimneys

An open fireplace sucks the warm air out of a house. If people could feel the stream of warm air that flows continuously out from a chimney (even without a fire burning below), they wouldn't be so nostalgically attached to open fires. Fit a stove instead.

Floor insulation

From a solid floor, heat flows out through the ground to the cold air outside. From the edge of the floor, the distance travelled is obviously less than from the middle, ie, the thermal resistance is less. In short, the U-value depends on the size and shape of the floor.

If the house has only single glazing, the Building Regulations expect the floor to attain a U-value of ·45. Some insulation is necessary. Approved Document L gives tables of the thickness of insulation required for floors of different dimensions to attain the U-value of ·45. The assumption is that the insulation is laid in a uniform thickness beneath the slab (or screed). (About $3\frac{1}{2}$ cm of polystyrene is usually sufficient.) But as mentioned in Appendix 2, vertical insulation of the perimeter may be more cost effective. With strip foundations, edge insulation can be easily installed. $2\frac{1}{2}$ cm thick sheets of polystyrene attached to the foundation walls to a depth of 60 cm reduce the U-value of the floor slab by about 20%. That is not a great difference, so it is only allowable on double glazed houses. But the work is easy and cheap. It is worthwhile as it can't be done once the house is built. The insulated floor slab acts as a good heat reservoir.

Insulation of a timber floor is easy and effective. Before boarding, tack plastic netting to the underside of the joists, and lay loft insulation on it. To find what effect this has on the U-value, use Table 4, Appendix 2, for the uninsulated floor. For example, if the floor is 7·5 m square:

Floor perimeter / area = ·53 $(4 \times 7{\cdot}5 \div 7{\cdot}5^2)$.

From the table the U-value is about ·75. Its Resistance is 1·3 (1 ÷ ·75). If the insulation is 10 cm thick, with

λ = ·035, its Resistance, R = 2·9 (·1 ÷ ·035). So the Resistance of the insulated floor is 4·2 (1·3 + 2·9).

The U-value is knocked down to ·23, a substantial reduction!

Thermal capacity

Insulation is not the only factor affecting the thermal performance of a building. The effect known variously as thermal capacity, thermal mass, or thermal inertia also plays a part. This is the capacity of the fabric of the house to store heat – to absorb heat when the room temperature is high, and to give it up when the temperature is low. This effect is desirable in two respects:

Firstly, an even temperature feels more comfortable.

Secondly, heat that is available on warm days is not wasted but stored for use on cold days.

The effect known as 'passive solar gain' relies on the thermal capacity of the building to store the radiant heat (sunshine) entering through the windows. Some experimental houses utilise this effect to the full by using special materials to store the heat. Though the effect is most pronounced in an Alpine-type climate, even in the muggier British climate it is still an effect worth considering. As a rough rule of thumb, the thermal capacity of a material increases with its density. So use heavy building materials rather then light ones. This is unfortunate – heavy materials make for heavy work!

A concrete floor obviously has a much greater thermal capacity than a suspended timber floor. And in this case, its construction is easier too.

You might like to build your partition walls downstairs in dense concrete blocks rather than aircrete blocks. And upstairs, you could use blockwork instead of studwork. (The heavier materials will aid sound insulation too.)

Ventilation

In the modern draught-proof house some controlled ventilation is necessary. In fact, the Building Regulations expect a background ventilation area of 40 sq cm for every habitable room, though this seems a rather excessive requirement. Some window fasteners have a second locking position which leaves the window very slightly ajar. This is the simplest way to attain background ventilation. Otherwise, trickle ventilators can be used – some windows have them fitted as standard, some can be fitted with them to order. Alternatively, you can fit 'hit-or-miss' vents yourself.

In bathroom and kitchen, the Building Regulations require extractor fans. The capacity of the fan should be at least 15 litre/sec for the bathroom, and double that for the kitchen (where it can be incorporated into a cooker hood, if required). The holes for the vents are best made at the end of the build, rather than being built in.

The loft must be ventilated too. This may seem surprising but there is a good reason for it. Water vapour diffuses through the ceilings into the loft from the warmer, more humid rooms below. In the cold loft it may condense; eventually the dampness could rot the roof timbers. To counteract this, the Regulations expect the loft to be ventilated at the eaves with a centimetre air gap all the way along (or the equivalent of that spaced out as larger gaps). This requirement must obviously be designed into the eaves detail. As an extra, you could fit air-bricks in the gables, though this is seldom done nowadays.

27
GENERAL TECHNIQUES

☆

☆

☆

☆

☆

☆

☆

Handedness
Symmetry
Straightness
Levelness
Plumbness
Squareness
Geometry
Gravity
Rods
Pinch rods
Scribing
Beams

THE FOLLOWING TECHNIQUES, of general use in different crafts, involve a slight hint of geometry – but so slight you may not even notice!

Handedness

Some years ago, the author asked a blacksmith to make up a pair of wrought iron brackets. The design included a twisted strut. (Incidentally, a twist in ironwork is not only decorative, it also strengthens the iron – a pleasing combination of ornament and utility.) With one of the brackets completed, the blacksmith asked how the second should be made. "Exactly the same" the author replied. Fortunately, the blacksmith persuaded him otherwise. The twist had imparted 'handedness' to the bracket. To match the first, the second bracket needed to be of opposite hand, with its twist in the opposite direction. Identical brackets would have looked unbalanced.

Handedness occurs under several guises in construction, but it is especially prevalent in the bonding of brickwork, eg, a pair of piers, such as for a gateway or chimney breast. (See Fig. 1.)

Figure 1: Matching pairs of objects

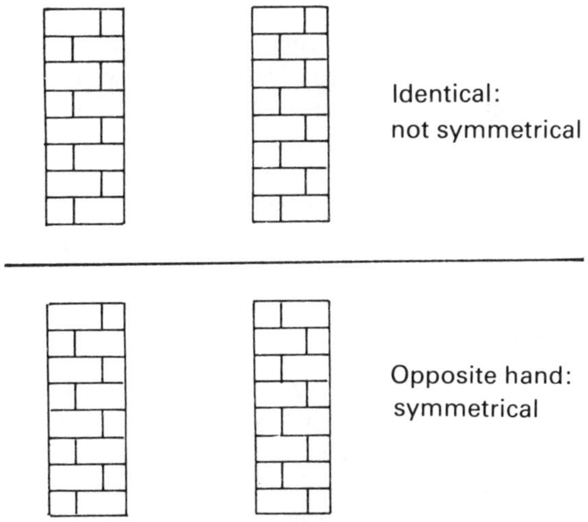

* If an object is handed and a pair of them are required to match, then they should be of opposite hand (mirror images).

Figure 2: Symmetry of tiles

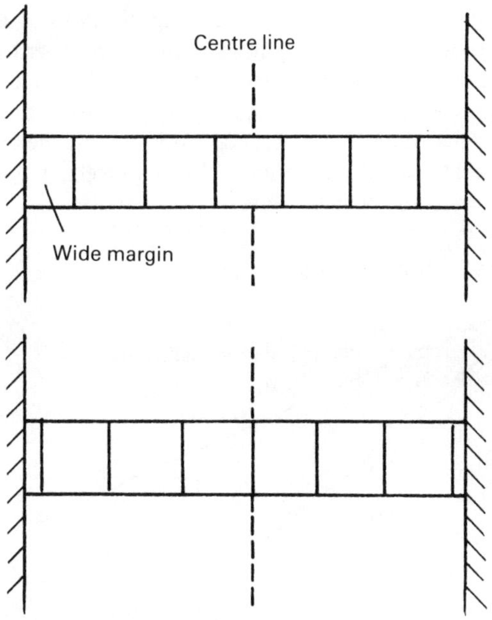

* There are always two symmetrical layouts possible. In general, choose the one with the wide margin.
* Similar considerations apply to matchboarding, etc.

Symmetry

In our culture, a repetitive pattern generally looks best when it is symmetrical about the centre. This factor is frequently met with in the tiling of walls and floors. If the tiling is symmetrical about the centre line, the margins at each side will be the same.

There are always two ways of achieving this symmetry, and both options should be considered to see which is more suitable. Either the centre or an edge of a tile can be placed on the centre line. (See Fig. 2.)

Generally, it is better to choose the layout which gives the wider part-tile at the boundaries.

Similar considerations apply in cladding walls with matchboarding.

Straightness

A string which is stretched tight must be straight. That fact is being used all the time by bricklayers 'laying to the line'. This technique is so easy and convenient that it explains the rarity of curved walls.

A quick practical test to check that a line is straight is to look along it. A straight line should appear as a point; any deviation shows up easily. (See Fig. 12, Chapter 24.)

Levelness

Levelness is easily tested by the ubiquitous spirit level. (To check that a spirit level is accurate, put it on a surface that it shows to be level, and swivel it 180°. It should still show the surface to be level.)

In outside work which involves long distances, a longer level is required. For this purpose, use a level-board about three metres long, with two straight and parallel edges. Lay the spirit level along the top edge of the board to give a much extended instrument. For accurate work, reverse the board's direction at successive positions, thus cancelling out any untrueness in the board.

Figure 3: Boning rods

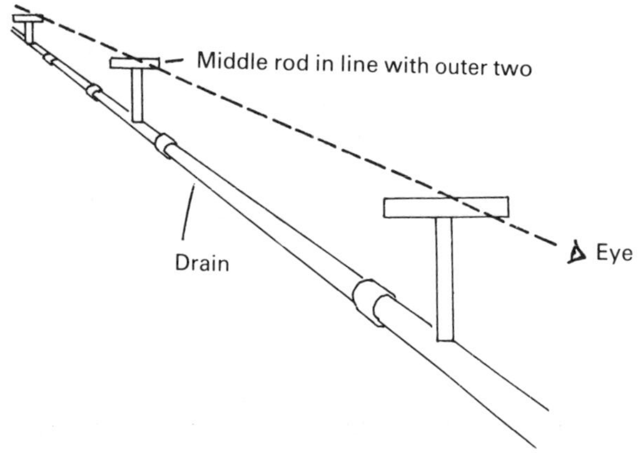

* Used for establishing a straight line over long distances.

To maintain a constant fall, as for drains, support one end of a level with a shim (or block) of the appropriate thickness. (Or some spirit levels have a bubble that can be rotated as required.)

Sometimes boning rods are used. A set of three of these can easily be made up. They are large wooden 'T' shapes, with the cross-piece square to the stem. They are all the same height, about a metre. When a rod has been positioned at each end, then the level at any intermediate position can be found by sighting across the tops of the rods. (See Fig. 3.)

Two fixed sight rails can be used instead of the end rods, and this reduces the number of people required to hold the rods. But boning rods don't often have an application on a selfbuild site anyway.

A water level uses a long tube filled with water. You can make your own with a long length of clear plastic tubing with a bore of about 1 cm (as sold in home brew shops). Tape each end to matching graduated rules about half a metre long. Nearly fill the tube with water, making sure that no bubbles are trapped. (Dyeing the water helps.) To move the level about, a stopper is required for each end – but take these out when using the level.

Before use, check the instrument by holding the rules side by side. The levels can be upset by air bubbles trapped in the tube, or by temperature differences (eg, if one half of the tube is in sun and the other half in shadow). Assuming the two levels are the same, mark them on the graduated scales.

In use, the instrument needs a person at each end. Stand the rules upright on the levels to be compared, and check the water levels against the scales. In practice, water levels are a little cumbersome, but they can be particularly useful in awkward situations where a level-board would be obstructed.

A Cowley level is an optical instrument supported on a tripod. It is easy to use, though a helper is needed to hold the staff. Unlike the older 'dumpy' level, it is self-levelling and requires no adjustment to set it up. The instrument is used in conjunction with a graduated staff, up and down which a cross-piece can be slid (by the assistant). The instrument produces a split image. When the two images of the cross-piece are in line, then the cross-piece is at the datum level of the instrument. (See Fig. 4.)

Figure 4: Views through a Cowley Level

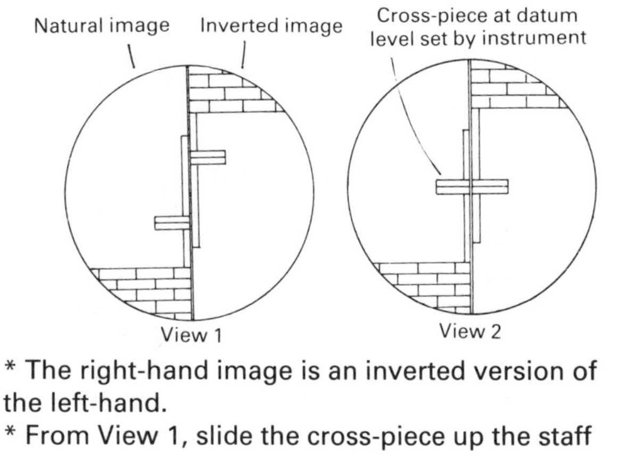

* The right-hand image is an inverted version of the left-hand.
* From View 1, slide the cross-piece up the staff until its two images meet (View 2). The cross-piece is then at the datum set by the instrument.

If the staff is moved to another location, the instrument can be rotated to follow it, and the cross-piece slid up or down again to re-establish the datum level. By comparing the readings of the cross-piece on the graduated staff in the two positions, the levels can be compared. The instrument can be hired, but it is very optional for a selfbuilder.

Occasionally, levelness can be transferred by eye. For example, when plastering, the soffit of a window reveal can be lined up with the window head by eye.

Plumbness

Plumbness can also be checked by eye against a neighbouring vertical line. This is useful when fixing door linings. In fact, it is often more important that a line should look right rather than be right, ie, it should match other out-of-true lines, rather than be true in itself. (But this is more relevant in renovations than in a new selfbuild.)

Plumb bobs are nearly obsolete, since they are slow to settle and liable to wind disturbance. Spirit levels have neither disadvantage.

Squareness

The term 'square' is not used in the same sense in building work as in geometry. To builders, it means 'right-angled'.

To form a right angle, Pythagoras's theorem is invoked. As you doubtless remember from your schooldays, in a right-angled triangle the square of the longest side equals the sum of the squares of the other two sides. Don't worry if you don't understand that! You only need to remember a particular instance of it:

$5^2 = 4^2 + 3^2 \quad (25 = 16 + 9)$

So a triangle with sides of length 3, 4, and 5 units contains a right angle. If a piece of string is taken and lengths in these proportions marked off on it, when it is stretched into a triangle, the two short sides will contain a right angle. This is a very accurate method; it can be used on a large scale for setting out on site. (See Fig. 1, Chapter 4.)

Figure 5: Squareness of a frame

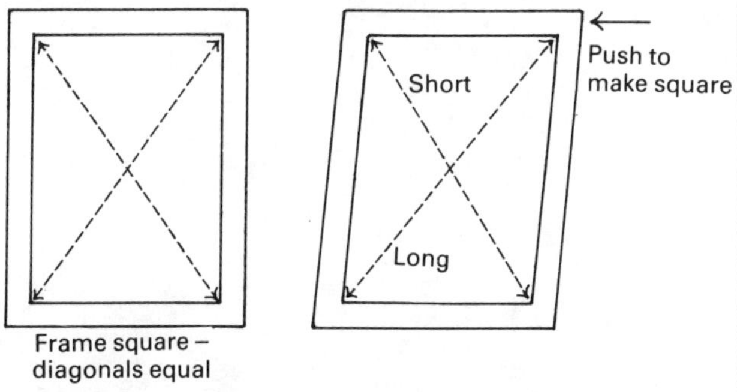

* Shorten the longer diagonal to make the frame square.

On a smaller scale, a builders' square is sometimes useful. This is composed of three pieces of straight timber assembled together as a right-angled triangle. Useful lengths for the sides might be 45 cm (3 × 15), 60 cm (4 × 15) and 75 cm (5 × 15) – the 3,4,5 triangle again. (Actually, an easier way to make a square is simply to cut a large corner off a sheet of ply.)

There is a quick way to test for the squareness of a rectangular figure: The diagonals must be equal. This simple test is often used, especially in woodworking. If the two diagonals are unequal, shorten the longer one. (See Fig. 5.) (The required length equals the average of the two unequal diagonals.)

The commonness of the right angle in building has two sources:

Geometry: Two right angles are the simplest subdivision of a straight line. (This can be used to test the trueness of a builders' square. Rotate the square to mark off two successive right angles; the result should be a straight line.) The right angle has a lot of other special properties, such as Pythagoras's theorem above.

Gravity: A body tends to topple unless its centre of gravity is over its base. Thus if walls are to be self-supporting, they need to be vertical. On the other hand, for a surface to be 'neutral' to gravity, it needs to be horizontal; so tables, floors and the like need to be horizontal. The horizontal and the vertical are at right angles, so the need to counteract gravity produces many right angles. In outer space, it might be different... ?

Rods

The term 'rod' can have a special meaning: a straight piece of timber with particular lengths marked on it. It is used for repetitive marking out: Marks on the rod can be quickly and reliably transferred over to a workpiece.

Rods are frequently used in a joiners' shop. In bricklaying, a gauge rod with coursing marks every $7\frac{1}{2}$ cm is useful. The simplest of all rods is just a spacing stick, used, for example, in spacing roof battens.

Rods are not only quick, they are also reliable. Marking a measurement from a rule is always liable to error. With a rod you do it once and you make sure that you get it right.

Pinch rods

A pair of pinch rods are used for transferring a distance to another location. Usually a tape measure can be used, but pinch rods are less liable to being mis-read and are sometimes easier to use. They simply consist of two long, light rods. They must be long enough to extend out together to span the required distance. Mark the position of one relative to the other. (See Fig. 6.)

The required distance can then be transferred elsewhere. The method is useful, for example, for checking the (equal) diagonals of a frame.

Scribing

'Scribing' is a widely used term in carpentry. It means shaping an edge to fit against a surface. This surface may be not quite flat, such as a kitchen wall is often found to be when a worktop is being fitted. Or the surface may have a pronounced profile, such as when moulded skirting boards meet in a corner. Techniques to suit these two circumstances are described under 'Scribing', Chapter 24.

Figure 6: Pinch rods

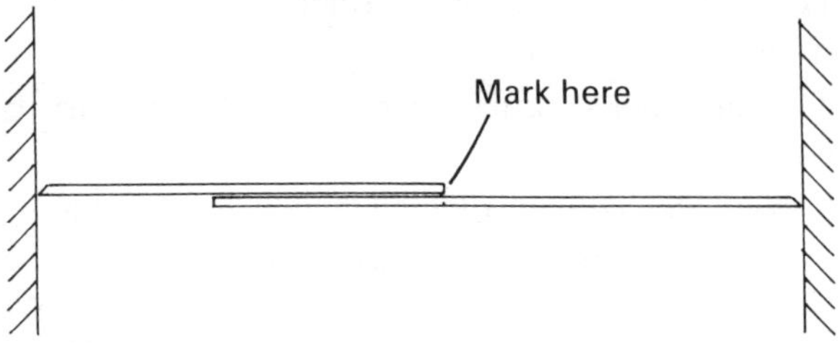

* Used to transfer a distance from one place to another – more reliable than measuring.

Figure 7: Scribing a tile at a margin

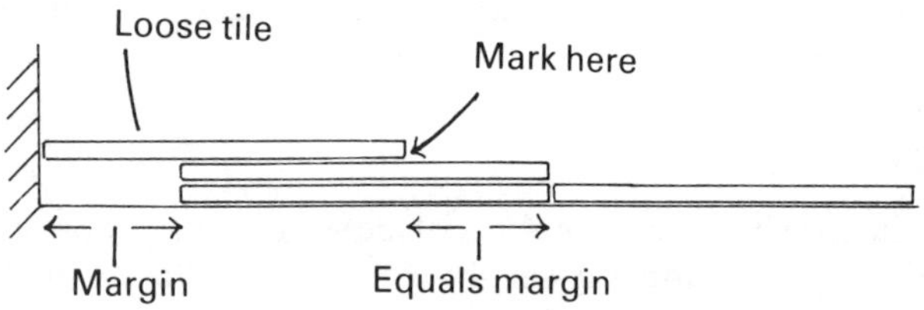

* Quick and accurate method of marking a tile for a margin.

Often the actual width of the workpiece is also important. This occurs, for example, when a wall is being tiled. A part tile may be needed to fit against a boundary such as a corner. To scribe a tile to fit, superimpose it over the nearest whole tile. Take a spare tile and, lining this up with the boundary, mark off its other edge onto the tile. (See Fig. 7.)

Cut the tile to this line, and it will be an exact fit.

A similar technique can be used when cladding walls with matchboard, or when plasterboarding studwork. (See Fig. 2, Chapter 12.)

Beams

When a beam which is supported at each end is loaded, it sags. The bottom of the beam stretches, but the top is compressed. In the middle, it is neither compressed nor stretched – the neutral axis. (See Fig. 8.)

Figure 8: Bending of a beam

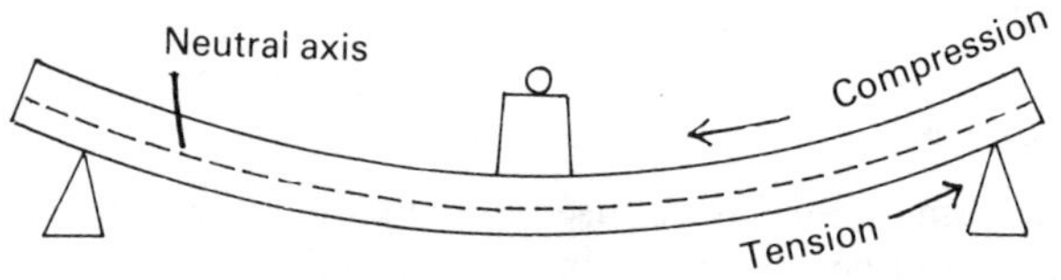

* The beam is stretched below and compressed on top. In the middle it remains unchanged: the neutral axis.
* Small holes drilled close to the neutral axis have very little effect on the strength of the beam.

This is why the strength of joists is hardly affected when holes for cables or pipework are drilled half-way up. And it is the reason why reinforcing rod is placed near the bottom of concrete lintels. There, it counteracts the tension in the concrete beam. Rods are not needed near the top because concrete is strong enough in compression.

28

SCAFFOLDING

☆

☆

☆

☆

☆

☆

☆

Putlog scaffolding
Erection
Other forms of scaffolding

'PUTLOG' SCAFFOLDING is often used for house-building – a form of scaffolding used for the building of the medieval cathedrals. In those days, they used timber lashed with rope; it was only at the beginning of this century that steel scaffolding came into general use in Britain. In the USA, even up to 1927 (when there was a disastrous fire involving scaffolding), skyscrapers were built with timber scaffolding. And today in China and Hong Kong, bamboo and twine are used, no matter how high the building.

In Britain, the common system of scaffolding is 'tube and fittings'. This uses steel tube (4·8 cm diameter) to which steel fittings are attached. In addition, there are proprietary systems where the fitting is an integral part of the tube (eg, 'Cuplock'). These systems are quicker and easier to put up, but more expensive. For selfbuild, the small saving in time for erection is unimportant, so go for the cheaper tube and fittings.

Putlog scaffolding

With putlog scaffolding, a series of upright 'standards' stand around the perimeter of the building, about 1·25 metres away from the walls. (Leave space for five scaffold boards, plus a little clearance at the wall for the bricklayer's spirit level.) These standards, together with the walls themselves, support the successive 'lifts', or platforms, as the walls are built up. (See Fig. 1.)

At each lift, the standards are connected together with horizontal 'ledgers' parallel to the walls. A series of putlogs span from the ledgers to the walls, and they support the scaffold boards. The putlogs themselves are tubes about a metre and a half long, with one end flattened to fit into a joint in the brickwork. (Instead of a purpose-made putlog, a putlog adapter can be fitted to a short length of plain tube.) As the walls are being built, cross joints are omitted, or bed joints raked out at the required places. The putlogs are placed into these when the lift is raised. The National Association of Scaffolding Contractors recommends that the spade ends of the putlogs should lie flat in the bed joints, although in fact, it is still fairly common practice for the cross joints to be used.

('Independent' scaffolding, on the other hand, is free-standing; the wall gives no support. Instead, a second series of standards and ledgers is put up adjacent to the wall, and 'transoms' span from ledger to ledger in place of putlogs. Obviously, this uses more tube and fittings, so only the putlog method is described below. However, the independent method does have the advantage that there are no putlog holes to be filled in after the scaffolding has been stripped.)

Scaffold boards are usually 3·9 m long, 3·8 cm thick, and 22·5 cm wide. Boards of this thickness need to be supported at least every metre and a half by the putlogs. The end of a board should overhang its putlog by only a short distance; else it lies in wait as a dangerous trap when stepped upon. So where a pair of boards meet, there should be a pair of putlogs one or two bricks apart, one putlog for each board end. Standards should stand within two metres of each other; and within 30 cm of a standard there should be a putlog secured to the ledger.

Something else that needs consideration is how to arrange the boards at corners. Make the platform (ledger, putlogs and boards) one brick course lower along a return wall. At the corner, the boards can then be overlapped.

It is convenient to have lifts at intervals of about 1·6 metres (shoulder height). For convenience when roofing, let the platform be about half a metre below the wall plate.

Erection

Firstly, sort out the fittings. Some of these will be putlog couplings, and they can be recognised by having only one bolt. They do not give a strong joint, and they are only suitable for holding putlogs in place on a ledger. The right-angle coupling, with two bolts, gives a much stronger joint, and is used to hold a ledger to a standard. A swivel coupling is used for diagonal bracing.

Standards can be extended upwards, if necessary, by a spigot coupling, which fits inside the tube. For extending the ledgers, a sleeve coupling is used which fits over the tube.

The most difficult part of scaffolding is starting it. One approach for the selfbuilder would be to get a scaffolder to 'base out' the scaffolding for him, with further lifts being put up by the selfbuilder. But if you want to do it all, here is an outline of the method.

The novice might find it useful to lay boards out on the ground around the building in order to work out where to put the standards and putlogs.

The standards need metal base plates stood on a board on firm ground. If the standards are as high as will eventually be required – fine. If not, they can be extended later with spigot couplings.

The sequence for starting the scaffolding is:

1) Fix a standard and putlog.
2) Fix another standard and putlog several metres away.
3) Fix a ledger for the first lift across the two standards.
4) Check the plumbness of the standards and the levelness of the ledger and putlogs.

Figure 1: Putlog scaffolding

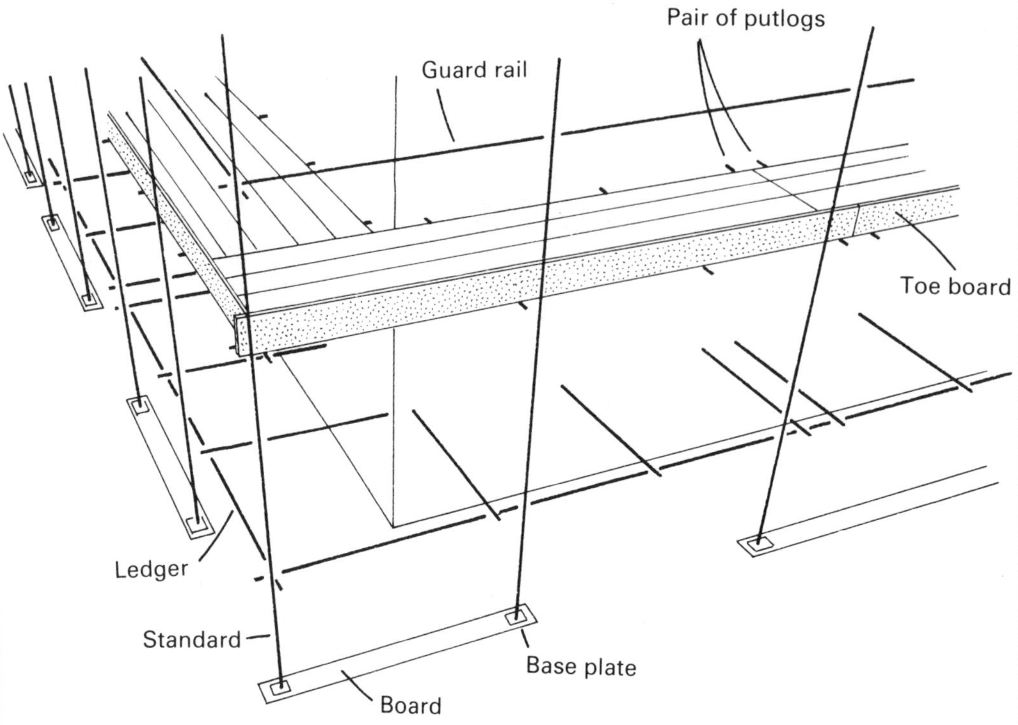

* Firm base to support standards.
* Pair of putlogs where boards meet.
* Ledgers inside standards.
* Add diagonal facade bracing for more stiffness.

Figure 2: Scaffolding at an opening

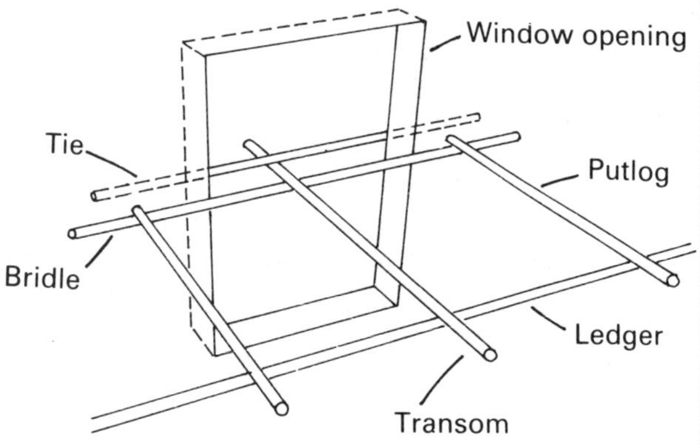

* The bridle, slung beneath putlogs on each side of the opening, supports a transom.
* As an option, the transom can be used to secure a tie against the back of the opening. This prevents the scaffolding from falling away from the wall.

5) Fix a ledger along the foot.
6) Fix a 'bridle' about 10 cm from the wall (ie, a tube slung beneath the two putlogs).
7) Secure diagonal braces from the bridle to the foot tie.
8) Secure a facade brace from a standard to the foot tie.
9) Fix intermediate standard(s) and putlogs.

Obviously a helper is useful, though a professional can manage single-handed. Once the scaffolding has been started, it can be easily extended, using braces to stiffen it as required. There are several points to note:

The ledgers are fixed inside the standards. There should be a putlog near every standard, with other putlogs put in as required to support the boards. (These extra putlogs can be removed later and used for the next lift if required.)

At window openings, there is, of course, no walling to support a putlog. In this case, a 'bridle' stretches along the wall – a tube is slung beneath the putlogs on either side of the opening. One end of a transom is then fixed onto this bridle. For more security, the transom can be turned into a tie: Use a long transom extending through the opening and fix a tube across it to bear against the inside wall. (See Fig. 2.)

The tie will prevent the scaffold from falling away from the wall. Ingenuity may be needed to get around, or over, obstacles (such as garages).

For safety, the platform should have a guard rail about a metre above the decking, and also toe-boards. (These are scaffold boards on edge, fixed to the standards with toe-board clips.) Heavy loads of bricks on the platform should be concentrated near the standards.

A ladder should extend a metre above the platform and be lashed at the top to the scaffolding. (For a safe angle, the foot of a ladder should stand out by a quarter of its height.) And when moving a ladder, keep it either vertical or horizontal – on a slant, it is difficult to control.

Other forms of scaffolding:

1) No exterior scaffolding. It is possible to build a bungalow, or even a house, from the inside – off the floor slab, then the floor joists (if a house), and then the roof timbers.

2) Lightweight tower scaffolding is widely available, and is useful for the gables of a bungalow.

3) Builders' trestles are useful for low heights.

4) Jack scaffolding is a form of DIY scaffolding rarely seen – is it dangerous?

It is very simple to make. The scaffolding is merely propped up against the wall with props such as scaffold boards. Details are given in *A Manual of Building Construction*. (See 'Books', Appendix 4.) Take care!

Appendix 1

THE METRICATION SHAMBLES

In the building industry, Britain's attempt to metricate has been a sorry story. The Metrication Board was set up in 1969 with the aim of complete metrication by 1975. That didn't happen, and it still hasn't. In 1980 the Board was abolished, and any remaining impetus towards metrication was lost. The result is a shambles. Some people work in metric, some in imperial, and some in a mixture of the two. By and large, architects are metricated and tradespeople stick to imperial. Youngsters are trained in metric, but when they go into their trade, they switch to imperial as though to show that they have been initiated into the rites of a mysterious craft. Plans are designed in one set of units but often built in another – how many mistakes has that lead to? At builders' merchants, the talk over the counter is usually in imperial – or even a mixture of the two, eg, 'ten metres of four by two' (inches).

A lot of metrication is a sham, as though quoting the size in millimetres metricates the product. Look at these standard thicknesses for sawn softwood, prescribed by the British Standards Institute in 1988:

16, 19, 22, 25, 32, 36, 38, 44, 47, 50, 63, 75, 100,...mm.

This bizarre set of numbers only makes sense if you translate it into imperial. (As British Standards are changed to conform to Eurocodes during the Nineties, this sort of British bodge will hopefully be consigned to the dustbin.)

'Covert imperialism' – the quoting of a precise figure in metric for what is really a round figure in imperial – is widespread. Plasterboard is not 1 cm thick, but 9·5 mm – because it is $\frac{3}{8}''$ in disguise. Totally new factories have been built – producing plasterboard in imperial thickness.

These are but two examples of the many that abound. They indicate a reluctance to exploit the metric system. Lip service has been paid to it while the imperial measures have been preserved. The result is a classic case of 'falling between two stools'.

The popular rejection of metrication must be due partly to the bodging and partly to a wrong choice of unit. The metre is fine and widely used. The millimetre is not; it is too small for convenient use in the building trade. It fills the head with spurious zeros and overworks the tongue. Compare the neat 'six by two' inches with 'one hundred and fifty by fifty' millimetres; or who can picture the area of 4,000 sq mm – the Building Regulations' approved area for background ventilation in habitable rooms? (Expressed as 40 sq cm, the quantity becomes comprehensible.) On the Continent, the centimetre is widely used for practical work. We should do the same here. (The example above would be 'fifteen by five', not 'one hundred and fifty by fifty'.)

With centimetres, those useful numbers 'half' and 'quarter' have some relevance. With millimetres they find no application.

And there is another, subtle advantage of using centimetres. They can be used to imply a degree of precision. Consider an instruction like 'Take a board 15 cm wide'. That is slightly different from 'Take a board 15·0 cm wide'. If you find a board which is 14·7 cm wide, it will probably suffice in the first case but not in the second. With millimetres, this difference is lost. Both cases become 'Take a board 150 mm wide'.

The use of millimetres is not only cumbersome and pedantic, but it also impedes the adoption of the metric system. How? – By not making use of its simplicity. For example, the standard thicknesses for softwood probably ought to include '4 cm'. What it actually is, '3·8 cm', looks awkward. However, expressed in millimetres there is little difference in awkwardness as written figures: '40' and '38'. So $1\frac{1}{2}''$ lives on. That is what practical people still call it, and how they still use it. If centimetres were the unit used, 3·8 cm would not be tolerated as a 'standard' thickness, no more than $1\frac{13}{16}''$ (say) would have been in the imperial system.

In 1981, the International Standards Organisation, of which the British Standards Institute is a member, issued a specification for standardised metric (SI) units (ISO 1000 – 1981). They recommended that sub-multiples of a unit be chosen so that numerical values are usually between ·1 and 1,000. In building work, the centimetre conforms to this very nicely. The millimetre does not.

So, adding to the present confusion of units – inches or millimetres – in this book, centimetres are used. Perhaps in the building trade the situation has to get worse before it can get better!

Appendix 2

THERMAL SUMS

U-values

The Building Regulations originated in a concern for people's safety and health. In the course of time, insulation became one of the requirements, primarily from a health point of view. Since the energy crises of the early Seventies, the insulation requirements have been greatly increased, and heat conservation is now required for its own sake. The standards required are quite high, but that is not to say that they are the economic standard. Commercial builders and their customers are content with the standards decreed by the Building Regulation. Selfbuilders are interested in the future running costs and comfort of their home, not just the initial capital cost. It usually makes sense to insulate beyond the standards required by the Regulations. Insulating during construction is relatively cheap and easy. Adding to it afterwards is costly and difficult. Moreover, the cost of insulation can be partially offset by the lower capital cost of a smaller heating system.

In any discussion of the insulation of buildings, the term 'U-value' is widely used: the coefficient of thermal transmittance. This is a measure of the ease with which heat is transmitted through any particular element of construction, eg, cavity walling. The higher the U-value, the more easily heat is transmitted across it. (It's unfortunate that the term has become so widely used. It would have been better to have used the coefficient of thermal resistance, R ($R = 1 / U$). This is simpler to understand and mathematically more direct, as we will see later.)

Warning: The rest of this appendix is somewhat mathematical. Though you may not follow the mathematics, you may find the results of interest. Or you may want to skip it altogether!

The conduction of heat

Let's look first at the factors involved in the conduction of heat across a slab of material.

For heat to flow at all, there needs to be a temperature difference, t, between the two faces of the slab. The bigger the temperature difference, the bigger the heat flow. The exact relationship has been found experimentally: The heat flow, F, is proportional to t. This is the simplest of relationships, as is so often found to be the case with physical laws.

Another factor is the area of the slab, and as would be expected, doubling the area, A, doubles the heat flow. So once again the relationship is simple: F is proportional to A.

What about doubling the thickness, L, of the slab? As you might expect, this halves the flow of heat. F is inversely proportional to L.

One last factor depends on the material itself of the slab. The flow of heat through a slab of concrete will be greater than through a similar slab of polystyrene. The conductivity, λ, depends on the nature of the material.

So Nature, or the cleverness of our minds, allows us to put these factors together in a very simple way:

$$F = \frac{\lambda A t}{L}$$

This is the basic law for the conduction of heat.

The thermal resistance, R, for the slab is defined by:

$$R = \frac{L}{\lambda}$$

(The thicker the slab and the lower its conductivity, the higher its resistance to heat flow.)

So we can also write:

$$F = \frac{A t}{R}$$

Using U instead of R, this can be expressed as

$$F = A t U$$

Now let us find out why the thermal resistance, R, is more useful than U.

Imagine a second slab, of the same area, A, but of a different material. Press this slab against the first. Consider the flow of heat through this combined slab. We can write the above equation for the first slab as:

$$F_1 = \frac{A t_1}{R_1}$$

And for the second slab:

$$F_2 = \frac{A t_2}{R_2}$$

But treating the combined slab as just one slab, we can also write:

$$F = \frac{A t}{R}$$

It's easy to see that the flow of heat through the first slab is the same as through the second, and indeed, the same as the flow through the combined slab, ie,

$$F = F_1 = F_2$$

So: $$\frac{A t}{R} = \frac{A t_1}{R_1} = \frac{A t_2}{R_2}$$

ie, $$\frac{t}{R} = \frac{t_1}{R_1} = \frac{t_2}{R_2}$$

So: $t_1 = \frac{t R_1}{R}$ and $t_2 = \frac{t R_2}{R}$

Now t, the temperature difference across the combined slab, is the sum of the temperature differences across the two individual slabs, ie,

$$t = t_1 + t_2$$

Replacing t_1 and t_2 in this, we have:

$$t = \frac{t R_1}{R} + \frac{t R_2}{R}$$

Or, our result:

$$R = R_1 + R_2$$

This states that the combined resistance is simply the sum of the individual resistances. That is a very useful result.

Expressed with the more cumbersome U-values, it is:

$$U = \frac{U_1 U_2}{U_1 + U_2}$$

As an example of the use of the previous equation, let's consider the thermal resistance of a cavity wall. Given the conductivity (λ) of brick, we divide this into its thickness (L) to obtain its thermal resistance. (Note: Remember to express the thickness in the SI unit of length, the metre – not in centimetres or millimetres.) Likewise, the resistances of the blockwork and plaster can be calculated. (Building Regulations suggest that the effect of mortar joints in brickwork and blockwork can be ignored for convenience.)

But what about the cavity? Heat is hardly transmitted across it by conduction – air is a bad conductor. Most of the heat transmitted is radiated across, from the warm to the cold surface. Some is also convected by moving air currents. To calculate accurately the heat transmitted is very complex, so a rather arbitrary assumption is now introduced: The cavity is assumed to be equivalent to a slab with a fixed resistance. It has been found by experiment that this assumption gives satisfactory results.

Similarly, at the inner and outer surfaces of the wall, there is a twofold effect: A layer of still air increases the thermal resistance, whereas radiation decreases it. Again, a rather arbitrary assumption is made that the resistance can be given by a fixed figure. (And again, practical measurements justify the assumption.)

So now we can add together all the resistances to obtain the overall resistance of the cavity wall:

	λ (W / m °C)	L (m)	R (m² °C / W)	
Outer surface			·06	(from table 1)
Brickwork	·84	·1	·12	
Cavity			·18	(from table 1)
Aircrete 650	·17	·1	·59	
Lightweight plaster	·16	·015	·09	
Inner surface			·12	(from table 1)
Total thermal resistance			1·16	

The U-value of the wall is ·86 watts / m² °C (1 ÷ 1·16).

The target U-value in the Regulations is ·45, so the insulation of the wall needs to be increased.

What happens if the cavity is $7\frac{1}{2}$ cm wide and we fill it with mineral wool? The value of λ for mineral wool is ·035, giving a thermal resistance, R, of 2·14. Replacing the cavity resistance (·18) with this gives a total thermal resistance of 3·06. This corresponds to a U-value of ·33. Quite cosy!

Table 1: Conductivities (λ) of some common materials

	(W) λ (watts / m °C)
Brickwork (outer leaf)	·84
Dense concrete blocks	1·1 *
Aircrete blocks (650)	·17
Aircrete blocks (480)	·11
Mineral wool	·035
Expanded polystyrene	·037
Lightweight plaster	·16
Render	·50
Timber	·13

* This figure is for 2,000 kg / cu m blocks – the conductivity varies with density.

Table 2: Some standard resistances (R)

	R (m² °C / W)
Unventilated cavity (over $2\frac{1}{2}$ cm wide)	·18
Internal surface	·12
External surface	·06 (wind!)

Table 3: Standard U-values for windows

	U (W / m² °C)
Single glazed	5·7
Double glazed	2·8
Low-e double glazed	2·0
Triple glazed	2·0

These U-values for windows – given in Approved Document L of the Building Regulations – don't take any account of solar gain, which can greatly improve the figures. (See 'Window insulation', Chapter 26.) This shows up the rather arbitrary nature of standard U-values.

Using values given in the tables, we can calculate the U-values for walls of different constructions (as above).

Working out the U-value of a roof is more complex, but fortunately, in Approved Document L, the work has already been done. The Document shows that the thermal resistance, R, of a pitched roof without insulation is ·41. The increase due to adding loft insulation of any particular thickness can easily be added. For example:

	R (m² °C / W)	
Uninsulated roof	·41	
20 cm of mineral wool	5·71	(·2 ÷ ·035)
Total thermal resistance	6·12	

The U-value of the roof is ·16 (1 ÷ 6·12) – another cosy result. (The target U-value for a roof is ·25.)

What about the floor? Calculating a U-value for this is even trickier than for a roof. In fact, the Approved Document doesn't give a method of calculation, only tables that give the thickness of insulation required for various shapes and sizes of floor. As long as you are using double glazing and meeting the target U-values for walls and roof, the U-value required for the floor is unspecified. (But if single glazing is being used, the target U-value for the floor is ·45.)

Nonetheless, for your own satisfaction, you may want to know the U-value of the floor. The Building Research

Establishment has produced a very simple method of finding the U-value of an uninsulated floor (Information Paper 3–90). The U-value is determined by the ratio of the perimeter of the floor to its area, as in Table 4.

Table 4: U-values for ground floors

Perimeter / area (m / m²)	·3	·4	·5	·6	·7	·8
U-value (W / m² °C)	·49	·61	·73	·82	·91	·99

(In the table, the conductivity of the earth has been assumed to be 1·4. In fact, it varies from ·7 to 2·1, so the figures are obviously not very precise.)

Surprisingly, this table applies to all types of uninsulated floors next to the ground, whether a concrete slab (of whatever thickness), a suspended timber floor, or whatever. For a suspended timber floor, the additional thermal resistance due to the under-floor space is counter-balanced by the heat losses due to the under-floor ventilation.

The insulation of a timber floor is accomplished by adding a layer of mineral wool beneath the boards. The thermal resistance of the extra layer can be added in the normal manner to obtain the overall resistance.

For a solid floor there are further considerations:

Heat is lost from the slab when it flows out through the ground under the perimeter of the slab. It has been found that insulating the foundation walls around the perimeter is nearly as effective as insulating beneath the whole slab (Building Research Establishment Digest 145). There are thus benefits in using insulation blocks in the foundation walls of strip foundations in preference to trenchfill concrete, dense concrete blocks, or bricks. (More effectively, polystyrene sheets can be fixed to the inner face of foundation walls.)

Heat losses:

Transmittance Losses

With U-values for the whole structure, we can now work out the rate at which heat is lost though the envelope of the house (for a given temperature difference).

Here are the figures for the author's well insulated, detached house. (The temperature difference, t, is taken to be a mere 1°C. Later, we will calculate something more useful.)

For insulated cavity walls of area 174 sq m and U-value ·31, using F = A t U:

Rate of loss of heat = 54 watts (174 × ·31)

(Note that a flow of heat is expressed in watts. A householder is familiar with this through the use of electric fires, etc.)

The windows of the house have sealed units with low-emissive glass. The figures for the heat lost through them become somewhat arbitrary. The standard U-value for these windows is 2·0. (See Table 3.) But if solar gain is taken into account, the effective U-value is greatly improved. For north-facing low-e units, the U-value is 1·0, and for south-facing units it is virtually zero. (See 'Window insulation', Chapter 26.) These figures are for the glazed area, not the whole window. But some 30% of a contemporary window is the timber with a U-value of about 2. Although the windows are not, in fact, north-facing, if we take an average U-value of 1·0 over all the whole window openings we may be about right. And equally arbitrarily, we'll assume that the doors have the same U-value – the door panels have been insulated with polystyrene.

So for windows and doors of area 26 sq m and U-value 1·0:

Rate of loss of heat = 26 watts (26 × 1·0)

For the solid floor, the ratio of perimeter to area is ·52 m / m², giving an uninsulated U-value of ·75 (from Table 4). The thermal resistance, R, is 1·3 (1 ÷ ·75). But perimeter insulation has been used. The inner leaf of the foundation walls is composed of aircrete blocks, and attached to the blockwork is polystyrene of $2\frac{1}{2}$ cm thickness.

In the calculations for the cavity wall, we found that the thermal resistance of 10 cm blockwork was ·59. The resistance of the polystyrene is ·66 (·025 ÷ ·037), so the combined resistance is 1·25. Now according to *BRE Digest 145*, perimeter insulation gives 'nearly as good results' as overall insulation. If we make the assumption that '80%' is a measure of 'nearly as good', then the resistance of the perimeter insulation is equivalent to a thermal resistance of 1·0 (80% of 1·25) as overall insulation. Adding this resistance to that of the uninsulated slab (1·3), we have that the thermal resistance of the insulated slab is 2·3. So the floor has a U-value of ·43 (1 ÷ 2·3) – quite satisfactory.

The area of the floor slab is 65 sq m, so:

Rate of loss of heat = 27 watts (65 × ·42)

As calculated earlier, the roof, which has 20 cm of loft insulation, has a U-value of ·17. The area of the roof equals the area of the floor slab, ie, 65 sq m.

So for the roof with 20 cm of loft insulation, area 65 sq m, U-value ·17:

Rate of loss of heat = 11 watts (65 × ·17)

Adding these figures, the total rate of loss of heat through the fabric of the house is 121 watts (for a temperature difference of 1°C).

Ventilation losses

There is, however, another source of heat lost – ventilation. The ventilation in old houses was excessive, but modern houses, without open flues and with good weather-stripping, cut it right down. However, some ventilation is necessary. People give off water vapour, about 40 g / hr. Some of their activities produce water vapour – washing-up produces about 1 kg of water vapour in the course of a day. People also give off carbon dioxide and body odours. A rather rough and ready way to express the ventilation requirement is the rate at which the air in a room should be changed for it to remain unobjectionable. Half an air change per hour is nowadays regarded as satisfactory – much less than used to be recommended.

This fresh air has to be warmed up from the outside temperature. There is a simple formula for calculating the rate at which heat is required to do this:

$F = \cdot 36\ V\ a\ t$

F – Flow of heat in watts
V – Volume of room or house in cubic metres
a – Air changes per hour
t – Temperature difference between outside and inside in °C.

(For the scientifically inclined, the specific heat of air is included in the factor, ·36.)

As an example, consider the author's house once more. The volume of its habitable space is 325 cu m. For a temperature difference of 1°C again, and half an air change per hour:

Rate of loss of heat = 59 watts (·36 × 325 × ·5).

Though this is less than the heat lost directly through the fabric (121 watts), it is still appreciable.

In well sealed houses with few air changes, diffusion can help to keep the air acceptable. Water vapour and odours can diffuse through the fabric of the house. (But this is prevented when a vapour barrier is installed, as is necessary for timber-frame construction to stop unwanted condensation in the panels.)

Adding the transmittance and the ventilation losses, the total rate of loss of heat is 180 watts for a temperature difference of 1°C.

Maximum heating requirements

As an example of the use of the above figure, let's consider a very cold winter's day, with the temperature at –5°C outside. We wish to keep the house inside at 20°C (ie, a temperature difference of 25°C). The rate at which heat is lost is 4·5 kW (25 × 180 watts). This is the modest amount of heat that is required to keep the house warm on a cold winter's day – for a well insulated house.

That's a useful figure to know when deciding upon the size of the boiler – the smallest available! (Though an allowance should also be made for the hot water requirement.)

In a similar manner, the maximum heat loss from any particular room can be worked out. This corresponds to the maximum heat requirement, ie, the size of radiator required. (Though in fact, the approximation given in 'Radiator sizing', Chapter 9 is good enough.)

Annual heating costs

We can calculate the likely heat losses over a whole heating season. For this we need a new concept, the 'degree-day'. This has nothing to do with mumbling in Latin at an ancient university. Rather, it is a measure of sustained coldness. It has similarities with the 'man-hour' concept. One man working for two hours is equivalent in man-hours to two men working for one hour. In a like manner, a temperature difference of one degree (between the outside air temperature and a given base temperature) over a period of two days is equivalent to a temperature difference of two degrees over one day. They both yield two degree-days. The concept was originally used in horticulture, but now it has a wide application in heating calculations. The reason for this is that it gives a measure of the heat lost from a building. The heat lost for a temperature difference of 1°C over two days equals the heat lost for a temperature difference of 2°C over one day. The heat lost must equal the heat required if the building is to stay warm.

For measuring degree-days, the base temperature is taken to be 15·5°C, and it is assumed that no heating is required if the outside temperature is above this value. (By now, the reader of this book should be suspicious when they see arbitrary temperatures expressed so precisely – 15·5°C indeed. Have you guessed it? 15·5°C is, in fact, the same as the nice round figure, 60°F. This example of covert imperialism is being put out by the Government's Energy Efficiency Office in their booklet *Degree Days*.) If, for example, the average temperature over a day is 5·5°C, then we have ten degree-days. From historical data for a particular locality, the average degree-days for each day of the year can be found. (In the summer, there are zero degree-days, of course.)

There are tables that give these values month by month for different areas. Adding them, we get the number of degree-days for a whole heating season. For the Midlands for example, the total is 2,300, but it ranges from 1,800 for South-West England, to 2,600 for North-East Scotland.

These figures can be used to work out heating costs over a year. As an example, consider again the author's house in the Midlands. We have found previously, that the rate of loss of heat is 180 watts for a temperature difference of 1°C. Since there are 24 hours in a day, over a heating season:

Total amount of heat lost = 180 × 2,300 × 24 watt hours
= 9,940 kW hr

At a cost of 1·8 pence per kW hr (for gas), the value of this heat lost is £179. But the boiler has to generate somewhat more heat because it is not totally efficient.

Assuming the boiler is 80% efficient, the cost of the gas consumed over a heating season would be £224.

(In practice, up to the time of writing, the gas consumption has been about half this figure. This is probably because of mild winters, and the fact that most of the house is generally cooler than 20°C.)

Economic value of insulation

The intrepid reader can adapt the above calculations to find the savings due to improving the U-value of any particular component of a house. Bearing in mind the cost of the extra insulation (and interest rates) are the savings worthwhile?

Appendix 3
QUANTITIES

Approximate densities of materials:

	tonnes / cu m	
Sand, dry	1·6	
damp (as supplied)	1·5	
very damp	1·3	
Crushed stone, gravel	1·7	– nearly a half consists of voids
All-in ballast	2·0	– about a third consists of voids
Cement	1·4	– a bag of cement occupies ·035 cu m
Lime (hydrated)	0·59	– a 25kg bag of lime occupies ·042 cu m
Dense concrete block	2·0	– varies
Aircrete block 650	0·65	
Aircrete block 480	0·48	
LBC brick	1·5	– including hollows (equivalent to 2·2 tonnes per 1000 bricks)
York stone	2·4	
Oak	0·8	
Red deal	0·6	

Brick size

Actual size: $21\frac{1}{2} \times 6\frac{1}{2} \times 10\frac{1}{4}$ cm

Format size: $22\frac{1}{2} \times 7\frac{1}{2} \times 11\frac{1}{4}$ cm (includes 1 cm mortar joint)

Format ratio $1 : \frac{1}{3} : \frac{1}{2}$

A square metre of stretcher-bonded brickwork contains just under 60 bricks and ·017 cu m of mortar.

0·06

Block size

Actual size: $44 \times 21\frac{1}{2} \times 10$ cm

Format size: $45 \times 22\frac{1}{2}$ cm

(This format size equals two brick lengths by three brick courses. Other block sizes are available.)

A square metre of blockwork contains 10 blocks and ·0067 cu m of mortar.

0·02

Overall, about three wall ties are needed per square metre of cavity walling.

Mortar and concrete

A cubic metre of 1:1:6 mortar requires approximately 1·6 tonnes of sand, 5 bags of cement, and 4 25-kg bags of lime.

A cubic metre of concrete requires approximately 2 tonnes of ballast, with 4 bags of cement for a 1:3:6 mix (eg, foundations), or 6 bags of cement for a 1:2:4 mix (eg, floor slab, paths).

Quantities of materials for VAT Schedule 1:

For Schedule 1 of a VAT claim, the total quantities of the main materials used in the construction of the house are required. (So when you are subcontracting work, ask the subcontractor to supply you with a list of the Schedule 1 materials that he has supplied – he'll probably find this an unusual request.)

To give the reader a feeling for the quantities involved, here are some of the quantities used in the construction of the author's house:

Ready-mixed concrete: 28 tonnes
Sand: 40 tonnes
Stone: 47 tonnes
Cement: 82 bags
Lime: 21 bags
Bricks: 16,500
Blocks: 2,700
Carcassing timber: 760 metres (of all thicknesses!)
Roof trusses: 34
Concrete roof tiles: 1200
T&G flooring chipboards: 65
Plasterboards: 140
Plaster: 59 bags
Glazing: 31 panes
Copper tubing: 200 metres
etc.

What do the Customs and Excise do with all these statistics?

APPENDIX 4

FURTHER INFORMATION

Books

(Don't be deterred from selfbuild by the length of this book list. Some selfbuilders manage without any. Besides this present book, the most useful one is probably *Collins Complete Do-It-Yourself Manual.*)

TALKING ABOUT SELFBUILD by Robert Matthews
ISBN 0 9515295 0 1 £7–50
First Published 1990, by Blackberry Books.
Contains eight in-depth interviews with selfbuilders, three case studies by the author, and two interviews with professionals who are commercially involved in selfbuild. A lively introduction to the subject.

THE SELF-BUILD BOOK by Jon Broome and Brian Richardson
ISBN 1 870098 23 4 £15
First Published 1991, by Green Books.
The authors describe their own selfbuild experiences, and then give accounts of several group selfbuilds. These are followed by an action guide on how to set up your own selfbuild project. Part Four of the book is a practical description of the Segal method of house building. Lastly, the authors ask "Why don't we all self-build?" and they look at the politics of the subject.

BUILDING YOUR OWN HOME by Murray Armor
ISBN 1 85327 055 5 £8–95
13th Edition 1991, by Prism Press.
A popular perennial, covering the story of the selfbuild movement. Lots of case histories with smiling faces.

BRICK BY BRICK: the Leading Edge Guide to Building Your Own Home
ISBN 0 948135 10 7 £6–25
First published 1989, by Leading Edge Press and Publishing.
A good introduction to the many options possible in selfbuild. Covers the managerial rather than the practical aspects.

BUILDING TECHNOLOGY by Ivor Seeley
ISBN 0 333 43350 5 £11–99
3rd edition 1986, by Macmillan Press.
A very useful standard textbook.

PRINCIPLES OF CONSTRUCTION by R. Greeno
ISBN 0 582 41366 4 £9–50
First published 1986, by Longman Scientific & Technical.
Useful textbook.

COLLINS COMPLETE DO-IT-YOURSELF MANUAL by Jackson and Day
ISBN 0 00 412403 0 £22–99
New edition 1988.
Superbly produced and packed with information. The best of the many DIY manuals.

DICTIONARY OF BUILDING by John Scott
ISBN 0 14 051115 6 £6–99
Third edition published 1984, by Penguin Books.
Explains briefly the many technical terms used in building.

GETTING WORK DONE ON YOUR HOUSE
ISBN 0 340 48935 9 £7–95
Published 1988, by the Consumers' Association.
Useful advice on using subcontractors.

THE NATURAL HOUSE BOOK by David Pearson
ISBN 1 85029 326 0 £9–99
Published 1989, by Conran Octopus.
The sub-title is 'Creating a healthy, harmonious and ecologically sound home'. Lavishly illustrated with colour photographs of houses around the world. A shame that so few British houses are thought worthy of inclusion.

Particular aspects of selfbuild:

A SIMPLE GUIDE TO PLANNING APPLICATIONS by Robert Cooke
ISBN 0 86025 419 4 £4–95
First published 1987, by Ian Henry Publications.

HOME PLANS by Murray Armor
ISBN 1 85327 009 1 £9–95
First published 1988, by Prism Press.
Update of an earlier book, with 230 plans for conventional or timber-frame construction.

THE BUILDING REGULATIONS EXPLAINED AND ILLUSTRATED by Powell-Smith and Billington
ISBN 0 632 02401 1 £21–50
Eighth edition published 1991, by BSP Professional Books.
A straightforward guide to the law of building control in England and Wales.

BUILDER'S DETAILS SHEETS by Sam Smith
ISBN 1 85032 023 3 £15
Revised edition 1987, by International Thomson.
Useful practical book.

TIMBER FRAME CONSTRUCTION
ISBN 0 901348 63 5 £30
Published by the Timber Research and Development Association, 1988. (See address under 'Info centres'.)
For the designer or builder of timber-frame buildings.

CANADIAN WOOD-FRAME HOUSE CONSTRUCTION
ISBN 0 660 10231 5E £3–50
Published by the Canada Mortgage and Housing Corporation, 1984.
Don't be mislead by the low price – this has stacks of information for designing and building your own timber-frame house. Obtainable from the Council of Forest Industries of British Columbia, 131 Upper Richmond Road, London, SW15 2TR. They also distribute useful booklets and leaflets.

A MANUAL OF BUILDING CONSTRUCTION by Rev. H.K. Dancy
ISBN 0 903031 08 6 £7–95
4th edition 1982, by Intermediate Technology Publications. Originally published in 1948 as *Mission Buildings*. An off-beat book for the self-sufficient builder: how to make your own bricks, doors, windows, timber roofs, dry closets, jack scaffolds, etc.

INITIAL SKILLS IN BRICKLAYING by P.J. Tempest
ISBN 0 08 025424 1 £15–75
First published 1981, by Pergamon Press.
Over-priced, but a most useful book for novices, with practical exercises.

ROOF CONSTRUCTION FOR DWELLINGS by C.N. Mindham
ISBN 0 632 02308 2 £18–95
Published 1989, by BSP Professional.
Useful for an understanding of different types of roof construction.

MANUAL OF ROOFING by J. Wickersham
ISBN 0 7153 8698 0 £16
Published 1987, by David and Charles.
A well illustrated book for the amateur.

THE SKILLS OF PLASTERING by Mel Baker
ISBN 0 333 49981 6 £7–99
First published 1990, by MacMillan Education Ltd.
Includes floor screeding and external rendering, as well as plastering. (Shame about the see-through paper used by the penny-pinching publishers.)

HOMEOWNER'S COMPLETE OUTDOOR BUILDING BOOK by John Brimer
ISBN 0 809 5796 4 £12–95
Third edition 1985. Paperback edition 1989, by Sterling Publishing Co. Inc.
Nearly half a million copies have been sold in the USA since the first edition in 1959. A well illustrated and practical book that shows lots of imaginative ways to build in the garden.

Reference publications:

Some reference libraries will possess some or all of the following:

THE BUILDING REGULATIONS 1985, and *APPROVED DOCUMENTS* and *1990 AMENDMENTS*
Various ISBN's About £50 for the whole lot
Published by HMSO, PO Box 276, London SW8 5DT.
The Regulations and Approved Documents are published in several (expensive) documents.

SPON'S ARCHITECTS' AND BUILDERS' PRICE BOOK
ISBN 0 415 14980 5 £45
Published yearly by Spon.
There are other similar books, eg Laxton's, at similar prices. Widely available in reference libraries.

SPECIFICATION 90
ISBN 1 870308 03 4 £75
84th edition in 1989, by MBC Architectural Press.
Three volume set containing an abundance of information on techniques, products and specification clauses. May have an answer to your problem.

MANUAL OF BRITISH STANDARDS IN BUILDING CONSTRUCTION AND SPECIFICATION
ISBN 0 09 170760 9 £25
Published 1987, by Hutchinson.
Outlines the subject matter of the many British Standards that relate to building.

BRITISH STANDARDS
Published by the British Standards Institution.
Large reference libraries have shelves full of these standards – masses of information in a rather indigestible form. They are made even more indigestible by being printed on red paper (to prevent photocopying). The BSI also issues a few 'Codes of Practice', some of which apply to building.

Trade publications:

Two large booklets by the British Cement Association (Wexham Springs, Slough, SL3 6PL – for other publications, ask for their catalogue):

BUILD IT WITH CONCRETE £3–50
Covers blockwork, render and paving, as well as *in situ* concrete – clear and useful.

HOUSE FOUNDATIONS £6–00
Describes a large variety of foundations, eg, rafts for soft soils.

The Glass and Glazing Federation (44 Borough High Street, London SE1 1XB) produce several leaflets including:

GLAZING TECHNIQUES FOR INSULATING GLASS UNITS £1–25

British Gypsum Ltd (Ruddington Hall, Loughborough Road, Ruddington, Nottingham, NG11 6LX) supply a free book:

BRITISH GYPSUM POCKET BOOK
Lots of useful information about British Gypsum's plasters and boards. It needs a fat pocket!

Salvo 91 (PO Box 1295, Bath, BA1 6TJ) produce a directory for recycled building materials:

RECLAMATION DIRECTORY £4–75

Books for people forming their own selfbuild group:

BUYING YOUR HOME WITH OTHER PEOPLE by Dave Treanor
ISBN 0 901242 79 9 £5–95
First published 1987, by Shelter and the National Federation of Housing Associations.
If you want to form your own selfbuild housing association, this may help your understanding of the legal labyrinths.

COHOUSING by Kathryn McCamant and Charles Durrett
ISBN 0 945929 29 3 £14–50
First published in 1988, by Habitat Press.
An American book of co-operative housing schemes in Denmark. A delightful inspiration of how our lives could so simply be so much richer. If you are forming a selfbuild group, why not continue co-operation when the building has finished?

Out-of-print books:

Worthwhile books that can be ordered from your library:

THE SELF-BUILDER by Nicholas Snelgar
ISBN 0 7153 9794 X
First published 1987.
A practical but rather brief guide to traditional house-building.

THE SELF-SUFFICIENT HOUSE by Brenda and Robert Vale
ISBN 0 333 25868 1
First published 1980.
Lots of ideas for saving energy at little cost.

THE OWNER-BUILT HOME by Ken Kern
ISBN 0 684 14223 6
First published 1972.
An American classic embracing many methods of building. An inspiring book, but frustrating unless you're prepared to emigrate – our Planning authorities allow for very little imagination.

HOUSE by Tracy Kidder
ISBN 0 330 29388 5
First published in Britain in 1985.
An account by a Pulitzer Prize winner of the building of a house in New England. Almost a saga.

Periodicals

BUILD IT! £1–95, monthly.
The first glossy magazine for selfbuilders, with a useful section on building plots for sale.

INDIVIDUAL HOMES £1–95, quarterly.
Another glossy, for people 'designing, building and renovating their own homes'.

THE SELF-BUILD HOMES ANNUAL £3–50, annually.
And another glossy, this one promoted by Potton Ltd, manufacturers of timber-frames.

FINE HOMEBUILDING £3–50, bimonthly.
An American magazine distributed in Britain. Both beautifully produced and practical – a rare combination. An emphasis on timber construction.

THE SELF-BUILDER
£1 for two issues a year, from Homesmith plc, The Spire, Leeds Road, Lightcliffe, Halifax, West Yorks, HX3 8NU.
Mainly about managed selfbuild projects.

PROFESSIONAL BUILDER
Free from the counters of some builders' merchants every month. Useful for its advertising.

Videos

TRENT TELEVISION
552 Hartshill Road, Hartshill, Stoke-on-Trent, ST10 4DU.
They publish *Build It Yourself: a practical guide to selfbuild housing* and several diy videos.

ESSEX VIDEO PRODUCTIONS
1a Cjrdinal Way, Rainham, Essex, RM13 9RB.
The Self-Built House is a four part video showing a real life self-build project, 'warts and all!!'

Courses

CONSTRUCTIVE INDIVIDUALS
1 The Cottages, Hambleton, Selby, North Yorkshire, YO8 9JE.
Practical building courses at various locations. They use a modular post-and-beam technique especially designed for selfbuild.

JUVAN COURSES
Lower House, Mill Lane, Longhope, Gloucestershire, GL17 0AA.
Weekend courses in selfbuilding, plastering, bricklaying, plumbing, electrics, etc.

THE SELF-BUILD TRAINING COMPANY
Park House, 106 Park Road, Teddington, Middlesex, TW11 0AN.
Usually one-to-one tuition – almost consultancy.

CENTRE FOR ALTERNATIVE TECHNOLOGY
Pantperthog, near Machynlleth, Powys, Wales, SY20 9AZ.
Weekend courses in the Segal method of selfbuild, solar energy, and much else. Also have permanent displays and a bookshop.

BRITISH GYPSUM
Run various courses at Erith (Kent), Cocklades (Cumbria), and East Leake (Leicestershire). Contact the Training Manager, British Gypsum Ltd, East Leake, LE12 6JU.
Courses include dry lining, but not the use of wet plasters. (Cost – about £90.)

REDLAND PLASTERBOARD
Unit 10, The Alpha Centre, Great Western Business Park,

Yate, Avon, BS17 5NG.
Courses in dry-lining, etc.

KNAUFF UK
PO Box 133, Sittingbourne, Kent, ME10 3HW.
At the time of publication, their dry-lining course is free.

For particular crafts: Try local adult education classes, or technical colleges.

TV PROGRAMS
(especially in the winter): for DIY techniques.

Info Centres

ASSOCIATION OF SELFBUILDERS
Lower House, Mill Lane, Longhope, Gloucestershire, GL17 0AA.
This newly formed association acts as a forum for selfbuilders to exchange ideas and experiences. It produces a quarterly newsletter and holds occasional conferences, site visits, etc. Twelve-months' subscription is £15.

THE BUILDING CENTRE
26 Store Street, London, WC1E 7BT.
Comprehensive bookshop; commercial exhibits and information. Send £1 for their book catalogue.

ROYAL INSTITUTE OF BRITISH ARCHITECTS (RIBA),
66 Portland Place, London, W1N 4AD.
The very useful library is open for reference to the general public. There is also a bookshop.

The RIBA also has small bookshops and/or a Clients' Advisory Service in Birmingham, Bristol, Cardiff, Knutsford (Cheshire), Leeds, Manchester, Newcastle, Nottingham, Winchester (Hampshire).

The *ROYAL INCORPORATION OF ARCHITECTS IN SCOTLAND* is in Edinburgh, and the *ROYAL SOCIETY OF ULSTER ARCHITECTS* is in Belfast.

Other bookshops:

Design Centre, 28 Haymarket, London SW1.

Housing Centre Bookshop, 6 St Olaves Mansions, Walnut Tree Walk, London, SE11 6DW.

Planning Bookshop, 17 Carlton House Terrace, London, SW1.

Stobart Davies Ltd, 67 Worship St, London, EC2.

Intermediate Technology, 103 Southampton Row, London, WC1B 4HH.
(If you want to use 'Third World' building technologies – thatch, mud, stone – IT has a range of books on such techniques.)

Books by post:

Blackberry Books, 10 Bartholomew St, Leicester, LE2 1FA.
Besides their own publications, Blackberry Books sell a wide selection of building books from other publishers. Send two first-class stamps for their Selfbuild Catalogue.

Ryton Books, 29 Ryton St, Worksop, Nottinghamshire, S81 2AY.

BUILDING RESEARCH ESTABLISHMENT
Garston, Watford, WD2 7JR.
Publish a wide variety of 'Digests' and 'Information Papers' based on their research (often available in reference libraries). Send for their list of publications. They sell technical advice.

TIMBER RESEARCH AND DEVELOPMENT ASSOCIATION
Hughendon Valley, High Wycombe, Buckinghamshire, HP14 4ND.
TRADA produce diverse publications about the use of timber. They also have an advisory service.

BRITISH BOARD OF AGRÉMENT
PO Box 195, Bucknalls Lane, Garston, Watford, WD2 7NG.
If you are interested in Agrément Certificates (they often have useful technical information), send for the index.

SOLID FUEL ADVISORY SERVICE
Hobart House, Grosvenor Place, London, SW1X 7AE. Regional offices in Birmingham, Chesterfield, Doncaster, Exeter, Market Harborough, Leeds, Lincoln, Nottingham, Edinburgh, and Belfast.
They give advice and practical help to selfbuilders about chimneys, solid fuel central heating, etc.

THE INSTITUTE OF BUILDING BIOLOGY
16 Church Street, Saffron Walden, Essex, CB10 1JW.
A house may look pretty and be structurally sound, but is it a healthy place to live in? The Institute publishes papers on this neglected subject.

WALTER SEGAL SELF-BUILD TRUST
Room 212, Panther House, 38 Mount Pleasant, London, WC1X 0AP.
The trust promotes the post-and-beam method of selfbuild pioneered by architect, Walter Segal. This method can be quickly mastered by anyone without prior building experience. Many of the skills traditionally needed are circumvented. The trust can also advise on setting up a selfbuild group. Their pack 'You build' is a comprehensive guide to selfbuild for those in housing need. For a description of Segal's method, see Architect's Journal, 5.11.86.

THE COMMUNITY SELFBUILD AGENCY LTD
18 Northampton Square, London, EC1V 0AJ.
A collaboration of the Housing Corporation and building societies. The Agency promotes the formation of selfbuild groups for people 'in housing need'. It has large amounts of money to dispense, but your group needs large amounts of patience to get any of it.

THE NATIONAL FEDERATION OF HOUSING ASSOCIATIONS
Warwickgate House, Warwick Road, Manchester, M16 0DD.
Give advice on forming selfbuild housing associations. Their book *Selfbuild* (£6–95) suggests fair working arrangements for selfbuild groups.

Manufacturers' free advisory services:

I.G. LINTELS LTD
Avondale Road, Cwmbran, Gwent, NP44 1XY.
Prepare a lintel schedule from your drawings.

IMI YORKSHIRE IMPERIAL PLASTICS
P.O. Box 166, Leeds, LS1 1RD.
Advise on the design and layout of their plastic drains. Also give on-site demonstrations of their jointing and laying.

BRITISH GYPSUM LTD
Their regional offices in Cumbria, Leicestershire, and Kent offer technical advice and training. (See 'Courses'.)

In fact, technical advice is available from most manufacturers.

Heating design services:

The following suppliers of heating equipment will design a heating system for a modest fee:

Central Heating Supplies, Moss Grove, Kingswinford, West Midlands, DY6 7LN.

Harrison McCarthy Ltd, Little Moss Lane, Pendlebury, Manchester, M27 2PX.

Ravensbourne Heating Ltd, 34 Cemetery Road, Lye, Stourbridge, Worcestershire, DY9 7EQ.

Stores: Do-It-All, Texas, Payless (free).

Exhibitions

The first national exhibition about selfbuild was held in 1990, at Alexandra Palace, London. The success of that exhibition, and the growing interest in the subject has resulted in four exhibitions being held in 1992:

IDEAL HOME BUILD SHOW, Earls Court, London, March 26-29 (promoted by the *Daily Mail*).

SELF BUILD HOMES SHOW, GMEX, Manchester, April 10-12 (promoted by *Build It!* magazine).

INDIVIDUAL HOMES EXHIBITION, NEC, Birmingham, April 18-21 (promoted by the *Daily Telegraph*).

SELF BUILD HOMES SHOW, Alexandra Palace, London, September 24-28 (promoted by *Build It!* magazine).

A general building exhibition is:

INTERBUILD EXHIBITION, NEC, Birmingham, November in odd-numbered years. A vast exhibition with plenty of interest to selfbuilders. (It is the largest exhibition of any sort in Britain.)

Finance

Many building societies and quasi building societies make provision for selfbuilders. Of particular interest are those which make some advance for the purchase of the plot, eg, National and Provincial, Birmingham Midshires, Bradford and Bingley, Bristol and West, Cheltenham and Gloucester, Halifax, Leeds, Nationwide Anglia, Norwich and Peterborough, Skipton, and Yorkshire building societies, and Abbey National plc. (The advance may be 20% – 90% of the value of the plot.)

JIG-SAW BUSINESS CONSULTANTS
Unit 14, Chingford Industrial Centre, Hall Lane, London, E4 8DJ.
Financial consultants for selfbuild.

Management packages

PACKAGE BUILD
Barnwell House, Barnwell Drive, Cambridge, CB5 8UJ.
They claim to be the largest source of land for selfbuilders. For a registration fee (£57-50) you are sent details of plots in your search area. They can also arrange finance and a selfbuild kit. If you wish, you can use their Build Management Service – throw away this book and stay at home in your armchair!

CONSULTANTS
Consultants to selfbuild groups have been active for a quarter of a century. Rather suddenly, there have appeared a large number of consultants who aim to help the individual selfbuilder. See the magazines for their adverts.

Insurances

NORWICH UNION INSURANCE
Either direct, or via DMS Services, Orchard House, Blyth, Worksop, Notts, S81 8HF.
Offer an insurance package for selfbuilders to cover the construction period. They also offer personal accident cover.

FOUNDATION 15
P.O. Box 71, Farnborough, Hants, GU14 0NT.
Offer a fifteen-year structural insurance once the house is completed.

BROKERS
eg, Davenport Stoll Ltd, 372 Palatine Road, Northendean, Manchester, M22 4FZ. They specialise in insurance for group builds, but they can also help the individual selfbuilder.

Some Building Societies offer insurances along with their selfbuild loans.

GLOSSARY

Aggregate: Sand or stone, or both mixed together.

Aircrete blocks: The common type of block used in house-building. It is made from aerated 'concrete', which is a good insulator and easily worked. (Eg, 'Thermalite', 'Celcon'.)

Architrave: Wooden strips around a door opening which hide the joint between the door lining and wall.

Arris: The edge along a corner of an object, most often along a length of timber .

Baluster: One of the set of posts that fill the gap between a handrail and the stairs or landing. (See also 'Spindle'.)

Barge board: The board which hides and protects the outside of a gable ladder; it follows the slope of the roof. There are two at a gable end, meeting together in a point at the ridge.

Barge foot: An extra timber piece added at the bottom of a barge board. It blocks off the gap under the eaves.

Bat: A part brick (from a whole brick cut across its width).

Batt: A slab of insulation.

Bed joint: A horizontal mortar joint in brickwork or blockwork.

Bevel: An edge that meets a face at an angle that is not 90°. (See also 'Chamfer'.)

Bonding: (1) The pattern of mortar joints in brickwork (or blockwork).
(2) The connecting together of metalwork (eg, plumbing pipes) and earthing terminal by an electrical conductor.

Browning: A Gypsum plaster (ie, similar to Plaster of Paris) premixed with lightweight material to bulk it out. Used for the floating coat (ie, undercoat) of plasterwork. (See also 'Render'.)

Butt: To press up against. Eg, if two boards are butted together, their ends (or edges) are simply pressed against each other.

Carcassing: As far as the carpenter is concerned, this consists of the joists and roof timbers.

Casing: See 'Door lining'.

Cement: A powder, usually grey, which forms a paste with water that sets hard. It is invariably mixed with aggregate to give concrete, mortar, render, etc.

Chamfer: A bevel at 45°.

Compactor: A machine with vibrating plate that compacts the material (eg, hardcore) beneath it.

Concrete: Made by mixing cement, stone, sand and water. Their proportions can be varied: the more cement, the stronger and more expensive the concrete. Common mixes are 4:2:1 and 6:3:1 (stone : sand : cement). Used for foundations, solid floors, paths, etc.

Corbel: A projection from a wall that supports a load above it. Necessary with flush verges to support the small area of gable projecting beyond the main wall. Often built in stepped-out brickwork. (See Fig. 21, Chapter 6.)

Course: A course in brickwork is a level layer of bricks.

Cross joint: A vertical mortar joint in brickwork or blockwork. Sometimes called a 'perpend'.

Diverter: A motorised valve forming a T-junction in plumbing. It diverts the flow to one arm or the other.

Door lining: At internal door openings, these boards hide the edges of the wall and support the door. Sometimes called a 'casing'.

Dpc: Damp proof course. Wide plastic 'ribbon' laid along the base of a wall to prevent rising damp.

Dpm: Damp proof membrane. Plastic sheeting laid beneath a concrete floor to prevent rising damp.

Dry lining: Finishing wall surfaces with plasterboard. Necessary with timber-frame construction and studwork. An alternative to plastering on blockwork.

Eaves: The lowest part of a roof, where it overhangs its supporting wall.

Fascia: The board that protects and hides the bottom ends of rafters or roof trusses. Often carries a gutter, hence its alternative name of 'gutter board'.

Fatty: Refers to the composition and feel of a wet mix of mortar, concrete, render, etc. A fatty mix is rich in small particles and feels cohesive and easy to work.

Felt and battening: Slaters' felt is nowadays laid beneath tiles (or slates) as a second line of defence against the weather. It is fixed in place by the rows of battens which support the tiles.

Finish plaster: Plaster used for skimming. (See 'Skim'.)

Flashing: Material (usually lead) used to cover the joint between a wall and roof.

Float: A type of trowel used to make plaster or concrete flat and smooth. (Can also be a verb: to use the float.)

Floating coat: The thick undercoat of plaster which flattens out the irregularities of the wall beneath it. On internal work, it is finished off with a skim coat.

Frog: A hollow in the top (or bottom!) of some types of brick.

Gable: The triangular wall that meets a ridged roof.

Gable ladder: A timber framework that carries a roof out over a gable. (See 'Verge'.)

Gauge: The distance between successive bed joints of mortar, ie, the height of a course of brickwork. (Has several other meanings.)

Hoggin: Natural mix of ballast (sand and gravel) with some clay.

Jamb: (1) The vertical edge of a wall at a door or window opening.
(2) The vertical member of a door or window frame attached to a jamb as in (1).

Joist: A beam for supporting a floor or ceiling.

Kerf: A saw cut.

Kite: Found sometimes where stairs turn a corner. One of the winders may be shaped like a kite (ie, a squashed diamond shape). (See 'Winders'.)

Laying to the line: In bricklaying, two corners are first put up. Then a line is stretched tight between them, and this is used to guide the laying of brickwork in between.

Leaf: A cavity wall combines a leaf of brickwork and a leaf of blockwork, separated by a gap (usually 5 cm) but tied together at intervals by wall ties.

Lintel: A beam (nowadays steel) which supports the brickwork above a door or window opening.

Low-emissive glass: Glass with a transparent coating on one face; it reflects radiant heat back into a warm room.

Matchboard: Tongued and grooved board with a decorative 'V' channel along the joint.

Mortar: Mixture of cement, sand and water (sometimes with lime also), which is used for sticking bricks together.

Mortise: A traditional way to join two pieces of wood is the mortise-and-tenon joint. The mortise is the hole (usually rectangular), and the tenon fits into it.

Moulding: A length of timber with a profiled surface (usually machined on a spindle moulder).

Newel: The stout post at the top or bottom of a stair that helps support the handrail.

Nogging: A short cross-piece of timber used, for example, in studwork. (See 'Studwork'.)

Overhand: Laying brickwork from the back face, not from the fair face in front.

Oversite: The concrete base laid over the plan area of a house.

Plate: A length of timber, laid horizontally and supported along its length, which supports the construction above (eg: a wall plate along the top of a wall supports roof trusses or rafters; a sole plate along a floor supports studwork).

Profiles: These are used to transfer the plan outline onto the ground. They are boards about a metre long fixed in place by a couple of stakes. By stretching a line tight between marks on a pair of profiles, the position for a wall can be fixed.

Ptfe tape: Polytetrafluorethylene(!) tape has replaced tow for wrapping round screw threads to make them watertight. Some plumbers even use it instead of a small washer by wrapping the tape round many times.

Purlin: A strong beam found in traditional roof construction. It supports the rafters midway up the slope.

Putlog: A short scaffold tube fixed level, one end supported in a joint of the wall and the other end by scaffolding. The scaffold boards are laid across the putlogs.

Rafter: A sloping timber of a pitched roof. Tiles are held in place by battens nailed across the rafters.

RCD: Residual Current Device. This is a sensitive safety device to protect an electrical circuit. If there develops a fault in the circuit such that some current starts flowing to earth, the device will break the circuit.

Render: A sand-and-cement mix used for plastering, either outside or as the floating coat inside – although for this, browning is more popular.

Reveal: When a window or door frame has been fixed in position, the part of a jamb left exposed is called a reveal. It is usually plastered.

Rive: To split timber apart along its grain.

Rodding eye: A short length of drain pipe that runs from ground level down into a drain so that the drain can be rodded.

Sash: A frame that holds one, or more, panes of glass. It is usually restricted to a frame that is movable, ie, a 'window' that opens. Nowadays, the frame may be hinged (a casement window), but originally it slid in grooves (a sash window). The word is a corruption of the French word 'châssis' (frame) – with less corruption of the word, it is also applied to motor vehicles: 'chassis'.

Screed: (1) A sand-and-cement 'plaster' applied to a floor rather than a wall to make it flat and smooth.

(2) A fillet of plaster or timber; several are used to divide up a wall to give true levels for plastering (or to divide a floor for screeding).

Scribe: To mark and cut a workpiece to fit against a non-flat surface.

Scrim: Strip of woven jute or cotton which is used to cover the joints between plasterboards before skimming. This prevents the skim coat from cracking later.

Setting out: Marking out on the ground the plan area of the house to be built.

Sharp sand: Coarse sand suitable for concrete. Soft sand contains more fine particles and is suitable for mortar.

Skim: In plasterwork, the skim coat is the top coat, ie, a thin coat of finish plaster with a smooth surface. (Also used as a verb: to apply the finish coat.)

Soffit: A flat undersurface, eg, beneath the eaves.

Sole plate: See 'Plate'.

Spindle: A baluster which has been turned on a lathe.

Stack: (1) The soil pipe that runs from the top of the house, where air can be sucked into it, down to the drain. Individual soil pipes from WC's, and waste pipes from basins, etc, run into it.
(2) Chimney stack.

Stair: A single flight of steps. Often there are two flights broken by a landing and so the word is more often used in the plural. A 'staircase' includes the newels, handrail, balusters, and small landing.

Stretcher bond: The ubiquitous bond used for cavity walls; every brick half-laps a brick below. All the bricks are 'stretchers', ie, laid horizontally exposing the long face. (Contrast a 'header', which exposes the end of the brick.)

Studwork: Timber framework which is usually covered with plasterboard to make a wall. The studs are the vertical members from floor to ceiling. They are stiffened with short horizontal pieces called noggings.

Texturing: A rather inadequate word used to describe the finish achieved with 'Artex' and the like.

Topping out: A ceremony that celebrates the construction of the highest part of a building. Traditionally, it includes the flying of the Union Jack and drinks all round!

Transom: A horizontal cross-member of a window frame, dividing the window into parts.

Trimmer: An extra strong joist which supports the ends of other joists (trimmed joists) at an opening for a stairwell, etc. The term has a corresponding meaning in roof carpentry: a bearer which supports the ends of cut rafters at an opening for a chimney stack, etc.

Trusses: Triangular frames used in the construction of a roof. They are prefabricated in a factory for an individual house.

U-value: A measure of the ease with which some form of construction used for the fabric of a building allows heat to escape. A low value is desirable.

Verge: Edge of the roof at a gable end. (It can also mean the brickwork where the gable meets the roof.) The fashion in the Sixties and Seventies was to project the verge out over the gable with a gable ladder. The contemporary fashion is for a flush verge: The tiles project only a few centimetres beyond the gable.

Winders: If there is sufficient space, the best way to turn a corner on a staircase is with a landing. If the stair itself has to turn, the triangular-shaped treads are called winders. (See also 'Kite'.)

Window sill: Like 'jamb' this has two associated meanings:
1) The bottom of a window (or door) opening. On the outside, the sill has to be designed to shed water. Nowadays, this is commonly achieved by a broad timber sill forming part of the frame. On the inside, the window sill is usually covered by a 'window board' – called the window sill by a householder.
2) The bottom member of a window or door frame.

INDEX